HOUGHTON MIFFLIN COMPANY
BOSTON
New York
Atlanta
Geneva, Illinois
Dallas
Palo Alto

PROBLEMS AND POLICIES IN PERSONNEL MANAGEMENT
A Casebook
Second Edition

Joseph W. Towle
Sterling H. Schoen
Raymond L. Hilgert
*Graduate School of
Business Administration
Washington University*

Copyright © 1972 by Houghton Mifflin Company. Copyright © 1965 by Joseph W. Towle, Sterling H. Schoen, Raymond L. Hilgert. The selections reprinted in this book are used by permission of and special arrangement with the proprietors of their respective copyrights. All rights reserved. No part of this work may be reproduced or transmitted in any form or by any means, electronic or mechanical, including photocopying and recording, or by any information storage or retrieval system, without permission in writing from the publisher.

Printed in the U.S.A.

Library of Congress Catalog Card Number: 78-176373

ISBN: 0-395-13400-5

Preface

With each succeeding stage of experience, an individual acquires a deeper understanding of the world around him. This lifelong process operates alike for the child, the youth, the businessman and businesswoman, and the scholar. In an attempt to accelerate it, formal education and training programs employ a variety of teaching techniques: classroom discussions, internships, work-study sessions, simulations, case studies. Of these techniques, case studies have proved to be among the most effective and most popular. Indeed, in organizational development work and in the education and training of managers and supervisors, they have unique values. For, within the cultural framework of an organization, they highlight the knowledge and skills needed to solve human problems and to make decisions.

The second edition of *Problems and Policies in Personnel Management* presents individual case studies, corporation policy statements, and part introductions drawn from experience with a wealth of business firms. Of the fifty-nine cases, almost half are new to this edition; the ten policy statements are new; the nine part introductions are either new or revised. New cases center on contemporary situations which impinge on employer-employee relationships: for instance, in "Equal Employment Opportunity" (Part Six), on the employment and supervision of minority workers. Certainly, the time is overdue to discuss and to proceed with the integration of minority workers into the labor force. Other new cases focus on college, government, and hospital organizations, on student protest, on the increasing importance of the not-for-profit sector of our society. All of the cases, both new and old, reflect the results of research studies which have probed innumerable aspects of group behavior and have brought us to the conclusion that, in many respects, "an organization is an organization of many organizations."

As we stated in the preface to the first edition, our aim has been to design a volume to meet two specific needs. First, it constitutes a convenient and relatively inexpensive set of materials to supplement the theory found in basic personnel management and organizational behavior textbooks. Second, it forms, in and of itself, a "short course" for executive development programs and supervisory training courses sponsored by universities and business firms.

Instructors will notice that the cases are presented without supplementary questions or study suggestions. We assume that the instructor will develop his own tools for case analysis and group discussion. For the instructor who wishes to avail himself of additional tools, we have provided an *Instructor's Manual.* It takes an overview of the use of the case study method and of various approaches to case analysis and it gives in detail suggestions for role playing, arbitration case simulations, and other instructional devices.

We are indebted to many case writers, business leaders, fellow professors, and others, who cooperated with us. (On page vii, we list contributors of cases presented here.) We are grateful to Professor Andrew R. Towl, Director of the Intercollegiate Case Clearing House of the Graduate School of Business Administration, Harvard University; to Mr. John D. Stewart, President of the Bureau of National Affairs, Inc., who gave us permission to use cases taken from *Labor Arbitration Reports;* to the many executives who contributed to the policy statements and allowed us to use them; and to our colleagues and students at Washington University.

Finally, we acknowledge, with many thanks, the cooperation of Dean Karl Hill in helping us to develop our manuscript and in providing us with the services of Mrs. Ruth Scheetz, of the Washington University secretarial staff, who typed the entire manuscript and who endured patiently changes, corrections, and delays

Joseph W. Towle
Sterling H. Schoen
Raymond L. Hilgert
Graduate School of
Business Administration
Washington University

Case Contributors

Cutler, T. H. (University of Denver)—"Tri City Utility Company"
Cronin, Justin C. (Boston College)—"Novac Company"
Dauten, Carl A. (Washington University)—"The Ozark Foundry"
Grimshaw, Austin (The University of Washington) and John Hennessey (Dartmouth College)—"Martha Burleigh," "Valley Metal Products Company"
Haimann, Theo (St. Louis University)—"A Problem of Tardiness"
Harries, Hu, and the Faculty of Commerce (University of Alberta)—"Telecronics, Inc.," "Paragon Pulp & Paper Company, Ltd."
Hennessey, John W., Jr., (Dartmouth College)—"The Worthington Case."
Hill, Clayton (University of Michigan)—"Carl Lohman—Lineman"
Hodgetts, James C. (Memphis State University)—"Oscar Metz Tool Company"
Hundley, John R., III (Washington University)—"Melba Moore," "Willis B. Johnson"
Knudson, Harry R., Jr. (The University of Washington)—"The Trouble with Lester," "The Jamison Furniture Company"
Learned, Edmund P. (Harvard University)—"The Larger Company," "John Edwards"
Ling, Cyril (American Association of Collegiate Schools of Business)—"The Night Shift Group"
Lombard, George F. F. (Harvard University)—"John Edwards"
Mullen, James H. (Temple University)—"The Forsythe Chemical Company"
Preshing, William A. (University of Alberta)—"Beaver Glass Company Limited"
Rogers, H. Barrett (Northwestern University)—"Jones Manufacturing Company"
Schoppenhorst, William (Emerson Electric Co.)—"The Allen Company"
Shah, Vasant (Bombay, India)—"Poona Metal Company"
Smith, Howard R. (University of Georgia)—"Too Many Bosses"

Vlerick, A. J. (State University of Ghent, Belgium)—"Textilcolor"
Ullrich, Robert A. (Vanderbilt University)—"A Matter of Priorities

Contents

Preface		v
Case Contributors		vii
PART ONE **The Personnel Management Function**		1
CASES		
1.	The Jordan Company	7
2.	The Russell Company (A) and (B)	10
3.	The Trouble with Lester	21
4.	The Midvale Plant	26
5.	The Night Shift Group	32
PART TWO **The Cultural Framework of Personnel Management**		35
CASES		
6.	Textilcolor	49
7.	Sonning Mead Boilers, Ltd.	51
8.	The College Protestor	61
9.	The Assembly Line: The U.S.A. and Japan (A) and (B)	64
10.	The Worthington Case	70
11.	Poona Metal Company	73

PART THREE
People at Work
79

CASES

12.	Carl Lohman—Lineman	87
13.	Telecronics, Inc.	89
14.	Martha Burleigh	93
15.	Frazer's Department Store (A)	97
16.	The Case of Tom Mendola	103
17.	The Jamison Furniture Company	105
18.	Tri City Utility Company: A Problem of Alcoholism	108
19.	Too Many Personal Calls	113
20.	A Matter of Priorities	116

PART FOUR
Organization for Management
121

CASES

21.	The Larger Company	131
22.	The Ozark Foundry	135
23.	Too Many Bosses	141
24.	The Adjustment Department	143
25.	The General Electric Company (A), (B), and (C)	147
26.	Hill City Junior College	157
27.	Oscar Metz Tool Company	164
28.	The Allen Company	167

PART FIVE
Selection and Development
175

CASES

29.	Frazer's Department Store (B)	180
30.	Paragon Pulp & Paper Company, Ltd.	183
31.	Simmons Retail Chain Store	203
32.	Valley Metal Products Company	·205
33.	John Edwards	211
34.	Petri Chemical Company (A) and (B)	215
35.	Management Development at the Ford Motor Company	222
36.	Incident in a Government Agency: The Unqualified Examiner	229

PART SIX
Equal Opportunity Employment 233

CASES

37.	Ten Women at the Employment Office	245
38	Melba Moore	250
39.	Sarah Jones	253
40.	The Reluctant Employee	257
41.	The Leadership Skills Conference for Supervisors	261
42.	Willis B. Johnson	265
43	A Problem of Tardiness	267
44.	The "Fixed" Election	269

PART SEVEN
Compensating the Workforce 273

CASES

45.	Novac Company	284
46.	Petri Chemical Company (C)	290
47.	Boynton Department Store	292
48.	The Filmore Electric Company (A)	294
49.	The Superintendent's Vacation Pay	298
50.	Jones Manufacturing Company	300
51.	The Kaiser Steel Long-Range Sharing Plan	305
52.	Charges of Discrimination Among the Library Staff	314
53.	The Engineering Department Salary Administration Plan	318

PART EIGHT
Employee Representation—The Role of the Labor Union 323

CASES

54.	On Organizing a Labor Union	329
55.	The Olympic Corporation (A) and (B)	332
56.	The Forsythe Chemical Company	339
57.	Beaver Glass Company Limited	348
58.	The Filmore Electric Company (B)	352
59.	Petri Chemical Company (D)	357

PART NINE 361
Statements of Company Personnel Policies

POLICIES

1.	The Monsanto Company	364
2.	Ralston Purina Company	366
3.	American Cast Iron Pipe Company	368
4.	The Continental Oil Company	374
5.	General Mills, Inc.	376
6.	Union Electric Company	378
7.	St. Luke's Hospital (St. Louis, Mo.)	379
8.	Motorola, Inc.	381
9.	Printing Industries of St. Louis, Inc., and Local 252, Lithographers and Photoengravers International Union	383
10.	U.S. Army Mobility Equipment Command (St. Louis, Mo.) and National Federation of Federal Employees (N.F.F.E. Local 405)	384

PROBLEMS AND POLICIES IN PERSONNEL MANAGEMENT
A Casebook
Second Edition

PART ONE

The Jordan Company
The Russell Company (A) and (B)
The Trouble with Lester
The Midvale Plant
The Night Shift Group

The Personnel Management Function

People, working together, produce most of the goods consumed in the world today. People, working together, provide most of the business and institutional services in our modern society. In fact, this "togetherness" is absolutely essential to the operation of our complex economy, which consists of a multitude of enterprises—all based on people, working together.

Organization is the term used to describe a group of people working together to achieve common objectives. An organization may be as planned and formal as a large business corporation, or it may be as informal as a picnic or a fishing trip. Regardless of purpose or size, any association of individuals for the attainment of common goals is an organization.

An organization is more effective in the pursuit of its goals if the individual efforts of the people within the enterprise are coordinated and directed properly. In a business organization, the coordination and direction of the efforts of others is a major part of the management job. In any organization each supervisor, foreman, and executive is a *manager* in the area of his responsibility. His success depends in part upon a capacity to understand how people work together and an ability to use this understanding in directing the efforts of his subordinates.

SUPERVISORS ARE MANAGERS

Some managers seem to be gifted with the ability to organize work and direct others without consciously knowing the "how" and "why" of their accomplishments.

1

Other managers have achieved similar success only through careful and thorough study of organizational and human relationships. Nevertheless, most managers are able to improve their leadership ability by increasing their understanding of certain principles of organization: how and why people work, and how they can be motivated to work together.

The titles of managers are not standardized. Job titles may have special meanings in certain organizations, but in the broad sense all supervisors, foremen, executives, and administrators are managers. Any individual is a manager when he is given authority over others and when he is responsible for their activities and the operations of the enterprise or a division of the enterprise. In the study of management functions, such terms as "supervisor," "executive," and "manager" may be used interchangeably.

FUNCTIONS OF MANAGEMENT

Frederick W. Taylor, the early pioneer in industry who was known as "the father of Scientific Management," once stated that management is "knowing exactly what you want men to do and then seeing that they do it in the cheapest and best way." Most authorities agree in one form or another that *the essence of management consists of the accomplishment of predetermined objectives with and through the efforts of other people.* In performing this overall management function, managers think ahead and *plan* work assignments and work schedules for the individuals in the organization. In addition, managers are required to *organize* and *staff* activities and jobs, as well as people and facilities, which require them to know what they want, where something is to be performed, and who is to perform it. Managers also must *direct, control,* and *coordinate* people who execute their plans and the operations of machines and the flow of materials and products. *Planning, organizing, staffing, directing,* and *controlling* frequently are called the functions of management. *Coordinating* is the all-pervasive and unifying effort which orders and schedules management activities properly. Management activities are not necessarily separate functions or parts of a total activity; they are interrelated and refer to overlapping duties of organizational management. They should be viewed as separate functions only for purposes of analysis.[1]

Planning is the forecasting of business activity and the preparing of work schedules and assignments. It requires that the manager look ahead, think about operations and problems in advance, and then prepare for future activities. It requires a preliminary analysis and the establishment of both long-range and immediate objectives of operations. With the goals established, policies and plans for action are developed to achieve the objectives. All of this analysis, the establishment of objectives, and the determination of policies and plans of action involve

---

[1] A variation of these management functions is called the "management process" in the text, *The Process of Management*, Second Edition, by William H. Newman, Charles E. Summer, Jr., and E. Kirby Warren, (Englewood Cliffs, N.J.: Prentice-Hall, Inc., 1967). The functions of management were presented as a part of his *Principles of Administration* by Henri Fayol, a Frenchman, in 1908. Also see, Theo Haimann and William Scott, *Management in the Modern Organization* (Boston: Houghton-Mifflin Company, 1970).

decision-making. Proper decision-making in the planning stage can avoid difficult problem-solving in the execution of plans. Decisions made in the planning of an operation involve the questions: What is to be done?, How is it to be done?, Where is it to be done?, When is it to be done?, and Who is to do it and be responsible for the results? As each of these questions is posed regarding any single operation, the manager usually has several alternatives. Thus, planning involves decision-making and becomes a process of choosing among various alternatives for future action.

Organizing basically involves answering the question, How shall activities and work be divided and accomplished? This function requires division of the work to be done, clarification of responsibilities and work assignments, and delegation of the necessary authority for carrying out the assigned activities. Organizing means to establish proper relationships among various responsibilities within an enterprise. As the duties of each job are clarified and described in the organization, jobs are grouped together into departments or divisions. In this establishment of departments or larger units, jobs must be related properly to one another. A coordinated and efficient enterprise requires the achievement of balance in the organizing of activities. Usually, the assembly and allocation of facilities and resources are considered to be parts of the organizing function.

Staffing is related intimately to the planning and organizing functions of management. It involves recruiting new workers and determining that there are enough qualified employees to fill the positions in the organization. Staffing includes the selection and training of employees, the appraisal of their performance, and provision for their development and advancement within the organization. Staffing further involves such matters as devising an appropriate wage and salary compensation plan, and administration of various benefits and working conditions surrounding the work environment. Some of these staffing functions are performed typically in a personnel or industrial relations department, but the basic responsibility for all of them lies with each manager in an organization.

Directing operations and individuals at work is another fundamental management activity which is related closely to all the other management functions. Directing means the guiding, teaching, motivating and supervising of subordinates. It includes careful instruction of workers by giving them complete and accurate information regarding their duties and responsibilities. It involves the continuous dispatch of directives, adequate communications, and proper consultation. Many authorities prefer to use the term "leading" or "motivating" to describe the directing function of management. By this, they mean that a managerial climate must be developed which will encourage employees to give more than just the minimum amount of performance expected on the job. *Since most management problems revolve around the management of people, the proper motivational climate is one of the most important of all managerial responsibilities.* Various approaches to developing positive motivation—(such as Theory Y,[2] System 4,[3] and (9,9) man-

---

[2] See Douglas McGregor, *The Human Side of Enterprise* (New York: McGraw-Hill, 1960), pp. 47-48.
[3] Rensis Likert, *The Human Organization* (New York: McGraw-Hill, 1967), pp. 3-77.

agement[4])—have been developed and frequently are called consultative or participative management. The proper motivational approach to directing subordinates encourages greater employee cooperation, enthusiasm, and job satisfaction, and thus enhances performance of employees on the job.

Controlling is the management function of maintaining operations at a continuous and efficient pace in order to achieve the objectives of the enterprise. Policies and plans of action established for operations form the basis for work standards. The quality of achievement desired for the activities of an organization constitutes the form of standards, which are essential in order to compare the results of performance with objectives and plans of action. For managers in the organization, this comparison constitutes a review of performance. Briefly, organizational control requires: 1) the establishment of standards of performance; 2) the review of actual results and their comparison with the established standards; and, 3) the analysis and correction, if necessary, of deviations from standards. To maintain satisfactory control over operations, serious deviations from standards must be corrected.

Coordinating generally is recognized as the overall synchronization of organizational efforts in the achievement of organizational objectives. It is accomplished through the establishment of policies and the actions of managers in executing those policies. It is through the use of authority that a manager works with people and is able to execute policies and plans in his area of responsibility. In the formal organization, this authority takes the form of a right delegated to the manager by his superior. Informally, it takes the form of a right earned—one which is given by a subordinate to a manager because of his competence and ability. To achieve upward delegation of authority, leadership ability must be demonstrated and recognized. The coordination of workers is achieved more readily when the manager communicates well with his subordinates by talking with them, listening to them, and understanding their needs and goals. Proper timing of orders and fair treatment of all subordinates are important in the use of managerial authority.

In addition to the coordination of human effort, there are technical aspects to the management functions. Coordination is aided by properly designed systems and procedures which integrate the technical details of work assignments. Departmentalization in an organization, resulting from the grouping of work activities, provides for the building of effective relationships and the coordination of workers as they carry out their assignments. Thus, work is directed and coordinated not only by personal leadership but also by the proper use of schedules, systems, and organizational planning. *In the final analysis, coordination will be achieved only if all of the managerial functions have been performed properly and well.*

THE NATURE OF PERSONNEL MANAGEMENT

Although managers are responsible for numerous resources, this book on problems and policies of management is concerned primarily with the management of

[4] R. R. Blake and Jane Mouton, *The Managerial Grid* (Houston: Gulf Publishing Co., 1964).

people, the "function" of *personnel management.* Currently, many writers prefer to use the term *human resources management* to describe this basic area of management responsibility. The personnel management function focuses upon planning, organizing, staffing, directing, controlling, and coordinating the activities of the human resources, the personnel, in a working organization.

Although personnel management is recognized as a basic management responsibility, one which permeates virtually all management functions and activities, there are conflicting viewpoints as to its scope and goals. Lawrence A. Appley, a long-time president of the American Management Association, made a classic statement many years ago: "Management and personnel administration are one and the same. They should never be separated. Management is personnel administration." As a workable definition of personnel management, Appley's concept emphasizes the importance of human resources in every management situation. However, this definition standing alone and out of context has been criticized for being too general. It fails to distinguish personnel activities from other basic areas of management responsibility.

Some theorists emphasize that personnel management activities should have as a primary objective the accomplishment of productive work, with little concern for individual and group needs. Managers and writers who primarily are inclined to be "profit-minded" or "production-centered" usually are credited with this concept of personnel management. Other managers and writers in the field believe that personnel management should include as a prime objective the recognition of individual worth and the realization of individual potential for all workers within an organization. This emphasizes the "human relations" approach to personnel management, an approach which would suggest that both the needs of an individual and those of an employer can be satisfied harmoniously.

The writers of this book advocate the following point of view: *Personnel management consists of those management functions and activities related to the acquisition, development, and maintenance of human resources in a working organization. Successful personnel management implies that these functions and activities integrate the efforts of people with the other resources of an organization in such a manner that the objectives of the company, the goals of individual workers, and the goals of society at large are all attained in the highest degree compatible with the work situation.*

LOOKING AHEAD

The present and future courses of personnel management in industry promise to be fraught with change. Dean John Hennessey of the Amos Tuck School of Business Administration at Dartmouth College, in a letter to the authors, has commented on our changing industrial world as follows: "Advances in automation and other aspects of technology are producing serious strains inside the business corporation, and I see the personnel manager as an important member of the executive group which needs to study and anticipate the broader ramifications of these developments."

Managers are challenged constantly by situations and events which reflect the dynamic nature of business operations. The tempo of change is accelerating. Firms throughout the country continuously are mechanizing labor and automating production processes; clerical and management work is being delegated to electronic computers; the expansion and acquisition of plants in some companies and the disposal of production facilities in others is a frequently occurring pattern. The steady flow of new markets, new products, and changing processes places new demands on the continued requirement for the proper utilization of personnel.

Change is everywhere. The course of business enterprise is being influenced by intense economic, political, and social forces which also create problems for managers of human resources. The impact of a changing composition of the labor force is being felt. Rising education levels coupled with technological advances have created many new jobs for technical, clerical, and managerial personnel, but have eliminated many unskilled and semi-skilled job opportunities. Labor unions and minority and racial groups are at the forefront of political and other types of pressures for more jobs, greater job security, and other forms of economic and social advance.

In light of these developments, personnel managers are compelled to ask and study such questions as: How can job satisfactions be provided for employees in the face of the rising expectations of people in an affluent society? Can drastic changes in production and operations be planned far enough in advance to minimize disturbances of the work force? Will work groups be developed which are flexible enough to permit reorganization and transfers within vacillating production units? What long-run training and development programs will be required for the movement and the upgrading of employees because of new demands for professional, technical, and managerial skills? What is management's responsibility for the welfare of workers who are displaced or are affected adversely by industrial change?

As all managers recognize these problems and acquire an understanding of their impact on society, the role of personnel management will assume a more important position among the responsibilities of business administration. Although the cases in this volume are not always concerned directly with these future problems of personnel management, approaches to new tasks are usually developed from experience in handling problems of the past or the present. Most case studies take place in a broad environment of dynamic change, and students in the field of personnel and industrial relations are urged to develop an awareness and a sensitivity to change. Through recognition and analysis of change, the problems ahead for the managers of people at work can become more apparent and can be anticipated. Realistic programs can and must be developed which will accommodate effectively the many conflicting pressures confronting managers of the future.

THE JORDAN COMPANY   CASE 1

The Jordan Company manufactures automobile piston rings, pistons, valves, and related products. The plant is located near South Bend, Indiana. The company is relatively small, employing 350 production workers, in addition to 125 office and sales employees and executives. Growth has been rather rapid—from an initial twelve employees to the present number in eleven years.

The founder and president, Thomas Jordan, also holds the title of sales manager in his company. Before organizing the Jordan Company, he had been the sales manager of a large automobile parts manufacturer. Believing that his extensive contacts in the automobile industry and his proven sales ability would enable him to own his own company, he went into business for himself, after obtaining additional capital from two friends, each of whom owns 20 per cent interest in the firm.

Jordan never gave much attention to the production aspects of business. In fact, he devoted about 25 per cent of his time to contacting important customers and the twenty manufacturers' agents representing the company in the southern and western states. Frank Elliott, his plant manager, started with the company at the time of its organization. He laid out the plant, established production and quality standards, and hired all the production executives under him as well as several of the first production workers.

It was the practice of the company to allow each foreman and office supervisor to hire, discipline, transfer, promote, and otherwise make his own decisions about personnel matters within his department.

Jordan observed that as the company grew in number of employees, morale appeared to degenerate. He commented to Elliott that "The one-big-happy-family spirit which pervaded our people during the first few years of the company disappeared during the past two years." Consequently, Jordan decided that the company should employ a personnel manager.

John Graham, chief cost accountant, learned of Jordan's plans through one of the secretaries with whom he had lunch in the plant cafeteria. John had wanted to get into personnel work for some time. As he put it, "I always did prefer working with people to working with numbers."

John had worked with the Jordan Company for seven years. He joined the company in the bookkeeping department immediately after graduating from college. Since the company was small and work was not highly departmentalized, he had many contacts with people in both production and sales. Elliott and Jordan both believed that he was an alert, conscientious employee who "generally is well liked by all."

John applied for the position of personnel manager, and he was selected for the job.

After much debate, it was decided to make the personnel manager a part of the production management section, the manager of which reported to the plant manager.

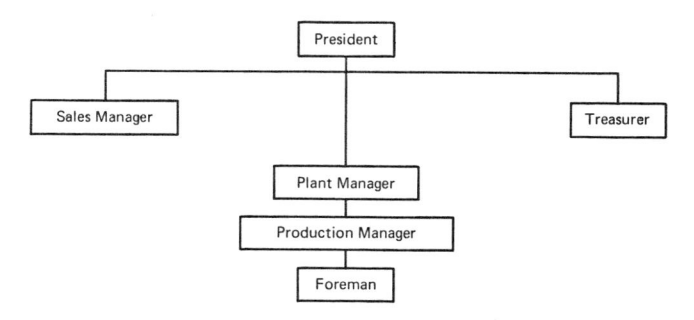

```
                        President
         ┌──────────────────┼──────────────────┐
   Sales Manager            │              Treasurer
                       Plant Manager
                     Production Manager
                          Foreman
```

John was given an office near the entrance of the plant and a secretary was assigned to him. The president told him at the time of his appointment that "the scope and success of the personnel department's activities will be pretty much what you make them."

John immediately sent a memorandum to all foremen, over the signature of the production manager, advising them that "the personnel manager will hire all new employees in the future." In addition, the memorandum stated that the personnel manager would henceforth initiate all transfers and changes in pay, and that all disciplinary action and other personnel decisions must be approved by the personnel manager before being acted upon.

Upon receiving the memorandum several of the foremen expressed considerable resentment against this organization change. They agreed that John had the "bighead."

After a short time, the production manager began to receive complaints from foremen to the effect that "new employees aren't what they were when we hired them." On one occasion when he questioned a foreman about a drop in production, the foreman said that his hands were tied; he could not hire, discipline or otherwise control his men. And, if he could not control his men, how could he be expected to get out production?

One day an employee came into John's office and protested that his foreman had just discharged him "for no reason at all." John telephoned the foreman and the following conversation took place:

JOHN: Hello, Jim. This is John Graham. What's the story on Joe Ralfing?
FOREMAN: I fired him.
JOHN: Yes, I know, but why?
FOREMAN: I don't like him.
JOHN: But that's no reason. You know that you can't fire him without an O.K. from my office.

FOREMAN: Well, I did it.
JOHN: But you can't, Jim. There has to be a good reason, and . . .
FOREMAN: I don't like him—that's reason enough.

The foreman hung up.

John presented the matter to the production manager who finally insisted that the employee be reinstated. Soon the number of complaints concerning the hiring of poor workers and the lack of control over personnel began to increase. The foremen agreed to "stay clear" of the personnel department as much as possible.

Finally, the production manager advised the plant manager that he did not believe that the firm was large enough to warrant a personnel department. He further recommended that the company return to the former plan of having foremen make their own personnel decisions. Finally, he urged that John be returned to his former job.

The plant manager thought about the production manager's recommendations for a few days and then passed them on to the president, recommending that they be accepted.

THE RUSSELL COMPANY (A)   CASE 2

While Lawrence Sloan, a case writer from Northwestern University, was visiting the Russell Company,[1] a large manufacturer of precision tools and machine parts, the assistant personnel manager, Homer Mills,[2] called his attention to certain happenings which are described in this case.

MILLS: You might be interested in this situation, Larry. Walter Wood, the foreman of the grinding department of the machine shop, has just suspended an operator, Jim Rand, for making too many scrap pieces. Rand is an operator on piecework, and in a two-day period he made 162 scrap units out of a completed 176 units. Before you came in, I called Rand down here and asked him what the facts in the situation were. He told me the machine was at fault. He said that if his machine had been working properly, he wouldn't have made so much scrap.

While Homer Mills was talking, Allan Thompson, the personnel manager walked into the office.

THOMPSON: What's the situation, Homer?

MILLS: I just finished talking to Rand and he said his machine was at fault, but Walter Wood told Donald Price at the time of the suspension that Rand had just been careless in his work again.

THOMPSON: Wasn't Rand suspended once before for making scrap?

MILLS: Yes. Six months ago he was suspended for four days for making about thirty pieces of scrap. This time, on the same machine and making the identical part number, he's turned out 162 bad pieces out of 176 completed units.

Reprinted with the permission of Northwestern University School of Business. Copyright, Northwestern University.

[1] All names and organizational designations have been disguised. Northwestern University cases are reports of concrete events and behavior, prepared for class discussion. They are not intended as examples of "good" or "bad" administrative or technical practices.

[2] The following list contains the names and titles of persons mentioned in this case:

Homer Mills:	Assistant personnel manager.
Walter Wood:	Foreman of the grinding department of the machine shop.
Jim Rand:	An operator in the grinding department.
Allan Thompson:	Personnel manager.
Donald Price:	Superintendent of the machine shop.
Lloyd Clark:	General foreman for the grinding and polishing department.
Bill Ewbank:	A shop steward.
Bob Dougherty:	President of the local union.
Charlie Jones:	An operator in the grinding department.
Irwin Flinn:	Vice-president of the union.
Curt Kimball:	Secretary of the union.
Johnny:	An electrician.

THOMPSON: How could he have made so many before the foreman discovered it?

MILLS: I don't know, Al. Price said that Rand told Wood around ten o'clock this morning that his machine wasn't running properly. When Walt took a look at Rand's completed parts and saw how much scrap he had made, he told him to stop work. Then, about an hour later, Price, Clark, and Walt called Rand and Ewbank, the shop steward, into the office. They told Rand then in Ewbank's presence that he was suspended as of eleven o'clock. It was around that time I got the phone call about the situation.

While Mills spoke, Thompson looked through Rand's file.

THOMPSON: I see that besides being suspended before for the same offense Rand has been warned about the quality of his work on two separate occasions by the foreman and the general foreman of the department.

MILLS: I just called Bob Dougherty on the phone and told him. Dougherty is going to appeal the case immediately. He's asked for a meeting at three o'clock this afternoon. That's pushing the hearing pretty fast, but I told him we'd do what we could to arrange it.

THOMPSON: Besides his seniority with the company, wasn't Rand an officer in the union?

MILLS: Yeah. He lost out in the election last year, however. (Pause.)

THOMPSON: Why don't you see what the department supervisors have to say.

MILLS: Okay, Al...

About an hour later, Mills met in Price's office with Lloyd Clark and Walter Wood.

MILLS: Walt, are you prepared to state your reasons for suspending Rand?

WOOD: Yes. Rand made 162 pieces of scrap. When I asked him about it, he had no reasonable answer.

PRICE: Homer, this is an open and shut case. Rand could easily have told Walt about the situation long before he did. But he went right on, hour after hour, making bad pieces. Then, when he knew he was really in trouble, he came to Walt complaining about the machine. Walt brought me the scrap parts, and I've got them locked up here in the office.

CLARK: As I told both Don and Walt, we've tried to be fair to Rand in this situation, but he's been asking for it for a long time. He made the bad stuff and that's about the size of it. I don't like to do this, but what are you going to do with someone who ignores every suggestion you make?

MILLS: None of us like to do something like this, Lloyd.

WOOD: Frankly, he could have been fired on the spot. We talked it over here in Don's office, and we thought that might be hard to make stick. The guy must be worth something. He's worked for the company for nearly twenty years.

CLARK: You know, Homer, that we try to meet any worker halfway. Many times, both Walt and I have excused a mistake when it was an honest one and the operator was willing to be a man about it and own up to it. But in this situation, well, Rand just went on making bad stuff until he saw he was in trouble. Then he decided to blame the machine.

MILLS: What about the machine? Is it all right?

PRICE: I checked the machine at the time Rand was suspended. There is nothing wrong with it. Also, I talked with the electrician and he said everything was functioning properly. He mentioned something about a switch not working quite right a few weeks back, but he repaired it, and it has worked properly ever since.

WOOD: Charlie Jones worked the same machine a week ago and he had no trouble at all.

MILLS: Well the meeting is set for two o'clock this afternoon in my office, if that's agreeable.

PRICE: What's the hurry? Why rush into this? We may need a little more time to get our materials together. Why don't we set it for tomorrow?

MILLS: Well, Dougherty asked for the meeting this afternoon.

PRICE: I say tomorrow. Let some of the smoke clear away. We'll be better prepared tomorrow.

MILLS: Okay, Don. I'll call Dougherty and tell him. How about ten o'clock? Does that sound all right?

PRICE: That's more like it.

MILLS: Well, I guess I've got the relevant facts in the situation. Oh, one thing. What did you say to Rand at the time you discovered the scrap, Walt?

WOOD: I didn't say anything. I took a micrometer and checked the parts and when I saw they weren't up to specifications, I told him to stop work. Then I took the parts into the office here and went to see Don and Lloyd about the situation. About an hour later, we called Rand and Ewbank in and told them our decision.

MILLS: Good.

WOOD: Also, I told Rand that if this ever happened again, he'd be discharged.

PRICE: We've got a case this time. It's not the man's personality I'm judging, but his failure to do the job properly. His work is not up to specifications, and we must be objective about that...

The suspension hearing for Jim Rand was held the next day at ten in Homer Mills' office.

Those present, in addition to Jim Rand and the case writer, were: for the company, Allan Thompson (Personnel Manager), Homer Mills (Assistant Personnel Manager), Donald Price (Superintendent), Lloyd Clark (General Foreman) and Walter Wood (Foreman); for the union, Bob Dougherty (President), Irwin Flinn (Vice-President), Curt Kimball (Secretary), and Bill Ewbank (Shop Steward).

Bob Dougherty of the union started the discussion of the suspension as follows:

DOUGHERTY: Now as I understand the situation, the company claims that Jim Rand here made 162 pieces of scrap out of a total of 176 completed pieces over a two-day period. Is that right?

MILLS: That's right, Bob. Because of that, Rand was suspended by his foreman, Walt Wood. And I think we should note that Rand was suspended for a week six months ago for the same offense, while working on the same machine, and making the identical part number.

DOUGHERTY: But he's not being suspended for that, is he?

MILLS: No. He's being suspended for the scrap he made yesterday and the day before.

RAND: They are trying to blame me for something that happened months ago and it's . . .

DOUGHERTY. Now, now, Jim, we'll all get our turn before this hearing is over. Let me run things right now. I'm still trying to get the facts straight. You say Rand made 162 pieces of scrap. What's the procedure down there, Walt, on checking machines and parts? What do the job standards call for?

WOOD: Rand is supposed to check every tenth piece he grinds.

DOUGHERTY: Okay. Did you check his setup before he started grinding?

WOOD: When Rand set up his machine the day before, I checked to see whether or not the first part he made was correct.

DOUGHERTY: And was it?

WOOD: Yes. From then on, he was supposed to check every tenth part. I don't have time to look at every piece he makes. That's his job.

DOUGHERTY: And you say you didn't look at his work again until the 162 so-called scrap pieces were discovered several work hours later? Is that right?

WOOD: His job is to check the machine and parts. He's supposed to dress the wheel every time it needs it, usually after making thirty pieces. If he had done what his job calls for, he wouldn't have made all that scrap.

DOUGHERTY: Is this one of the so-called defective parts on the table here?

PRICE: It isn't so-called. The part is defective. It doesn't come up to specifications, and if we put such parts in a machine, there's no telling what the results might be. If you look closely on the sides of that piece you're holding, you can see that he brought the grinding wheel too close to the center and damaged the unit.

DOUGHERTY: Lloyd, can you see the damage that Don speaks of with the naked eye?

CLARK: Yes, I'm not saying it's easy to detect, but the damage is there.

DOUGHERTY: Does it require 20-20-vision? Could Jim see the damage without the use of a magnifying glass? You know there is water running over the parts continuously.

CLARK: As I said, Bob, it's not easy. You have to look carefully, but you can see it. The part fails to meet specifications.

DOUGHERTY: Would someone inform me just how this so-called scrap was discovered? Jim, why don't you tell us exactly what happened?

RAND: I told Walt on several occasions that my machine wasn't operating right. Then around ten o'clock yesterday morning, I told him again. He checked some of my parts and told me to shut down the machine. He picked up the two trays of parts and took them off to Price's office. A little later, he told me I was suspended.

WOOD: Now, let me tell what happened. Around ten o'clock yesterday, Rand approached me and said that he didn't think his machine was grinding properly. I took a look at it and checked his last part. Then, I told him to make another one. When I saw what he was doing, I got a micrometer and checked the spacing on the parts. It was obvious at once that the parts were not ground properly. Then I saw that practically every piece he had made for a day and a half was bad. I told him to shut down his machine and I took the parts to the office. Later, Rand was called in, as well as the shop steward, and was told that he was suspended for two weeks for making scrap.

MILLS: I think it should be said also that earlier this year Rand was told twice that his work was not up to quality.

DOUGHERTY: Was that on this machine?

MILLS: Once it was, I believe.

RAND: I was given hell for something that was the machine's fault. I told Wood that the diamond of my machine was worn out. I couldn't dress the wheel properly as a result.

DOUGHERTY: That brings up another point. Was the machine inspected before Jim was suspended?

PRICE: Yes, and there's nothing wrong with that machine. Others have worked on it without any difficulty. And, heaven only knows how many parts Rand has made on that machine.

DOUGHERTY: Then he has been making quality parts right along?

PRICE: I guess he's made some 10,000 or 15,000 parts since he came back to work last spring after the lay-offs.

DOUGHERTY: Did you look at the machine, Walt?

WOOD: We looked at the machine. There's nothing wrong with it. Charlie Jones made plenty of good parts on it just a couple of weeks ago when Rand was working on another job. Rand knows how to operate that machine. This situation is the result of his carelessness.

DOUGHERTY: Shortly after Mills told me that Jim had been suspended, I sent Curt Kimball down to look at the machine and to talk to the electrician and the other operators. Curt, why don't you tell us what you found out? Curt, as you know, has worked on similar grinding machines.

KIMBALL: The operator next to Jim told me that on several occasions he had pointed out to Jim that his magnetic light wasn't on. As you know, the light is always on when the magnet is functioning properly.

PRICE: The electrician told me just yesterday that Rand's machine was functioning properly.

KIMBALL: Well, it might be functioning properly when Johnny (the electrician) is about, but the operator next to Jim said that on several occasions he's had to tell Jim that his light wasn't on.

DOUGHERTY: What did you do on those occasions when the light for the magnet didn't come on right, Jim?

RAND: I've had that magnetic trouble before. The switch box just isn't worth much. I usually have to hit it with my hand so that it will work. Sometimes it goes off.

KIMBALL: Lloyd Clark here will tell you that it's possible for the magnetic switch to go out.

CLARK: Well, sure, it's possible, but whether it did in this case, I don't know. When I talked with Johnny, he told me that switch worked all right.

RAND: Do you remember some time back when I told Johnny that the switch wasn't working right? He said he didn't have a new one, so he fixed up the old one. Also, the times I was called down by Walt about my work, I had a worn out diamond. I told him about it and he gave me a new one. Then, once when I told the shop steward that the machine wasn't working right, he told Walt about it and Walt told me to mind my own business. He said to come to him when I had machine difficulties. He said I wasn't to bother the shop steward.

DOUGHERTY: Listen, Jim, the contract says you can contact either your steward or the foreman, whenever you have any trouble.

WOOD: I didn't tell you to mind your own business.

RAND: You said to get to work.

KIMBALL: Look, the electrician says that the switch might be defective, and besides, the diamond used in dressing the wheel must have been bad.

WOOD: It was a little worn.

THOMPSON: Now, the problem here is whether the machine was at fault or whether Rand was at fault. Isn't that the issue?

PRICE: Of course. Rand wasn't watching what he was doing. How could a worker, who is supposed to check every tenth part and redress his machine wheel frequently, stand there and work hour after hour, making 176 parts, 162 of which are scrap?

KIMBALL: Lloyd, you know those machines. What are the specifications for Jim's work?

CLARK: Well, Curt, a good grind makes a part acceptable for use.

DOUGHERTY: And what about this part? Isn't it a good grind? You mean to say that you can tell with the naked eye that this part has been damaged beyond use? I could make a good grind with sandpaper.

CLARK: A good grind, Bob, means that the work be within .043 of an inch of tolerance. Now, Bob, we both know that there's nothing complicated about Jim's work. I could probably train anyone to do the job in a few afternoons. The work involved in meeting the specifications isn't difficult; the difficulty is in the worker's willingness to meet the specifications.

PRICE: A good grind isn't the issue. The issue is whether the parts made by Rand meet the specifications as indicated by the blueprints. Now here is the blueprint for his part, and that part you're holding just doesn't match it.

DOUGHERTY: You say that Rand made 162 defective parts. Where are they?

PRICE: We've got them upstairs.

DOUGHERTY: Well, upstairs isn't down here. Let's bring them down here if they're evidence.

THOMPSON: Well, Bob, it wasn't convenient to bring down. But if you want to look at them, we can go upstairs and get them.

PRICE: Sure, if you want to see them, I'll be glad to show them to you.

DOUGHERTY: I'm not upstairs. I'm down here.

PRICE: Look, you heard what the electrician said, that the switch was functioning properly. It wasn't the machine's fault.

DOUGHERTY: That's another thing. I think the electrician should be here, for evidently he told you one thing and Curt another. Also, let's call in the operator that Curt talked to as well.

MILLS: Can't we continue without these men? The issue is whether Rand was doing his work properly.

DOUGHERTY: What's going to happen to these pieces when the case is over?
PRICE: They will be scrapped.
DOUGHERTY: Walt, what would you do with these pieces if Jim hadn't made them?
WOOD: What do you mean? I'd scrap them regardless of who made them. They're defective.
EWBANK: Now, Walt, I know for a fact that you have used parts like these before. Just the other day we turned out some parts like these and they passed. Just because Rand made these parts, you won't use them.
WOOD: That's not true, Bill. I'm not dealing in personalities. I'm saying that these parts are scrap. They aren't acceptable for use.
RAND: He's had it in for me for a long time. They're always picking on me. Isn't that right, Bill?
EWBANK: If Jim hadn't made these parts, they would be passed. And, also, they will work in the machines they were designed for, just as they stand.
PRICE: Whether they will or not has no bearing upon the situation before us. For that matter they might be shipped to Alaska, but they aren't going to be. They are scrap. As Walt said, we don't want to bring personalities into this discussion. Let's look at the facts and the situation objectively. Regardless of who made these parts, they are defective. They are defective because they fail to meet specifications. And because they cannot be used, they have cost the company money. I say the situation is one of negligence and carelessness.
DOUGHERTY: If you don't use these parts, you ought to fire your foreman for not doing his job properly and costing the company money. These parts are salvable.
THOMPSON: Bob, is the question here whether the parts can be used or whether Rand was doing his job properly?
PRICE: Would you, Al, want to use these parts when they fail to come up to specifications? I don't think so. I don't think the company wants their name on such parts.
THOMPSON: The parts are defective, Don.
DOUGHERTY: I ask for full re-instatement of Jim Rand. I believe he was suspended for something for which he was not to blame. I think he should be fully re-instated and paid accordingly.
The union officials left the room. Mills turned to Thompson.
THOMPSON: We are on solid ground. I think much of what Bob said was just for the benefit of the grandstand. He's saying a lot because he hasn't much of a case. The issue boils down to whether the machine was at fault or whether the worker was careless. I think the latter is true.
PRICE: Dougherty's tactic is to get everyone sore, but it doesn't work with me. The parts do not meet the specification. The issue is why 162 pieces of scrap were made.
CLARK: I'm willing to meet any man halfway. If a man makes a mistake and is willing to admit it, I'm willing to give him another chance. But we've given Rand so many, and it's never worked out.

WOOD: I can remember many instances when I've told him to do something and he just gets mad. You can't tell him anything. That job he works isn't complicated. I could train a girl in half a day to do that job. It's his attitude. It's all wrong. Very few in the department speak well of him. I'd call him a trouble-maker.

MILLS: Well, then I'll have to give Dougherty our decision tomorrow. Do we agree on what it will be?

THE RUSSELL COMPANY (B)

The events described in this case took place subsequent to the suspension hearing for Jim Rand which was described in the Russell Company (A).

On the day following the hearing, Homer Mills, the assistant personnel manager, reported to Robert Dougherty, the union president, that Jim Rand's suspension had been upheld by the company's representatives at the hearing. Dougherty then appealed the case to the plant manager's office, and a week later another hearing was held. After that hearing, the plant manager upheld the decision made by the foreman.

When Jim Rand returned to work in the grinding department after his suspension, he was put back on the same machine, to make the same parts he had made previously. He had been at work a little over a week when Lawrence Sloan, the case writer, went to the department to talk to Walter Wood, the department foreman. As they walked about the department, Wood commented about Jim Rand:

WOOD: I don't know whether or not you gathered this from our conversation, but of the jobs I've described to you, Jim Rand has one of the simplest. Frankly, as far as skill is concerned, there is no reason at all why he should have had the trouble he has had.

SLOAN: How has he been doing, Walt, since he returned?

WOOD: Oh, he's been back a little over a week now, and his work still isn't quite up to standard. But he hasn't made any stack of defective parts, either. Lloyd Clark (the general foreman) says he sees some improvement in Rand's attitude. But I don't know. He's not easy to talk to, that's for sure. Other workers in my department take my suggestions without giving me any trouble. "Sure, Walt," is the reply most of them give me if I tell them to do the work one way instead of another, or ask them to improve their work a little when I inspect it. But ask Rand to do something differently and his usual comeback is: "What's the matter? Don't you think I know my job?" He's got a belligerent attitude. For instance, just the other day I asked him to do a certain job a little differently and his only remark was: "That's probably the way you'd do it—that's not the only way."

I've been supervising people for many years and I've seen things change. I guess it's only right that the foreman can't be the bull of the shop anymore. But in the old days, we got the work out. Today a foreman has to take a lot of abuse from the workers. The days when you told a worker what was expected of him and got rid of him if he didn't do it are gone forever. Nowadays, it's a major project to get a worker transferred or discharged, even though he's costing the company plenty of money.

Why, in order to remove a bad worker you've really got to have the goods on him. You've got to prove dozens of things, write him up at least twice, and suspend him at least once before you can ever hope to discharge him. And, like I said, all the time he's costing the company money, causing you one headache after another, and screwing up the work for others. Frankly, Rand's a troublemaker. Few of the other fellows have much to do with him. The union steward sticks up for him, but that's because of their past union connections. (Pause.)

SLOAN: He's just not much good at all?

WOOD: Well, sometimes I don't think he's really a bad guy at heart. Why, he's an excellent gunsmith—at least I'm told that—and can do beautiful work fixing guns. And frankly, working on a gun is far more complicated than the grinding job he does. Sometimes I think he wants to be a gunsmith instead of working here. That may be his problem, but I don't know. Also, as I said in the meeting upstairs a few weeks back, he's got good in him because he's been with Russell for nearly twenty years. Any man who's willing to give that much service to the company is bound to have many good qualities about him. I wouldn't want to discharge him for that reason. He's not a young man as you can see. But he's asked for a transfer and I hope it goes through. He wants to go on day work, and maybe his personality is better suited to that type of work.

While he was in the department, Sloan spoke to Rand at his machine.

SLOAN: I don't know whether you remember me or not, Jim, but I was here a few weeks back when the suspension hearing came up.

RAND: Oh yes, I remember you. So you were there when I got my arm caught in the wringer, eh? (Laughed.) Well, that's what I should expect, I guess.

SLOAN: How's that?

RAND: You see, I used to be an officer in the union. I lost my place by a few votes. I shouldn't have lost, but I did. And, well, now I'm not too active. Say, you're from a university; you ought to come to some union meetings. I could get you in. (Pause.)

I was a steward once, too, and I could be the steward here if I wanted the job. Of course, the union has got a good man in Bill Ewbank and I wouldn't want to take the job away from him. But as I was saying, the foremen here are out to get the union people. Otherwise, I can't figure out what all this fuss is about. Scrap has been made in this department before.

SLOAN: The machine was at fault?

RAND: Sure it was. Don't you think so? (Pause.)

On the day I had all the trouble with the parts, I told Walt Wood about it several times. I said that the grinding wheel was bumping the inner ring too much. He told me to go to work and not to bother him. So I did. Since that's the way he wanted, I just went on grinding parts. I had an idea they weren't any good. Frankly, Wood is always trying to tell people off. It doesn't work with me, however. I just don't pay him any attention and that just burns him up. He's got some idea that he knows more about these machines than I do. But he doesn't. The day I made all those bum pieces, that wheel just wasn't working quite right. I told him but he's got some idea that I bellyache all the time. He thinks I don't know my business, but I do. (Pause.)

So you see, when he gets something on me, he really wants it to stick. He's out to get me, that's what I think. At any rate, I've asked for a transfer to day work. I don't like this piecework any more. Besides, most of the workers in here aren't too interested in union matters like they should be.

Later, Sloan talked with Homer Mills, the assistant personnel manager.

MILLS: Suspending Jim Rand for two weeks wasn't an easy thing to do, but frankly we didn't have any choice in the matter. The company can't afford to tolerate that quality of work. Why he did such a thing, I don't know. If he did it intentionally, why? If he was just careless, why? The work had been carefully explained to him and he knows his business. He has had years of experience and the operation is not too difficult.

Frankly, I don't like to suspend a man any more than anyone else. But when a worker does something like this and it's obviously due to carelessness, we don't have any other alternative. Now, you know yourself that when you were a child in school, you had some teachers who were pretty strict and you didn't like them, but when you left school and thought back on those teachers, you saw that they did what they had to do. Then you began to appreciate them for the first time.

As you know, Jim Rand is back at work now. The foreman tells me he's asked for a transfer. In a way that may be a good thing. Of course, he had to ask for the transfer. The company can't arbitrarily change workers around. The contract provisions must be followed in all transfer cases.

But, you know, Larry, this situation, small as it is, has important implications for our cost and production. What would happen if all of our workers were permitted to turn out work like that? I don't think I've ever told you that the machine shop and, in particular, the grinding room make precision parts that are vital to our customers. And customers aren't growing on every bush any more. We are moving into a highly competitive era, in which cost and quality determine whether or not we stay alive economically. We have strong competition nowadays. No, the problem can hardly be taken lightly. It's only one incident—that is true—but multiply it by many more, and before long Russell wouldn't be in business any more. Not only would we suffer as a company, but the community in which we supply thousands of jobs would suffer as well.

THE TROUBLE WITH LESTER   CASE 3

One February morning, George Healey, the personnel director of the Lester Manufacturing Company, received a document entitled "The Trouble with Lester" from Mike Bossart, one of his assistants. It had been given to Bossart by Frank Baxter during the customary exit interview which had followed Baxter's voluntary resignation the day before.

THE TROUBLE WITH LESTER

DEDICATED TO THE FRUSTRATED SOULS WHO SPEND THEIR WORKING HOURS IN THE SUFFOCATING JUNGLE OF THE ACCOUNTING DEPARTMENT

Without the Lester Company the economy of our city, and the state would collapse. This statement, constantly reiterated, is undoubtedly true. But even with Lester, unemployment in the state has reached one of the highest figures in the nation.

It follows that with the current changing product emphasis, Lester, like others in the field, will, in the future, be operating with less manpower. Thus, inevitable cutbacks, and mounting unemployment will follow.

Lester couldn't care less. They have their defense contracts. The Lester products, both military and commercial, are universally respected. The company will still reap financial profit.

But what will become of the state, and the people who live here? They have suffered, and are doomed to suffer more, from the weaknesses of an overbalanced economy. Nearsighted leadership, and moss-backed legislation have made it difficult to attract new industry. In contrast to other states which promote new industries with lease-free land, our state offers prohibitive taxes.

A remedy must be found.

In the meantime, Lester, without competition, floats like a fat shark in a pool of shellfish, taking all, giving nothing, and spitting out the bones.

No, the picture isn't that morbid. Actually, Lester is benevolent. They provide a huge payroll. They have a rewarding Suggestion System, which

---

Case prepared by Professor H. R. Knudson, Jr., College of Business Administration, University of Washington, Seattle, Washington. From *Human Elements of Administration* by Harry R. Knudson, Jr. Copyright © 1963 by Holt, Rinehart, and Winston, Inc. Reprinted by permission of Holt, Rinehart, and Winston, Inc.

benefits the ingenious employee (as well as the company). Cash awards are made on everything from designing a labor-and-expense saving casting to suggesting that Maintenance install signs over the restrooms for nearsighted personnel. Suggestions concerning the value of specific employees, or groups of employees, or where they should go, are not accepted.

Lester supports the Community Chest, and they have a personal Blood Bank. They, also, have a Credit Union, where an employee can obtain a loan at a reasonable interest rate. Payments are deducted from the second paycheck of every month. It is not advisable to borrow too much, however. It is difficult to take a $500 loan payment out of a $175 termination check and end up with any money.

The company protects its employees with insurance. The rumor that they were forced into it by the Federal Government is false.

The company has a Pension (?) plan. However, unless you work for Lester for 120 years, don't expect to retire to the Bahamas on the money they give you. Better line yourself up with a part-time job as a Western Union boy.

Lester provides schools where the employee can better himself. The courses are related to the company and its business. Supervision urges that employees take advantage of this built-in education system, and attend as many classes as possible. The fact that you have taken some classes goes in your personnel folder, and will help you advance. I know a fellow who has been with the company six years and taken 24 classes. (That's an average of four a year.) He's an expeditor—at the next to bottom grade.

The company stimulates leisure activities. It has hobby clubs, and athletics.

In addition, different departments (for example, the Accounting Department) sponsor social functions for their employees. This promotes a feeling of "togetherness" in the section. There are dances, picnics, mixed-overnight camping trips, and assorted orgies.

For the employee working in Accounting, the Accounting Dance is a social must. This gives the peon a chance to cultivate his supervisor. An interchange of dances is a good approach. What do you care if his wife is a foot taller than you and has halitosis? So she wants to lead? When dancing, try to Charleston in front of the Chief's table. In this way you may be able to strike up an acquaintance with him. This is especially true if you kick him in the mouth.

Bowling is the best of departmental athletics. The whole gang is down at the alley. You can joke, and kid, and drink beer with your supervisors. It's a hell of a lot of fun. But don't try and win, or you'll be permanent second shift. (This is comparable to being permanent K.P., or permanent latrine.) And for God's sake don't laugh if some superior falls down delivering the ball, or gets a split.

Lester provides for Sick Leave. But if you work in Accounting, don't take it unless you have polio. If you break an arm, put it in a splint and come to work. If you have malaria so bad your clothes are soaked through, put on another change and come to work. Supervision stresses attendance, and if they don't like the color of your ties, a bad attendance record (missing over two days a year) is a ready-made excuse for stopping your progress.

What happens to the employee working in the Accounting Department at Lester?

Foremost his individualism is crushed. The bigness of the company, and its socialistic structure make him small. It is no wonder that he loses incentive.

He must conform. The proper dress is a white shirt and tie (conservative), and preferably a business suit. To get ahead, you should keep your suit coat on, even though it may be a rather sticky 95, and four stenos have fainted.

Be intense. Furrowing the brow, and scowling, indicates that you have a businesslike attitude, and are serious about your job, and not that you have a bad case of hemorrhoids. And for gosh sakes don't laugh during working hours. Laughing conveys frivolity, and may give some supervisor the idea that you don't give a damn about your job. (A small chuckle is permitted at lunchtime.) Don't grin, and smile only at superiors.

When traveling to another area, walk briskly. Don't loiter. An efficiency expert may be watching. Carry a piece of paper. A paper gives the carrier an air of importance.

Being on good terms with your supervisor is essential at Lester. Cultivate him. Asking him questions about the job is one method. Chances are he won't know the answer, but he can direct you to some experienced employee who will. Asking questions show that you're enthusiastic. That's the image you must create.

Discover your supervisor's interests. If he cuts out paper dolls, buy a pair of scissors.

Be cautious in talking with your supervisor, or, for that matter, any supervisor. The relationship is a delicate one. Never disagree, even though you know he's dead wrong, and a jerk besides. Contradicting the supervisor means that you are out of line, have a bad attitude, and are not pulling with the team.

Your supervisor can make or break you, depending on his whims, and whether or not he's had his coffee. Despite all the "hogwash" about a "scientific" Personnel Evaluation System, all individual progress at Lester is based on the personal relationship of the supervisor with those under him. The man who thinks he can succeed through merit alone is living in an "ivory tower."

If the supervisor likes you, and considers you "sharp," it's one step into the "Up" elevator. If he doesn't think you "fit in," or aren't aggressive, it's the basement.

Stock cover-up phrases are used by supervisors in the "P.A." interview to conceal personal feelings. Such mouthings as "You don't communicate well," "you don't write an effective memo," or "you don't show enough initiative" are typical.

Movement is vital in the Accounting Department. Many a good man has stayed at the same desk month after month, watching new hires pass him by, because a supervisor has taken a dislike to him. This man may be a good, conscientious employee, well-qualified for a better job, but he won't get it. Eventually this man must go out the door. He isn't moving.

Once you are stopped, start reading the Want-Ads.

Security is a hollow word at Lester. Nobody uses it, unless they're talking of the market. Anybody who thinks they have it here, should be advised to see a psychiatrist. When the cutbacks come, they can strike anywhere, both bottom and top. They will get worse.

After reading the document with a great deal of interest, Mr. Healey reviewed the personnel record of Frank Baxter. This record is reproduced in part as follows:

FRANK BAXTER

Work History

Hired in	3-16-53		
Transferred to Accounting	5-25-54	Clerk C	$ 69.60/week
Reclassification	4-22-55	Accountant C	76.60
Merit Raise	4- 6-56		80.40
Reclassification	7-13-56	Accountant B	94.60
Merit Raise	1-25-57		97.60
Merit Raise	8-23-57		104.40
Reclassification	9-19-58	Controller B	110.60
Resigned	2- 2-61		117.80

Evaluations (from Personnel Evaluation Reports)

W. Bostrom 4-15-53 to 2-15-54. Group 4 to Group 3. Good steady worker. Improve accuracy factor

R. Kast 7-20-54 to 7-18-58. Rating 60 to 72. Hard worker, good job knowledge. Needs to attain self-confidence and aggressiveness.

B. A. Lootkens 2-59 to 9-59. Comments same as above.

V. R. Cone 11-59. Reliable and cooperative, needs initiative.

J. R. Lockover 6-60. Improve initiative, productivity, judgment. Shown some improvement over last P.A.

Merits (From Merit Increase Evaluation Form)

M. R. Ballert 1-57 to 8-57. Good improvement. Above Average.

H. A. Berg 12-58. Average.

B. A. Lootkens 3-59. Show more initiative and drive. Above Average.
9-59. Below Average—not concentrating.

J. R. Lockover 3-60. Room for considerable improvement in job performance. Below Average.

H. E. Martin 9-60. Improved over past 6 months. Average.
Memo dated 3-2-60, J. R. Lockover, regarding job performance. Placed on 30-day probation. Remarks: Needs to improve—initiative, reliability, response to Company needs, productivity and judgment. Has capability to do good work, but needs to apply himself and show interest.

A few days after he had received the document, Mr. Healey made the following comments concerning Frank Baxter.

"I've really never talked with him, so these are just observations that I have. I became acquainted with him, originally, or rather I noticed him originally, because of his sloppy dress. He has a real talent for looking sloppy if you know what I mean. You know the kind of guy who makes the best clothes look unkempt. I really don't think he would comb his hair if he were paid for it. He's balding, about 36 or 37 years old, single, and a university graduate.

"He is very interested in sports—really an authority on them. He's the kind of guy, for example, who can quote batting averages for years back, knows who is playing whom three years from now, and how many night games the Yankees played in 1958. He is also a participant in sports to some degree, and I've heard that he's been active in some of the company's recreational programs.

"He is a man who has frequently been suggested to me as a man who might fill vacancies of higher positions in the accounting department. But just as frequently I've said 'not interested.'

"He's obviously quite well liked by his fellow employees. I've received many indications through the grape-vine that they have been asking if something can't be done to get him moved up the ladder or some way worked out that he could progress faster than he had been. There is no indication at all that he had any difficulty in getting along with his people. Indeed, quite the opposite. It is strange, though, in noting the comments on his personnel evaluation reports and merit evaluation forms, that this matter of sloppy appearance never came up. Yet this was what first attracted my attention to him.

"I've done nothing about the document. The guy has some good points in there. There's a real message, I think. For example, his comments about 'conformity' may be quite pertinent. Some of the people I've talked with about the document have suggested that we get it reproduced and distribute it to all of our supervisors. I'm not sure this is the right approach, though. I think we should try and gain what good we can from this incident. And I'm not sure that circulating it with wide distribution will let us realize any of the benefits that are here. You can get good ideas from this or anything like this, but I'm afraid that if we circulate the document those supervisors who weren't directly involved might treat it facetiously and tend to ride their fellow supervisors who had had contacts with Baxter. Maybe a better approach would be to discuss it with the chief supervisors who were involved and see if there is, in fact, any good that we can get out of the situation. I'm really not sure what I should do. There's probably some element of 'sour grapes' involved in this but on the other hand Baxter does make some good points."

THE MIDVALE PLANT   CASE 4

The Midvale Plant of the Abacus Corporation is located in a suburb of Metro City, some 15 miles from the corporate main office and major manufacturing facilities in the central city. The plant has been established as the principal source for small coil windings and sub-assemblies for the company's radio and television production. In its 15 years of operation, the plant had experienced a slow, steady growth; by 1967, 300 employees worked at Midvale, 25 of whom were management or supervisory personnel. Many technical and managerial services were provided by home office personnel whom the Midvale people referred to as "city-folk" located at "the city."

PLANT ORGANIZATION—1967

The plant manager at Midvale, George Whitfield, had 25 years service with the company and had been on his present job for eleven years. He was interested primarily in the production work at the plant, constantly striving for increased output, and he had displayed very little interest in personnel administration. He left routine personnel matters in the plant to the supervisors and his secretary, Miss Martin.

The employee group at Midvale consisted primarily of female production workers. The plant was not highly regarded by male employees in the company, because many of them had said that Midvale was a "dumping ground" and that anyone who was assigned to it probably had little future with the company. Until 1965 the women at the plant had resisted all attempts to be organized by labor unions. About that time, however, the morale of most departments was not good, and a majority of the women felt a need for some form of employee representation. One of the unions which represented employees in the main plant became interested in the group at Midvale and decided to organize them. The union organizing campaign met little resistance, and a short time later the union won recognition from the company as the bargaining agent for Midvale production employees. For management, the union relations activities and collective bargaining were carried on by representatives from the central manufacturing office.

PLANT GROWTH AND REORGANIZATION

Beginning in 1967, the Midvale plant started to grow rapidly. In three years time, production at the plant almost doubled. The payroll of production employees grew to 650, and the management employee group increased to 60 personnel. This growth necessitated the expansion of manufacturing facilities which formerly occupied a one-floor building. An adjoining two-story warehouse was taken over by the Midvale plant, and several new production units were installed in it. Once the decision to expand was made, major changes occurred frequently in every department and unit. Many times the girls found that their workbenches or desks had been moved or their supervision changed before adequate explanations were made to them. The union found numerous occasions when situations of this kind had to be handled as complaints or grievances to be discussed with the plant manager.

With rapid growth and many personnel changes in the plant, a complete reorganization of line and staff functions took place in 1970. The parent Abacus Corporation sent several new managerial people to Midvale from other manufacturing plants. George Whitfield, who previously had had four departments and the office manager reporting to him, was relieved of all other responsibility and was given supervision over the assembly department. He moved his office from the attractive quarters in the front of the plant to a small room in the warehouse building in which the assembly department was relocated. Two of the men who assumed departmental supervisory jobs in the new organization were brought in from other company plants.

A new plant manager, Oliver Hawk, an experienced manufacturing executive, was transferred from the company's main office to Midvale. After participating in the reorganization of other Abacus plants, Mr. Hawk had become a strong proponent of decentralization in management and organization. He insisted upon the transfer of accounting, production control, labor relations, and personnel functions from the home office to the Midvale plant. In addition, he appointed one of his former assistants to the position of plant controller with responsibility for certain records, bookkeeping, cost and payroll activities. Some of these functions, especially payroll and employee records, had been handled by the office manager, whose responsibilities, after reorganization, were reduced to office services, the purchase of supplies and the stenographic pool.

In spite of these changes and rapid growth, the work in the plant continued to be handled quite well. Production and financial results improved each year even though the changes taking place had created many problems.

PERSONNEL ADMINISTRATION

Before the reorganization, the personnel work in the plant, consisting primarily of hiring, general wage and salary administration, union relations, and the like, was theoretically provided by the industrial relations section in the home office. Actually, the department heads at Midvale employed most of their workers personally, even though the paperwork and formal procedures required services from the employment office at "the city." Over the years the majority of the work concerning routine salary and wage administration, employee benefits, vacations, incidental absences, and so forth, had been handled by Miss Martin, (George Whitfield's secretary) who acted as an unofficial chief clerk. Everyone at Midvale had come to look to her for answers to routine personal questions and she had accepted these reponsibilities willingly. She took a great deal of pride in being "busy," and

*The Midvale Plant
Organization Chart — 1967*

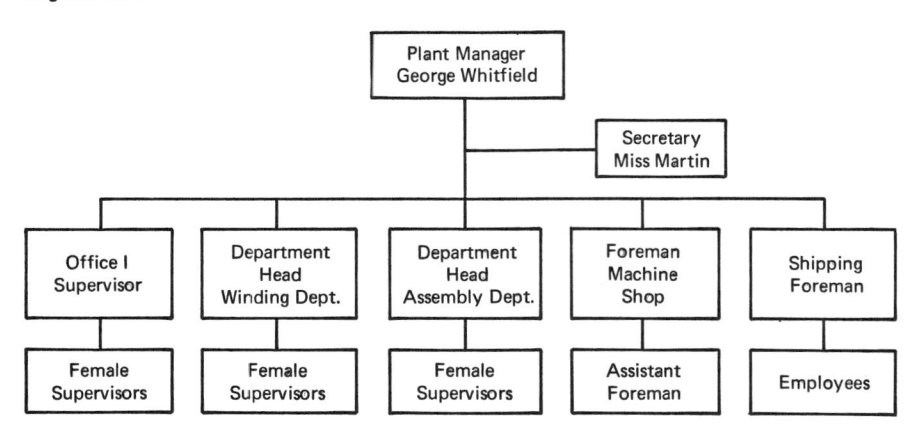

```
                    Plant Manager
                    George Whitfield
                         |
                         |————————Secretary
                         |          Miss Martin
     ┌───────────┬───────┴───────┬──────────────┬──────────┐
  Office I    Department    Department       Foreman     Shipping
 Supervisor      Head           Head          Machine    Foreman
              Winding Dept. Assembly Dept.     Shop
     |            |              |              |            |
  Female       Female         Female        Assistant    Employees
 Supervisors  Supervisors    Supervisors     Foreman
```

derived pleasure from telling her associates that she didn't "know what" they would do without her. With Miss Martin assuming authority and responsibility in routine personnel matters, supervisors usually did not try to answer questions from their employees involving personnel policies, but instead referred them to Miss Martin. Few of Miss Martin's rulings, procedures, and practices were in writing, and she stated frequently that she preferred to keep most personnel policies "flexible, and juggle them around in my head as needed." Miss Martin was well liked by the union stewards at Midvale, and most union grievances were minor and quickly settled.

At the time of the reorganization in 1970, Mr. Hawk decided that a full-time personnel supervisor was needed in the plant. A young man named Tom Jones, a college educated junior executive with several years experience with the parent company, was appointed to this new post. Most department heads and supervisors at Midvale welcomed this appointment, because they believed that Tom Jones would handle all their problems in much the same way that Miss Martin previously had done, and with more expertise.

Tom Jones was given wide latitude in setting up the personnel department. A general description of his authority, provided by Mr. Hawk, was as follows:

> To be responsible for labor relations activities and to represent the company in bargaining with the union. To be responsible for the hiring, placement and induction of employees in the plant. To be responsible for wage and salary administration. To be responsible for the liaison of all plant matters with the Benefit Department in the home office. To be responsible for employee activities, leaves of absence, disability, incidental absence, etc. and to act in a staff capacity on personnel matters for the entire plant.

In setting up the new department, a female personnel assistant was appointed to whom Tom Jones delegated most of the responsibility related to the employment of female workers. Miss Martin (Whitfield's former secretary) was assigned

The Midvale Plant

Plant Manager — Mr. Hawk
- Secretary
- Assistant Plant Manager

Reporting to Plant Manager:

- **Plant Controller**
  - Supervisor Bookkeeping
  - Supervisor Payroll

- **Office Manager**
  - Production Planner
    - Female Supervisors

- **Personnel Supervisor Tom Jones**
  - Personnel Assistant
  - Chief Clerk

- **Department Head Winding**
  - Female Supervisor

- **Department Head-Assembly George Whitfield**
  - Male and Female Supervisors

- **General Foreman Machine Shop**
  - Foremen

- **Department Head Warehouse**
  - Foremen

- **Department Head Ship. and Receiv.**
  - Employees

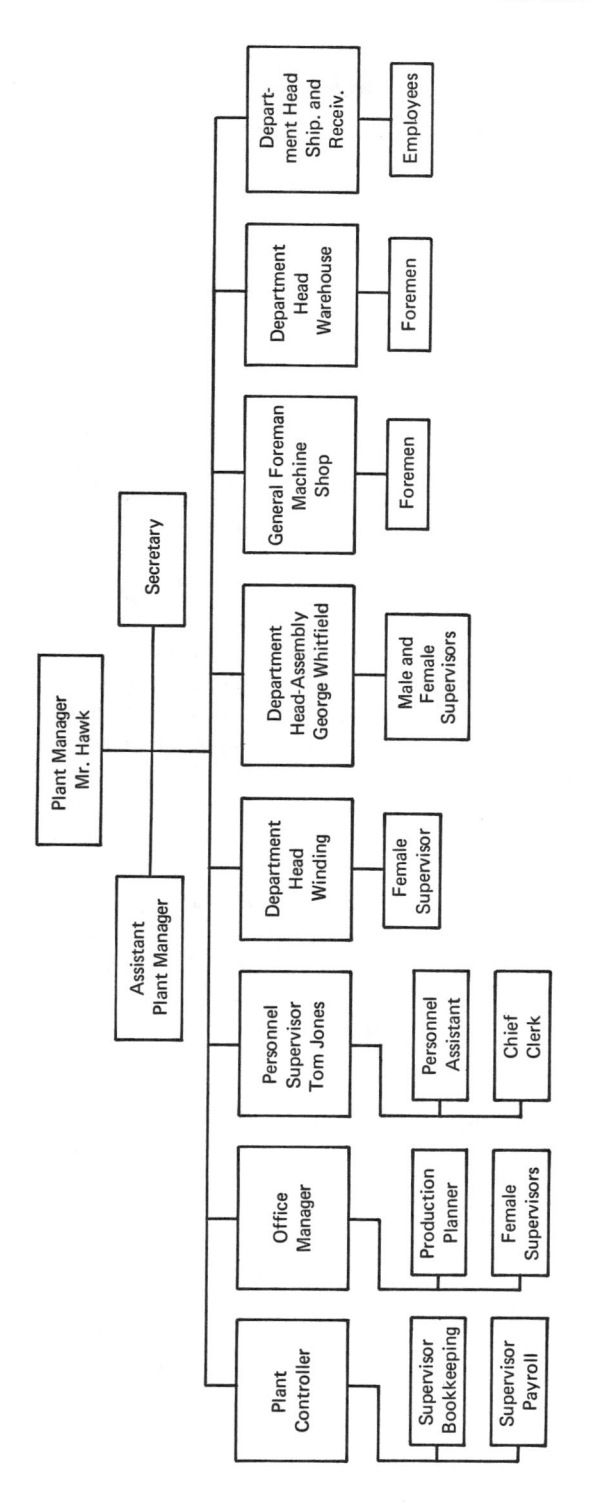

The Midvale Plant Organization Chart – 1970

to the personnel office and given the title of chief clerk. Salary-wise, this was not a demotion, but neither was it a promotion. Miss Martin did not look upon it too kindly and she appeared to be envious of the new personnel assistant. She decided to retire a few months earlier than necessary. Miss Martin left the company shortly after Tom Jones arrived to take over his responsibility; consequently, he promptly appointed a new girl to the chief clerk's job. This new appointee, Miss Eiler, was entirely unfamiliar with the work which had been handled by Miss Martin.

ORGANIZATIONAL RELATIONS

The majority of the managers and supervisors in the plant had been trained under George Whitfield and believed that technical and production aspects of their jobs were more important than personnel and human relations problems. One department head was quoted as having said, "I hope this new fellow Jones doesn't have to hold a lot of meetings and keep my people off the job." However, the newer supervisors and department heads who had transferred into Midvale had worked in plants which had personnel supervisors. They seemed to be more accustomed to the new organization and the services to be provided by a personnel department.

After assuming his job as personnel supervisor, Tom Jones found that the new chief clerk, Miss Eiler, was being consulted on personnel matters in the way that had been customary with Miss Martin. He was disturbed by a telephone call from George Whitfield, who said: "Tom, I know that you are new on this job, but you'll have to do something about vacation plans. One of our gals on the assembly line was told by Miss Martin that she could take her vacation in May, and now your new chief clerk says she has to wait until June. You'll probably have to talk to her.

"And there's another thing. A month ago we started to hire a young fellow named Jorgenson on benchwork, filing, polishing and miscellaneous work. Miss Martin and I thought we had him hired, but the employment office over at the city stopped it, saying we can't hire anyone who's not a high school graduate. Why in the hell does a filer have to be a high school graduate? Now this applicant isn't a relative or a friend or anything special, but I have a supervisor who's going to be very unhappy until we get that young guy on the payroll. You're going to have to do something about these problems and get them handled the way Miss Martin used to do."

Tom tried to interrupt and answer but Whitfield went right on talking: "And I think you ought to know that the union reps are stirring up a fuss about some of the things going on around here. The stewards in my department are concerned that you haven't met with them and talked about union problems, grievances, and negotiations. They think you've got the company bighead, and that personnel problems are going to be hard to settle around here without Miss Martin!"

During the telephone conversation Tom Jones tried to explain several new policies designed by the home office to upgrade Abacus plant personnel. For example, the company management had decided that for an indefinite period of time only high school graduates were to be employed for all jobs other than custodial work. Tom was not successful in convincing Whitfield of the merits of this policy. Upon completing the call, Tom decided to make a list of matters pertaining to plant personnel relationships which he should discuss with Mr. Hawk.

THE NIGHT SHIFT GROUP   CASE 5

Mrs. Jean MacDuff, night nursing director of St. Amos Hospital in Midwest City, was disturbed by a memo from the administrator, Mr. Paul Seay. Reports from the controller's office indicated that linen replacement costs, particularly for bed sheets, had doubled within the past three months. A check by the day staff of the laundry room procedures and nursing floor supplies had not accounted for the continued shortages. Mr. Seay's memo concluded, "In view of rising operating costs, I suggest that you institute immediate close checks on all of your personnel."

The design of the hospital included two sections with eight floors each, and one north wing consisting of three nursing units. Soiled linen was collected from two main laundry chutes in the basement of the two sections and from linen hamper trucks in the adjoining north wing. The hospital laundry operated at peak capacity for eight hours six days a week starting at 9 a.m. Daily supply orders were filled and checked by the laundry manager before the laundry closed at 5 p.m. At 11 p.m., the night orderlies began distribution of the loaded hampers to each of the eighteen nursing divisions and the operating room. Floor personnel stored the linen in the closets during the night as time permitted. The empty hampers were returned to the basement chutes by the orderlies before they checked out at 6:30 a.m.

The night staff was a very close-knit group, and its employment turnover was the lowest in the nursing department. Since the hospital was located in the far southwest area of the city, many of the night employees, including several of the professional nursing staff, came to work together from inner-city downtown areas in car pools. There were many relatives and long-time employees and several second-generation nurses' aides and orderlies in the night shift group.

The director, Mrs. MacDuff, was of pure Irish extraction and, being of ample proportions, was affectionately referred to as "Miz Mac" directly and "Big Mac" indirectly. With her approval, the shift's 2:30 a.m. break had become a respected ritual; personnel birthdays, anniversaries, and pay raises were always observed with shared food and fellowship between the units. Henry Sharon, the head orderly, often added an original poem in honor of any special occasion. Of undetermined age and handicapped with a lower prosthesis, Henry nevertheless was the most agile and light-hearted worker on the staff. He carried his "keys" proudly

In this actual case situation all names and places are disguised. Contributed by Dr. Cyril C. Ling, Executive Vice-President, American Association of Collegiate Schools of Business.

dangling from his belt, which indicated that he was in charge of laundry cart deliveries. He had been at St. Amos for more than twenty years, and he guided new orderlies with skill and understanding in their jobs. Many student nurses learned much, too, from Henry in handling difficult patients and expirations, during their early night duty experience.

Because of the size of the hospital and her many administrative duties, Mrs. MacDuff considered the directive from Mr. Seay for an immediate check on all night personnel to be an impossibility. On rounds that evening, she simply read Mr. Seay's directive to each of the floor charge nurses, and asked them to observe the handling of linen closely, to report any irregularities, and to make suggestions for changes. During that same night during the break, Mrs. MacDuff asked Henry if he had noticed any "outsiders" hanging around while the linen hampers were being moved from the laundry. Henry reminded her there were six exits to the hospital, which fire regulations stated must be kept open at all times, and only one night watchman was on duty who was usually helping at the "Emergency" entrance. No suggestions or ideas were reported to Mrs. MacDuff by any of the night personnel. Since there was no apparent shortage of clean linen during the 11-7 shift, nothing further was done by Mrs. MacDuff and the night shift staff concerning the linen problem.

Two weeks later a second memo from Mr. Seay advised that "Due to continued shortages in linen sheets, effective immediately, all linen closets on nursing units will be kept tightly locked. Sheets will be dispensed only upon request by the floor charge nurse, and delivery and storage of the next day's linen must be personally supervised by the charge nurse on each division."

This regulation was met with much opposition and resentment by the night staff, because of the time and personnel involved in the storage procedure. Orderlies who were tied up with floor linen hamper unloading were often called off the floor, and patients' lights could not be handled as promptly. Due to the excessive workload, the 2:30 a.m. break was frequently delayed until 3:00 or 4:00 a.m., or on some floors was omitted entirely. On two occasions Mr. Seay was observed counting hampers and checking the basement laundry room at 6 a.m. Return of the empty carts, which had never been a problem, often filled the service elevators when the day staff reported for duty. Henry Sharon explained to Mrs. MacDuff that his orderlies no longer had time to get the empty hampers back to the basement, because the floors were too slow unloading them. Nurses' aides reported frequent backaches from too much heavy unloading, and complained that they could not guide the hampers even when they were empty and blocking the hallways.

Absenteeism, which had never been a problem on the 11-7 shift, became more frequent, and several aides asked for transfers to the day shift. One very capable aide who resigned from the hospital was questioned by Mrs. MacDuff about her reason for leaving. She said, "It just ain't fun working here like it used to be. Everybody's got to be so careful and looking at each other. What do they think we would do with them sheets that's missing anyway, Miz Mac? We're all double-bed sleepers! You can ask anybody!"

The following month, St. Amos began receiving new linens with large blue-center name markings. In spite of the addition of two new guards at the employee exits and check of all personnel parcels, linen losses continued, although at a reduced rate.

About three weeks later, Mrs. MacDuff resigned as night nursing director complaining that she simply "couldn't take all this bickering and suspicion anymore."

Six months later, the hospital administrator had not secured a qualified replacement for Mrs. MacDuff. Nursing care during night hours had been reduced sharply, and many staff doctors were admitting acutely ill patients to St. Amos only if they had private duty night nurses available to them.

PART TWO

Textilcolor
Sonning Mead Boilers, Ltd.
The College Protestor
The Assembly Line: The U.S.A. and Japan (A) and (B)
The Worthington Case
Poona Metal Company

The Cultural Framework of Personnel Management

The concept of culture is most important in understanding and carrying out the personnel management function. Personnel policies and procedures evolve within a cultural framework. Policies must be consistent with the values, sentiments, and beliefs of the larger society of which the organization is a part.

CULTURE

Culture may be viewed as the values, beliefs, and sentiments internal to individuals in a society or its subdivisions. Culture, at any given point, is a product of man's continuing response to the problems he encounters in his life struggle. It includes all the accumulated customs, traditions, and habits, as well as the social institutions and material objects which embody and sustain them. Culture is learned and is transmitted from one generation to another through the ages.

In other words, it is a way of life of a group of people possessing some configuration. Though it is dynamic, diversified and everchanging, the basic patterns tend to remain integrated and evolve slowly. Thus, Barnou described culture as:

> The way of life of a group of people, the configuration of all of the more or less stereotyped patterns of learned behavior which are handed down from one generation to the next through the means of language and imitation.[1]

[1] Victor Barnou, *Culture and Personality* (Homewood, Illinois: The Dorsey Press, Inc., 1963), p. 5.

35

The culture of a society, or one of its subordinate organizations, provides a number of ready-made solutions to problems which people encounter. It is the means by which a man can adapt to changes in his environment. It is the means by which he passes on to his children the learnings which he has acquired from his ancestors, and his home, social, and work experiences. In other words, "the purpose and function of culture are to make life secure and enduring for the human species."[2] Culture consists of habits which are shared by members of a society or one of its subordinate groupings, such as a business organization. The larger and more general the group which shares the habit, the broader this cultural trait will be. The sharing may be general throughout a society, as is frequently the case with language habits. The sharing also may be very restricted, as is the case with work, recreation and living customs in a fire department.

COMPONENTS OF CULTURE

The components of culture may be classified into two major categories: the intangible and the material (including the habitat).

Intangible Culture

The intangible culture includes the philosophies, ideologies, attitudes, habits, sentiments, and other concepts which reflect the value system that a group of human beings have developed in order to survive within an environment and to give meaning to their lives. It includes all those forms of social organization and technologies which people have evolved to achieve their individual and group goals.

Many facets of the intangible culture are of significance to the manager. For example, the American democratic ideal manifests itself in political institutions, educational institutions, family relationships, and in business organizations. The emphasis upon "bottom-up management" participation, and consultation in all types of organizations reflects the American culture of which we are a part. Contrast this with the Mexican culture which is much more authoritarian. Authoritarian values affect government, family, religious, and business institutions alike.[3]

Status systems are culturally determined. Status symbols are subtle, frequently intangible signs of social ranking. They vary from one culture to another, and from one subculture to another.

Other features of culture include the use of *rituals.* Newcomers into organizations frequently encounter ritualistic ceremonies, sometimes called *rites of passage,* which serve to introduce them to the organization. Similarly, retiring members participate in banquets and other ceremonies designed to ease their departure. Practitioners of labor relations often refer to the "ritual" of union-management negotiations in which union and company negotiators ritualistically provide calculated theatrics to impress members of the union, members of management, and the public, with the importance of the issues and the seriousness of

---

[2] Leslie A. White, *The Evolution of Culture* (New York: McGraw-Hill Book Co., Inc., 1959), p. 8.
[3] John Fayerweather, *The Executive Overseas* (Syracuse, New York: Syracuse University Press, 1959), pp. 24-25.

the deliberations.[4] The *taboo* is another cultural phenomenon; it is that behavior which is prohibited or discouraged because it violates some value, belief, or sentiment of the group. Thus, in some organizations, one does not address his superior by his first name; in others, an individual is expected to respect the output standards established by the group. Taboos are powerful inhibitors of proscribed behavior because group members exercise constant surveillance over each other and are able swiftly and effectively to impose sanctions.

Many groups develop distinctive language and terminology; this is identified as *jargon*. Occupational groups, such as railroaders, develop a distinct terminology.

Material Culture

The material culture includes all those things that man produces as a result of his technology. Intangible and material cultures are not completely separate. For example, food, clothing and many other objects possess both a utilitarian and a symbolic value.

There are many examples of material culture in business organization: the telephone, the air-conditioned office, the company airplane, the mass production assembly line.

The material culture of a society constitutes a part of the environment of any individual or group thrust into it; hence, the material environment for an individual or group becomes a "given" in the same manner as the natural environment. For example, the railroad represents one aspect of material environment. It constitutes one technique by means of which society met many of its transportation and communication problems. On the other hand, for anyone entering into the railroad industry as an employee, the railroad becomes a part of the environment to which he must adapt.

The Habitat

While the natural environment, the habitat, is not a direct part of culture as defined here, habitat affects patterns of behavior. The climate, natural resources, and other natural factors influence human needs and the behaviors which will be selected to satisfy them

SUBCULTURES

Culture as a system is universal in the experience of man. Culture as a body of content, however, is more or less unique to each individual. Thus, a considerable variation in behavior patterns and beliefs actually exists in the larger society, because individuals are exposed to different parts of the culture and natural environment. They show individual differences in their capacity to learn from their exposure to the culture and environment, and each individual responds to his experiences in his own unique manner.

While the members of the society may share many values, beliefs, and feelings, few "universals" exist. Even such cultural traits as language, dress, and housing

---

[4] For an interesting example of this 'ritual," see: "Motor City Ritual," *Wall Street Journal* (Vol. 163, No. 128, June 29, 1964), p. 10.

vary from one individual to another, depending upon the social class, age grouping, occupation, geographic area, and creed to which one belongs. These groupings constitute systems within the larger social system. Members accept the values, beliefs, and sentiments of these subsystems, or smaller societies. They are committed to them; hence, these subsystems influence the behavior of the members. Individuals identify themselves with subsystems within a larger social system.

The subsystems within the scope of our interest are oriented around organizations, professions, racial and ethnic elements, geographic location, and social class. Individuals develop common values, beliefs, and sentiments as a result of their membership in these systems. While their behavior is in part determined by the larger culture, the small cultures hold to values which direct the behavior of the members. The subculture which is built around an organization is somewhat different from that built around a concept such as social class. These are not "pure" types, however. For example, an engineering society may constitute elements of both types. Further, the former type is vertical and internal concerning a single organization from lowest to highest levels. The latter is horizontal and external, extending across many organizations.

The Organizational Subculture

Members of organizations tend to develop behavior patterns which will enable them to meet the expectations of the organization toward them, and also enable them to achieve the personal goals and objectives they have set for themselves. Such behavior patterns, if they persist, become known as *customs.* These, plus the values, beliefs and sentiments of the members of the organization, constitute their subculture.

Some organizations possess subcultures which are more distinct than others. For example, there are distinct subcultures which exist in such organizations as newspapers, aircraft crews, educational institutions, ships, fire and police departments, railroads, mass production assembly lines, prisons, hospitals, and religious institutions. The distinctiveness of the behavior patterns and beliefs in these organizations varies in large measure according to the total environment of the organization. In general, such factors as isolation from the larger society, the degree of commitment by the members to the organization, the nature of the work performed, and various sociological factors determine the uniqueness of the subculture and its persistence in the face of outside influences.

Two organizations producing the same product, serving the same market, and situated in the same community may be quite different from one another as a result of the unique personalities and philosophies of the founders, method of organization, production processes, competitive pressures at critical times in the history of the organizations, and similar other variables. Further, each major functional group within an organization tends to possess its unique value system. The values and orientation of the research and development group in an organization tend to be quite different from that of marketing or production; and accounting and finance tend to be very different from all of the other three. For example, research groups tend to be quite individualistic and idealistic. They place high value on perfection, "theoretical yield," "100 per cent purity." Finance and accounting groups tend to be conservative in orientation and usually are identified as always asking "But who will pay for it?" These differences in value and orientation frequently cause misunderstanding and conflict.[5]

The Professional Subculture

The increasing complexity and specialization of occupations in modern society have produced an attitude of professionalism among the members of these occupations. While it is difficult to identify a profession, certain attributes are common to occupations classified as professions: (1) advanced education; (2) special training through an internship; (3) certification or licensing by a governmental agency and/or a licensing board made up of members of the occupation; (4) a code of "ethics" or some other set of minimum standards to which the members are held; (5) a process or procedure for disciplining members who violate the code of performance or conduct; (6) one or more organizations which grant membership only to members who meet requirements of the profession. The most common of professional groups are medicine, law, engineering, the clergy, accounting, and teaching.

The development of professional value systems gives members an entity with which they may identify. Organizations with large numbers of middle management personnel whose functions and duties cannot be easily or precisely defined provide a fertile ground for the development of professionalism. A profession gives members an opportunity to enhance their status both inside the organization and outside it. It gives them a means of obtaining recognition from their superiors. It may even provide a means for enforcing demands on the organizations by invoking sanctions upon the superior by the profession. There is considerable pressure inside organizations for certain groups to develop professional organizations: Personnel administrators, cost accountants, internal auditors, office managers, training directors, transportation directors, safety directors, and even secretaries have all attempted (and some have succeeded) to establish "certified" positions.

Cultural Change

A society is dynamic, always changing. Changes in culture generally have their origin in some significant alteration in the life conditions of the society. Any occurrence which changes the conditions under which collective behavior occurs, so that the customary and habitual factions are discouraged and new responses are favored, may lead to cultural changes.[6]

The forces making for change may arise either from outside the society or from within it. Among the more important sources of change are the following: Interactions with other cultures; epidemics and crop failures; planned and accidental

---

[5] Paul R. Lawrence and John A. Seiler, *Organizational Behavior and Administration*, Revised Edition (Homewood, Ill.: Richard D. Irwin, Inc., 1965), pp. 578-581.
[6] Harry L. Shapiro, *Man, Culture and Society*, Ch. 11, "How Culture Changes," by George Peter Murdock (New York: Oxford University Press, 1960)

discoveries; education; changes in population; complex changes in technology; and, such events as the death or rise to power of a strong leader.

IMPLICATIONS OF CULTURE FOR PERSONNEL MANAGEMENT

Since culture has such an important influence upon the values, beliefs and sentiments of the individuals in an organization, and since these values are so important in determining the needs and drives of individuals, it is important that managers take cultural factors into consideration in carrying out their personnel management function. Every organization operates within a larger cultural environment, and the values, beliefs, and sentiments held by those comprising the society set the limits within which the organization must function. At the same time the organization itself may be considered a culture. That is, from the point of view of society, the organization comprises a subculture. The business organization is assumed to acquire its own value system and patterns of conduct, which although not the same as those of the larger cultural pattern, are consistent with it.[7]

In industry there are many examples which illustrate the impact of organizational culture upon the individual. For example, young adults entering upon a work career probably possess no fixed beliefs or values with respect to quality or quantity of work which they should turn out in a day. The socialization process of a large number of workers, however, involves education by other workers in the work group. If other workers in the work group establish low output and quality standards, they will attempt to convince the young adult that these standards are reasonable and fair and that he should do the minimum necessary. If this young adult learns to accept these standards as his own, then the factory culture will have played an important part in establishing norms with respect to work for this individual.

An awareness of the culture concept is useful to the manager in five important ways. First, it enables the manager to understand the behavior of the people in his organization. Perceptions, attitudes, and behavior have all been in large measure learned from cultures. For example, in understanding the resistance of the southern worker to unionization, it is important to realize that the southern agrarian is likely to regard an employer's right to control wages, hours, and working conditions as in some sense natural and proper. As a result of this, the southern factory employee, who in all likelihood formerly was an agricultural worker, is apt to be relatively satisfied with his lot in the factory. He is not apt to experience the discontent which is a frequent prerequisite to unionization.[8]

Second, the patterned life experience of people in large measure determines how they will behave in a certain situation. As examples: A professional or

---

[7] Talcott Parsons, "A Sociological Theory of Organizations," *Administrative Science Quarterly* (Vol. I, 1956), p. 29.

[8] Ray Marshall, "Ethnic and Economic Minorities: Unions' Future or Unrecruit?," *The Annals of the American Academy of Political and Social Science* (Vol. 350, November 1963), p. 70. See also: J. A. C. Brown, *The Social Psychology of Industry* (Baltimore: Penguin Books, 1954), p. 232.

managerial employee will be more likely to oppose the unionization of an organization than a blue-collar worker; an American manager, more likely to utilize participative techniques in carrying out his management functions than a German manager; a group of coal miners, more likely to share the available work in a time of unemployment than a group of automobile workers.

Third, a knowledge of culture will enable the manager to exercise control over his employees. While the social scientist may be content with understanding and predicting human behavior, the manager in guiding the organization toward its goals also must manipulate various resources at his command, including human resources.

Fourth, it provides a substitute for experience:

> In many respects, the "experienced" person is the one who has developed a sensitivity to the culture in which he operates. This is particularly true as one climbs the management ladder and, therefore, operates at the level where decisions tend to have a high component of value judgments. Awareness of these cultural factors, then, could possibly reduce the amount of time a person has to "live" in an organization, assimilating its value system.[9]

Fifth, it aids in facilitating change. Behavior patterns within groups, just as within individuals, tend to become permanent and are changed only with considerable effort. However, organizations, just as individuals, require flexibility. Organizations must be able to adapt to a rapidly changing environment. An organization, while itself a subculture of the larger society, also encompasses within itself one or more smaller subcultures. These smaller subcultures arise out of such factors as specialization of labor, social stratification, and so forth. Managers of organizations must understand the nature of the subcultures and the needs which they serve for their members if they wish to effect change within the organization.

Let us explore at this point some of the more important influences of culture and cultural change upon the performance of the personnel management function in organizations.

Time, Tempo and Space

Americans tend to be very time-conscious, probably more so than other Nationals. DeGrazia concluded that, "Other commercial societies have had the feeling of urgency and of many things to do, similar to ours, but ours can be more tightly scheduled and made almost escapeproof by the ubiquitous clock and the machines geared to it."[10]

We must be careful, however not to ignore the great subcultural differences which exist in the use of time in our country. For example, Hall found that

> In Utah the Mormons have developed promptness to a degree that is unknown in the rest of the country . . . On the northwest coast the traditional

[9] John M. Pfiffner and Frank P. Sherwood, *Administrative Organization* (Englewood Cliffs, New Jersey: Prentice-Hall, Inc., 1960), pp. 253-254.
[10] Sebastian DeGrazia, *Of Time, Work and Leisure* (New York: The Twentieth Century Fund, 1962), p. 310.

feelings about time are altered and are not experienced in as pressing a manner as they are elsewhere. The Northwest uses the same time structure as the rest of the country, but nobody seems particularly driven by it.[11]

Ethnic subcultures also may use time differently from what we consider to be the typical American style. For example, Horton found that unemployed, uneducated blacks use time in a very flexible manner: "Negro street time is built around the irrelevance of clock time, white man's time, and the relevance of street values and activities."[12]

In great measure culture influences the way people use and feel about space. We become most aware of cultural differences when we compare other cultures with our own. For example, Latin Americans typically stand closer together than Americans when conversing. When two people from these different cultures interact, the Latin American attempts to reduce the physical distance between them, while the American backs up in an attempt to restore the physical distance to what is comfortable for him. The Latin American feels uncomfortable with the greater distance. He feels that the retreating American is unfriendly and cold, while the American feels that his counterpart is crowding in on him.[13]

Motivation

Allison Davis, from studies of lower-class white and black workers, concludes that the behavior of the underprivileged worker is learned from the socioeconomic and cultural environment in which he lives, and that he must be trained to work for the rewards offered in a middle-class society and to which middle-class workers respond. Davis points out that:

> ... administrators' emphasis upon punctuality, responsibility, and the desire and drive to get ahead in life is part of their culture. They have *learned* all these traits through training, family pressure, work opportunities, and through encouragement and reward on the job . . . they become so integral a part of their behavior that they tend to regard these virtues as entirely their *individual* achievement . . . the underprivileged workers act also in accord with their culture. The habits of "shiftlessness," "irresponsibility," "lack of ambition," absenteeism and of quitting the job, which management usually regards as a result of the innate perversity of underprivileged white and Negro workers, are, in fact, *normal responses* that the worker has learned from his physical and social environment.[14]

Thus, the learned work habits of the middle class, as opposed to the underprivileged white and black, are different because the individuals of these different

---

[11] Edward T. Hall, *The Silent Language* (Greenwich, Conn.: Fawcett Publications, Inc., 1959), p. 131.
[12] John Horton, "Time and Cool People," *Trans-action* (Vol. 4, No. 5, April, 1967), p. 8.
[13] See Hall, *Ibid.*, Ch. 10.
[14] From William F. Whyte, Editor, *Industry and Society* (New York: McGraw-Hill Book Company, Inc., 1946), pp. 85-86.

socioeconomic statuses and cultures are reacting to different realistic situations and psychological needs. Their values and social goals are different. Further, the standards of the community and society in which an employee lives greatly influence his perception of his needs.[15]

Worthy, in an analysis of employee motivation and morale in a large retail organization, concluded that motivation and morale tended to be higher among workers in the South than in the North because of religious and parental upbringing which emphasized the rightness of hard work for its own sake and the moral obligation to give a fair day's work for a fair day's pay. He further concluded that social integration is an important determinant of motivation and morale. Thus, he found that morale tends to be lower in the large, industrialized, metropolitan centers and higher in the smaller and less complex communities; that morale is lower in eastern as opposed to western regions; and, that the simpler the industrial base of a community and the more homogeneous its population, the higher the level of employee morale.[16]

Organizational Structure

Pfiffner and Sherwood speak of the "gospel" of decentralization. During the 1940's and 1950's a number of influential managers espoused the restructuring of American industry in order to produce a decentralization of the decision-making process in organizations. In large measure, they accepted the philosophy of decentralization on faith and without much scientific evidence to support the philosophy they were promoting. It was a philosophy imbued with considerable idealism, a concept with deep ethical roots in democracy. Most important, however, was the fact that the promoters of this form of organization were attempting to affect cultural change.

> ... it is in the beginning a more difficult way of life because it involves a change in behavior running counter to historically rooted cultural patterns of mankind. That is why the new literature of decentralization dwells on how to bring about a change in organization behavior. Men find it difficult to delegate, to think in terms of the abstractions required by long-term planning, to listen rather than to give orders, to evaluate other men and their work in terms of overall results instead of the irritations and tensions of the moment. Yet this is the very key to the behavior required of leaders in a decentralized organization ... decentralization will always experience a certain amount of endemic conflict between those whose purpose is to learn a way of life in which the coordinating process will be the least restrictive, in which people can pursue individual goals to the maximum and yet work in harmony toward group goals with others who look upon things

---

[15] Harold L. Wilensky, "Human Relations in the Workplace: An Appraisal of Some Recent Research," in, *Research in Industrial Human Relations,* Conrad M. Arensberg, *et al.*, Editors (New York: Harper and Brothers, 1956), p. 45.
[16] James C. Worthy, "Organizational Structure and Employee Morale," *American Sociological Review* (Vol. 15, 1950), pp. 169-179.

differently. It takes considerable experience and organizational maturity to do this.[17]

The concept of participation is an old one in our society. The signers of the Declaration of Independence affirmed that "all men are born equal"; the Constitution of the United States and the constitutions of the states of the union affirm the concept of political and social equality. Lincoln's Gettysburg Address reiterated the fact that this was "a government of the people, for the people, and by the people." The philosophy of participation has been introduced into our educational system. The authoritarian role of the father has gradually given way to a more permissive role. The mother and children take a more active role in making decisions that concern the family. It was inevitable that this participative philosophy should invade the authoritarian industrial setting.

Leadership Style and Culture

The leadership style practiced in an organization is in large measure determined by the culture of the organization. For example, Halpin found that the leadership style most successful in the administration of a public school differs considerably from that on a combat aircraft.[18] He found that the same elements—initiating structure and consideration—were the two most important in leadership style. However, in the case of aircraft commanders, the element of initiating structure was more important than that of consideration, while in the case of school principals, the element of consideration was much more important than that of initiating structure. The difference in these two situations can be attributed to many factors. School teachers expect to work in a more permissive environment than do members of the military; school teachers generally are better educated; their problems are less immediate and critical, although equally important; errors have less serious consequences, hence more judgment may be left to the individual.

Selection and Placement

There is little doubt that the American culture has influenced, and even shaped, the nature of personnel policies and practices in American organizations. In our society considerable emphasis is placed on individual merit and ability. Employees should be selected, promoted, compensated, and otherwise rewarded according to their performance. This concept is not accepted in all cultures. In many societies employees are selected on the basis of family relationship. The employer does not necessarily hire persons on the basis of ability but rather hires them on the basis of whether or not there are any members of the family, immediate or distant, who are seeking employment. For example, the owner of a large construction company in South Korea agreed that certain personnel policies

---

[17] Pfiffner and Sherwood, *op. cit.*, pp. 190-191.
[18] Andrew W. Halpin, "The Leader Behavior and Leadership Ideology of Educational Administrators and Aircraft Commanders," *Harvard Educational Review* (Vol. 25, Winter 1955), pp. 18-32.

could and should be revised in his firm; however, he added, "As to hiring people on the basis of their qualifications without regard to family relationship, that will take a long time!"

Collective Bargaining

Management's attitude toward labor unions in our society has long reflected the attitude of the larger culture, especially the middle- and upper-class culture. However, a gradual change in the attitude of management toward labor unions and collective bargaining has evolved. It reflects, in large part, the changing attitudes of the broader culture, and also reflects a change within cultures of the firms. The owner-manager tends to have a different outlook than the professional manager toward unions. As one company president stated, "After all, we are all employees; we perform different functions within the organization; we have different duties and responsibilities; we receive different amounts of pay; however, whether we are a janitor or a vice president, we are all employees." This growth in the attitude of "employeeism" has undoubtedly had a profound effect upon the culture of firms.

Wage and Salary Administration

The individual wage incentive system has found wide acceptance mainly in America. It has not been adopted widely in any other industrialized society. The incentive system is individualistic, pitting the worker against some objective work standard and also against his fellow employees.

Profit sharing, stock ownership plans, and suggestion systems have long been utilized as a means for enlisting worker support and enthusiasm. A new wave of interest in these plans seems to be pervading management circles. Managers are seeking ways to stimulate and maintain the interest of the work force with its rising expectations. Education, increasing technology, and the many promises for a better life tend to create a situation in which many employers find it difficult to meet the rising expectations of workers. These changes within the work place force employers to look for new and different ways to stimulate workers. Employers hope that profit sharing, stock ownership, and suggestion plans will stimulate workers through participation. They hope that workers will work harder waste less, and become better ambassadors of good will for the company. The changing culture of industry is requiring managers to look for new ways to arouse and maintain the enthusiasm of workers in their work.

Layoff and Termination of Employment

It is customary in business, voluntary, and governmental organizations in the United States to terminate the employment of workers whose services are no longer needed as a result of decline in output, increases in efficiency, or geographic relocation. By and large, this principle has been accepted by employers and employees alike. This individualistic outlook is not common, however, in other countries. For example, workers in Japan usually are retained on the payroll even though no work may be available for them.[19] The life-employment system and seniority systems operate for management and non-management personnel alike. Further, while undergoing some modification they appear both stable and functional in Japanese industry.[20] This practice also occurs in European countries. In 1962, two American companies operating plants in France closed down their plants and terminated employment of persons working in them. The terminations were consistent with company policies and practices in America. However, employers in France do not suddenly terminate employment of their workers. When it is necessary to terminate employment, elaborate arrangements exist to cushion the impact of the terminations. The actions of these two American companies were consistent with American practice but contrary to French practice. The reaction of the French Government and the citizens of France was quite violent, resulting in a minor "international incident."[21]

Ours is a changing culture. We now are witnessing a decline in the former individualistic competitive attitude toward layoff. American workers are placing increasing stress upon job security and the protection of "job rights" which they associate with length of employment. Many collective agreements specify the rights of workers when a plant closes down or is moved. Some agreements provide that workers who are displaced when a plant is moved shall have first claim upon jobs at the new location. In some instances they also receive reimbursement for the costs of moving to the new location. Workers who do not elect to move to the new plant or who are not qualified to perform the new jobs frequently receive dismissal compensation.

Discipline

Discipline, whether it is meted out in the home or in the factory, traditionally has been considered the prerogative of the parent and the employer. Just as the administration of discipline has changed in the home, so it has changed in the work place. While the responsibility for maintaining work discipline remains with the employer, this discipline has become more complex in recent years. The rising expectations of employees has required a greater emphasis upon the wise administration of justice. Employees both in union and non-union groups insist that justice be administered fairly, and also insist upon the right of appeal to higher management any decision which they believe to be unfair.

Social Security and Social Welfare

Traditionally our society had maintained that each individual was responsible for his own welfare and security. Hence social security measures did not receive widespread attention in this country until the mid-1930's. Mass unemployment, a realization that ours was an affluent society, and an awareness that many people

---

[19] Domen Toyonobu, "Employee and Customer Policies in the International Company," *Proceedings, CIOS, XIII Annual Management Congress* (New York: Council for International Progress in Management, Inc., 1963), pp. 438-439.
[20] William Brown, "Japanese Management—The Cultural Background," in Ross A. Webber, *Culture and Management* (Homewood, Ill: Richard D. Irwin, Inc., 1969), pp. 428-442.
[21] "Freedom to Fire in France," *Business Week* (No. 1725, September 1962), p. 96.

find it impossible to provide for their individual security in a complex society, all resulted in a re-examination of traditional attitudes toward self-reliance in providing for economic security. The Social Security Act was passed in 1935. It provided for Old Age and Survivors Insurance, aid to dependent children, aid to the blind, and aid to the aged indigent. It also provided for an unemployment insurance program. Labor unions have negotiated many other security measures to be provided by the employer, such as pension plans, supplementary unemployment benefits, hospital, medical, and surgical insurance, accident and life insurance, and major medical insurance. Further, a large number of people in our society believe that the federal and state governments should liberalize the benefits now received and also should increase the scope of security programs to include medical care for the aged, total disability, and other welfare measures. There is little doubt that employers will feel further pressure for increased security and worker benefits. There is little doubt, too, that these pressures are a reflection of the broader changes in attitude that are taking place in the American society.

Minority Groups

Americans traditionally have looked upon their country as the "great melting pot." They have pointed with pride to the successful assimilation of huge numbers of immigrants from every part of the world. Industry has successfully employed men and women of every nationality, race, and religion. Most of our entrepreneurs and executives are the sons and grandsons of men and women who came to America to seek a better life for themselves and their children.

We have been forcibly reminded, however, during the past decade that the assimilation and integration process has been far from perfect. Blacks, Puerto Ricans, Mexican Americans, Indian Americans, as well as certain other groups, such as the Poles, feel that they have been the subject of serious discrimination.

Women constitute one of the most important "minority" groups in industry; they now comprise over one-third of the labor force. While women have improved their status in employment, they continue to receive lower wage rates for comparable work, possess less opportunity for advancement, and are considered less competent than men. [22]

The traditional role assigned women at all levels in our society has been that of wife and mother, whose primary interest was in the family and the home. She has not been expected to compete in the labor market on an equal basis with men. In fact, men usually have held the female to be inferior in intelligence, mechanical ability, creativity, and physical and mental stamina. While these beliefs in large part have been proven false, they have helped the male sustain his self-image as the superior sex and his role as the protector and breadwinner in our society.

The role of the woman is changing. Increased job opportunities, changing attitudes toward the employment of women, increased mechanization, labor-saving appliances in the home, and the rising expectations of highly educated

---

[22] *American Women, Report of the President's Commission on the Status of Women* (Washington: U.S. Government Printing Office, 1963), pp. 27-34.

women—all of these are creating a situation in which women increasingly seek employment opportunities outside the home. The Women's Liberation Movement represents a rebellion against the role assigned to women in our society. It seeks not only equality, but also freedom of choice in determining careers.

Nevertheless, the changing role of women in industry creates problems for the manager. Women threaten both the security and status of men. They perform some tasks better than men, such as clerical work. If they work at lower rates than men, the men fear for their jobs; if the employer pays them the same amount, the status of men is lowered. There are many examples of women entering an occupation or job classification only to "drive" the men off!

The movement of blacks from the agricultural South to the industrial North has paralleled somewhat the movement of European and Asian immigrants to American industrial centers. Blacks tend to occupy the low status and unskilled positions formerly held by other ethnic minorities.

Assimilation is much slower for the black, however. His color sets him apart, and the "white society maintains a strict caste system with effective controls for keeping Negroes separate and subordinate."[23]

While the greatest damage results from the denial of human dignity and the waste of human lives, the economic loss in terms of wasted human resources is also incalculable. Attitudes toward blacks and women are changing slowly. The Civil Rights Law of 1964 was enacted to prohibit discrimination against blacks and women in the exercise of certain economic, social, and political rights.

The problems facing the manager are enormous. If he seeks to reduce discrimination against minority groups in his organization, he can effectively accomplish this only by changing the culture of his organization. Since his organization constitutes but a small part of the total culture which shapes attitudes, his efforts will have to be directed towards his employees as members of his small "society," and his employees as fellow members of the larger society.

SUMMARY

Culture is defined as the patterned behavior of groups of people in their endeavor to meet life's problems. Culture is learned. It consists of the values, beliefs, and sentiments elicited under various conditions.

The business organization is a subculture of the larger culture. The values, beliefs, and sentiments of the business organization must be consistent with those of the larger culture. An organization may be divided further into still smaller subcultures, such as the professional subculture.

The concept of culture is most important to the manager. Culture influences organization structure, leadership philosophy, selection, discipline, wage and salary administration, and many other areas of personnel policy.

---

[23] Burleigh B. Gardner and David C. Moore, *Human Relations in Industry,* Fourth Edition (Homewood, Ill.: Richard D. Irwin, Inc., 1964), p. 436. Also see: Gunnar Myrdal, *An American Dilemma* (New York: Harper and Brothers, 1944).

TEXTILCOLOR   CASE 6

Textilcolor is a firm situated in a small community of East Flanders, Belgium. A total of 550 persons are employed by the company. The company's activities consist of the dyeing and finishing of woolens. The production division is divided in ten departments, each of which performs an entirely different activity. The workweek runs from Monday morning through Friday night.

The organizational structure of the firm is very centralized. Mr. Boddens, the director general, not only is in charge of general management, but also of the production division. Commercial, personnel, and accounting directors report as staff-functions to the director general. An "executive committee" (the director general and the directors of the three staff-functions) meets monthly.

Miss Hanssens reports to this executive group. She is a nurse, whose job at the same time is considered to encompass the function of social assistant. She often comes in direct contact with the workers, assisting them in case of individual social difficulties, and dispensing medical care when necessary (in case of accidents). Occasionally she also performs administrative work for the personnel department.

The department heads, with approximately 50 workers under their immediate supervision, are subordinate in line responsibility to the director general and are appointed by him. These appointments are partially based upon individual technical abilities. Other factors which bear on these appointments are more subjective: department heads often are successors of one's father or a close relative of a person holding an important job in the production division. Within his department, the department head has practically absolute power.

Demand for the firm's products often make the firm subject to strong seasonal fluctuations. The department heads have full authority to lay off workers temporarily in periods of diminished activities.

Workers in the various departments usually know each other very well and in many cases are members of the same family (neighborhood and family-groups). Management has encouraged this policy of having family-groups in the firm, because it feels this can more effectively restrain a potential "deserter" (to a competing firm) through the influence exerted on him by his remaining relatives. "This

---

Case prepared by the Seminarie Voor Productiviteitsstudie En-Onderzoek (Center for Productivity Study and Research) of the State University of Ghent, Belgium. Copyright, by the Belgian Productivity Agency, Brussels, Belgium. Reprinted by permission of Dr. A. J. Vlerick, Director of the Center, and the Belgian Productivity Agency.

is very useful," said a top management representative, "because our production techniques are unique and very secret."

The nature of the work in the plant results in the fact that most workers are very dirty when leaving the plant in the evening. Miss Hanssens, being of the opinion that the hygienic welfare of the workers was of greatest importance, proposed to the management about a year previous that management should provide bathrooms to give the workers an opportunity to get a thorough washup before leaving the plant and to take a complete bath on Friday night.

Management was rather pleased with the idea and was ready to pay for the installation of a sufficient number of bathrooms. Management, however, was skeptical about unanimous acceptance by the workers.

Therefore, management decided to organize an opinion survey on this matter. If the majority of the workers agreed, work would be started immediately and every worker would be obliged to use the bathrooms.

Whenever management deemed it necessary to have decisions communicated to the department heads and to the rank-and-file workers, the department heads usually received a notification in their office. In this case, each department head received a letter which stated as follows:

> A proposal has been accepted by management to install bathrooms in the plant. This will make it possible that you and your subordinates can get a washup by the end of the day and take a complete shower on Friday night. Attached is a list of your personnel. Your name is on top of the list. Fill in "yes" next to the name if the person concerned agrees with this proposal, "no," if he does not agree. If the majority of the workers are in favor, work on the bathrooms will be started immediately. Return this list to Miss Hanssens the day after tomorrow.

The department heads, after having written down their opinions on these sheets, went their rounds through their departments and gathered the "votes."

The results of the opinion survey were not encouraging. The majority of the personnel voted against the initiative. In the seven departments where the department heads answered "no," about 90% of the workers were also against the proposal. The three remaining departments on the other hand, where the department head said "yes," gave favorable reactions with a majority of 70%. The "no" voters in the favorable groups were mostly people which management knew to be on bad terms with the department head.

Closer analysis of the survey results showed that female workers voted against the proposal in greater numbers than the male workers. The "yes" voters were predominantly men. There was also a significant difference between the old workers ("no") and the young workers ("yes"). The department head "no" voters were all "veteran" employees. Two female department heads, who had mainly female subordinates, had voted "no."

Management was unpleasantly surprised by these reactions of their personnel. Despite these results, at the insistence of Miss Hanssens, two bathrooms were installed for trial usage anyway. The workers could use them without being obliged to, but for several months the installations were used only on very rare occasions.

Management pondered what its next move should be in this matter.

RS, LTD. CASE 7

lerbert Pressel had played golf. The incessant
s impossible. Besides, as Managing Director of
he had found himself regularly working at week-

ed to combine a day of relaxation with a needed
Board of Directors had called for a report on
management supervisory staff for the company's
Mr. Pressel invited Mr. Seymour Glasser, a lec-
known Midlands Business School, as well as Mr.
lver, members of his own staff, for a day of golf

ube Boiler Makers, Sonning Mead Limited was
am generating plants for the Central Electricity
ent projects included both conventional and
s.
capacity of 60 megawatts. It is normal to
boiler in terms of the equivalent electrical
oday it is common to have a series of four
on one site.
n vast changes in the technology, logistics, and
he need for qualified staff to implement these
tion to the question of management education.
had become increasingly aware of the impli-
ct. Under this Act, Regional Councils had
ered to make substantial levies based on a
ge bill. This wage bill included executives as
well as hourly paid personnel. For the Boilermakers the levy was 2½% of total wages. The company could then claim back any of these funds which were used in the direct training of workers or management personnel.

The Industrial Training Act created a strong incentive for the companies to finance training up to the amount which had been levied by the government.

Case material of the Management Case Research Programme, The College of Aeronautics, Cranfield Bedford, England. Prepared as a basis for class discussion and made available through the cooperation of a company which remains anonymous. © Copyright reserved by Department of Education and Science (May 1966). Used by permission.

Sonning Mead expected a levy of over £200,000 in 1966. Questions of how such a sum should be allocated had become a matter of some urgency.

After greeting his guests at the car park, Mr. Pressel led the way to the clubhouse and suggested that before they changed they should have some coffee.

HERBERT PRESSEL, Managing Director: Gentlemen, I thought that while we enjoyed our golf we might have a useful discussion on the company's plans so far as training is concerned. Why don't we start with the qualities we are looking for in future site supervision.

W. E. CULVER, Training Manager, Sonning Mead Ltd.: Existing site staff are, in many cases, die hards. They have their own ideas on construction and often are not amenable to modern techniques. They are generally capable but have difficulty imparting their wisdom to juniors.

My experience is that resident site engineers have an excessively high opinion of their ability to improvise and consequently don't spend enough time planning at the start of a job.

SIDNEY JORDAN, Resident Site Engineer, Sonning Mead Ltd.: That which you call an excessively high opinion of themselves, Mr. Culver, I'd call a reflection of the inadequacy of the juniors, section engineers, and labour that have to be supervised. Remember, the design of boilers has changed drastically in recent years. Most of our top site staff have come from the ranks. They were good foremen and have extremely strong personalities. The new systems needed to build a modern station are foreign to many of them.

HERBERT PRESSEL: That's right. The older members of our site staff have not all had formal technical education. In one sense the influx of young people with such education is a threat to them and in itself builds resistance to new methods.

SEYMOUR GLASSER, Lecturer: I've noticed that your section engineers are generally young men and that there is a fairly high rate of turnover. In particular I've noticed a lack of understanding in labour relations and in handling of the men.

SIDNEY JORDAN: Seymour, you can't teach your grandmother to suck eggs and similarly the only way you can learn labour relations is to spend years fighting these problems on the job.

SEYMOUR GLASSER: In one sense you are right but you must admit that living with a problem can develop a hard line orientation that results in a lack of perspective in a particular situation. Antagonism, even when it's a result of experience is not a healthy condition.

HERBERT PRESSEL: I'm convinced that the administrative aspect of site supervision needs more emphasis. Work on site needs to be more sequential than work in the factory because of the heights involved, access problems and the close integration of one operation with another. In the factory they can more easily go back to things; on the site they can't because they'd be putting up cranes and derricks and involved in all kinds of erection equipment and plant.

SIDNEY JORDAN: The quality of supervision is critical. Men have to respect the supervisor. The foreman is number one. A good foreman will make the job; not a good section engineer, not a good resident, but a good foreman.

W. E. CULVER: So what you are saying is that the section engineer should be a planner and an administrator rather than a technical expert.

SIDNEY JORDAN: Yes, but he must understand the technique and gain enough respect to be the leader. And the chief engineer must be a born organiser.

SEYMOUR GLASSER: The term "resident engineer" would seem to be a misnomer. On large C.E.G.B. contracts he is more of a general manager than an engineer. He controls a large labour force, consisting in the main of relatively unskilled labour. And he has to apply discipline in his organisation by negotiating from a position of strength. And today he oversees the planning, progress and budgetary control of the contract. All of this is much beyond the definition of a "resident engineer."

HERBERT PRESSEL: I agree. It's not enough to be a qualified engineer. He also needs a firm grounding in Trade Union Law, National agreements, Current Planning methods and Proper Site Organisation as well as the legal aspects of employment.

SIDNEY JORDAN: The ideal site man should have a working knowledge of all the construction trades and have held direct responsibility for erection work himself, and a man needs at least five years as a section engineer before he is ready to become a resident. The important point is that a man should be fully educated and experienced before real site responsibility is given to him. Full practical experience is of much greater value than a ton of theory. You can't create the aggressiveness and enthusiasm it takes to be a leader by studying books. You can only find out who possesses the ingredients of leadership on the job itself.

W. E. CULVER: Considering the complexity of today's site work, you need young people with National Certificate or HNC qualifications. They need lots of experience in the works and drawing office but formal management education is also necessary; particularly in human management, self expression, report writing, communication techniques, and work study methods. It's the lack of this formal education that needs our attention. No one will argue that experience is not vital. The point is that in today's world experience is not enough.

And as you know, formal education at the site is difficult. Men can't be spared for part time courses. The location and working hours make it difficult particularly among juniors. And it's difficult to convince management of the value of formal training. They say that since they didn't have formal training and are successful why can't today's juniors manage without it.

HERBERT PRESSEL: The fact that we are here discussing this subject seems to contradict you doesn't it, Mr. Culver?

W. E. CULVER: Yes Sir, it would appear to.

As the group moved into the dressing room to change it began to rain so they agreed to continue their discussion in the bar.

HERBERT PRESSEL: Mr. Glasser, could you review for us the kinds of formal training that are currently available.

SEYMOUR GLASSER: I brought along some pamphlets for you to inspect. Why not take a few minutes and we can talk around them. (See Exhibits 1 to 4 on pages 57-60.)

What you are really looking for is the best way to spend your educational funds. Remember that very few programs will satisfy every requirement unless they are specifically tailored for your company. Also a programme might include some subjects which seem to have no immediate relevance to your needs. Therefore your choices in formal education will be usual business decisions in that there will be a full measure of uncertainty involved.

HERBERT PRESSEL: I understand management education to mean three things; it means developing the ability to make rational and informal decisions. It also means increasing a man's effectiveness in working with and through people as well as enlarging his capacity for taking responsibility.

W. E. CULVER: What we want is a course that is valuable to men who have proved their effectiveness as junior managers, in a specialist's role, and are considered ripe to take on greater responsibilities, either within their specialist function or by assuming a broader cross functional responsibility.

HERBERT PRESSEL: We want our men to develop substantially in a variety of ways. They should increase their understanding of the business world and its environment and they should develop greater powers of analysis and decision making. They should develop skills in human relations, both in relating themselves to others and predicting human reactions to change. They should develop a more conceptual framework in which to lead out their business lives. And finally, they should develop a greater perception of the interplay in different business functions.

SIDNEY JORDAN: But do we want to prepare men for wider responsibility in the company? Or should they be more effective in discharging predefined responsibilities? It should also be pointed out, that by being mistakenly prepared to take greater responsibility, a man is likely to develop heightened expectations of the role he is able to play. Thus it is important that when a man is elected by his company to attend a programme, serious thought be given to the question of his future career, if the programme is apt to give him ideas of grandeur.

SEYMOUR GLASSER: The quality of a programme must depend in part on the quality of the participants. It is assumed that when a man is nominated for attendance, the company will have selected a man of genuine potential and demonstrated competence.

SIDNEY JORDAN: Yes, but you are still assuming we are training potential managing directors.

SEYMOUR GLASSER: No, not really, but what I am saying is that business schools are not in the business of readjusting misfits. Good men can ill be spared. But the loss of such a man for a time must be weighed against the continuing benefit of a brighter, more knowledgeable manager over the many years of active life remaining to him in the service of the company. The new ideas and enthusiasms which such a man brings back with him do not remain locked within him, but are an injection into the company as a whole, and spread to the man's associates in widening circles.

W. E. CULVER: It seems to me that a smaller and smaller number of good young men for recruitment as managers will be available from non-university sources. And that to get the right men business will have to increase its intake of graduates. The graduates while, highly educated in their particular subjects, have in most cases, acquired little familiarity with the business world and will be arriving three years older. All these factors will make them less suitable, less willing subjects for the historical training and indoctrination which they normally would have received.

SIDNEY JORDAN: This sounds rather general to me. A man will never find out the proper way to rig a tackle except on a site. And what conceivable relevance does the determination of National Income have to building a boiler.

SEYMOUR GLASSER: It all depends on your goals, Sidney; a manager must have broad perspectives. There are, however, special programmes arranged to suit particular needs. Such courses have been arranged for the services, Technical College teachers, trade union officials, and nationalised industries.

HERBERT PRESSEL: I can see that it is critical that we define specific goals for our training. There appears to be such a diversity of courses offered that unless we target our purposes we will go off in many directions at once.

We seem to be troubled by the question of the relevance of offering a broad spectrum of courses to a man who will be concerned essentially with production planning and human management. Perhaps management development cannot be a once for all exercise. In a world of cumulative change, ever more intricate complexity, expressively increasing knowledge and constantly widening horizons, what could suffice today would almost certainly be inadequate tomorrow.

SEYMOUR GLASSER: For the individual man, a single course, however, good, at any one stage in his life, will not be enough.

W. E. CULVER: That is why there are series of general courses for trainees, younger managers, middle managers, senior managers and directors of companies, each complete in itself, but together providing a progressive system of courses available to the manager at the decisive levels throughout his career.

SIDNEY JORDAN: If anything I prefer a large number of specialized courses, conferences and seminars in particular subjects or for particular types of managers.

SEYMOUR GLASSER: You can see, gentlemen, that many schools are active in the field of business education. There are many more than the programmes we have noted. However, these are representative. And the number of so called business schools is growing rapidly. You will not lack in choices of direction. Fees, in each of these institutions, vary considerably, but in no sense will the fees be out of proportion, if you have chosen the right man, the right institution, for the right reason.

W. E. CULVER: Of course, the least expensive means of training is within our own company.

HERBERT PRESSEL: The difficulty is in achieving new perspectives in the individual man when he is taught generalist subjects on the job within the atmosphere of the company's existing value system. What we are really looking for is constructive change and there is a strong argument for injecting new thought, new ideas, new techniques, into the thinking of our younger men. These new ideas will then be modified by the facts of life within the company, when they return from a particular institution. Nevertheless, they will make their mark.

W. E. CULVER: Should the method of instruction mean anything to us? There has been a good deal of controversy in this country over the best way to develop management skill in the classroom.

SEYMOUR GLASSER: At one extreme you have the pure lecture method in which the teacher imparts his knowledge directly to the students. At the other you have a pure participative scheme in which the students discuss the materials they have studied with only guidance and control supplied by the teacher.

The answer as to which is the best method depends on what is to be taught, the calibre of the students, and the aim of the particular course.

For example, in your case, subjects such as labour relations might deserve a different approach from method study techniques.

SIDNEY JORDAN: If we are going to have courses I think they should be individual company training schemes. I think formal training in things like labour relations would be next to useless. Practical on-site experience is what's required.

HERBERT PRESSEL: We must insure that we give special training only to men whom we expect to stay with the company. This raises the question of how early in a man's career we should spend money on his training. I feel initially direct site contact should be maintained to give a realistic basis for the labour relations education, and an awareness of site conditions and erection procedures. Perhaps by employment as an inspector, plant erection procedure can initially be studied. If possible employment as a section engineer should take place on a small job where every aspect can more easily be studied in detail. For erection procedures and heavy lifting, a transfer to a large project would be preferable. At that point perhaps, training and theoretical aspects of site work from organisation to planning to human relations could be phased into the training.

SIDNEY JORDAN: There is no substitute for experience provided you are willing to learn from and by it. Thus, the highly qualified man, academically speaking generally does not make the best site man. He must above all be practical, and somewhat a jack of all trades. Therefore I would recommend an apprenticeship period that would last 4 to 5 years that would be spent in the drawing office, works, design service, maintenance department, and planning and estimating departments, as well as in periods of learning trades, such as welding, fitting, rigging, pipe fitting stores. I would also advocate periods of working in gangs or with gangs of men, perhaps as a foreman, then a period as a section engineer and within this period, perhaps a course of workstudy or method study. I frankly can see very little value in the company spending its money on broad academic courses.

W. E. CULVER: My personal observation after 12 years in the business world, working for two different boilermakers, is that I have never known or heard exactly what a company's objectives were with regard to management training and I think it would probably be found that nobody else has heard either. One can only guess.

SEYMOUR GLASSER: I think this is the point of our discussion today . . . In terms of basic value of formal education, it is interesting that those individuals who have had it are those that endorse it. And those individuals who haven't are those that decry it. There is a lesson in the examination of this fact as well.

HERBERT PRESSEL: Gentlemen, thank you very much indeed. I think we have had a fair statement of the qualities we are looking for in future site supervision and a representative glance at the kind of formal education that is available. It is now up to us to equate the two.

Exhibit 1

Programme A

This is a 10 week residential course taught by lectures and participative method. The programme is broadly divided in two phases, approximately equal length. In the first phase, the focus is on the development of background knowledge in three major areas; analysis and measurement, human behaviour, and the environment of business. Analysis and measurement is covered by problem oriented instruction in quantitative methods, in financial and cost accounting, in the analysis and measurement of demand in costs, and in the economics of production.

The human behaviour course develops an understanding of the nature of the individual, group and intergroup behaviour as it occurs in a business setting, and draws creatively on the behavioural sciences to increase the individual's awareness of the nature of his own behaviour and his own attitude.

The study of environment concentrates on three major aspects. These are: (a) the overall workings and management of the British economy, including an introduction to national incomes accounts, balance of payments, and national planning. (b) social control of industry which covers problems of monopoly, competition, restrictive practices, and resale price maintenance. (c) the corporate legal environment which is studied through an introduction to the underlying principles of company law, and the law of contracts, sales payments and labour relations.

The second phase of the programme is directed toward the application of the knowledge acquired in the first phase to actual business situations. The programme is divided along the lines of the major functions of business, production, marketing, finance, industrial relations, personnel management. The work is largely based on actual situations drawn from business and effort is concentrated on the development of skill for dealing with particular problems. There is also a section in operations research methods which introduces many of the newer techniques and indicates both their potential and their limitation.

The last element in the second phase is a course in policy making which offers the opportunity to develop skill and the integration of functions through the concepts of setting objectives, and the development of coherent strategy with the subsequent formation of policies, and the organisation development and motivation of people to achieve objectives.

Exhibit 2

Programme B

Instruction in techniques—a series of operating courses taught by lecture and laboratory work where appropriate.

Course number 1: A one week course in recent developments in management techniques.

A survey of contemporary management services with particular reference to management sciences. The course covers the modern scope of work study, ergonomics, cybernetics, operational research, industrial dynamics, linear programming, statistical methods for managers, control of stocks, investment policy making, distribution, modern organisation theories, organisation and methods of computer studies, the current economic background to management activities, and finally the integration of management services.

Course number 2: Network Analysis.

This course consists of critical path planning, PERT and other related methods, and the general technique called network analysis. The course offers sufficient practical training in network analysis to enable those who successfully complete it to introduce the technique in their own organisations. Case studies from industry are worked through in considerable detail. The students are also required to complete a practical project. The application of electronic computers in this field is dealt with and a computer is used for a demonstration in critical path analysis.

Course number 3: Statistical Methods for Solving Industrial and Commercial Problems.

The course aims to give a thorough but simplified instruction in a limited but powerful range of statistical techniques. Areas covered include the use of sampling procedures to give better control of quality, lower inspection costs in the office as well as the factory. The course includes the use of computers as an aid to statistical analysis, and the design of experiments and research to obtain the required information with a minimum of experimentation. The course provides a valuable introduction to statistics for managers and supervisors. A high level of mathematical ability is not required. Only elementary algebra is used in the course. The approach is essentially practical, formal theory being reduced to absolute minimum.

Course number 4: Materials Handling.

A two week course with emphasis on the solution of problems by the use of critical analysis. The aim is to maximize utilization of resources at least cost, an approach which is often absent in the field of management.

Course number 5: Data Processing and Computer Studies.

This is a three week practical course in data processing for which no other knowledge of computers is required, and which develops a sound critical approach to the problems of electronic computers.

Course number 6: Method Study.

This is a four week course which prepares individuals to return to their organisations capable of carrying out method study investigation under some guidance from management. The course therefore meets the need for sound basic training which few organisations are able to provide from their own resources.

Course number 7: Organisation and Methods.

This is a course in administrative work study, and covers such subjects as analysis of procedures, office and work measurement, office equipment, organisation theory, management information analysis, and elementary statistical theory.

Course number 8: Production Planning and Stock Control.

This two week course has been drawn from actual methods in current use, carefully selected so as to illustrate most modern principles in practice. It is essentially concerned with teaching practical techniques in production planning and stock control.

Exhibit 3

Programme C

Course number 1: Short lecture courses in Specialised Subjects.

These short courses include balance sheets for the laymen, business tax, corporate taxation, cost and profit evaluation techniques, a profit planning seminar, production control, critical path analysis, value analysis seminar, work-study appreciation, organisation and methods appreciation, industrial marketing, new product development, market forecasting, capital expenditure decisions, interviewing skills for managers, systematic selection methods, management by objectives, and appraisal by results, the negotiation of productivity agreements, as well as others. These short courses run from one day to ten weeks and can be selected to the particular needs of an individual company or industry.

Exhibit 4

Programme D

Course number 1: Weekend Residential Lecture Courses.

These courses are held in both England and N. Ireland. They offer a series of elementary as well as advanced courses. The number of students accepted for each course is limited in order to give ample opportunity for discussion. The advance course includes job evaluation, incentives, increasing cost consciousness, organising for production, weighing up people and jobs, men, money and trade, and supervisory decision making.

THE COLLEGE PROTESTOR   CASE 8

Jane Washington, a student at Hill City Junior College,* was nineteen years old at the time of this case and in the second semester of her freshman year. In order to support herself while attending college, Jane had accepted employment with Sanders Supermarket Store, a unit of a major chain of food stores in Hill City.

The store in which Jane worked as a "check-out girl" is located in a predominantly white community, populated primarily by blue-collar (or working-class) families. Jane worked approximately 15 to 20 hours a week, during evenings and on weekends as she was available and needed. Her performance had been rated as satisfactory by her supervisors during her six months of employment.

CAMPUS UNREST

A series of events at Hill City Junior College led to a serious situation of student unrest on the campus. On one occasion dissident students occupied several buildings, and frequent protest demonstrations by black students culminated in a severe demonstration protesting against the Vietnam war. The partial burning of a building during this demonstration led to the closing of the campus for several days. Jane Washington became interested in campus problems and she was quite sympathetic with the student protests and issues that had been raised. Following a major student demonstration involving anti-war sentiments and protests of the killing of several students on other campuses in the United States, Jane Washington could contain herself no longer. She decided that she had to make known her feelings to everyone, including people with whom she came in contact on her job at Sanders Supermarket.

Jane reported for work on a Saturday morning at the supermarket with a black band around her left arm clearly displayed over the neat uniform which had been furnished by the store. In addition, several large buttons were attached to her uniform which stated various protests against the Vietnam war and discrimination against blacks. Her supervisor, Miss Helen Dulo, noticed these items but she said nothing to Jane because she didn't know what action would be appropriate.

CUSTOMER PROTESTS

Within several hours after Jane Washington had come to work, numerous customers whose groceries had been checked by Miss Washington had commented

* See Case 26 in Part Four for further information concerning Hill City Junior College.

on the armband and the protest buttons. Several went directly to the store manager, Mr. George Jamieson, to complain. These customers said they thought it was very inappropriate for a college student to express herself politically in a store which was supposed to be neutral on political matters. Mr. Jamieson, after hearing several of the customers' complaints, agreed with them. He proceeded to tell Miss Dulo to tell Miss Washington to remove the buttons and the protest armband.

THE ULTIMATUM

At 11:45 a.m., about fifteen minutes before Jane was to go to lunch, Miss Dulo asked her to come to her office for a conference. The general nature of the conversation between Miss Dulo and Jane Washington was as follows:

MISS DULO: We have received several complaints about your protest buttons and the black armband. We do not care what you do or what you say off the job, but while you are at work here in our store, you must remove these armbands and buttons and wear only the authorized uniform.

JANE WASHINGTON: And if I choose to do otherwise?

MISS DULO: If you choose to do otherwise, we will have no recourse but to suspend or discharge you, since we need to maintain the confidence of the customers we have in this community. We will give you a little time to think about it, but before you report back to work next Monday, you'd better make up your mind. We hope you will come to work as usual without the band and buttons.

THE NEWSPAPER STORY

That afternoon, Jane Washington went to Mr. Jamieson's office and told him that she was resigning her position from the supermarket because she could not, in good conscience, work at a store where she was denied freedom of speech. After telling Mr. Jamieson this, she went to her home where she called a reporter at the local newspaper to relate the situation as it had occurred. She told the reporter that she had been fired because she was not permitted to exercise her individual freedom of expression while being an employee at the supermarket. The newspaper reporter contacted the supermarket manager, Mr. Jamieson, and asked for his version of the story. Mr. Jamieson replied that the company had to protect its business. He stated that no employee while in the store was allowed to wear unauthorized clothing or buttons which openly expressed opinions about controversial political or social issues.

The next day, the story was a front page item in the local newspaper. On the following Monday morning, many students at Hill City Junior College were irate because of the supermarket's treatment of Jane Washington. They suggested a boycott of the Sanders' chain and they organized a brief afternoon protest demonstration outside the store. A number of store employees—particularly part-time students working in the supermarket—joined in the protest demonstration, and several employees and numerous citizens wrote letters of protest to the management.

Several days after the protest demonstration and the publicity in the newspaper,

Mr. Jamieson called a meeting of supervisors in his store as well as supervisors from several other Sanders Supermarkets operated in Hill City. He opened the meeting by raising several major questions for consideration by the management: "Should we rescind our actions in the Jane Washington situation? Secondly, What policies do we need in order to cope with future situations of this sort? Further, should we have any different policies or rules to cover employee dress, behavior, and appearance, and if so, how should these be developed?"

THE ASSEMBLY LINE: THE U. S. A. AND JAPAN (A)— THE GRUELING LIFE ON THE LINE

CASE 9

For eight hours every day, says Henry Belcher, a 40-year-old welder, "I am as much a machine as a punch press or a drill motor is." With that comment, he sums up a crucial reason for the auto-worker militancy that led to the strike against General Motors. Most of the men on the assembly line hate their jobs— with a bitterness that can hardly be understood by anybody who performs interesting tasks in comfortable surroundings. At best, reports *Time's* Correspondent David DeVoss, the auto worker's routine is a daily voyage from tedium to apathy, dominated by the feeling that he sheds his identity when he punches the time clock. At worst, in the industry's older plants, his life is one of physical discomfort as well.

LESS THAN A MINUTE

One such factory is the 60-year-old Dodge plant in Hamtramck, Mich., where Belcher works. Promptly at 6 a.m., the assembly line begins sending cars past his work station, and from then on Belcher is a part of the line, like the well-oiled gears and bearings. The noise is deafening: Belcher could not talk to the men at the next stations three feet away even if there were time. There never is. Partially assembled cars move past him at the rate of 62 an hour; in less than one minute he is expected to look over each auto, pound out a dent in a fender or reweld an improperly joined seam. Cars that cannot be fixed that quickly are taken off the line. In the winter, drafts from ill-caulked windows chill Belcher's chest, while hot air blasts from rust-proofing ovens 30 feet away singe his back. After two hours of standing on the concrete floor his legs ache, but the whistle does not blow for lunch until 10 a.m.

Then the line stops, and Belcher gets 30 unpaid minutes to eat. That is not long enough for him to walk down from his sixth-floor work station to the second-floor cafeteria, buy a hot meal and get back before the line starts again. So he munches a sandwich from a bag—often while standing at the back of one of the long lines of men waiting to use the urinals. The chance to visit the bathroom cannot be passed up, since Belcher can rarely leave the assembly line. Besides the lunch period, he gets breaks of eleven minutes in the morning and twelve minutes in the afternoon. After the lunch break, the whistle blows again at 10:30 a.m., and the men put in four more hours of work until the shift changes at 2:30. Says Belcher, who makes $3.82 an hour: "Everything is regulated. No time to

Reprinted by permission from *Time*, September 28, 1970, pp. 70–71. Copyright, Time, Inc., 1970.

stop and think about what you are doing; your life is geared to the assembly line. I have lost my freedom."

Complaints like these have been heard almost from the days when the first assembly line started rolling. In fact, the conditions that so depress Belcher are not as bad as they once were. Under union pressure, companies have made some improvements. Shifts are a bit shorter now than the 3:30 p.m. to 1 a.m. stint that Walter Reuther worked at Ford in 1927. Over the years, the union has won regular relief breaks, the system of roving relief men, and doors on toilets. Some workers who do especially dirty jobs such as painting, now get company-paid special clothing. Many plants now have enclaves away from the line where men on their breaks can sit down, smoke or get a cup of coffee from a vending machine.

For the workers, that is not enough. The amenities are greatest in the industry's newer plants, but a large proportion of union members labor in aged factories. The very nature of the work remains the worst problem. Auto managers concede that most assembly jobs are hard and boring, but they figure that little can be done about it. Managers commonly complain about shoddy workmanship. Union members vehemently retort that the line moves too fast for them to do as good a job as they would like to.

WELCOME OLD AGE

For many workers, the only escape is retirement on a pension. Old age is not unwelcome in the auto plants; it is common to hear young men talk longingly of retirement. That is why the union's demand that workers be allowed to retire after 30 years, regardless of age, on minimum pensions of $500 a month, has become a key issue in the G.M. strike. Says Pete Tipton, 34, a welder for Cadillac: "All I have to look forward to is '30 and out!' I only have a ninth-grade education, so I can't do anything else, but my children are going to stay in school so that they will not have to be subjected to this kind of life."

Some men, of course, work up to jobs that are free of much of the tough labor. Al Powarowski, 32, has advanced from loading boxcars for Ford to driving completed autos off the assembly line, at $3.72 an hour. Like many Ford workers, he believes that the company is more understanding than G.M. or Chrysler. But Powarowski feels insecure because of the unsteadiness of the work. He has spent 14 months of his seven years at Ford waiting out eight separate layoffs: the first, lasting one week, started on the 89th day of his 90-day probationary period as a new employee. "In the years when you are making money, you don't have time to spend it, and when sales go down and layoffs come, no one has any money at all," says Powarowski. His own annual income has dropped from $12,000 to $7,000 because his hours have been sharply reduced during this year's auto-sales slump. Besides, he finds the job maddeningly dull, if not physically taxing. "The only fun I have," he says, "is getting a few cold beers after work."

Richard Jankowski, 29, is happier—but only because he will soon realize the auto worker's dream of leaving the line for good. During the last three of his eleven years at G.M.'s Fisher Body plant in Ypsilanti, he went to night school, and this fall he will become a high school teacher. "I almost cry when I see kids coming into the shop today," he says. "Working in a factory is nothing to be ashamed of, but you look at men who are 35 and look 50 and you say, is that going to be me?"

As the nation's labor force becomes better educated, the automakers may run into trouble finding enough new men willing to enter the plants. Even before the strike, the once long queues outside plant hiring offices had disappeared, and for the first time in years in some factories, supervisors had begun hiring women for the line.

THE ASSEMBLY LINE:
THE U.S.A. AND JAPAN (B)—
JAPANESE LABOR'S SILKEN TRANQUILLITY

Compared with his blue-collar counterparts in the West, the Japanese worker is underpaid and overworked. Still he seems surprisingly contented with his lot. Rarely does the Japanese factory hand walk out on a long and costly strike. His energetic work habits are reflected in his country's productivity, which has been rising at an annual rate of 11.8%, helping to make Japan the world's fastest-growing industrial power. More and more Western businessmen are beginning to envy the tranquil relationship between Japanese labor and management.

ALL IN THE FAMILY

Much of the reason for this productive peacefulness lies in the psychology of the Japanese people. Their swift passage out of feudalism in little more than a century has not completely erased the stoic acceptance of a fixed hierarchical order. In contrast to most Americans, Japanese workers are quite willing to bow to managerial authority and place their own desires second to the goals of the company that pays their wages.

Toyota Motor Co., Japan's largest automaker, is a prime example. Like all car manufacturers, Toyota finds it increasingly difficult to hire young men to fill achingly monotonous jobs on the assembly line, which rolls off 60 cars an hour. "The work is simple and boring, and it is hard to get a sense of accomplishment from it," says Kentaro Sasaki, a 25-year-old personnel officer, who spent six months on the line. But whatever their feelings, the plant's workers apply themselves diligently. "They try to increase their output to show that they can do the job well," Foreman Schoichi Tsuchida told *Time* Correspondent Edwin Reingold.

The company's attitude toward the worker is also important in keeping labor peace. It is often said by economists that a Japanese company is not in business so much to make a profit as to fulfill its obligation to employees. Like most Japanese firms, Toyota practices a silken but binding paternalism designed to make the company's 38,500 employees feel that they are part of a large family rather than corporate cogs. Veteran workers are encouraged to spend hours of their own time helping newcomers improve their skills, and bosses generally attend subordinates' weddings.

In common with all Japanese workers, Toyota employees are never laid off— even during the slack period of model changeovers. The comforting sense of security is exceedingly important. The only serious strike Toyota ever had was in

Reprinted by permission from *Time*, October 5, 1970, pp. 81–82. Copyright, Time, Inc., 1970.

1950, after 2,000 workers were let go. Before the strikers returned to their jobs, President Kiichiro Toyoda had to accept personal responsibility for the firings and commit a kind of corporate hara-kiri by resigning.

RISING SALARIES

Job hopping is unusual. The deeply rooted Japanese system of pegging raises and promotions almost exclusively to seniority is an inducement for young people to stick with one company. If a worker stays with Toyota, thus proving his loyalty, he is almost certain to be advanced every seven years through a system of fixed, regular promotions. After 21 years he can bank on becoming a foreman. During this time he is likely to undergo periodic retraining and be transferred from one department to another. No Toyota employee has to look forward to a lifetime of doing nothing but tightening nuts and bolts or welding cardoor frames.

A new worker at Toyota earns only about $100 a month for a six-day, 42-hour week. But the fact that wages at the company have risen at an annual average of 20% for the last four years at least gives him something to look forward to. Moreover, he gets more than a month off in paid vacation and holidays. In addition, the company inspires productivity through a generous system of bonuses geared to profits; this year profits were high enough to allow every Toyota employee to collect a handsome bonus of 6.1 months' pay.

DISCOUNTS AND DIAMONDS

Fringe benefits cushion almost every aspect of a worker's life. Toyota provides free bus transportation to and from work and pays for the gasoline of workers who commute in their own cars. Company cafeterias offer cheap and diverse menus, including the popular hamburger. Rolling clinics visit the factories each day for sick call, and the company maintains a 344-bed hospital with 20 doctors in attendance.

Off the job, single workers can rent space in Toyota's tatami dormitory for as little as $2 a month. If married, employees are eligible for company apartments, which cost between $3 and $17; commissaries sell food at a 10% discount. A worker who wants to buy his own home can borrow money from the company.

His employer also provides a plenitude of sports and recreational facilities—swimming pools, meeting halls, tennis courts, golf courses, baseball diamonds and rugby fields. Hundreds come out to cheer the Toyota teams in competition with those of other companies. Classes are offered in flower arranging, sumo wrestling, water skiing, skating, weight lifting, squash and judo. A worker or his wife can learn to play a guitar and join a company band. For vacationing employees, Toyota maintains a string of mountain and seaside resorts, which charge about $1.40 a day, including food. These benefits are motivated less by union pressure than by management's desire to reinforce worker loyalty.

Unions in Japan are vastly different in structure and outlook from those in the West. Instead of banding together by craft, small Japanese unions have jurisdiction over individual plants and thus have far less clout than huge American unions. Japan has an estimated 56,000 unions, some of which are allied in four federations.

The individual unions tend to be led by men who have been brought up in the company and maintain a strong loyalty to it.

UNBEATABLE MISTRESSES

Massive industrialization in Japan is less than 40 years old, thus there are no bitter memories of labor strife like those that nourish the militancy of U.S. workers. Far from viewing management as an enemy, most Japanese believe that in working to improve the company, they are helping themselves, the economy and the nation. Indeed, they are. Last year, for example, Japan produced 2,600,000 cars, of which 281,162 were shipped to the U.S., including 150,000 Toyotas.

More than anything else, it is the worker's attitude toward his job that accounts for Japan's labor peace. The average machine-tool operator at Toyota was raised in an atmosphere of obedience that he has never really shed. He is not overly attached to such Western values as individual liberty. He views the company as an extension of all his other social relationships, not, as many Westerners see it, a world apart. A worker's job is often more important to him than his home life, a fact that most Japanese wives accept with equanimity. In Japan, the company is a hard mistress to beat.

THE WORTHINGTON CASE   CASE 10

The Worthington Bank and Trust Company has extensive national and international operations. In total assets, it ranks among the top ten banking institutions in the nation. The Worthington maintains a system of approximately one hundred branch banks in New York City, where its headquarters is located.

One afternoon in April, Mrs. Juan Rodriguez, a woman of about seventy, walked into Worthington's main-office branch in downtown Manhattan at about 1:30 p.m. She went to a teller's window, presented her passbook, and explained that she wanted to see her money and count it.

"I don't quite understand, Mrs. Rodriguez," the teller replied. "Do you wish to make a withdrawal, or are you referring to our tour service?"

"My book says I have one thousand dollars and one hundred and seventy-two dollars, no?" said Mrs. Rodriguez.

"Yes, ma'am, your balance is eleven-seventy-two."

"Well, I only want to see it and count to see if it is all there," she calmly and politely answered.

The teller, taking into account her age and obvious foreign background, felt he understood her problem. Therefore, he tried to explain briefly to her how a bank works. He explained that her funds were pooled with those of others and that a bank uses such funds to help people who need capital. As the teller talked he began to realize from Mrs. Rodriguez's confused expression that she did not understand. She apparently was upset over the realization that her money was not tucked away in its own box somewhere in the vault. Her confusion seemed to turn to fear, and she was quite upset over the whereabouts of her money.

At this point, the head teller, who had heard part of the conversation and who was becoming concerned over the commotion, stepped into the teller's cage and politely introduced himself to Mrs. Rodriguez. He realized that she had become quite excited so he very cordially invited her to come into his office and speak with him. Mrs. Rodriguez seemed somewhat placated by the intrusion of this "higher authority." She went quietly into the office of the head teller, Mr. Scott Weiss.

Mr. Weiss tried to assure Mrs. Rodriguez that "everything's all right now." Mr. Weiss quietly and patiently explained the problem to her.

Case prepared by Professor John W. Hennessey, Jr., of the Amos Tuck School of Business Administration, Dartmouth College. The primary source of information was a Worthington employee who witnessed the events recorded in the case. All names disguised.

"Yes, of course you're concerned over your savings, and you should be. That is precisely why we have good sound banks for people to keep their money in. You see, we at the bank keep your savings safe and sound for you ...." Mr. Weiss went on to explain how Mrs. Rodriguez's money was watched closely. He invited her to come in on any Tuesday and take a tour of the bank to see its "large vault" and its new machines which "ensure all depositors against any mistakes in the records of their savings."

Mrs. Rodriguez listened patiently and politely while Mr. Weiss explained the situation. When Mr. Weiss felt that she was sufficiently calmed he smiled obligingly and asked her if everything was now all right.

"Yes, I understand fine," she answered, sounding satisfied with his explanation. "Now, if my money is all safe and there are no mistakes, it is all right that I can see it and count it, no?"

Mr. Weiss realized, to his dismay, that he had solved nothing. He tried to explain how her money was kept in a "common pool" with other people's savings and how other people, who had no savings could borrow some of this money.

Immediately, Mrs. Rodriguez seemed to become nervous over this idea. She could not understand why her money was not kept separate. She did not want others using her savings. Now, she seemed convinced that she had better "see and count" her money to make sure it was all there! Mr. Weiss tried several new explanations; however, Mrs. Rodriguez insisted that she had the right to see her money.

Although reluctant to have Mrs. Rodriguez make a withdrawal of her funds, Mr. Weiss felt that this might be the only solution. Therefore, he decided to check on her balance himself and then let her make a withdrawal of the entire amount if she so desired. He rose and excused himself, explaining that he would be right back.

Mr. Weiss checked the Rodriguez account and the balance was all in order. However, one additional complication now arose. Mrs. Rodriguez's account was, in fact, a joint account with her daughter. Mr. Weiss realized that he could not allow her to make a withdrawal without her daughter's signature. While Mr. Weiss was at first dismayed by this new complication he decided that this could serve as his "out." Telling Mrs. Rodriguez that she needed her daughter's signature would be a way of getting rid of her temporarily, and then maybe her daughter would be able to explain the whole misunderstanding to her. With this "perfect solution" in his mind, Mr. Weiss returned to Mrs. Rodriguez.

He laid the bank's record of her account in front of her and explained how that proved that her money was all there and was accounted for. He said nothing more for the moment, hoping this would satisfy her. She agreed with this account perfectly; however, she still wanted to see her cash.

"Well, Mrs. Rodriguez, all I can suggest then is that you come down with your daughter and then the two of you can make a withdrawal of any or all of your money. This is your money in this account and any time you and your daughter wish to withdraw some or all of it, you may do so."

"My daughter is away. She cannot come here. She is away now. Why can I not have my money? It is your money, no? I put it in here to keep it safe, no? Now, if I want to make sure it is safe, I cannot. You show me papers and numbers and say my money is safe, but you do not let me see my money or have it. This I do not understand."

Mrs. Rodriguez's confusion was apparent. She was becoming increasingly upset. Mr. Weiss offered to give her a withdrawal slip to send to her daughter to sign. She could not understand this. It seemed as though nothing but the $1,172 in cash would calm her. However, Mr. Weiss did not feel he could possibly present her with the money even to count it. If she got that far she might decide to take it with her.

Suddenly Mrs. Rodriguez rose and announced that she wanted to see Mr. Swanson, the President of the Worthington Bank, for he would certainly help her. Mr. Weiss, taken by surprise, did not know what to say. Mrs. Rodriguez had apparently seen Mr. Swanson's name in the papers and she felt that he could handle her problem. Mr. Weiss tried to explain that this would be impossible, that Mr. Swanson did not handle problems of this nature, and that he was not in anyway. He really did not know what to say. Mrs. Rodriguez quite firmly stated that she was going to see Mr. Swanson and that was final! She would wait until he returned if he were out, but she very firmly stated that she absolutely would not leave until she had spoken with Mr. Swanson and had made sure her money was safe.

By this time Mrs. Rodriguez had become quite agitated. She said that she would not be "fooled or cheated," just because she was "a foreigner." She stated further that if she could not see Mr. Swanson and check on her money, she would call the "police, the newspapermen, and the pastor!" At this point she walked into the lobby and there took a seat on a bench.

While Mr. Weiss stood somewhat dumbfounded by Mrs. Rodriguez's closing ultimatum, Mr. Theodore Hall, the assistant manager of the branch, went to Weiss' office. Mr. Hall knew nothing of the matter under discussion, but he had apparently seen that Mr. Weiss was having some difficulties. Mr. Weiss explained Mrs. Rodriguez's confusion and told Mr. Hall of her closing ultimatum. The two men discussed what had happened. Then Mr. Hall left with this parting remark:

"Well, Scott, you get these nuts from time to time. I'm sure you can straighten out the situation. Personally, I don't think Big Bob (Mr. Swanson, the president) would have time to chat with her today," he added facetiously. "You sure can't give her any cash because it's probably her daughter's savings anyway. And whatever you do, don't get the damned newspaper guys in on this. Those tabloids would make some tear-jerking, 'wicked-big-business' story out of this, sure as hell!"

At this point, Mr. Weiss was confused as to what he should do.

POONA METAL COMPANY   CASE 11

The Poona Metal Company, located in a small city approximately 125 miles east of Bombay, India, has operated for five years as a manufacturer, merchandiser, and distributor of kitchenware, pots and pans and other metal household items. The firm was organized originally as a partnership with two brothers, Maganbhai and Prakashbhai, as investing partners without management responsibilities, and two active partners, Narandas and Mansukhlal, directing the firm. A nephew of the silent partners named Ramlal is employed in the firm as well as Maganbhai's son, Nutan. It is a common form of business organization in India for capitalists to invest funds in a partnership and establish relatives in the organization for observation of the activities involving their investment.

The office of the Poona Company is located in the center of the main business district of the city; the plant is in a suburb, approximately twelve miles from the office. The operations of the company are partially manufacturing and partially merchandising. For the manufacturing process, metal ingots are obtained in the market and are sent through a process where they are melted and cast into strips and then sent through a continuous heat and rolling process until the strips reach the desired thickness. Brass and alloy sheets are produced in this mill process, but brass and stainless steel sheets also are purchased on the market and used in the other manufacturing processes.

In the manufacturing process, metal sheets are sent through a production line where they are sheared, punched and pressed into various shapes and forms of utensils and then sent through a heating and deep drawing process until the proper depths and shapes are achieved. Final spinning, trimming, polishing, and buffing activities complete the finished products. The operations of the machines in the mill and in the shops and the conveyance of all materials and products are performed by hand.

MANUFACTURING AND LABOR

The production process as shown in Figure 1 takes place in the factory, which consists of a series of four small shacks housing the rolling mill, furnaces, presses, and lathes. The machines are arranged to accommodate a maximum number of operations and workers in a given space without a very efficient layout pattern for flow of materials. The finished goods are packed in "jute" bags which are

Case written by Dr. Vasant Shah, Malabarhill, Bombay, India. All names, titles, and other identifying factors have been disguised, weighed and stacked in an open space at the end of the line of small buildings. No material handling equipment is available for moving the materials or the finished products.

The factory is operated on the basis of a 48-hour week. Power shortages and the scarcity of raw materials make it impossible to operate a second shift. In normal times, about 150 people work in the factory.

The management of the Poona Metal Company does not employ the majority of the people working in the factory. Within each department or principal activity, such as the rolling mill or the shearing and punching department, a private contractor employs the workers and subcontracts the work for his department from the management. Most of the people in the factory are employed by the contractors who have accepted responsibility for their specific operations. The contractors are paid for their jobs on the basis of the available work and their output. (See "Organization Chart," Figure 2.) For the company management, the employment of workers through contractors has the following advantages:

1. The company does not pay overtime rates for any additional work required of employees.
2. Workers employed by contractors are on a temporary employment basis, i.e., they are never employed by one contractor for more than six months. At the end of the six-month period, workers either are laid off for a day or they sign up with a different contractor. For these temporary workers, the company is not required to make deductions from their pay or contribute to health insurance or pension benefits. Both of these plans are operated by the government.
3. Layoffs and transfers of workers during the slack seasons are less costly for the company.
4. The threat of unionization of workers is averted because the majority of the employees are working for contractors and are on temporary payrolls.

THE LATHE OPERATOR

In checking his production reports one morning, Ramlal noticed that there was no production from the machine lathe in the trimming department for a three-day period. On inquiring about this condition, he found that the lathe operator, Raju, had been absent from work during this time. Raju was called in to the office and the following conversation took place:

RAMLAL: We've missed the output from the lathe, Raju. Where have you been recently?

RAJU: Sir, my wife was sick. I had to take her to a doctor. We had to travel by bus for 45 minutes and wait several hours to see the doctor. He asked us to go to the hospital for some tests. Once again, we had to travel by bus and wait in a queue. However, the Outpatient Department was closed before our turn came. Next morning we went to the hospital early and waited in a queue to get the papers, then to see the doctor, and finally for the tests. It was late in the afternoon by the time we got home. Yesterday I spent most of the day at the insurance office getting approval for treatment and for the bills. The office is at the other end of town and it is very difficult to get there.

Sir, you deduct insurance premiums and pension contributions from our small wages, and we have to run around so much to get any treatment.

RAMLAL: Well, those deductions are required by law and we contribute to the pension plans, too. When you retire you will collect your pension.

RAJU: God only knows if I will live that long! Besides, the pension may not mean much with our rising prices. Most of us are poor, unschooled people, and we don't even know how to go about collecting our pensions. I would rather use the money to get better treatment for my wife. Other workers with contractors don't have to contribute to all these plans. I would rather work for a contractor!

Mr. Ramlal thought for a moment, scribbled a note on a piece of paper to his family physician, and handed it to Raju.

RAMLAL: Raju, you are one of our permanent workers and you know how to operate that lathe. Actually, your pay is much higher than temporary workers who work for the contractors. They can barely exist on their wages, and we can't contract this machine operation. Take this note to our family doctor. He will treat your wife and it won't cost you anything. Soon you will receive our Diwali bonus.[1] This year, you will get about eight weeks pay which should help you meet your wife's doctor bills and other expenses.

PROBLEM AREAS

For some time Ramlal had been considering a recommendation to his uncles that the Poona Metal Company be dissolved and reorganized at a later date. A friend named Desai had recently returned to India from the United States where he had completed his college education and a graduate program in business administration. He had worked for three years with a group of management consultants in New York City and was considering the establishment of his own consulting firm in India. Desai had sought out Ramlal as a potential client at the same time the Poona Company operations were being reviewed. Their discussions included these remarks:

RAMLAL: I'm afraid that I can't discuss all aspects of our business with you. But you are highly recommended by our partner Narandas, so I will tell you something about our business. Please keep these remarks confidential.

DESAI: You can be assured that anything you say will be kept confidential. In my business this is always necessary.

RAMLAL: Our accounting records are extremely poor. Our production, sales and inventory records do not truly represent our actual operations. Only a small

---

[1] Diwali represents the end of the year for the followers of the Hindu Sanwanta calendar. To most Hindus, Diwali is the most important festival of the year and can be compared to Christmas. It is customary for most business organizations to give a special bonus to employees at this time. The bonus can amount to a maximum of six months pay. However, wages for unskilled workers in India are usually less than $1.00 per day.

part of our business transactions are recorded. Raw material supplies are regulated by the government, and we receive an allocation each month on how much of any material or product we can procure. These allocations are based on a quota system, supposedly dividing up all metals available. However, our allocations are too small to meet our requirements, so we have to buy raw materials on the second market[2] at much higher prices. We do not receive bills of sale for these purchases. Hence, all phases of operations and final transactions connected with the purchases on the second market never enter our records.

DESAI: The raw material shortage should result in substantial over-capacity for your company.

RAMLAL: This situation exists in most of the small-scale businesses in India. These conditions force us to concentrate mainly in obtaining import licenses. This is a more important function than manufacturing. A concern like ours does other things than produce and develop products. Production sometimes plays a small role in the survival of a company like ours. We obtain import licenses and we buy metal on the second market also. Any consultant we use must have a considerable influence in government circles and help us in obtaining import licenses. We tie up a lot of our capital in inventory, and the appreciation of the inventory is a major source of the company's profit.

DESAI: What do you do about purchasing new equipment for expansion?

RAMLAL: Most of our profits are from the second market and not on the records. They cannot be utilized for investment purposes. Usually the expansion of any business is restricted because of the shortages of raw materials and of skilled manpower, and we frequently lose money on our manufacturing operations. In these times, speculation in the markets is more profitable.

DESAI: I think we have more than enough manpower in our country. Much training is needed, but I do not see how manpower can be a limiting factor for growth.

RAMLAL: Due to the restrictions and the operations in the second market, we have to put our family members in most of the supervisory positions and guarantee them employment. Further, we have to deal personally with government employees. Otherwise, we might not be able to control our expenses and maintain adequate relations with various agencies in the government.

DESAI: I think I understand your position. It appears that a management consultant can do little about the improvement of management and labor, but must be effective in working with government officials.

RAMLAL: Give some thought to our principal problem. The government has informed us that next year we will not receive any import licenses for the raw materials we need. If we can't find something else to do, we will just have to close the plant. We don't want to close down and lay off workers; for some of our people, jobs are just not available. We have pressures from the local government to keep the plant open, and this influence may help us to obtain our import licenses. If you have any ideas on how we can continue to operate profitably, we would like to employ your services.

2 Black market

DESAI: My knowledge of the Indian market is inadequate. Let me think about your problems, and if I can do anything for you I will call again. On the other hand, I think I should consider returning to New York.

RAMLAL: Wait, Desai, maybe you can help us before you go. My uncles, Maganbhai and Prakasbhai, have invested in several businesses and this one is probably the least profitable. The returns from the second market operations do not appear on the official reports, and they are not sure that all funds are accounted for. Narandas takes care of the bookkeeping and they trust him pretty well, but there's just no way to audit the situation. If you could develop a plan to insure our share of import licenses and then give us better control over our second market business, it would be a great help. And sometimes I think we don't save as much through the use of contractors for hiring laborers as we think. How would we find out about our labor costs if the company employed the whole work force?

DESAI: Let me give it a try. I know of several other partnerships in Bombay which are dissolving. Our tax regulations make incorporation almost prohibitive so the partnership is most common. But, with problems like yours the life cycle of a partnership is short—every two or three years the partners think they have to reorganize. I'll take a look at some of these problems.

Figure 1
Manufacturing Process
Poona Metal Co.

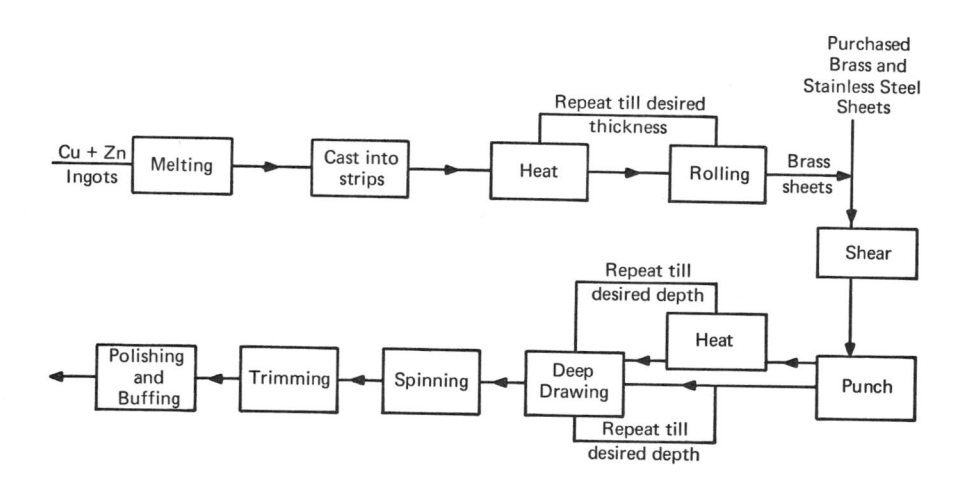

Figure 2
*Organization Chart
Poona Metal Co.*

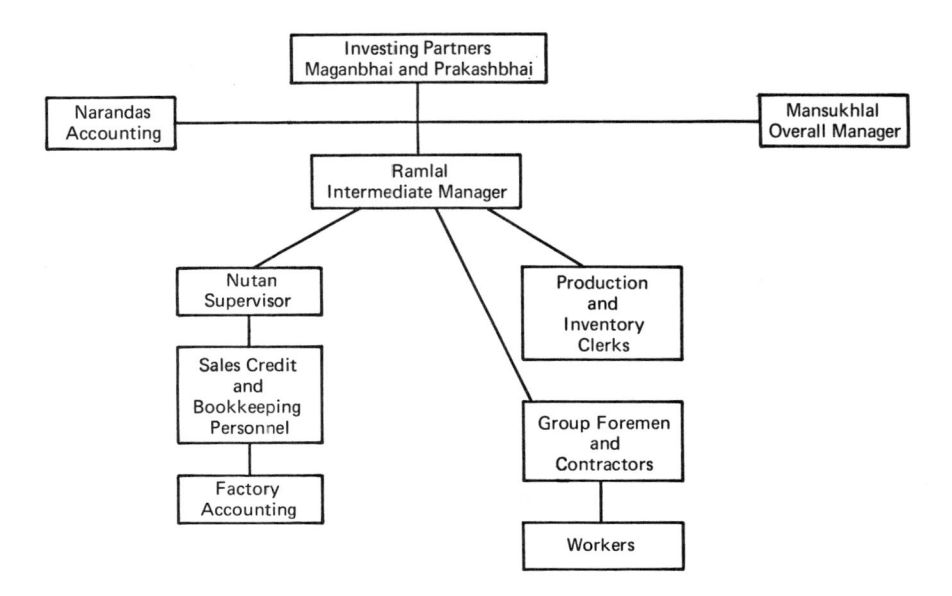

PART THREE

Carl Lohman—Lineman
Telecronics, Inc.
Martha Burleigh
Frazer's Department Store (A)
The Case of Tom Mendola
The Jamison Furniture Company
Tri City Utility Company: A Problem of Alcoholism
Too Many Personal Calls
A Matter of Priorities

People at Work

The members of a business organization may be classified into two broad categories, managers and workers. In a larger sense everyone in the organization is a worker, each contributing in his own way to the enterprise. Managers, however, perform a particular kind of work which is responsible for the planning, the organizing, and the directing of the efforts of others, especially the activities of the work force. It is a "law of the situation" that someone in the operating enterprise must assume the leadership or supervisory activities. The appointed manager becomes the leader of the work group because of this need for supervision, not merely because of his appointment or because of his special abilities. Normally, someone is selected for management responsibilities in preference to others because he is considered by higher authorities to be the best-qualified person available. But managers as well as the members of the work force are recognized as individuals with personal needs, wants and aspirations.

The behavior of people at work is primarily a matter of individuals endeavoring to satisfy their needs and wants. However, it is not always easy to recognize the causes of individual behavior. Some managers attempt to explain differences among individuals by developing classifications or types into which men fall. For example, in an organization a person may be stereotyped as being a selfish, materialistic individual, mostly interested in self-preservation and advancement. In another situation a man is judged to be a high-minded extrovert, interested in the people and the world around him. These efforts to classify individuals can be misleading, for a first principle of psychology is that all individuals are different. In some instances the "labels" placed on people at work are an injustice to the individuals and also handicap management in obtaining maximum utilization of its important resource, human effort. To understand the actions of people in dynamic work situations, it is necessary for the supervisor to constantly ask himself why human beings act as they do.

A second major principle contributed by psychologists to theories of personnel management is that "all human behavior is caused." Sometimes causes of behavior (causes of performance, problems, complaints, etc.) are difficult to assess, for they are frequently buried in the personal background of the individual. By searching and finding the causes of incidents of behavior, a supervisor is better able to understand the situations involving workers. This perception and understanding which comes to the manager through careful study of each individual worker's strengths and weaknesses leads to more effective approaches to personnel problems.

INDIVIDUAL NEEDS AND DRIVES

Research in human behavior has revealed that an individual's needs and ambitions constitute the underlying factors which motivate him to action. Some of these human factors seem a part of nature itself. For example, the infant and young child have a great need and desire for security, clinging to mother's apron strings and feeling safe in father's arms. The somewhat older child, moving away from the mother's care, is driven by an egocentric desire for recognition and a desire to be the center of attraction. The dominant drive of the adolescent is usually conformity, a desire to belong and be like the other members in his group. The dominant drive of the young man or young woman is more apt to be economic, a desire to be independent and to earn, to accomplish and to win the rewards of achievement.[1]

Related to these basic drives are other needs and wants recognized in most normal beings. Many psychologists have classified an individual's needs and wants as physical, social, and egoistic. Physical needs are requirements of individuals for food, clothing, shelter, and the material things necessary to nurture and protect human life. Social needs are the desire for companionship and love. This includes the desire to belong to family groups, social organizations and work groups and to generally satisfy the gregarious instincts. The egoistic needs of individuals include desires for recognition and praise, the desire for accomplishment, and the desire to express one's self and feel that one's talents and abilities are being used and appreciated.[2]

---

[1] For an interesting discussion of the growth of individuality, see Harold J. Leavitt, *Managerial Psychology*, Second Edition (Chicago: University of Chicago Press, 1964), pp. 13-27.

[2] For a discussion of these needs appropriate for managers see, Henry Clay Smith, *Psychology of Industrial Behavior* (New York: McGraw-Hill, 1964), pp. 21-41. The hierarchy of needs theory is discussed by Abraham H. Maslow, *Motivation and Personality* (New York: Harper & Brothers, 1954)

WHAT WORKERS WANT FROM THEIR JOBS

Numerous surveys have been made which go directly to workers and ask them to identify values or satisfactions they want from their jobs. The underlying questions in these studies were asked in different ways, such as "What does a worker expect from his job?" "What can a supervisor provide or do to properly motivate workers?" and specifically "Why do people work?" While the results of these surveys vary considerably, the answers are usually related to certain wants or needs which individual workers readily admit.

In some studies it is reported that the compensation of workers is far down the list of important things that workers want from their jobs. Security, recognition or praise, and fair supervision frequently appear to be more important in the minds of workers than the amount of pay which they receive. Other studies, however, place good pay high on the list of the most important wants of workers. There is the implication that in the work situation where the majority of workers believe their compensation is adequate, they will report other needs as being more important. However, in those situations where workers generally feel that their wages are inadequate or where attention is being focused on worker demands for higher pay, the compensation factor is most important among the needs of workers. Among the basic wants of workers are the following:

1. *Security* (steady work): Most workers are interested in finding and keeping steady jobs in order to ensure a continuous supply of the necessities and some of the luxuries of life. Although real security is hard to define and even more difficult to find, the assurance of continuous employment is a basic factor in relieving a worker of worry about the future and concern for the welfare of his family and himself. In addition, the social security program, various supplementary pension plans, insurance programs, and other benefits provide more security and peace of mind for modern industrial workers.

2. *Good compensation:* In our socio-economic system most workers depend upon wages or salaries for their livelihood. A worker's status in society as well as his standard of living depend to some extent upon his level of monetary compensation. Naturally, adequate compensation and the opportunity to improve one's standard of living by obtaining higher rates of pay are essential to employee job satisfaction.

3. *Justice* (fair bosses): Individual consideration and fair treatment from supervisors are desired but not always received by workers. In most organizations some weaknesses of supervisors and managers are accepted and tolerated by subordinates, but favoritism, prejudice, or nepotism are usually resented. The supervisor who is objective and endeavors to be impartial in his treatment of subordinates can have other shortcomings overlooked and excused.

4. *Good working conditions:* Most workers want to be as comfortable and neat as possible, and the efforts of employers toward good housekeeping are usually appreciated. In addition, employers find that attractive work places and cleanliness contribute to efficiency. Consequently, workers normally want the most comfortable and orderly working conditions that the nature of the operations will permit.

5. *A feeling of importance:* Most people want to feel that they are leading useful lives, and that their work is necessary and important. Every job in an operating organization is important or it should not exist. Although each individual worker is different, the need for achievement and the desire to create are usually strong motivating factors. Effective supervisors impress workers with the importance of their individual tasks.

6. *The opportunity for self-expression:* Most workers possess special talents or abilities, or at least they think they do. Each individual hopes to be able to use his own special strengths and abilities. He regrets lost opportunities and his failures to accomplish the things he is qualified to do. When employers provide opportunities for workers to improve and develop their talents, to increase their contributions to the organization, and to express their full potential, a tremendous new source of energy and power for the organization is developed.

7. *Sense of belonging to a group:* Belonging to a group means being a respected and appreciated member of an operating organization. It involves acceptance by one's working associates, participation in group activities, and opportunities for self-expression and achievement. Almost without exception workers like to feel that they are needed and wanted in their work groups.

8. *Opportunity to participate in decision-making:* The desire to belong to a group usually coincides with opportunities to participate in the group. In work situations most individuals want more than minimum opportunities to participate; they like to participate in the making of decisions which affect their own welfare. Few workers actually want to usurp management functions, but they do like to be consulted in matters pertaining to their employment, such as job assignments, working hours, vacations, work schedules, and similar matters.

9. *Recognition and praise:* Every individual likes to receive credit for his accomplishments, and workers respond as much to recognition and praise as to any other motivating factor. The supervisor who learns to give credit where it is due and to compliment workers for tasks well done usually has less trouble in winning employee cooperation. The boss who uses praise as a management tool generally accomplishes more through the efforts of others than does the supervisor who is too busy to recognize and note good job performance.

The importance of any single want or need to any worker at any given time depends upon his attitude and sentiments. The job he is performing, the behavior of his supervisor, his working conditions, and many external factors (including his home life) influence the worker's behavior and thinking. Since these dynamic factors are constantly changing, a study of individual behavior should not rely upon any single list of factors which generalizes what most workers want from their jobs. At best, any statement of why men work is only a modest guide toward the understanding of the behavior of people at work.

WHAT EMPLOYERS WANT FROM WORKERS

Although human needs and wants differ from one individual to another, there are some needs and desires common to most workers. Each employer also has certain needs as he hires one or more workers. The wants of employers in building and maintaining a work force might be summarized as follows:

1. *An adequate supply of workers:* Employers need an adequate supply of workers to carry on their operations without interruption. Most employers regret the existence of a large group of unneeded or unemployed workers, but they search the labor market and recruit job applicants in order to have qualified workers available for work requirements at all times.

2. *Low unit labor costs:* Employers want "a fair day's work for a fair day's pay." In other words, they want efficient, reliable job performance. In a free-enterprise economy, employers' products or services must compete in relatively free markets and are judged by customers. Although they desire competitive labor costs, this does not mean that employers necessarily want low wages for workers. Scientific developments and professional management, coupled with mass production techniques, have resulted in both lower unit labor costs *and* higher wages for workers. Since the industrial revolution, an ever-increasing supply of material things have been produced for more people at lower costs. This abundance is the result of the mechanization of work, improved methods, more efficient marketing programs, better management, and all the innovations of modern industry which bring lower unit costs and at the same time higher standards of living for workers.

3. *Ambitious and promotable workers:* Employers frequently need workers who are able to step up to greater responsibilities. As managers retire or resign from their positions, there is a turnover of supervisors and executives. At such times during periods of business expansion, employers must advance workers to more important assignments. While these opportunities vary greatly with employers, workers who are willing and able to work for advancement are always important company assets.

4. *Rights and prerogatives:* Employers usually claim certain basic rights because of the economic risks involved in providing jobs for workers. These are:

The right to discipline employees who do not comply with the demands of the organization, regulations, or standards for their job assignments.

The right to transfer workers from job to job or from department to department in order to maintain efficiency and balance in productive activities.

The right to dismiss workers for insubordination or serious infringement of work rules.

5. *Employee loyalty:* Employers want workers who are reliable and willing to make reasonable sacrifices for the good of the organization. This loyalty is expressed by acceptance of the employers' leadership, by reliable and dependable service, and in other ways. In some instances employers find their workers showing greater loyalty to their labor union leader or to an informal leader in the work group than to their supervisor or the company. This divided loyalty may be the result of poor employer or supervisory leadership. Nevertheless, most employers appreciate evidences of loyalty shown by their employees.

EMPLOYEE GOALS, INCENTIVES, AND FRUSTRATIONS

A worker seeks employment for one or more personal reasons, usually because he needs the income to live. He might also want the satisfactions of accomplishment, to be with certain people in the particular organization, or the opportunity to do a particular kind of work. At the time of employment he usually feels that the job he accepts represents an opportunity by which he can satisfy his own personal needs and goals. He sees in the organization an opportunity to achieve the things he desires from working.

It is possible, even desirable, for the management of a business organization to establish the type of environment and operating systems which assist the worker in accomplishing his individual goals while the company or the organization is achieving its objectives. One of the systems devised to integrate the personal goals of the individual worker with the objectives of the organization is an incentive program. Incentive plans for individuals (or for groups of individuals at work) permit them to earn greater compensation by achieving a higher standard of productivity, and they also provide a means for the recognition of superior performance. In some organizations the recognition of superior performance by supervisors simply takes the form of praise or encouragement which may provide a nonfinancial incentive which effectively motivates workers.

It is natural for an individual to be disappointed when he does not achieve his goals and when he does not receive what he wants and expects from an experience. A worker becomes frustrated when an obstacle blocks the promotion, the wage increase, a special work assignment, or some other benefit he is seeking. Such frustrations can result in minor disturbances of work patterns, or they can be deep-seated and seriously disturb the worker, greatly reducing his effectiveness on the job.

A worker's reaction to frustration might assume any of several forms. One typical reaction to frustration is aggression. When a worker has been greatly disappointed because he has not obtained something he wanted, he is likely to be emotionally upset. He might become aggressive and argue with his supervisor. If he is permitted to vent his emotions, even though he might appear abusive to his employer, it is possible that he can overcome this aggressive tendency and find a solution to his problem.

At the other extreme is resignation. When an employee is disappointed and fails to achieve his objectives, he may become quiet, no longer strive for his goals, and appear to resign himself to his fate. In many instances he loses enthusiasm and the desire to do a satisfactory job. Under these conditions the supervisor who understands the causes of this resignation might attempt to find new means of motivating the individual.

Sometimes a frustrated worker gives in to the desire to withdraw from the scene. He resigns his position, and finds employment elsewhere because he has not obtained what he wants from his job. If the possibility of his adjusting himself to his present environment is not good, this withdrawal may be a proper solution to his problem. On the other hand an understanding supervisor may prevent such a withdrawal.

Perhaps the most desirable reaction to frustration is reorientation. The worker who is frustrated because he has not reached his objectives often needs assistance in analyzing his problems logically and objectively. If he is able to reorient himself and substitute new goals for those which he did not achieve, he can maintain his interest and his enthusiasm in the work situation. This frequently requires that the worker admit that he was unrealistic in the establishment of his original goals or that he does not have the ability to achieve them. A supervisor may be able to effectively counsel a worker and help him to recognize his own abilities and to realistically establish attainable goals. By overcoming frustrations and working towards objectives, the individual worker is able to experience the satisfactions of achievement.[3]

THE CHALLENGE TO PERSONNEL MANAGEMENT

The manager at any level of an organization is constantly challenged to meet his production or operating schedules and at the same time to provide personal satisfaction for workers. Often there appears to be an unresolved conflict between the *wants of employees* and *the demands of the business enterprise.* How to resolve this common dilemma has long been a major challenge to personnel managers.

In recent years, many theories relating to the motivation of employees and to management practice have been contributed by various behavioral scientists. They have suggested that employer-employee conflicts can be mitigated if there is more creative effort on the part of managers to bring the objectives and motivations of individuals more in line or in harmony with the goals of the organization.

Professors Frederick Herzberg[4] and M. Scott Myers[5] have demonstrated in their research that certain traditional areas of concern to both employees and employers no longer strongly motivate workers and often are only taken for granted. Such factors as adequate pay, good working conditions, job security, supplementary benefits, and fair company policies and employment practices are expected by employees to be satisfactory and comparable to what other businesses and organizations are providing. Companies constantly strive to have these factors meet the needs and expectations of employees in order to attract and maintain a capable work force. But these factors are only basic foundations for the building of positive motivation. What is needed, more today than ever before, are opportunities in the job situation for employees to find continued personal growth, a sense of accomplishment or achievement, recognition, and opportunities to advance to more challenging work situations. Herzberg and Myers maintain that these types of factors are associated with the higher level needs of human beings, which if properly stimulated offer employers the most powerful opportunities for the motivation of workers to perform in directions of superior achievement and personal satisfaction.

Perhaps the most notable effort to tie management and motivational theory together in recent years has been the work of the late Douglas McGregor at Massachusetts Institute for Technology. In his famous book, *The Human Side of*

---

[3] See Edwin Flippo, *Management: A Behavioral Approach*, Second Edition (Boston: Allyn and Bacon, 1970), pp. 105-116.
[4] See Frederick Herzberg, "One More Time: How Do You Motivate Employees?," *Harvard Business Review* (Vol. 46, No. 1, Jan.-Feb., 1968), p. 57.
[5] See M. Scott Myers, "Who Are Your Motivated Workers?," *Harvard Business Review* (Vol. 42, No. 1, Jan.-Feb., 1965), pp. 73-88.

Enterprise,[6] Professor McGregor postulated the "Theory X" and "Theory Y" approaches to management which he recognized as being extreme styles on the scale of alternatives open to any manager. The Theory X manager views his employees as being indolent, unwilling to work, and stimulated to work only by coercion, control and various forms of monetary and tangible incentives. The Theory Y manager, at the other extreme, has a more positive outlook on the capabilities of human beings. He believes that workers seek responsibility and are motivated to perform well when they are committed to the objectives of the organization. This commitment can be developed by enabling employees to utilize their talents and to find a sense of achievement and accomplishment in work. Obviously, it is not always possible to create job situations in which Theory Y can be implemented. But Profesor McGregor maintained that with the changing nature of the work force, the Theory Y concept of management will become more important and more necessary if managers are to achieve an optimal use of their human resources.

There are no easy answers to this constant dilemma facing the manager in the human relations area. Many situations arise which create difficult conflicts that must be resolved between the wants of employees and the demands of the business. For example, employees may be seeking increased salaries and higher benefits when competitive conditions on the market require lower prices of products or a reduction of costs. Employees may prefer security in their current job situations, whereas the requirement of the business may mean the transfer of employees from one job to another or possibly a layoff of workers. How can these and other kinds of employer-employee conflicts be resolved? Among the greatest tasks facing all managers is the challenge to integrate and reconcile the desires and wants of employees with the goals and objectives of the business enterprise. In accepting this opportunity, the progressive organization strives to procure and develop intelligent, dynamic, and effective managerial leadership for all of its segments and at all levels within its organization. With such leadership in developing the full talents and capabilities of all human resources and with positive efforts to attain both group and individual goals, effective organization results are possible.

---

[6] Douglas McGregor, *The Human Side of Enterprise* (New York: McGraw-Hill, 1960), pp. 33-34 and pp. 47-48

CARL LOHMAN—LINEMAN CASE 12

The Tri-County Power Company operates in a midwestern state and serves numbers of relatively small typical country towns with populations running from 250 to 3,000. There are also two medium-sized cities in the area serviced by the company. A major part of the company's power users are small industries and farmers, the area being a prosperous farming center. It is company practice to work many of its line crews over wide areas, sometimes 25 to 35 miles away from their central headquarters. This generally requires the crews to spend one or two nights away from home, although they always return to their home town over the weekends. For many years it has been the practice of the company to schedule this away-from-home work on a rotational basis so that each crew in a given center assumed its share of these assignments.

Carl Lohman started work as an apprentice lineman with the company some 20 years ago. He was born and raised on a farm near one of the towns served by Tri-County Power. His father was a well-to-do dairy farmer. At the time he left the farm his father was resentful that his son decided to reject farming for a "city job." Carl worked for several years with the same line crew, eventually becoming a lineman-first class, and a very good one. Eight years after joining Tri-County Power, Carl Lohman married. Ten years later his father died and Carl's mother urged him to bring his wife and two young daughters to live with her on the dairy farm. Being the only eligible heir to the farm, and sensing that it would be the logical place to which he could eventually retire, Carl made the move. Chores on the farm were being done by an old hired hand who had been with the family for many years. Carl helped as much as he could in his spare time.

All went along satisfactorily until the hired hand became ill and could no longer carry the burden of caring for the cows and dairy work. Carl Lohman then reduced the size of the dairy operation to 12 cows and he, with his wife's help, took on the full responsibility, along with his lineman job with Tri-County Power.

On one particular evening, the foreman scheduled Carl's crew to begin work the next day in a locality some 30 miles away, remaining there for a period of three days. It was the crew's turn to accept the out-of-town assignment. Carl reported to the foreman that his wife was ill and that he could not take the work assignment because he had to be at home in the evenings and mornings to care for the cows. His foreman told him that he would have to either go along with

---

Case reproduced by permission of Professor Clayton Hill, School of Business Administration, The University of Michigan. All names, titles, and certain other identity factors have have been changed. In other respects, the facts are true.

the crew or go home. He explained that it was not the responsibility of the company what Carl did with his own personal time, so long as he reported regularly for work and carried out his assignments. In this instance Carl's off-duty activity was interfering with a regular Tri-County duty. He suggested that Carl had better arrange to get some assistance for the farm since failure to meet job assignments could not be tolerated.

Carl, somewhat disgruntled, turned on his heel and went back to the farm. The foreman assumed that Carl would realize that he would not be paid call-in pay or his regular pay as long as he could not report for work. But two days later Carl filed a grievance through the union requesting he be paid call-in pay and his regular pay for the time he remained "laid-off."

After the case had been heard by the proper management representatives, and all available information and data collected, the management reversed the action taken by Carl's first line supervisor. They reasoned that Lohman had been, as far as records indicated and from information picked up, a very satisfactory employee. He had never given any previous trouble and had always been willing to do the job assigned. The supervisors in that area knew he was running the small dairy farm on his off hours. They had made no criticism of the arrangement nor had they forewarned Lohman of what might happen if he couldn't take his turn at any time on the out-of-town assignments.

As a result of the management's decision, Carl was restored to his normal duties and paid for the days he was laid off. However, he was told, both by the company and the union, that if he planned to continue operating the farm, he should make plans to get the necessary help and that reasonable time would be granted to do this. He was given warning that if he could not maintain proper help on his farm, then the company would expect him to either perform his duties assigned or resign from Tri-County Power's employ.

Carl's first line supervisor was not happy with this decision. He felt that unless foremen had some authority, it would cause their men to lose respect for them. In this case he thought he was doing the best thing for both the employee and the company and something that was perfectly reasonable. He felt that Carl's attitude had been unreasonable since his main livelihood was his compensation received from Tri-County Power.

TELECRONICS, INC

CASE 13

For several months Steward Atkins, director of quality control, and Walter Erskine, director of industrial relations, had been aware of a peculiar morale problem in the machine shop area of Telecronics' test equipment design and construction department. There were 25 employees in this department of whom about 15 were machine operators. There seemed to be a distrustful atmosphere amongst the machinists and they seemed less friendly than those in other departments. With the passage of time the atmosphere of distrust became more evident, especially after Atkins and Erskine started to investigate the loss of mill supplies in the department. Loss of personal tools by the machinists became apparent with this investigation. Yet the operators "clammed up" as soon as they were aware that a review of the situation was in process. The tension rose and it began to affect the output of the department.

Telecronics was a major manufacturer of electronics equipment located in the Eastern United States. It produced radios, television senders and receivers, tape recorders, and a variety of special equipment for the United States defense effort. Telecronics expanded rapidly during World War II and took part in the post-war electronics boom. It was primarily noted for high quality equipment and design of equipment for specific new and unusual functional applications.

The rapid expansion required the purchase of additional facilities. One of these additions was a building in Hinton, ten miles from the main plant, which housed 300 employees engaged in certain electronic accessory assembling, the salvage of scrap materials and the design and construction of test equipment.

Because of Telecronics' work in the development and production of considerable military equipment, the personnel at Telecronics were all subject to security clearance review. The building in Hinton was classified and everyone working there had to be cleared. The company maintained its own guards.

The accessories assembled in Hinton were completed, packaged units which could be added to a major product.

The scrap and salvage department serviced this and other units of the company. Materials that were no longer useful in production operations were salvaged where possible and where economically worthwhile. Otherwise the materials would be sold for scrap value to a scrap dealer on a bulk basis.

Located next to the scrap and salvage department was the test equipment and construction department. This department designed and built special test equipment

Reprinted by the permission of the Faculty of Commerce, University of Alberta, Edmonton, Canada. All names, places, and dates disguised.

for proving out the company's various products. Since these products were nearly all designed by Telecronics to meet special needs, their final test embraced a high order of engineering skill and special test equipment was required. Initially new designs of electronic equipment were proved out on paper without the benefit of sample units which might be tested. Hence, the testing program following the manufacture of a new product included the type of tests that would normally be run in an engineering laboratory to prove out the design.

The test equipment department designed the test equipment that was needed. This included the drafting work where prints were required. Following design, materials and parts were ordered. Construction of the equipment was conducted in the department's own machine shop which included sneet metal equipment, drills, lathes, millers and spray painting equipment.

The department employed about 15 machinists. These were necessarily highly skilled operators. Often the specifications were not completely proven out and the definition on prints was incomplete. A great deal of ingenuity in building the equipment was therefore called for. The department was generally under pressure to complete the equipment so that a good deal of improvisation was necessary if delivery of the test equipment was not to delay the final testing of major electronic units.

As a result, production economics was a secondary consideration; time was primary. The machinists would do things very unconventionally at times. They would resort to many common or easily available materials from a hardware store or mill supply house. Where possible standard production parts were modified. Often the machinists were able to use some of the materials that were being scrapped by the scrap and salvage department and no longer useful in the production operations.

Since scrap and salvage was located right next to the test equipment construction group, the machinists were able to observe the type of materials being scrapped. These were actually parts of electronics gear being manufactured, but for various reasons they were not usable. With modifications, however, the materials could be used in the construction of test equipment. The machinists found this department one of the best sources of materials. So, whenever they ran into a "crash" program, they would actually search through the scrap and salvage department and pick up material they could make into something.

The work in the machine shop called for a high degree of skill. Though none of the men had an engineering education, their "gadgeteering" called for imagination, ingenuity and knowledge of diverse electronic components.

Each machinist had his own personal tools and tool box. Whenever he brought tools into the building, they were checked in. Whenever they were taken out, there was a check out. In addition, each machinist signed for additional tools supplied by the company through the tool crib. In this way there were separate records of personal and company property in the possession of each machinist.

Stewart Atkins, director of quality control, and Walter Erskine, director of industrial relations, were aware of a bad morale problem in the machine shop area. For several months they had not been able to determine the cause of it.

They considered Bob Shaw, the foreman of the group, to be the type of leader who would be attractive to the group. They characterized him as technologically very inventive; his approach to getting things done was of extreme expediency in nature. He was full of energy. He had attracted primarily a group of individuals that were quite like himself. The production of the test equipment department in terms of quality and quantity was felt to be satisfactory.

The first concrete evidence that something was seriously wrong was an increasing number of reports that individuals were missing some of their own personal tools that they had carried in. There were reports also of missing tools and mill supplies that had been drawn from the tool crib.

Atkins, Erskine and Shaw decided to investigate this and try to trace the disappearance of these materials. They didn't have much success, however. They reached the point where they could trace the loss of materials between specific times, but even this was not particularly helpful in explaining how the materials disappeared or who was involved. The machinists, themselves, didn't seem interested in helping to solve the problem.

By chance it was discovered that they had developed a practice of locking up their loose tools. They would place the tools in their tool boxes and lock them when they left their work benches. They did this even when merely turning their backs on their work position to work on another tool only a few feet away. Management was unable, however, to tell if they were distrustful of each other as a group, or whether they had some particular individual singled out of whom they were distrustful. Atkins, Erskine and Shaw were unable to learn, also, if the machine operators were trying to discourage borrowing by others or if they were guarding against the permanent loss of the tools.

As the investigation continued, the tension in the department rose, and it began to be reflected in reduced output. Though the men worked primarily independently of each other, the common use of facilities and the assignment of several men to the construction of a single piece of equipment demanded cooperation. The men were not cooperating as much as they had.

Production was also hampered by the disappearance of supplies ordered especially for test equipment construction. For example, one day a ¼ horsepower motor with a particular step-down worm-type gear drive was missing. This motor had been ordered for a specific application. The whole department looked for this motor and no one could find it. Another instance was a step-on lid design can used for receiving oily waste which disappeared the very same day that it was delivered. It was large and bulky. The time of its receipt one morning was documented by many persons in the area. The approximate time of its disappearance was identifiable. Yet no trace of it could be found.

For a time management appeared to be stymied in its efforts to explain the disappearance of tools and mill supplies. A lead was given by one of the janitors one day, however, when he voluntarily asked to talk to Erskine. He said that he had something on his mind, something that was bothering him, but that he did not want to tattle on anybody. Yet, he said, he felt a responsibility to Telecronics.

As related by Atkins, the janitor stated that a "specific individual in the test equipment department (Joe by name) had requested the janitor to cooperate with him to the extent that a janitor leave a particular door accessible." This particular door was involved with the safety regulations. It was not being used, with the exception that it was a safety door. It had escape-type hardware on it that was incapacitated to a degree, and since it wasn't used for traffic it would get occasionally blocked up with material, janitors' supplies and so forth. The degree to which Joe had asked the janitor to cooperate with him was to keep this area way open and clear. He didn't ask him to open it or anything like that, but it was merely, "Don't block this door, leave this area clear."

Atkins continued: "The janitor didn't give us any specific hint that would be accusing anyone of thievery, but he felt it would ease his conscience if he put a 'spot-light' in a particular area to guide us to gather our further information, if we so desired, but he was very careful not to be involved in it.

"Now Joe was one of the higher skilled, one of the more energetic individuals in the group that was constructing equipment. He was very versatile; he was very helpful in many cases... He, in no way, had caused us to have any suspicion directed toward him until he was named by the janitor."

MARTHA BURLEIGH   CASE 14

Ten years after the event John Sedgwick could remember vividly in its every detail what he called the "affaire Martha" and particularly his sense of personal outrage when he first learned of Andrew Joplin's decision. The passage of a decade, during which he had accumulated a substantial amount of administrative experience himself, studied a number of administrators-at-work, and read and thought a lot about administration, had left him still unsure as to whether his boss had shown a deep understanding of human nature in his handling of Martha Burleigh, clerk-stenographer, or whether he had been just plain lucky that the action he took turned out as well as it did.

John Sedgwick at the time had been working for the United States Air Force as a civilian employee in the aircraft structural design division, evaluation section. He was one of four engineers reporting to Andrew Joplin, the section chief. Assignments were divided as follows:

Sedgwick: heating and ventilating, fire protection
Anderson: production materials and processes
Berry: production materials and processes
Zernia: design strength minima for structural components
Joplin: supervision, integration of above assignments

Martha Burleigh was the clerk-stenographer for the section. Although she was under Andrew Joplin's direct supervision, she handled the clerical work of the entire group. She was about 40 years old, had been in the section for 15 years, and had the reputation of being the best quality (not quantity) producer among the clerk-stenographers in the aircraft structural design division. She was single and lived at home with her father, mother, and a brother about her own age, also unmarried.

John remembered Martha as sallow in complexion, thin and stringy in build, neat but drab in dress; and as impersonal and withdrawn in her daily contacts with divisional personnel. She wasn't exactly unfriendly, she just wasn't friendly. She addressed herself diligently to her work, did a minimum of talking, and never took part in the give and take of office badinage.

Floor space in the division was allocated to sections on the basis of a fixed number of square feet per employee. Footage assigned to each section was subject to immediate adjustment whenever its personnel increased or decreased. Layout of desks in the evaluation section was as shown in follows (see Stage 1).

From Austin Grimshaw and John Hennessey, *Organizational Behavior* (New York: McGraw-Hill 1960). Used by permission.

Stage 1

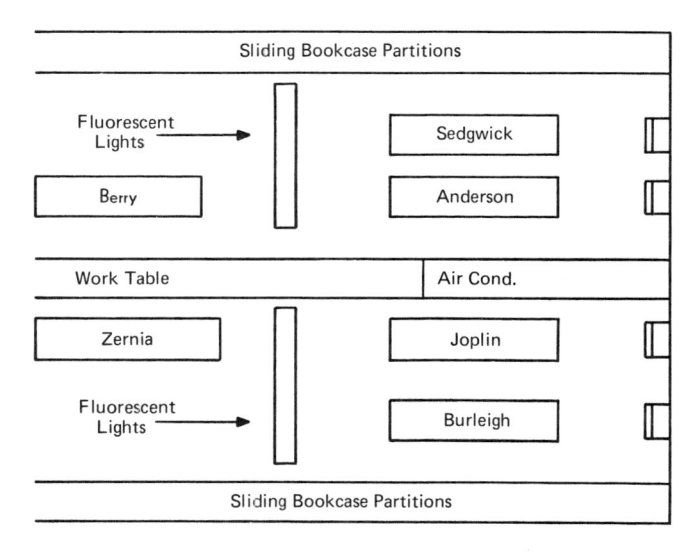

```
┌─────────────────────────────────────────────────┐
│           Sliding Bookcase Partitions           │
├─────────────────────────────────────────────────┤
│  Fluorescent  ──▶  │  │   ┌──────────┐       ▯ │
│    Lights          │  │   │ Sedgwick │         │
│    ┌─────────┐     │  │   └──────────┘         │
│    │  Berry  │     │  │   ┌──────────┐       ▯ │
│    └─────────┘     │  │   │ Anderson │         │
│                    │  │   └──────────┘         │
├────────────────────┼──┼─────────────────────────┤
│    Work Table      │  │      Air Cond.         │
├────────────────────┼──┼─────────────────────────┤
│    ┌─────────┐     │  │   ┌──────────┐       ▯ │
│    │ Zernia  │     │  │   │  Joplin  │         │
│    └─────────┘     │  │   └──────────┘         │
│  Fluorescent  ──▶  │  │   ┌──────────┐       ▯ │
│    Lights          │  │   │ Burleigh │         │
│                    │  │   └──────────┘         │
├─────────────────────────────────────────────────┤
│           Sliding Bookcase Partitions           │
└─────────────────────────────────────────────────┘
```

Sedgwick, Anderson, Joplin and Burleigh had window desks. Berry and Zernia had inside desks. The entire space was brilliantly lighted by fluorescent tubes and there were no shadow areas.

Andrew Joplin, before joining the section as chief a year earlier, had been an aircraft structures engineer. In his position his duties had been entirely technical in nature, with no supervisory responsibility. He was a graduate engineer, 36 years old, with 12 years of continuous service as an Air Force civilian employee. His appointment as chief of the evaluation section, aircraft structural design division, had involved a transfer within the aircraft design organization from one branch to another, an increase in grade and a higher salary. The four engineers under him had all been in the section for varying periods of time when Joplin took over—Sedgwick and Anderson for nearly four years and Berry and Zernia for one and two years respectively. All four had enjoyed working for Joplin and with each other. There was no conflict of interest among them because each had his own specialty.

The trouble with Martha began when Berry quit to take a job in industry. Her space by the window and the desk where she sat were assigned to another section in the square footage readjustment which followed Berry's resignation. He was not replaced. Joplin assigned Zernia to Berry's old location and Martha to the desk vacated by Zernia (See Stage 2). Martha was obviously disturbed. She became more tight-lipped and silent than ever.

Almost immediately after the move, Martha began to complain that the fluorescent lights bothered her. Joplin had the lights turned 90 degrees in an attempt to stop her frequent references to her newly developed headaches. When she continued to complain, he arranged to have light meter tests made. These indicated

Stage 2

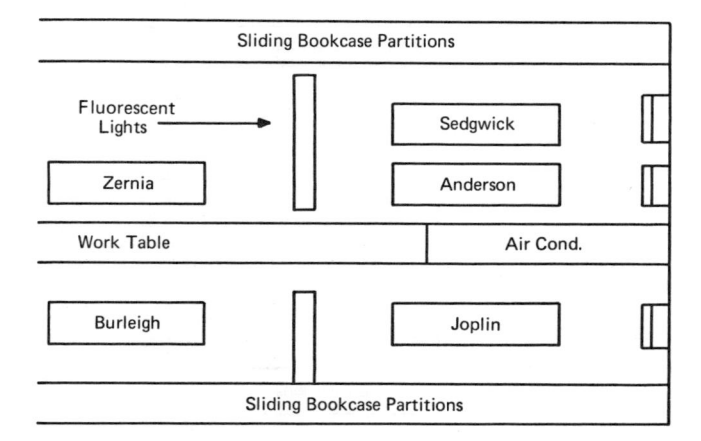

```
┌─────────────────────────────────────────────┐
│         Sliding Bookcase Partitions         │
│  Fluorescent                                │
│    Lights  ──→  ┃   ┌──────────┐         ┃ │
│                 ┃   │ Sedgwick │         ┃ │
│  ┌──────────┐   ┃   ├──────────┤         ┃ │
│  │  Zernia  │   ┃   │ Anderson │         ┃ │
│  └──────────┘   ┃   └──────────┘           │
│                                             │
│     Work Table        │      Air Cond.      │
│                                             │
│  ┌──────────┐   ┃   ┌──────────┐         ┃ │
│  │ Burleigh │   ┃   │  Joplin  │         ┃ │
│  └──────────┘   ┃   └──────────┘         ┃ │
│         Sliding Bookcase Partitions         │
└─────────────────────────────────────────────┘
```

that the illumination level at her location was slightly below the recommended standard, so he had blue tubes put in. These brought the lighting level at her desk slightly above standard.

During the following two weeks Martha still fussed about her headaches. She kept aspirin, cotton pads and eyewash, prominently displayed, on her desk and frequently used them. She bought a pair of dark glasses and a green celluloid eyeshade, which she wore constantly. Her production dropped to almost zero. Work she had previously handled in stride had to be sent outside the section to the typing pool, in order to get it done within a reasonable time.

Sedgwick, Anderson and Zernia were upset because Martha was not getting out the work they gave her. Also, they resented her attitude. Zernia, they pointed out to each other and to Joplin, had gotten along all right in the same location and his job involved much more eyestrain than Martha's. They severally said to Joplin: "Let's lay down the law, let her know who's boss around here. Send her to the doctor. If he says she's OK, get her reassigned out of the section and get someone in here who'll get some work done."

Instead of acting on this advice, Joplin horrified the three engineers by trading his window location for Martha's inside space (see Stage 3).

Martha immediately abandoned her aspirin, eyewash, dark glasses and eyeshade. Her productivity at once returned to its previous norm. She apparently took her return to a window desk as her just due. She made no slightest gesture of demurring when Joplin suggested the shift, nor did she ever thank him for it.

After a few days the section settled back into its former routine. Sedgwick, Anderson and Zernia, although still upset by Joplin's solution, decided to go along with it. Sedgwick and Anderson, however, did try individually to persuade Joplin to trade locations with them. Joplin refused to do so.

Stage 3

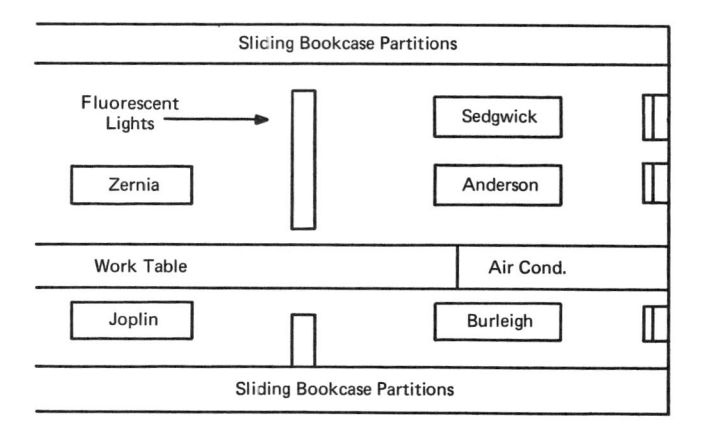

Slicing Bookcase Partitions		
Fluorescent Lights →	Sedgwick	
Zernia	Anderson	
Work Table	Air Cond.	
Joplin	Burleigh	
Sliding Bookcase Partitions		

FRAZER'S DEPARTMENT STORE (A)— CASE 15
COMMUNICATIONS

Mr Gordon Fiske, executive vice-president of Frazer's Department Store, returned from a conference held by the National Retail Dry Goods Association where he had been impressed by a talk he heard on the subject of communications. Soon after his return to the store, he discussed the conference with Mr. Stone, the personnel manager, and gave him the notes he had made on the talk about communications. Mr. Stone agreed that relationships between members of the Frazer organization might be improved, if more attention were given to management-employee communications.

A young man, George Prentiss, had recently joined the personnel department and was being trained for the position of employment supervisor. He was a graduate of the state university and had worked in a small department store while in college and for two years thereafter. He came to Frazer's directly from that position. It occurred to Mr. Stone that it would be good training and experience for his new assistant, if he made a thorough survey of the methods of communication used by the store personnel.

Mr. Prentiss was given this assignment, which he discussed with both Mr. Stone and Mr. Fiske. He was given the notes which Mr. Fiske had prepared at the conference, and he was told that he could interview any executive in the store. He was given permission to dictate his report to Mr. Stone's secretary, and he was asked to complete the survey within a week.

Four days later, Mr. Prentiss presented the following report to Mr. Stone and asked permission to discuss it with him after it was read.

STORE COMMUNICATIONS—REPORT BY GEORGE PRENTISS

Like many other department stores, Frazer's has established various channels for two-way communications between management and the workers. There is a need for making these means of communication more effective. This report suggests that improvements in store communications might result in greater employee understanding of store problems and could increase worker productivity, lower operating costs, and result in greater store profits

Means of Communication

Various types of communication are presently used at Frazer's. They include the following:

A. *Written Communications.* Several media make up this part of the formal system used by management to supply workers with information.

97

1. *House Organ.* "Frazer's Family" is a monthly publication written and edited by store employees. It is an attractive magazine featuring many employee pictures and brief copy. It concentrates on the "human element" and attempts to build group solidarity among store personnel. The store management makes little or no attempt to use this medium to tell employees of its philosophy or its problems.

2. *Door Handouts.* The employees receive these bulletins when they sign in for work at the beginning of the day. The handouts announce special events, such as an evening softball game, or they emphasize important sales promotions, Christmas sales, and other events. The handout bulletins are issued once or twice a week and primarily serve as reminders of store events. They frequently give employees information or instruction from management.

3. *Paycheck Inserts.* Another reminder that emphasizes important promotions, charity solicitations, or policies is a brief message placed in each employee's paycheck envelope. This method is particularly effective when the store is in the process of a charity drive. In general, the messages in pay envelopes are carefully written, and do not offend the reader when he is being asked for a contribution. Several supervisors feel that these inserts are less effective when used each week.

4. *Bulletin Boards.* Eleven bulletin boards, placed in strategic locations throughout the store, contain important and current information. Some workers pay very little attention to these postings. Perhaps the material could be presented in a more interesting and readable form. Some employees complain that items on the bulletin board are seldom changed, and current notices are carelessly posted.

5. *Intra-Store Correspondence.* One of the most useful channels of communication consists of intra-company correspondence and reports. Written matter travels between superiors and subordinates, and among people of equal rank. These reports are usually concerned with operating problems and policies, but they frequently clear up misunderstandings and solve problems which reach deeply into the human relations aspect of communications. Many individuals in the store do not write letters, memos, and instructions as well as they should.

B. *Meetings.* Department and store meetings constitute another segment of Frazer's formal communication system.

1. *Departmental Meetings.* In departmental meetings, employees receive merchandise information and hear about changes in operating procedures. New selling techniques are presented. The primary motive is to stress store operations, policies, procedures, and merchandise.

2. *Store Meetings.* Occasionally a meeting is held on the main floor for all 800 employees of Frazer's. Everyone is expected to come to work ten minutes early on the days of these meetings but half or more of the store personnel either miss the meetings or come in late. New policies or special promotions are briefly discussed. Detailed explanations are given

at the department level. The purpose of the mass meeting is to develop a feeling of group solidarity and to give employees the opportunity to hear a message from "top management." Supposedly, the workers will think that they are in "one, big, happy family," and thereby accept the submitted information more readily. These meetings are not as successful as the speakers think they are. Many employees complain about the early starting time, especially since they receive no compensation for the extra time spent in the store.

C. *Counseling.* In connection with employee attitudes and performance, there are two types of counseling, a six-month interview and the attitude survey. The objectives of both counseling methods are to determine and improve employee job satisfaction and job performance.

1. *Six-Month Interview.* Each employee is rated and interviewed by a member of the personnel department every six months. An attempt is made to see if an adjustment between job and worker is needed. Compensation problems, promotions, benefits, and transfers are the main topics considered. It is the responsibility of the personnel department to cooperate with an employee's supervisor if any action is needed after the interview. The interviews have more form than substance. In many cases, the worker and the personnel counselor differ in their opinions as to needed adjustments. The interviews seem to be guided too much by what the counselor feels is important. These impressions have been obtained from conversations with several employees.

2. *Attitude Survey.* Occasionally management attempts to determine general employee attitudes toward store policies and operations. A questionnaire has been developed which is used as a guide by a member of the personnel department to conduct a question-and-answer interview with each worker in those departments where morale or productivity seems to be at a low ebb. Some employees think the attitude surveys are a waste of time. Some of the younger stock boys take the interviews as a "joke," and the information is probably very unreliable.

D. *Informal Communications.* Some supervisors and department heads at Frazer's seem to be unaware of the fact that good management-employee relations depend upon continuous satisfactory relationships. These managers are frequently skilled technicians in merchandising or salesmanship, but they fail to realize that the cooperation and good will of subordinates is necessary in order to have an effective department. Lower levels of management in the store do not appear to be convinced of this.

1. *Manager-Employee Relationship.* There is a wide variance of supervisory effectiveness from department to department. In a few departments the employees seem to be reasonably contented and productive. Their bosses treat them as individuals and are willing to listen to their problems and questions. Too many Frazer supervisors do not know how to develop this permissive atmosphere. Their employees seem to be afraid and seldom care to speak with their superiors. Some even refused to talk freely with the author of this report.

2. *Grapevine.* The Frazer's grapevine is, perhaps, the quickest means of communication in the store. It travels up and down the management-employee ladder at a rapid rate. The "Black-Girl Case" illustrates the point.

A black girl was hired one afternoon to fill a sales vacancy in Department X. She was to report for work the next morning. That same afternoon a stenographer in the personnel office informed Sue Jones, one of the better sales ladies, that a Negro was going to work in her department. Sue, who originally came from Birmingham, Alabama, told another saleswoman in the department that she would quit if a colored woman were hired. The saleswoman mentioned that fact to the assistant manager. He told the manager. The manager wanted to retain Sue since she had an excellent record; accordingly, he quickly explained the situation to the personnel manager. Very shortly thereafter, the employment interviewer called the black girl and politely told her not to come to work the next morning. The black girl was promised a different job in another department to begin the next week. This entire process took place during a period of about three hours.

Conclusions

Some potential channels of communication in the store have not been included in this study. The most significant of these are relationships which exist between the training supervisors and employees. No doubt the activities of the store's training division could be a more effective channel for management communications. In training new employees and in training regular employees for transfer, the training supervisor and the departmental instructors could pass along more information regarding management policies and practice. In addition, these training supervisors could collect ideas, suggestions, and other information from workers which would be helpful to management. The meetings organized by the training supervisor for department managers and supervisors could be more effective. Apparently, higher-level executives have seldom participated in these meetings. One supervisor stated that he was sorry that his boss couldn't hear what was said at the last supervisory conference.

At this time, there are two suggestions which might be appropriate as a part of this report. First, it is recommended that the suggestion system, which was discontinued several months ago, be reconsidered. With careful study and reorganization it might be operated successfully to the store's advantage. Secondly, it is suggested that this report be carefully reviewed in management and supervisory meetings. Improvements in communications in the store can be made if the key people in the organization give their attention to the problem.

Respectfully submitted,

George Prentiss

Within an hour after the report on communications was submitted to Mr. Stone, he called Mr. Prentiss into his office. "It's a good report, George. You've covered a lot of ground. Don't you think you've been a little too critical in some spots? You've been pretty tough with our counseling program."

"Well, I hope not, Mr. Stone," said George. "I just didn't know how to write the report. I couldn't sleep night before last, worrying about it. I could have made it sound better, but I decided to call a spade a spade and tell you just exactly how I felt."

"Oh, it's not so bad—but, take something like the early morning meetings. A few employees gripe about the ten minutes' early start; but do our better people mind? Don't the meetings do more good than harm?"

"Possibly so, Mr. Stone, but I just feel that there have been too many lately. Mr. Bauer had two last week."

"Well, Mr. Bauer is superintendent over the whole store, but he probably does call too many meetings. Did you talk to him about the survey? How did he like it?"

"I think he was too busy to really understand what I was doing," replied Prentiss. "I had a hard time seeing him, and when I did have a chance to get into his office I waited behind a line of three other people. I don't think he liked the survey."

"But what did he say about communications in his department?" asked Mr. Stone.

"He said they were good; he thinks there is no problem. He says that when he wants to communicate, he just goes out and talks to whomever he wants to communicate with. Of course, I couldn't ask him many questions."

"I know what you mean, George. I need to reach him this morning. I've called three times, and I can't get him on the phone."

"Well, I want you to know, Mr. Stone, that I appreciated the opportunity to make this survey. If I seem critical it's just because I want to be of help. I don't expect any place to be perfect. I like Frazer's and I think I have a good job here."

"I'm glad you feel that way," replied Mr. Stone. "We want you to get into these store problems. I'd better mark this report 'Confidential'—and we'll see what Mr. Fiske says about it. He started all this, anyway. Is there anything else you have to say about it?"

"Yes, there is, Mr. Stone. As long as I'm sticking my neck out, I might as well go all the way. I met an old schoolmate of mine working in the basement. He's only been there two months, but he's not sure who his boss is. He says that he takes orders from two buyers and also from the basement manager.[1] But most of the time he just does what he thinks is right. It seems that both the buyers and the operating managers think they supervise the sales people. He told me that he'd been in the department about a week when a new girl came to him about 12:30 one day and asked him if it was all right for her to go to lunch. He looked

---

[1] Frazer's Department Store is organized in such a manner that merchandise managers are responsible for both buying and selling activities. Sales people report directly to buyers, but many basement activities are controlled by the basement manager.

*Frazer Department Store
Management Organization*

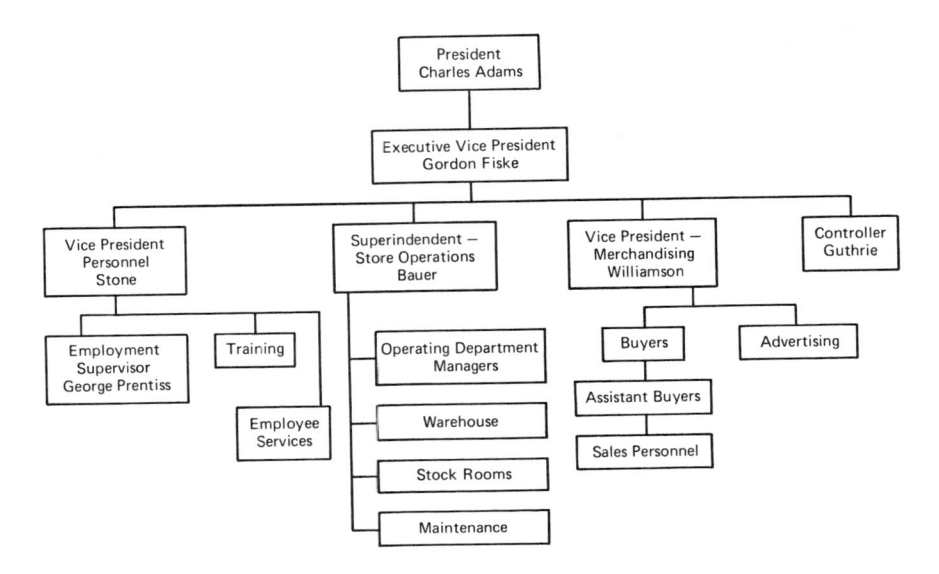

```
                        President
                       Charles Adams
                            |
                  Executive Vice President
                        Gordon Fiske
                            |
    ┌───────────────┬─────────────────┬──────────────┬──────────────┐
Vice President   Superindendent —   Vice President —    Controller
  Personnel      Store Operations    Merchandising      Guthrie
    Stone             Bauer           Williamson
    │                  │                  │
 ┌──┴──┐         ┌─────┼─────┐        ┌───┴────┐
Employment Training  Operating Department    Buyers   Advertising
Supervisor           Managers
George Prentiss          │               Assistant Buyers
         │           Warehouse                │
      Employee           │              Sales Personnel
      Services       Stock Rooms
                         │
                     Maintenance
```

around and saw that the floor was clear, so he said, 'Yes, I guess it's all right.' She went to lunch, and for several days after that she thought that he was the boss. It may not be a problem of communications, so I didn't see how I could put it in the report. But I did want to tell you about it."

"That's a good story, George, and I'm glad to hear it. We're really a buyer-operated store, but some of the operating managers still don't like it. But then, maybe the supervision of salesmen is weak when merchandisers have this much authority. If that's a communication problem, it's a tough one. Let me give this report to Mr. Fiske, and I'll see you later."

"Thanks, Mr. Stone," said George as he left the office.

THE CASE OF TOM MENDOLA CASE 16

Tom Mendola was employed in the machine shop of the Thornton Electric Company when he was 17 years of age. His parents had asked him to leave high school in his third year in order to go to work and help support the family.

Tom's first job was miscellaneous assembly, filing, and bench work in the shop. After a few months he was placed on a job where he could learn to operate a drill press. At first Tom was very enthusiastic, and he seemed to learn the work very quickly. Soon after the first month, however, he began to tire of the monotony of the machine, and he spent a great deal of time going to the tool crib, to the wash room, and looking for excuses to be away from his machine.

When his foreman noticed the drop in Tom's learning speed, he reprimanded Tom and told him to pay better attention to his work. During the next month second and third reprimands were necessary, but Tom still did not seem to take an average interest in his work. Tom also was tardy and absent from the job several days during this period.

In talking to Tom again, the foreman found out that Tom's wages were badly needed at home as his family was in very poor circumstances. Tom said that he was the oldest child in a family of ten children, and that his father had been in poor health and unable to work regularly for the past year. Tom also said that he didn't believe that he could get interested in the drill press job, and he would like to have a transfer to the assembly department. He said he was very interested in one job—spraying parts in the assembly department. He said he was sure that this was the kind of work he would like.

The machine shop foreman discussed Tom's case with the assembly department foreman, and they agreed to give Tom a transfer to the spraying unit of the assembly department.

When Tom first started this new job, he showed considerable interest and enthusiasm for the work. But once more this interest lasted for only about a month. A part of Tom's work in the spraying job was to deliver parts to the different departments in the factory. Tom soon acquired the habit of visiting and loafing in other departments, which also kept other employees from their work. Tom was again reprimanded, and the assembly department foreman made it plain that he would not tolerate such actions. It was later necessary for these reprimands to be repeated, because Tom did not improve in his work. He was finally told that he would have to be released. Tom made a plea that it was necessary for his family's sake that he hold his job. He said that he now wished that he had kept his job in the machine shop, because that would offer him the opportunity to become a machinist. He appealed to the foremen of the shop and assembly department and also to the personnel manager for another chance on the drill press job.

The foremen and the plant personnel manager pondered what their decision should be.

THE JAMISON FURNITURE COMPANY   CASE 17

"Let me tell you about a situation I got involved in several years ago that I still can't get completely out of my mind.

"Shortly after I finished college I took a job with the Jamison Furniture Company. I had really never thought of a career in the furniture industry but when I graduated, jobs were pretty hard to get. I'd finished my education on the GI Bill and I was quite low on money. Consequently, when the Jamison people made me an offer at a pretty attractive salary for those times, I took it. Formally I was the assistant to Bill Blackwell, the plant manager, but actually I was a jack-of-all-trades who did just about anything that needed to be done. I worked on the books, helped with the production scheduling and shipping, and was responsible for what we vaguely called 'personnel relations.'

"As you may know, the Jamison Furniture Company is located in a small town in Ohio. It manufactures a high-quality line of occasional furniture, dinette pieces, desks, and occasional tables and chairs. When I was with them they employed about 150-160 people and had sales of about $40,000 per week. Finished furniture was sold to a large number of independent furniture stores throughout the country. The company has been quite successful and I'd guess that at the present time their sales are four or five times what they were then.

"Most of the people who worked at Jamison were relatively long-time employees. Most of the jobs didn't really require skilled labor and almost anyone with the proper attitude and a reasonable degree of intelligence and physical dexterity could be trained in time to do what had to be done. Nevertheless, as the company did produce a high-quality line of furniture, it was very important that the employees do their work well, especially in the staining and finishing operations. If a table or desk was improperly finished, for example, it had to be sold as a 'second' and the company took a terrific beating on profit.

"Well, the particular situation I referred to took place in the department which manufactured and finished occasional tables. The people involved were Bill Blackwell, the plant manager, Stu Thurston, foreman of the department, and Betty and Alice Sawyer, mother and daughter who worked for Stu. Betty, the mother, had worked for the company about 12 years before Stu came with the company. Alice Sawyer had worked for the company for about two years and had been in

---

Case prepared by Professor H. R. Knudson, Jr., College of Business Administration, University of Washington, Seattle, Washington. From *Human Elements of Administration* by Harry R. Knudson, Jr., Copyright © 1963 by Holt, Rinehart, and Winston, Inc. Reprinted by permission of Holt, Rinehart, and Winston, Inc.

Stu's department since she had been initially hired. Before I go any further, let me tell you that Stu had a reputation as being quite a lady's man. Whether he was or not I never knew, but I do know that he did take a lot of good-natured kidding about 'liking the girls.' The 16 girls who worked for Stu liked to kid him a lot about this and often told him that if they didn't need the money so badly they wouldn't take the risk of working for such a lady's man.

"When I went to work for Jamison everything seemed to be fine in Stu Thurston's department. Production was high, the girls were meeting their quotas, and everyone seemed to be happy. Stu kidded the girls a lot and they kidded him right back. In retrospect, I'd say at that time that Stu's department was one of the best I had ever seen.

"After I'd been with Jamison about four or five months it became pretty obvious that Stu Thurston and Alice Sawyer were getting pretty serious romantically and about two months later they announced their engagement, to the apparent joy of the other girls in the department. I remember particularly well that Stu and Betty Sawyer did an awful lot of kidding about their forthcoming relationship as son-in-law and mother-in-law.

"When Stu and Alice got married all the girls chipped in and bought them a real nice wedding gift and everyone went to the wedding in a group. I remember one girl saying that 'This was the biggest thing that ever happened at the Jamison Furniture Company.' It was obvious that everyone was pretty much excited and enthusiastic about the wedding.

"After their honeymoon both Stu and Alice returned to work and things pretty much returned to normal. Stu was his own genial self, kidding the girls all the time and they in return continued to kid him right back. They had a big thing going about his being able to boss his wife and mother-in-law on the job but 'oh, how different it was when he was at home.' As I said, things went along swell for a while, but after about four or five months there was some inklings that the newly married couple weren't getting along as well as they might. Six months from the day on which they were married Stu started divorce proceedings against Alice on the grounds of mental cruelty. Then things really started to happen.

"At first, reaction was pretty well mixed concerning this sudden change of events. No one really knew what happened, but some of the girls felt that Stu must have had sufficient reasons for his action and attempted to keep things going as they had in the 'good old days.' The rest of the gals, headed by Alice and Betty, wouldn't have anything at all to do with Stu unless they absolutely had to. For example, the day that it became known that Stu had started divorce proceedings they stopped speaking to him unless it was in direct reply to a question or comment that he made. When they did speak they merely answered, 'yes sir,' or 'no, sir,' as the occasion demanded, and not in a very friendly tone of voice.

"As the date for the final divorce decree got closer, Betty Sawyer, in particular got more and more riled up. She started saying some pretty nasty things about Stu, and it wasn't too long before she had all the 16 girls so incensed that they weren't speaking to him either. It even got to the point where Betty led a delegation of the girls to see Bill Blackwell and demanded that Stu be fired for 'things that were going on in the department.' They maintained that Stu 'just wasn't a good foreman' and should be fired immediately. Bill handled the thing as well as he could, I guess. He tried to press the girls for specifics, but when it became apparent that the girls were so emotionally wrought up that they weren't making any sense, he just tried to get them quieted down and out of his office and back to work. I remember his talking to me about the girls' visit later. He said something like 'I sure don't know what to do, but we've got a real one on our hands.'

"Things got worse. The atmosphere in Stu's department was pretty icy, and it wasn't too long before the girls weren't making their quotas and rejects were rising at an alarming rate.

"Stu Thurston talked with me at length about the situation one day. I can't remember all of our conversation but I do recall him saying that what he did in his personal life was his own affair and that what happened on the job was business. He didn't see any reason for the girls to care about what he did on his own time. I do remember very distinctly how our conversation ended, however. Stu wanted me to fire both of the girls. He said, 'I don't care what you do—fire them—no matter what the reason, get rid of them.' His face was very flushed and he was quivering as he spoke. There was no doubt in my mind that if he had had any kind of weapon with him at the time he would have used it on either or both of the two women.

"Well, as you can see, we had a pretty bad situation on our hands. It got really bad for me personally the next day when Bill Blackwell came back from a visit to Stu's department and shouted at me, 'You're in charge of personnel relations. Do whatever you have to do to get that mess cleaned up!'"

TRI CITY UTILITY COMPANY
A PROBLEM OF ALCOHOLISM

CASE 18

Tri City Utility Company served some fifty towns in one of the major midwestern metropolitan areas. It had approximately 5,000 employees and an annual payroll of over $40 million. The operating employees were members of Local 1023 of the Federated Union of Utility Workers, AFL-CIO. At the termination of the labor agreement on June 1, a strike of approximately three weeks had occurred. The strike had ended when the employees had accepted management's proposals which included a wage increase, an improvement in group life insurance and the addition of major medical insurance paid by the company. During the strike period, which was orderly throughout, management, supervisory and other non-union employees had operated the essential company services without inconvenience to customers.

Mr. Robert Black, vice-president of industrial relations of Tri City, headed a department which consisted of four divisions (labor relations, safety, personnel and medical). In April, Black had hired a new medical director, Dr. Ward Medico. Medico had ten years as a very successful private practitioner but had not worked in a company medical division prior to his acceptance of the job with Tri City. Medico approached his new job with great sincerity and enthusiasm. He regarded his division as a service to all the people who made up the company. He thought the people should be in a position to confide in him with assurance that the conversation and records were completely private.

Dr. Medico was very much concerned about alcoholism. As a result of his analysis of medical statistics, he was of the opinion that it was the nation's number three killer, being exceeded only by cardiovascular diseases and cancer. He believed that with professional diagnosis and assistance at the proper time, many alcoholics and potential alcoholics could be cured. He had read that one of the manufacturing companies in the area by adopting a program on alcoholism had been able to reduce its overall rate of absenteeism from 8 per cent to 3 per cent. Dr. Medico was convinced that Tri City should also adopt such a program.

By December Dr. Medico had developed a program which he thought would be effective in dealing with this problem at Tri City. As a part of the program he planned to have all the employees of the company meet with him in groups to view a film, hear a lecture and discussion on alcoholism. He also proposed to distribute literature on the subject to the employees. Additional aspects of the program were set forth by him in a proposed policy bulletin (Exhibit 1) and a

Case prepared by Professor T. H. Cutler, of the University of Denver. Used by permission. All names disguised.

questionnaire (Exhibit 2) which he proposed to have employees fill out if they wished to do so. Medico discussed his program with Black and gave him a copy of the proposed policy bulletin and questionnaire.

Black had his secretary make copies of the proposed policy bulletin and the proposed questionnaire and sent them to the members of the personnel committee of the company with the following comment: "Dr. Medico is recommending the adoption of the attached policy bulletin and the use of the attached questionnaire. Please be prepared to discuss this matter at our meeting on Wednesday."

Exhibit 1
Policy Bulletin—Tri City Utility Company

PROBLEM DRINKING

    A. Since problem drinking or alcoholism is an illness requiring professional diagnosis and assistance, the Medical Division will offer treatment for the purpose of correcting problem drinking or alcoholism preferably before it has resulted in disciplinary action.

    B. Such treatment will be offered on a voluntary basis and in strict medical confidence to help the employee avoid jeopardizing his future and his job. Among sources of help to be used by the Medical Director are:

1. Alcoholics Anonymous
2. Tri City Committee on Alcoholism and Guidance Service
3. Tri City General Hospital and Clinics on Alcoholism
4. Private physicians and psychiatrists
5. Religious consultation services
6. Any combination of above

    C. If the employee who has a potential drinking problem prefers, he may be encouraged to go directly to any of the above services independently for help.

    D. Management personnel should, on a confidential basis, advise the Medical Director of subordinates whose dependability and job performance appear to be affected by the repetitive consumption of alcoholic beverages. The Medical Director will examine and consult with such employees and advise needed corrective treatment. If the Medical Director determines that the employee has failed to start, continue or otherwise cooperate in a rehabilitation program, the Department will be so informed.

    E. The Medical Division will periodically present teaching programs on the alcohol problem and will distribute literature which indicates where help may be obtained.

    F. Nothing contained herein is intended nor should be construed to limit or otherwise affect the continued responsibility and authority of management personnel to discipline employees.

                              Issued: _____
                                         Vice President

Approved: _____
                President

Date: _____

Exhibit 2
Tri City Utility Company Medical Division

The following twenty questions were developed by medical researchers at the Johns Hopkins University Hospital and are used by them as a test in the diagnosis of the sickness of alcoholism.

	Yes	No
1. Have you lost time from work due to drinking?	( )	( )
2. Has drinking made your home life unhappy?	( )	( )
3. Do you drink because you are shy with people?	( )	( )
4. Has drinking affected your reputation?	( )	( )
5. Have you gotten into financial difficulties because of your drinking?	( )	( )
6. Do you turn to lower companions and an inferior environment when drinking?	( )	( )
7. Does your drinking make you careless of your family's welfare?	( )	( )
8. Has your drinking decreased your ambition?	( )	( )
9. Do you want a drink "the morning after"?	( )	( )
10. Does your drinking cause you to have difficulty sleeping?	( )	( )
11. Has your efficiency decreased since drinking?	( )	( )
12. Has drinking ever jeopardized your job or business?	( )	( )
13. Do you drink to escape from worries or troubles?	( )	( )
14. Do you drink alone?	( )	( )
15. Have you ever had a complete loss of memory as a result of drinking?	( )	( )
16. Has your physician ever treated you for drinking?	( )	( )
17. Do you drink to build up self-confidence?	( )	( )
18. Have you ever been in an institution or hospital on account of drinking?	( )	( )
19. Have you ever felt remorse after drinking?	( )	( )
20. Do you crave a drink at a definite time daily?	( )	( )

Johns' Hopkins University says one "yes" answer indicates that a drinking problem may exist and two "yes" answers indicate a probable condition.

If three questions are answered "yes," it is reasonably certain that alcohol has become, or is becoming, a major problem for the patient.

NOTE: This test is for diagnostic purposes only and can be destroyed after consultation.

TOO MANY PERSONAL CALLS   CASE 19

THE ORGANIZATION

John Dixon, vice-president of operations for Consolidated Stores, Inc., is responsible for the Springdale region. Forty-four retail clothing stores and outlets in four midwestern states are in the region which is divided into three districts. Each district is supervised by a district manager and an assistant district manager. Managerial, accounting, merchandising, and advertising activities serving the stores are carried on in the Springdale regional office. A common clerical group in the Springdale office serves all managers and supervisors and is located on the second and fourth floors of the company building. A spacious, well-appointed lounge, used by office personnel, is located on the third floor along with the cafeteria and lavatories.

At the time of this case, John Dixon had over 35 years of service with the company. During his five years as regional manager in Springdale, he had been very successful in meeting the problems created by shortages of facilities and by an increase of nearly 40 per cent in store sales. Service and operating results for the region were above average for several years, and the current year had shown improvement over the corresponding months of the previous year.

In addition to the district managers and their assistants, a number of other managers and supervisors maintain offices in the Springdale building. A controller, a merchandise manager, and an advertising director each have private office space. Although a number of clerical employees work directly for the various managers and supervisors at Springdale, many employees report directly to several office supervisors who in turn report to the office manager, Miss Harriet Black.

Since most managers and supervisors travel frequently to the stores, all clerical employees are responsible to Miss Black for office procedures, practices, and discipline. Harriet Black is an experienced manager who has been in the Springdale office for over 15 years. She generally is recognized as being exceptionally capable, and other supervisors and managers often consult with her for help on various problems. All other office supervisors are former clerical employees who have been promoted and trained during the last five years.

THE PERSONAL CALLS PROBLEM

John Dixon devoted some time each week to operating and personnel problems within the Springdale office. Sometimes he observed various office activities jointly with one or more of the managers and supervisors, but he also made it a frequent practice to observe certain operations by himself.

113

Over a period of weeks, Dixon became increasingly aware that a number of personal telephone calls were being made by the office supervisors and certain clerical employees at their desks. He noticed that this was not peculiar to any one unit, but seemed to be a general practice. On several occasions when he was in the various offices, he had to wait for supervisors to finish their personal calls before he could discuss business matters with them. One morning, as he was observing activities alone, he noted a supervisor's telephone was tied up for almost an hour with two successive calls which Dixon believed to be personal in nature. He was not always sure that he was able to distinguish a personal from a business call, but it was obvious that company telephones were often used for other than business communications.

Company policy was not to prohibit personal calls, but such calls were to be strictly limited so that the telephone lines would be available for calls from stores, suppliers, customers and other business people needing to communicate with the regional office. Several complaints from store managers had been received by Dixon to the effect that it was difficult "to get through" to the regional office by telephone. Consequently, on two different occasions earlier in the year, Dixon had discussed the policy on personal calls in regular meetings with his management personnel, and he believed the policy was generally understood. Further, Dixon felt that the office supervisors and managers through their own observations should have been aware of the excessive number of personal calls currently being made by their people.

THE NEW POLICY

It seemed apparent to Dixon that the corrective action—if any—that had been taken by the managers and office supervisors had not been effective. He decided that prompt personal action on his part was needed.

In order to dispose quickly of the problem, as was his usual practice, Dixon issued the following memo, a copy of which was distributed to every person in the Springdale office: "To keep our telephone lines available for business calls, all personal calls by supervisors and employees should be made from the telephones that have been placed in the lounge." Dixon then arranged for four additional telephones to be connected in the lounge the same afternoon.

PROBLEMS

During his observations the following week, Dixon did not discern any personal calls. However, early one morning about two weeks after he had issued the directive regarding telephone calls, Dixon received a call from Janet Smythe, one of the most attractive and reliable stenographers in the secretarial pool. He invited her to come right up to his office. Miss Smythe had been a "Class I" stenographer for three years; she frequently was called upon for special assignments because she was popular and well liked by everyone. As she walked into his office, Dixon noticed that she seemed to be quite upset.

Miss Smythe, in her usual low voice, commenced by saying, "I would like to question the fairness of your ruling on personal telephone calls." She went on to cite her own experience on the day before. She had been informed of an overtime assignment by Miss Black, late in the afternoon. Feeling obligated to let her family know that she would be late, she started for the lounge to call home, when Miss Black questioned her as to why she would be leaving her desk since she had already taken her afternoon coffee break. After explaining her reason for leaving, she was told by Miss Black that the only time personal calls were allowed was during a normal rest period.

Dixon promptly told Miss Smythe that the directive had been issued for the purpose of stopping excessive calling from the supervisors and employees' desks, and he had not intended it to be interpreted as it had been in her case. He told her that he would like to investigate this incident, and that he would get in touch with her later.

Several days later, Dixon discussed the situation at a regular meeting of his managers and supervisors. He found that the supervisors and managers were unanimous in disagreeing with his directive. They pointed out that the instructions permitted no flexibility and were too severe. Dixon apologized to the group for not discussing the problem with them prior to issuing the directive, and he asked for their suggestions.

A supervisor in accounting was emphatic and insisted that the directive should be rescinded in its entirety. He said, "Really, Mr. Dixon, if you expect an order like that to be enforced by us, you should have let us give the instructions to the people ourselves!" The advertising department director commented, "This whole matter is ridiculous; it's a waste of time! Why not let employees make personal calls? To stop excessive calls would cost more than they are worth!" One of the assistant managers suggested that the employees should be allowed to make personal calls only with the approval of their supervisors. Several members of the group immediately disagreed with this suggestion, stating that the responsibility for policing personal telephone calls should not be placed on supervisors who are trying to motivate their people positively.

After a prolonged discussion of the telephone call problem and other matters, Dixon adjourned the meeting stating that they would hear from him or the district managers at a later date about the problem of personal calls.

As he returned to his office, Dixon wondered what alternate procedures could be used to reduce successfully the time wasted and the expense of excessive personal telephone calls. In addition, he began to speculate on what method of communications or supervisory practices could be used to help him obtain a better reception of management policies and decisions.

A MATTER OF PRIORITIES CASE 20

Ted Michod graduated from the Newark College of Engineering as an electrical engineer and went to work for a small but growing computer manufacturing firm in Philadelphia which employed about 10,000 people. His first position with the company was that of a junior engineer in the data processing systems division. He worked with twenty other junior engineers designing primary computer circuits and electro-mechanical linkages. Basically, Michod's job consisted of fitting various electrical and mechanical components into a package which would perform logical and arithmetic operations with the greatest reliability for the least cost. Most of the time he worked out designs on paper, although, on occasion, Ted actually tried his ideas out in the lab.

After two years, Ted received a promotion which, along with an increase in pay and status, provided him with an opportunity to expand greatly his knowledge of the industry. As an associate engineer in the programming systems division, he served as a liaison between his old design group and a systems engineering team which was responsible for the creation of new programming languages. Ted's duties were to make sure that the programming languages being developed were consistent with design capabilities which were being incorporated into new computer systems by his old work group. Thus, he was able to relate his previous experience with hardware (circuits) to the creation and design of software (program languages) and round out his technical education.

After a year in his new position, Ted began to realize that while he was mastering the technical end of the computer business, he was unprepared for the managerial responsibilities it entailed. Furthermore, it seemed to him that a graduate degree in business administration would improve greatly his chance for promotion in the future. After giving the problem considerable thought, Ted decided to take a two year educational leave of absence to work on an MBA degree. His decision was based on the fact that in addition to his need for managerial development, his interests had gradually shifted from the technical to the administrative aspects of the industry.

Ted Michod graduated from the local university finishing in the top twenty per cent of his MBA class. Within two weeks of graduation, he was married and he decided to return to work with his old company. This time, at his request, he was assigned to the midwestern marketing regional office in Chicago as a customer engineer. Ted felt that experience in the field of customer relations together with

Case prepared by Dr. Robert A. Ullrich of the Graduate School of Management, Vanderbilt University. Used by Permission.

his previous technical work would increase greatly his worth to the firm and thus his chances for success. For this reason both Ted and his bride viewed their move to the Chicago office as a "step in the right direction."

Once settled in Chicago, Ted reported to the customer engineering manager, John Lucas. Mr. Lucas assigned Michod to the customer education section as an instructor. The section's purpose was to train customer employees in the installation and use of computer systems. Since this was not considered to be a full-time assignment, Ted was given additional duties as the supervisor of a program modification team. This second job consisted of giving technical assistance and direction to a group, consisting of four programmer trainees, which was modifying existing computer programs written by the manufacturers for the customers to keep them consistent with improved methodology and technology. Both positions required that he report directly to Mr. Lucas. On the average Ted taught about thirty hours a week and devoted fifteen hours to his second job.

As a result of the group's work modifying a set of market forecasting programs, Ted hit upon the idea of using a form of the Markov Process to predict growth in sales of new industrial products. [The Markov Process is a statistical approach which basically views life as a series of probabilities that an event will (or will not) occur given that it has (or has not) taken place in the past.] Ted had learned about this technique in his MBA program. He studied the problem evenings at home and in mid-October submitted his idea to Lucas in the form of a well researched and documented proposal. Lucas seemed interested in the project but told Ted it would have to be shelved until the necessary manpower and finances became available.

About two months later, however, Ted's program modification team completed its assigned projects and the group was disbanded. When he reported to Lucas to be re-assigned, Michod was instructed to see Wayne Smith, the head of the computer installation department. Smith, like Lucas, was the head of a staff department. Smith and Lucas enjoyed equal rank within the firm and reported to the same district manager.

Smith outlined Ted's next assignment as follows. Ted would supervise two junior systems engineers in the installation of small computers and would have complete responsibility for each installation project. The job, at first, would require about twenty hours a week of his time. In addition Ted would continue to serve in his present capacity of instructor until the middle of the year. At this time, an additional instructor would be transferred to the midwestern Region and Ted would be relieved of his teaching responsibilities to devote his entire efforts to the installation department. Until then, however, he would report to Smith concerning installation problems and to Lucas for matters involving the education program.

The following day Ted received a note from Lucas to see him as soon as possible. Upon entering Lucas' office, Ted found himself engaged in the following conversation.

TED: You wanted to see me, Mr. Lucas?

LUCAS: Yes, Ted. Sit down. You know, I liked the proposal you submitted for forecasting with Markov Processes. I'd like you to work up some programs and make it operational. Do you think you could wrap up the job in two months?

TED: Well, I could if I had the time, but as you know I'm still working as an instructor and I've just taken over an installation team for Wayne Smith.

LUCAS: Yes, I know about that. You'll have some free time on Wayne's project though. I don't see why you won't be able to fit my project around your other work. It won't take long, will it?

TED: I just don't know. I can make a wild guess at a hundred and twenty man hours. I don't think I'll have the time to tackle it.

LUCAS: Sure you will, Ted. Smith's project won't take all your time. Besides, a hundred and twenty hours isn't very much. Why, it's not even two weeks' work.

After leaving Mr. Lucas office, Ted stopped in to see Wayne Smith.

TED: Hi. I was just wondering when I should start working for you.

SMITH: Today! Now! (Jokingly.)

TED: Well, what I mean is will it be full time at first or will I have some time on my hands?

SMITH: No. It should be a full twenty hours a week right from the start. Why did you ask? Any special reason?

Michod told Smith about his conversation with Lucas and explained that he didn't think he would be able to handle all three projects. Wayne Smith agreed but felt that there had been some misunderstanding. He told Ted that he would talk to Lucas that afternoon and that Ted should let the matter ride until it had been looked into further.

TED: Good. I hope this gets cleared up soon.

SMITH: Don't worry, Ted, we just have our wires crossed. Stop in and see me first thing in the morning.

The next day the following conversation took place between Ted and Mr. Smith.

SMITH: Ted, I saw John Lucas yesterday and I'm not sure I've solved your problem. He said that the project he had in mind wasn't very big and that you should have plenty of time to get it done.

TED: But I told him it would take a hundred and twenty hours. Since then I've been worried that my estimate was way too low.

SMITH: Well, you'd better talk with him again. I understood that I was to have you for twenty hours a week and believe me I need every bit of that time!

Ted saw Lucas a few hours later and explained again his commitments and lack of available time. He went on to suggest that he could instruct a new man to carry out the project if that was acceptable to Lucas.

LUCAS: I don't know who else would be available to do this type of work.... Look, Ted, just fit it in around your other work. You'll have time to do it.... Oh, before I forget, see Mary in Personnel on your way out. They need some information

Exhibit 1 *Midwestern Marketing Region Partial Organization Chart*

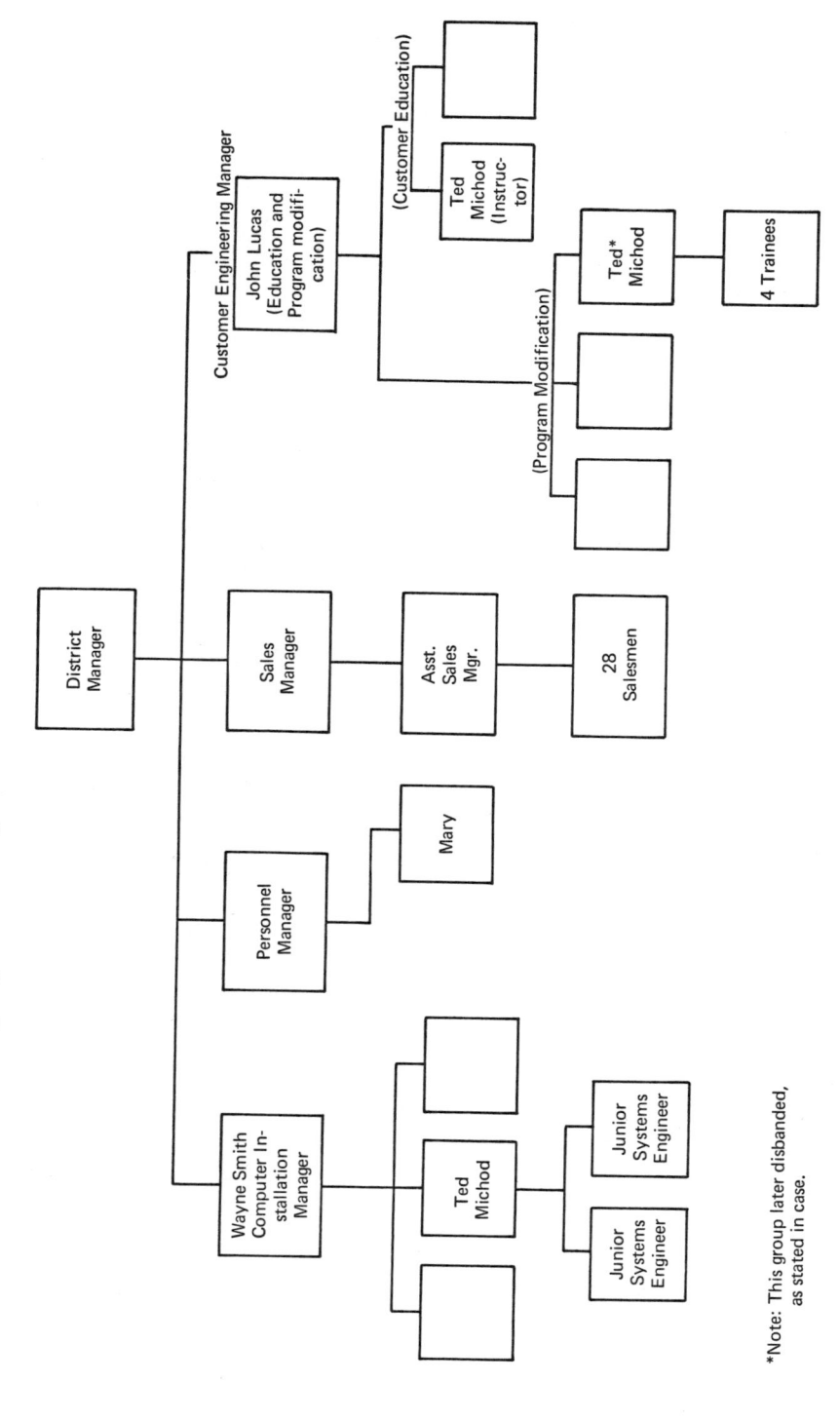

```
                          District
                          Manager
                             │
     ┌───────────────┬───────┴───────┬───────────────────┐
     │               │               │                   │
  Wayne Smith    Personnel        Sales           Customer Engineering
  Computer In-    Manager        Manager               Manager
  stallation        │               │              John Lucas
   Manager          │               │            (Education and
     │              Mary        Asst. Sales       Program modifi-
     │                             Mgr.               cation)
     │                              │                   │
   ┌─┴─┬──────┐                 28 Salesmen      ┌──────┴──────┐
   │   │      │                                  │             │
   │  Ted     │                          (Customer Ed.)  (Program
   │ Michod   │                                  │       Modification)
   │   │      │                              Ted Michod       │
   │ ┌─┴──┐   │                             (Instructor)   ┌──┴──┐
   │ │    │   │                                  │         │     │
   │Jr.  Jr.  │                                  □       Ted*  [ ]
   │Sys. Sys. │                                        Michod
   │Eng. Eng. │                                          │
                                                       4 Trainees
```

*Note: This group later disbanded, as stated in case.

A Matter of Priorities 119

for your records. And tell my secretary to come in, will you? I have a stack of letters to get out.

Ted walked down to Personnel wondering how he wound up in the middle of all this. Furthermore, he wondered what he should do next.

PART FOUR

The Larger Company
The Ozark Foundry
Too Many Bosses
The Adjustment Department
The General Electric Company (A) (B), and (C)
Hill City Junior College
Oscar Metz Tool Company
The Allen Company

Organization for Management

A business enterprise is directed towards specific objectives. Management must develop policies and plans of action for the achievement of these objectives and then organize tasks, people, and facilities for the execution of these plans in the most efficient manner. The result of this organizing activity is an association of people working together to achieve certain goals, and the form of their relationships is the organization.

Organization is the mechanism through which a management directs, coordinates, and controls business activity. This mechanism may be likened to the steering mechanism of a motor vehicle. If the steering mechanism is faulty or it is improperly operated, the vehicle is apt to go off course. Similarly, if the organization is poorly designed or if the management is lacking in personal leadership, the enterprise may not achieve its objectives.

Thus, managerial control in a business enterprise is largely affected by: (1) the organization structure; (2) policies and policy decisions, the courses of action taken by management; and (3) management's qualities of personal leadership. These elements, of course, are interrelated, but for purposes of classification this section concentrates upon the organizational aspects of management.

THE TRADITIONAL VIEW OF ORGANIZATION

Traditionally, certain fundamental principles which contribute to the operation and efficiency of any organization are stressed. It is suggested that an awareness of these concepts permits more effective planning and control of work activities. Their value, however, has recently been questioned by students of organization theory who doubt that there are universal principles or laws in work situations.[1] Nevertheless, at least three great principles of organization can be cited, which have been analyzed and described since Adam Smith wrote his treatise on the "Division of Labour" in his *Wealth of Nations.* These fundamentals—the *division of labor,* the *combination of labor,* and *coordination*—may be observed in every successful organization and can be briefly described:[2]

> *Division of Labor:* Since organization is the structure of human associations for the achievement of common goals, it involves individuals and groups of individuals. When two or more individuals join together to perform certain tasks, it follows that some division of the work is done. Properly or improperly, fairly or unfairly, work is divided among those who participate in a productive organization. With the effective planning and organizing in an enterprise, division of labor leads to the fixing of responsibility, the delegation of authority, specialization, and other conceptual schemes which are frequently called principles of organization.
>
> *Combination of Labor:* With work divided and assigned to members of an organization, the activities are grouped together in some logical manner. This grouping of activities brings tasks together, forming operations, and operations are arranged to establish systems and procedures. From a structural point of view this grouping of activities results in units, departments, and divisions of the organization. The basis for this grouping of activities may be the skills of the workers, the tools and machinery used, the nature of the product, the materials employed, or some other reason. Whether it is logical or not, there is always some reason for the arrangement of tasks in the work place.
>
> *Coordination:* This all-inclusive principle emerges because of the need in every organization for the integration of work activities and the coordination of individuals and groups of individuals performing the tasks. Coordination is implemented through leadership, and in the structural sense it involves the fixing of responsibilities and the delegation of authority. It establishes controls which provide for the efficient scheduling and performance of work activities. Coordination is frequently confused with personal leadership, but might be more accurately described as the technical need of the organization for planning and control through leadership.

---

[1] John M. Pfiffner and Frank P. Sherwood, *Administrative Organization* (Englewood Cliffs, N.J.: Prentice-Hall, 1960), p. 59, "We have generally refrained from talking about principles in this book because we have not been able to identify such regularities in organization practice."
[2] See Theo Haimann and William G. Scott, *Management in the Modern Organization* (Boston: Houghton Mifflin, 1970); and Harold Koontz and Cyril O'Donnell, *Principles of Management,* Third Edition (New York: McGraw-Hill, 1964).

Organization for Control

The typical large enterprise in business today is a corporation[3] with a line-and-staff form of operating organization. In this type of concern the stockholders or owners elect a board of directors who oversee the organization for them. At the top of the operating organization is this board of directors, presided over by a chairman of the board, who is elected by the board members.[4]

The officers of the corporation are appointed by the board of directors and are given the responsibility of directing the operations of the enterprise. They are accountable to the board. The chief executive of this group of officers and the active head of the line organization is usually the president. In some instances the chairman of the board is the chief executive officer. A chain-of-command, a direct line of responsibility and authority, moves downward through the vice-presidents, division heads, department heads, and supervisors to the workers. In this chain-of-command, each manager delegates responsibility and authority downward to two or more subordinates, usually to several.[5]

Every line officer from the president down to the lowest level of supervision has a responsibility for direct communications, namely:

1. To communicate to his subordinates policies, information, and instructions received by him from his superior.
2. To report to his superior conditions, information, and employee attitudes in areas under his supervision. This reporting should include technical operating problems as well as the sentiments and morale of supervisors and workers reporting to him.

In addition to the line organization, specialists and **staff** departments are usually added to assist the line operations. Wherever a unique service is needed, a staff specialist or a department of specialists may be attached to the chain of command regardless of the executive level. The primary objective of a staff department is to render a service to the line that requires a specialized ability or skill and/or undivided attention. Staff members may provide advice, information, controls or services which contribute to more efficient operations.

An organization structure of this type provides a mechanism of control through which top management can direct the activities and operations of the entire enterprise. This control mechanism is visualized in Figure 1. Its characteristic feature is the stratification of the management function to denote different levels of responsibility and authority. Thus, the board of directors of a corporation is the highest authority in the organization. Through the determination of policies and broad, over-all planning, the board performs a trusteeship function for the owners

---

[3] There are still many more proprietorships and partnerships, but most of the large enterprises are corporations.
[4] The approach used in this section is adopted from *Industrial Organization and Control*, a training manual prepared by William R. Spriegel and later revised by Joseph W. Towle for the International Harvester Co.
[5] The problems of "span of control" (the number of subordinates reporting to each manager) are not discussed here. See Haimann and Scott, Koontz and O'Donnell, or other management texts, for information on this subject.

124 *Organization for Management*

or stockholders. Members of the board are usually stockholders, and they select the major executives and direct the organization in the interest of all owners. Directly below the board in the organization is the general management group, consisting of the president and others who are responsible for the administration of company-wide policies and the management of the entire enterprise. Their interests include all divisions and departments of the business. Reporting to the general management is the divisional management organization, made up of those executives who are each responsible for the direction and control of a single major division of the company, such as sales, manufacturing, finance, engineering, personnel, etc. These three levels—the board of directors, the general management, and the divisional management—make up the top-management organization in the typical large corporation.[6] Further down the scale are the middle management and first-line supervisory levels.

Figure 1 *A Manufacturing Organization*

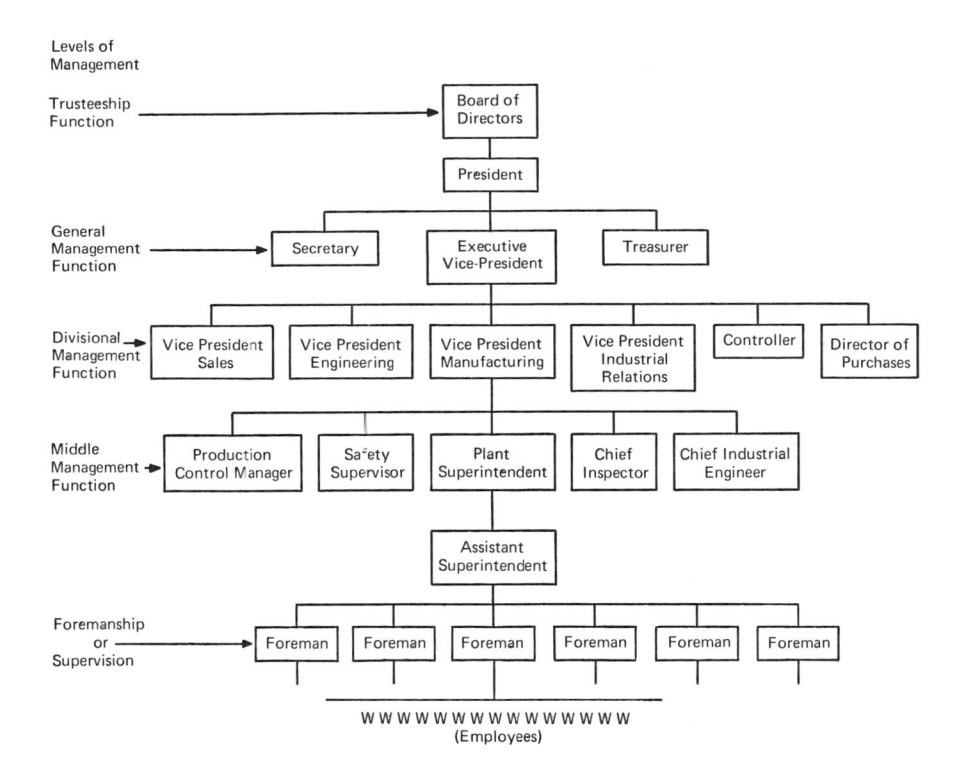

Levels of Management	
Trusteeship Function	Board of Directors
	President
General Management Function	Secretary — Executive Vice-President — Treasurer
Divisional Management Function	Vice President Sales / Vice President Engineering / Vice President Manufacturing / Vice President Industrial Relations / Controller / Director of Purchases
Middle Management Function	Production Control Manager / Safety Supervisor / Plant Superintendent / Chief Inspector / Chief Industrial Engineer
	Assistant Superintendent
Foremanship or Supervision	Foreman / Foreman / Foreman / Foreman / Foreman / Foreman
	W W W W W W W W W W W W W W W (Employees)

Organization chart indicating the levels of work in an enterprise. Managers, supervisors, and employees are all workers, but the levels theory points out that supervision and management consist of special classifications of work.

---

6 See Edwin Flippo, *Management: A Behavioral Approach*, Second Edition (Boston: Allyn and Bacon, 1970), pp. 170-190.

The concept of management levels as visualized on an organization chart is useful in studying and clarifying lines of responsibility and authority and channels of communication. On the other hand, in any single enterprise all executives at all levels are part of the same management team. Undue emphasis on levels is dangerous. To some members of management it may imply different classes or qualities of leadership, rather than differences in the type of work or the amount of authority involved. The charting of organizations into levels has many uses and greatly facilitates organization planning, but it should be done with the understanding that the chart itself is an oversimplification of complex technical and human relationships.

Committee and Group Management

There is a growing tendency in American business for executives to relegate more and more problem-solving and decision-making activities to councils or committees. Rather than to assume all of the responsibilities for detailed analyses and decisions, managers prefer to consult with and even to delegate problems to qualified groups of experts. In many instances the complexity and scope of problems in large business organizations make this procedure necessary. The growth and expansion of some concerns have required detailed investigations and careful analyses of large volumes of data and information. By using the combined judgment of several members of a management team, intelligent action can be taken in such situations and better results may be attained in solving problems and executing policies.

Committees in organizations are usually considered supplementary to line-and-staff activities and are frequently used to perform investigative or advisory functions for management. When directed properly, committees are effective in building teamwork and cooperation among personnel. Executives and supervisors usually understand each other's problems better and obtain broader views of the organization after serving together on committees. Although some committee meetings are inefficient and waste the time of committee members, this seldom happens when the committee has sound objectives and adequate leadership.

Group management is both different from and similar to the committee organization procedure. Group management may exist at various levels and in many areas. It is found at the top of an organization when the chief executive surrounds himself with an active executive council consisting of the principal officers of the corporation or a group of special staff assistants. The problems and policies considered by the chief executive are discussed and analyzed by the group. Frequently, the conclusions of the group actually control the organization and its activities.[7]

At lower levels in the modern organization the same form of group participation may be evident. When the department head or the superintendent consults with his staff of supervisors and permits a thorough airing of departmental problems, he depends upon the pooled judgment of these subordinates. This situation may approach group management, although the actual authority of the group

[7] For example, the Du Pont Company has an executive committee which performs these functions. This company is frequently cited for its "management by committee."

varies from one instance to another. In industrial and engineering projects, for example, the functions of task forces and the recently-developed operations research groups illustrate the trend towards cooperative management effort. It is an old saying that "two heads are better than one." In addition, these group activities provide the members of the group with a degree of participation in management, which usually contributes to higher employee morale as well as to a better quality of decision-making.

Conflicts of interest and personality differences may be temporary deterrents to the work of committees or councils. Their accomplishments and advantages, however, tend to outweigh these disadvantages. When effective leadership properly controls the conflicts between individuals in prominent groups, there is usually noticeable improvement in the coordination of activities and the cooperation of individuals throughout the entire organization.

As the operations of business enterprises continue to increase in size and complexity, there will be greater reliance upon group management. Administrators will find many jobs for teams. Small groups of managers working together will carry important responsibilities in an effort to minimize the risks of "one-man rule." Also, in the future more than in the past, enlightened managers will discover new values when they understand and employ those processes which require high degrees of cooperation and teamwork among executives.

Centralization vs. Decentralization

As managers have learned to share their responsibilities, their problems and their decision-making duties with subordinates, usually with good results, new concepts of delegation have developed. For several decades the General Motors Corporation and more recently the General Electric Company and other concerns have recognized that a company's growth and diversification into a variety of businesses is implemented by a management philosophy described as **decentralized operations and responsibility with centralized control.** Consequently, many growth concerns have endeavored to build not only geographically decentralized business activities but also decentralized managements with responsibility and authority for decisions and actions delegated to low organizational levels.[8]

Whether the management of an enterprise retains the authority for decisions in a central, top-management group or whether these rights are delegated down through the organization is a matter of philosophy, leadership style, and practice. Decentralized concerns usually divide the large organization into smaller, semi-autonomous units with total responsibility for each division delegated to a qualified division or branch manager. In such an organization, decisions are made near the points of action and at the lowest possible levels where judgment and ability exist. Obviously, greater knowledge and understanding of the problems are available and decisions are prompt when made "on-the-spot." But the costs of decentralized operations must be admitted. It requires more and better-trained managers in the decentralized organization. Elaborate executive development

[8] See William R. Spriegel and Ernest C. Davis, *Business Organization and Operation* (New York: Prentice-Hall, 1960); and Haimann and Scott, *op. cit.*, pp. 256-278.

programs and effective performance appraisal procedures are necessary, when executives and supervisors are expected to depend upon their own initiative and ingenuity in directing affairs under their supervision.

Although General Motors, General Electric, Johnson and Johnson, and other major concerns intentionally practice decentralization, it is not necessarily appropriate for all companies and all situations. In some firms the development of information centers using electronic data processing equipment suggests that centralized decision-making may be advantageous. Also, organizations with a shortage of competent managers or with a need for special and centralized controls might wisely decide against efforts to decentralize management authority. Certainly, the advisability of decentralization is a matter of providing adequate controls over operations and the desired degree of delegation of authority. Managers who tend to be autocratic find that decentralization is difficult. Those who are more democratic and who employ a participative style of leadership, find that decentralization can be an effective process, permitting more rapid organizational growth. It is for each organization to develop its own individual structure and pattern of management.

ORGANIZATIONAL THEORY AND THE BEHAVIORAL SCIENCES[9]

In recent years, the field of organization and management has been subjected to changing concepts. Contributions from researchers in psychology, sociology, anthropology, and social psychology have become an accepted part of management literature. In particular, organizational theorists have drawn upon the behavioral sciences, making organization theory a developing discipline, and its impact upon management thought is already evident in many areas.

Modern organization theory synthesizes and integrates many theoretical and empirical findings into a unified conceptual framework. This has led to the fundamental theoretical basis for most modern organizational theory, namely, its conceptual approach to the study of human organizations as systems.

The system concept of organizations transcends traditional concepts of organization such as line and staff, committee and group management, and span of control. It views an organization as a complex, dynamic system of interdependent but variable factors. These include the individual and groups of individuals, their attitudes and motives, the formal organization structure and its modification by the informal, the patterns of interactions which permeate all levels of the organization, the roles of status, authority, and goals. These and other behavioral aspects are both influenced by and also influence the organizational environment. Theoretically, an organization's environment includes all social, physical, legal, and economic factors associated with the organizational setting.

Finding a unified conceptual framework to integrate all these organizational concepts into a system has been approached from different points of view by a

---

[9] Parts of this section were taken from Raymond L. Hilgert, "Modern Personnel Philosophy Makes Sense to Me," *The Personnel Administrator* (November–December, 1963). Reproduced by permission.

number of theorists. E. Wight Bakke's organizational model is one of the most comprehensive. Bakke conceives of organizational behavior as operating within a framework of organizational bonds. These bonds are:

1. Identification Bonds to develop and legitimize an organizational charter including the organization's function and objective;
2. Perpetuation Bonds to provide and perpetuate the basic resources required;
3. Work-flow Bonds to produce a product or service;
4. Control Bonds to control and coordinate all operations and behavior;
5. Homeostatic Bonds to provide for ability, viability, and integrity of the organization in a state of evolving dynamic equilibrium.[10]

A close examination of this model reveals that personnel management activities are included in all organizational-bond categories. The most important concept of the model is the homeostatic-bond concept, which through a "fusion process" permeates throughout the organization to guide, preserve, and maintain an evolving organization. Bakke sees the fusion process as attempting to reconcile or fuse the expectancies of both the organization and the individual and to bring them into closer harmony with each other. In the fusion process the organization, the groups, and individuals are changed, and their behavior is changed.[11]

Chris Argyris has arrived at even more specific conclusions regarding a fusion process of organizations and individual behavior in his organizational model. Argyris describes industrial organizations as being highly structured and formalized and having objectives and purposes basically in conflict with the needs and interests of individual human beings. Argyris conceptualizes that workers adapt to their work situation by creating an informal employee culture which sanctions individual predispositions and needs of the workers. Informal activities of workers modify the formal organization, and the total behavioral system of the workplace becomes a composite of:

1. The behavior that results from the formal organizational demands;
2. The behavior that results from the demands of the informal activities;
3. The behavior that results from each individual's attempt to fulfill his individual needs;
4. The behavior that is a resultant of the unique patterning for each organization of the three levels above.[12]

(Interestingly, Argyris also hypothesizes that a principal function of the personnel department is to make certain that no one is hired who might either question or upset the organization as it exists.) [13]

These theorists have stressed the dynamic quality of the relationship of individuals to organizations. No neat organizational chart exists which can adequately

---
[10] E. Wight Bakke, "Concept of the Social Organization," from *Modern Organization Theory*, Mason Haire, Editor (New York: John Wiley & Sons, Inc., 1959), p. 72.
[11] *Ibid.*, p. 60.
[12] Chris Argyris, *Understanding Organizational Behavior* (Homewood, Ill.: The Dorsey Press, Inc., 1960), p. 24.
[13] *Ibid.*, p. 81.

describe the human processes which take place in an organization. A conflict between the needs of the individual and that of the business organization tends to arise. In order to reconcile this conflict, mutual adaptations which affect both the individual and organizational behavior take place.

William F. Whyte, another behavioral scientist, has proposed a conceptual system which emphasizes patterns of organizational interaction, activities, and sentiments mutually dependent upon each other and in relation to the forces of the environment. Similar to the Bakke and Argyris models, Whyte's theoretical system also visualizes an organization as a complex, interrelated, evolving process. Whyte describes it as an "interactional" approach in order to emphasize the dynamic qualities of the inter-personal aspects of organizations, and to show how even the sentiments of the workers play an important part in what happens within a working organization.[14]

ORGANIZATION AND PERSONNEL MANAGEMENT— A BROADER POINT OF VIEW

Although the impact of organizational theory and behavioral science research upon management thought is not precisely clear, recent trends in management literature give evidence of an expanding philosophy of organization and personnel management. This is an outgrowth of research and application of behavioral sciences.

For sake of convenience, personnel management still is (and probably always will be) spoken of in functional terms such as hiring, placement, wage and salary administration, and others. A functional approach is completely unavoidable in describing some organizational aspects and personnel management activities. However, in the future as even now these functions may be discussed from a somewhat different perspective than that of the past. In view of recent organizational theory and behavioral science research, modern personnel philosophy emphasizes personnel processes rather than mere functional activities. Personnel management is to be considered as part of a complex network of interrelated processes [15] of which the following are representative:

1. Since organizational theory and behavioral science research recognize that all aspects of organizational activity, (i.e., production, marketing, personnel, etc.) are interrelated and interdependent, personnel management activities are to be considered as but one part of the entire organizational process.
2. In this respect, personnel management specifically encompasses all activities related to the acquisition, development, and maintenance of human resources in a working organization.
3. Since organizations are dynamically held together by bonds of organization,

---

[14] William F. Whyte, *Man and Organization* (Homewood, Ill.: Richard D. Irwin, Inc., 1959), p. 65.
[15] For an excellent textbook approach to personnel management from this standpoint, see: Wendell French, *The Personnel Management Process*, Second Edition (Boston: Houghton Mifflin Company, 1970).

any personnel management activity must be considered a part of a continuing process, rather than a mere function in itself.
4. Personnel management activities should be evaluated in relation to the probable conflict between the objectives of an organization and those of an individual. If good personnel management means "optimizing" the objectives of the organization and the individual in relation to society, then the overall goals of personnel management must be assessed from a perspective that is cognizant of all behavior patterns in a business organization.
5. Personnel management activities should be studied, planned, and instituted in consideration of their effects upon the informal organization of workers as well as upon the formal one. And personnel management activities should be considered in relation to the total human processes involved. For example, communication becomes much more than a memo, a poster, or an interview; it becomes all interpersonal communications within the organization. Such a perspective would suggest reasons for possible barriers to effective communication due to the dynamic properties of the organization.
6. Organizational planning takes on new meaning as a personnel function. The proper structuring of formal organization, workflow, interpersonal linkages (as some authors refer to them), and other such factors, may be the difference between an effective blending of individual and organizational objectives or none at all. Organization planning implicitly means recognition of the informal organization, its functioning, and its channeling towards organization goals.

Although these statements deal with generalities, they reflect the philosophy suggested by behavioral science research and organizational theory for today's personnel managers. Modern personnel philosophy does not consider personnel management activities in a vacuum. Formal concepts of organization are not completely adequate as a conceptual framework for personnel management activities. Rather, modern personnel philosophy views all personnel management activities from a broader perspective, carefully observing and analyzing the dynamics of human behavior in our complex organizational systems.

THE LARGER COMPANY   CASE 21

The phone rang, and highly indignant words blared: "Masters, what do you mean by submitting a report to all the executives without first talking it over with the division manager!"

Masters replied, "My men made every effort to see him. They never got past his secretary. He instructed her to have them talk to the works manager."

"I don't believe a word of it. Vining is up in arms. He says the report is vindictive. What are you trying to do—embarrass the division manager? I don't believe your men ever tried to see Vining and I question the veracity of their statements!" The phone on the other end was hung up with a bang.

Masters said to himself, "Gunn must be hot under the collar or he wouldn't have called me when I was away from my own office, visiting another plant."

The next day Masters' office received Gunn's letter confirming this telephone conversation and demanding an explanation. A week later Masters received a letter from Gunn's superior, a Mr. Jordan, stating, "I have read the aforementioned report and discussed it with Mr. Gunn. He has advised me that the report is essentially untrue, inaccurate, and overstated. I am not satisfied to have such wide differences of opinion and have scheduled a meeting to be held in my office on _____. I would appreciate it if you would be present."

In light of the phone call and the two letters, Mr. Masters decided to reassess all events leading to this climax...

The case of characters is as shown in Exhibit 1. The Larger Company had an elaborate organizational structure as a result of its scale of operation. At the headquarters office of the corporation the president had a group of staff vice presidents in charge of functions. Mr. Masters was a staff department head reporting to the vice president-manufacturing. The headquarters staff departments assisted in policy formulation and made staff studies for the operating organization when requested. Members of such departments were encouraged to offer ideas for the good of the company. Their proposals were considered by a management committee consisting of the vice presidents at the headquarters level and the operating vice presidents in charge of product groups. Mr. Jordan of this case was the operating vice president-product group "B."

Case prepared by Professor Edmund P. Learned of the Harvard Graduate School of Business Administration and appears in George Albert Smith, Jr. and C. Roland Christensen, *Policy Formulation and Administration* (Homewood, Ill.: Richard D. Irwin, Inc., 1962). Case material of the Harvard Graduate School of Business Administration is prepared as a basis for class discussions. Cases are not designed to present illustrations of either effective or ineffective handling of administrative problems. Copyright © 1953 by the President and Fellows of Harvard College. Reproduced by permission.

132 Organization for Management

Exhibit 1
The Larger Company Organization Chart

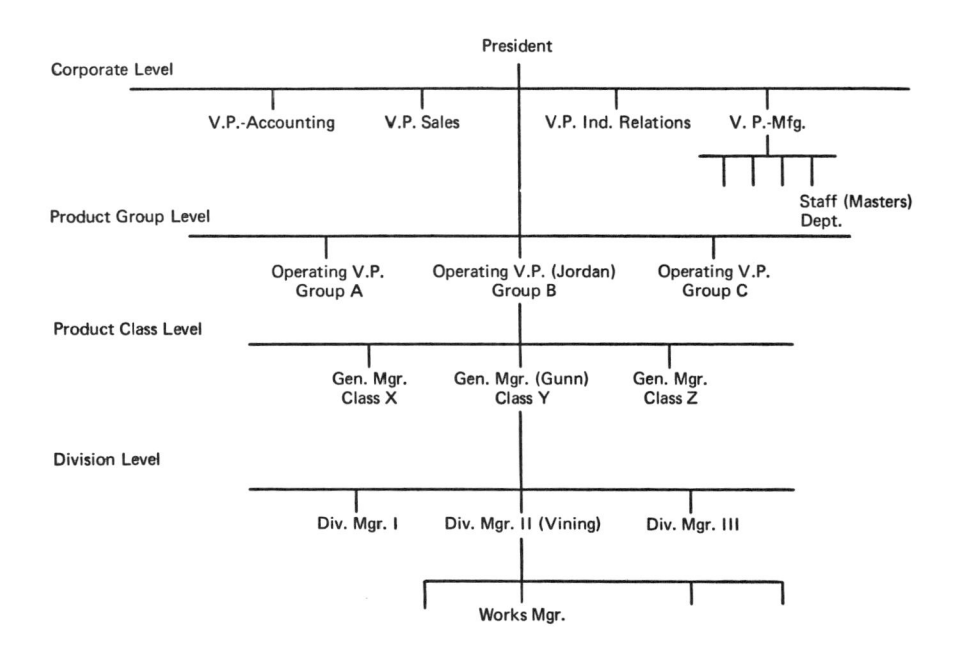

```
                              President
Corporate Level    ──────────────┬──────────────
              │         │        │         │
         V.P.-Accounting  V.P. Sales  V.P. Ind. Relations  V. P.-Mfg.
                                                    │
                                                ┌─┬─┬─┬─┐
                                                         Staff (Masters)
Product Group Level ──────────────────────────────────── Dept.
              │                  │                  │
        Operating V.P.    Operating V.P. (Jordan)  Operating V.P.
           Group A              Group B              Group C

Product Class Level ───────────┬──────────────
              │                │                │
         Gen. Mgr.       Gen. Mgr. (Gunn)    Gen. Mgr.
          Class X            Class Y          Class Z

Division Level ────────────────┬──────────────
              │                │                │
         Div. Mgr. I     Div. Mgr. II (Vining)  Div. Mgr. III
                               │
                         ┌─────┼─────┐
                           Works Mgr.
```

Under the product groups there were general managers of product classes. They supervised the division managers, who were in charge of the sales and manufacturing operations of one or more plants. Mr. Gunn was general manager of product class "Y." One of the four division managers under him was Mr. Vining of Division II...

Two years before this incident occurred, Mr. Masters' staff department proposed to the management committee, with the approval of the vice-president-manufacturing, that representatives of Mr. Masters' office join with representatives of the vice president-accounting to make studies in each plant of the procedures for and actual practices regarding expense control. The suggestion was approved, and enthusiastically endorsed by the general managers. They sent a letter through channels to each division manager advising that periodically a team of two men would visit each plant to make a comprehensive analysis of expense control practices and systems.

After a visit these field representatives of headquarters were to prepare a report giving findings and recommendations. They were to discuss it with the appropriate division manager and his staff. Thus they would be able to incorporate any specific plans of action set in motion by division managers. Next, a report was to be submitted to Mr. Masters. Both his department and the accounting office were to make comments. The final document was then to be submitted to the vice president-accounting, vice president-manufacturing, the operating vice president-product group, the general manager-product class, and the division manager concerned.

This general procedure had worked smoothly within the company until General Manager Gunn of product class Y exploded. In the first plant studied, the two team members spent approximately four weeks examining documents, interviewing line management, interrogating industrial engineers, observing operations, etc. The employees of this plant were very cooperative. Some of the facts revealed by them could have been embarrassing to the division manager. The team was enabled to make specific recommendations for improvement to the division manager. His reception of the report was good. According to him, the study had given an opportunity to review his situation and get his house in order. He intended to implement the recommendations unless they were changed in the review process at the higher level. Sixteen other plants were visited with reasonably good acceptance of the work of the team.

In his review of the Division II situation, Mr. Masters found that the team had observed all the required organization routines. Mr. Sawyer, representing Mr. Masters, had a master's degree in industrial engineering and had twelve years with the company. Mr. Peters, from the accounting office, had served that department for thirty years. Both men had shown ability to gain confidences and to use them discreetly. They were considered straightforward, conscientious, and unobtrusive in their work. In Division II the team obtained from plant personnel considerable information which pointed up a number of practices and procedures requiring improvement. In the opinion of the team members, the operating organization at the lower levels sincerely wanted to make these changes. The team thought that there was some resistance at some level within the division to these suggestions and, in fact, to any from headquarters.

While the study was in process, Mr. Sawyer advised Mr. Masters about the possible impact of the information which was being collected. Mr. Masters emphasized the necessity to report to the division manager, and Mr. Sawyer promised that he and Mr. Peters would do so.

The team made several efforts to see the division manager, but his secretary informed them that he was busy. They questioned the secretary closely to learn if the manager had knowledge of the procedural requirement that he and his staff go over the report with the team. She replied that he knew the requirements, but was too busy to discuss a headquarters program. He would ask his assistant, the works manager, and several staff members to go over it, and what they approved would be all right with him. Eventually this meeting was held.

The members of the local management staff took a very reasonable attitude; they admitted the bad situation portrayed in the analysis and offered their assurances that immediate steps would be taken towards improvement. The team members thought that the local management staff was glad to have their problem brought out in the open, and were delighted to have the suggestions of the headquarters representatives.

When Mr Masters reviewed the report, both team members expressed their complete dissatisfaction with the brush-off they got from the division manager. Masters took this as a cue to question them extensively concerning their findings and recommendations. In view of the sensitive character of the situation and the possible controversy that it might create, he was reluctant to distribute the report. It was the consensus of the remainder of the staff and the representatives of the accounting office that the usual transmittal letter should be prepared, and distribution made. Mr. Masters signed this letter and took no other action until the telephone call came from Mr. Gunn.

THE OZARK FOUNDRY   CASE 22

The Ozark Foundry was incorporated in 1906 by George Hampton who came to the Midwest from Massachusetts where he had been connected with the foundry business. Upon his arrival in St. Louis he purchased 20 acres of land in a nearby suburb and set up his foundry. In a small plant, Hampton started in a rather simple way to produce some of the iron castings which were needed most by the people of that area, things like gate latches, hinges, fixtures for cistern pumps, sash pulleys, radiators, and the old-time cook stoves which in that day served a double purpose—they were both the stoves for cooking the family meals and the central heating plant of most homes.

The business prospered and by 1913, Mr. Hampton's Ozark Foundry was one of the largest jobbers and producers of stove castings in the area. In 1915, however, Mr. Hampton sold his interest in the firm and Howard Smith took control and remained the principal owner until his death in 1941.

The first big expansion in the business came in the period from 1910–1915 as the development of modern machinery gave a great impetus to this nation's manufacturing activity. During this period of years, the Ozark Foundry tripled the size of its plant facilities.

The next important development of the company occurred during World War I and in the early postwar years. Ozark Foundry made castings for electric motors and for the manufacturers of automobiles. By 1920, the company was the largest producer of piston-ring castings in the entire midwestern area. The plant and personnel, of course, continued to expand through these years.

By 1925, the firm was out of the piston-ring business because of a change in production methods introduced by car manufacturers, and Ozark began to investigate and develop hi-strength mixtures and alloys. The move into the production of hi-strength iron led to the purchase of the firm's first electrical melting furnace about 1930. Sales were at a low level during the early Thirties, but the company was able to survive when others failed in this period of low economic activity, because it continued to develop special alloys and castings.

During World War II, Ozark produced parts for the machinery which turned out shells, castings for the engines on small aircraft carriers, pump castings, and castings for hydraulic turrets.

Case co-author is Dr. Carl A. Dauten, Graduate School of Business Administration, Washington University. Names, dates, and figures altered so as to conceal the identity of the company.

POSITION IN THE INDUSTRY

In the postwar years, foundries turned to research and advanced engineering for new products. Changes in consumer demands, new production methods, and new developments in metallurgy and chemistry presented many problems to the small foundry which sells its products in a competitive market.[1] Special melting procedures, heat-treatment and alloys have been developed to produce castings which will endure greater pressures and stresses and thus give longer life to many of the articles used in our daily lives.

The Ozark Foundry not only kept pace, but originated some of the developments that enabled the industry to progress. It was one of the earliest jobbing foundries to do electric melting and is known today as one of the first and most reliable firms to enter the specialty casting field. In 1963 the eighth electric furnace was installed at the Ozark Foundry, which then covered about twelve acres of land and employed about 680 persons. The installation of this electric furnace doubled the company's electric melting capacity. In addition, the company has a cupola furnace which has a melting capacity of 100 tons. The company's production at this time ran to about twenty thousand tons annually.

The present president of the company, Mr. A. R. Kraft, was one of the prime figures in the development of new methods. He started out as an apprentice boy with the Ozark Foundry, but later left the firm to work for other concerns. In 1938, he returned to Ozark as Superintendent and was made General Manager in 1943. He was promoted to the presidency of the firm in 1952. It was Mr. Kraft who encouraged a move to install a special-type of electric furnace for melting high-strength gray iron and alloy castings, so that these castings might have the special properties required for various industrial uses. He developed alloys and directed the sale of such castings to firms which could benefit from their use. Mr. Kraft is active in professional associations and has been cited by the Gray Iron Founder's Society for his important personal service to the industry.

CAPITAL STRUCTURE

The capital of the company consists entirely of $1.00 par value common stock and capital and earned surplus. Some short-term borrowing is done from time to time to help carry inventories for special orders. All of the stock was owned by the directors, the president and other key officials until the end of World War II. At that time it was decided to distribute the stock more widely. The directors, officers, and key employees now own just over 60% of the common stock, and the remainder is owned by more than 300 people, none of whom owns more than 3% of the total amount outstanding.

PERSONNEL RELATIONS

The company has a small personnel department consisting of a personnel manager, Harry Grow, and a secretary, Miss Helen Johnson. In addition to her secre-

---

[1] There are two kinds of foundries, *captive* and *jobbing*. Captive foundries are owned and operated by large manufacturing concerns primarily to produce castings for their own needs. Jobbing foundries do an engineering as well as a casting job producing metal castings to their customers' specifications

tarial duties, Miss Johnson does employment interviewing and assists the plant nurse, whose office adjoins the personnel department. Mr. Grow is responsible for all recruiting and employment, wage and salary administration, and miscellaneous related activities. All training of employees, counseling, and personnel supervision is considered to be a responsibility of the foremen, supervisors, and department heads.

The company has few written personnel policies and no formal retirement plan. Employees are not organized, but their wages exceed the average in the industry in the community. Most personnel problems are handled on an informal basis directly between worker and supervisor. On rare occasions Mr. Grow is asked to assist a line executive with such problems. More often the problem is taken to one of the higher ranking executives. Under these procedures personnel relations in the foundry have appeared to be good. One hundred and twenty-eight of the 680 employees in the company have 15 years or more service; fifty-eight have more than 25 years of service; and one employee, Henry Buckwalter, has been with the company for 48 years.

PLANS FOR FUTURE DEVELOPMENT

Re-building and expansion took place in the company during the ten-year period after World War II. The board of directors agreed early in 1964 that continued expansion could be expected. It was believed that an increase in sales of 20% or 25% would occur between 1965 and 1970. On the basis of this forecast, Mr. Kraft asked Harry Grow to give some thought to the development of the Ozark organization. Little attention had been given in the past to the planning of the organization structure, and Mr. Kraft wished to do some work along these lines.

Mr. Grow was called into Mr. Kraft's office to present the material on the company organization which he had developed. He reported to Mr. Kraft, "This is the first organization chart I've drawn for the company, but I think it gives the picture. You might find some improvements you can work into it." With that comment he handed the chart to Mr. Kraft.

After looking at the chart for several moments Mr. Kraft said, "It looks good, Harry. Let me keep it and I'll let you know of any suggestions I have. We might want to print some copies of it ... I don't know though. Everyone around here knows what everyone else does. I wonder if we really need it?"

"It might be useful when we hire a new man," answered Grow. "But, we've gotten along without one before. Maybe we don't need it now. We don't change very fast around here—and when we do make a change, everyone knows about it through the grapevine before we could get out a chart."

"Yes, I guess you're right," replied Mr. Kraft. "But what about those estimates of personnel changes in the organization?"

"One thing more about the chart. Mr. Kilgore might think that I should report to him. He treats me as though I work for him, but you told me once that I reported to Mr. Kilgore and to you. You had better check this. Here are the personnel estimates—and remember they are only estimates of our minimum requirements." With this statement, Grow handed the table to Mr. Kraft.

138 Organization for Management

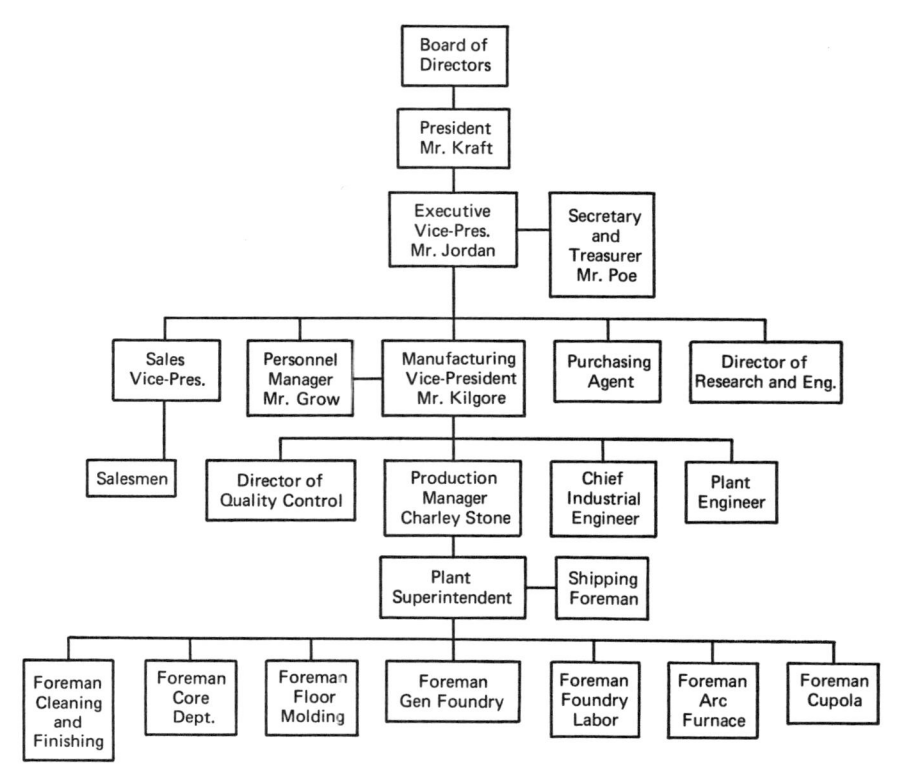

```
                    Board of
                    Directors
                        │
                    President
                    Mr. Kraft
                        │
          ┌─────────────┴──────────────┐
    Executive                      Secretary
    Vice-Pres.  ──────────────────  and
    Mr. Jordan                     Treasurer
                                   Mr. Poe
         │
 ┌───────┬────────┬────────┬────────┬──────────┐
 Sales  Personnel Manufacturing Purchasing Director of
 Vice-  Manager  Vice-President  Agent    Research and Eng.
 Pres.  Mr. Grow  Mr. Kilgore
         │
 ┌───────┬────────┬────────┬────────┐
Salesmen Director Production  Chief    Plant
         of       Manager    Industrial Engineer
         Quality  Charley    Engineer
         Control  Stone
                     │
               Plant ──── Shipping
               Superintendent  Foreman
                     │
  ┌──────┬──────┬──────┬──────┬──────┬──────┐
Foreman Foreman Foreman Foreman Foreman Foreman Foreman
Cleaning Core   Floor   Gen     Foundry Arc     Cupola
and     Dept.   Molding Foundry Labor   Furnace
Finishing
```

Note: The Secretary and Treasurer of the company directs all financial and accounting activities.

Anticipated Minimum Personnel Requirements of Ozark Foundry

	Today (1964)	1969	1975	1980
Total Employment	680	806	913	1056
Skilled Workers	150	190	205	240
Semi-Skilled Workers	92	110	120	140
Unskilled Labor	114	130	150	170
Molders	82	100	110	130
Core Makers	18	24	30	36
Supervisors, Office, Lab.	100	116	136	160
Adm., Exec., Sales	66	72	90	100
Foremen	36	40	44	50
Staff	22	24	28	30

"I presume you talked to the department heads about this—and let them look into your crystal ball," said Mr. Kraft as he looked over the personnel estimate.

"Yes, I did," answered Grow. "Some of them told me it was a waste of time. But, I really think they got a kick out of it. A few fellows took an interest in the figures—and several felt that they were in on the planning of company operations."

"I see some problems buried in these figures, Harry," said Mr. Kraft. "If we put in straight-line production and mechanize more of our molding operations, what happens to these figures on molders?"

"Well, Charley and the other fellows knew about those plans. We've estimated that by 1975 and 1980 we'll be doing a lot of our molding with machines—and we believe that 72 of those 130 molders in 1980 will be on mechanized lines. We don't know how far we'll be off, but one of the engineers says it is an 'educated guess.'"

"I don't know that I could guess any better. I presume that you have our pattern makers in your skilled workers' figures," said Mr. Kraft.

"Yes, they're in with other skilled jobs."

"Have you given any more thought to our pattern maker problem? We're sending most of our work out now, and our own men actually do little more than repair work. With this proposed expansion the time might be ripe for training our own pattern makers."

"You just can't find pattern makers anymore, Mr. Kraft. I don't know where those job shops get them. I've talked to manual training teachers at the high school and to trade school people in the city. They say that it's almost impossible to get young people to go into these skills. I've thought that we might take some of our own people who like foundry work and train them. It would require an apprenticeship program, and it probably should be a registered program under the government's department of labor," said Grow. "But, frankly, Mr. Kraft, such a program takes a lot of time. I really need an assistant, anyway, and putting in an apprenticeship program is impossible unless I get some help."

"Harry, you're talking just like a government man. You want the government in on the program and you want to hire more people and spend more money—that's typical!" said Mr. Kraft, laughingly.

"Well, we fill a lot of our jobs by just promoting and training, but we can't seem to get pattern makers that way," objected Grow.

"I'm kidding, Harry. You'll need an assistant before long. Give some thought to the building of the organization we need to meet this projected growth. Where will we get the professional and office people? There is the possibility that the board will decide we should go after some of those large orders we're missing. In that case we'd have to set up a real volume-production plant and expand even more."

"I guess business comes to us because of our engineering skill," said Harry. "We have only six salesmen and they're more engineers than they are salesmen."

"Yes," said Mr. Kraft. "If we put forth a real sales effort, we might get some of the automobile business we're now losing. Some of our customers have us develop their first castings and then send the business elsewhere when they want volume production. If we were set up to keep some of that business and could go out and get more, we might increase our business 50% in the next five years. An increase in business of 50% probably would not require any more office or lab people than a 25% increase. You might try to set up your personnel estimates on the basis of a 50% increase as well as the 25%. It raises a question though; would our engineering services and job work suffer? We don't want to do anything to hurt the reputation this company has built in fifty years."

"You're posing some interesting questions," said Harry. "Some sort of survey of the market might be worthwhile."

"We're thinking along these lines, Harry, but in the meantime we've got customers and castings to think about. I want to talk to Mr. Poe and see if he feels we can finance our expansion without running the risk of losing control to an outside group. I appreciate this work you've done—and let's talk further about an apprenticeship program in the next few months. Talk to Charley about it and see if he thinks it has merit." With that final comment Mr. Kraft dismissed Grow from his office.

TOO MANY BOSSES CASE 23

In February, the major jig and fixtures department of a large manufacturing company had opened a group of jigs to production. Some of these tools had been built by outsiders and shipped in presumably ready for use in building parts, but this was only the ideal. In practice many bugs had to be ironed out, and in some instances it was even discovered that sub-contracted tools had been built to obsolete tool design. This meant that major reworking would be required—occasionally even rebuilding the tool involved.

Where this was necessary, production was delayed until the tools could be ready to build the production assemblies which were needed to turn out parts in quantity. This might require as little as three days or as long as four weeks, depending upon the amount of rework required. It is not to be wondered at that this condition generated a great deal of pressure on the tooling organization from some of the upper echelons of management.

During the peak of this confusion Fred Larson, a supervisor, found his operation to be one of the hottest spots. Jess Bradley, his division superintendent, inaugurated the practice of walking through the shop a couple of times a day to see how things were moving along. At first he always came with Phil Hawthorne, Fred's foreman, and discussed the job chiefly with the supervisor in charge. Pretty soon, however, he was coming by himself and if the supervisor wasn't around he might talk at length with a lead man or even one or two of the workers. Then as time went on, he went a step beyond talking and asking questions, requesting job builders to tear down a set-up in order to incorporate some of his ideas.

Fred's was not the only work station in the tooling organization to receive this treatment. All of the operations reporting to Phil were also on Jess' itinerary, as were a number of those for which other foremen were responsible, and Phil and his foreman colleagues well knew what was going on. It was just that the straw which broke the camel's back, so to speak, was an incident that occurred in Fred's area about 10 days after all of this started. Already the morale of his men was at low ebb, since they did not know any more whether to go ahead with a given set-up as planned or wait for Jess Bradley to tell them how to proceed. Then one day Fred returned to his station after a brief absence to learn that

---

Case reproduced by the permission of Professor Howard R. Smith, Head of the Management Department and Director of Executive Development, the College of Business Administration, University of Georgia.

scheduled operations on a large job had just been changed, and that two days' set-up time for seven men had thereby gone down the drain.

Profoundly disturbed and thoroughly angry, Fred decided that things could not go on this way any longer.

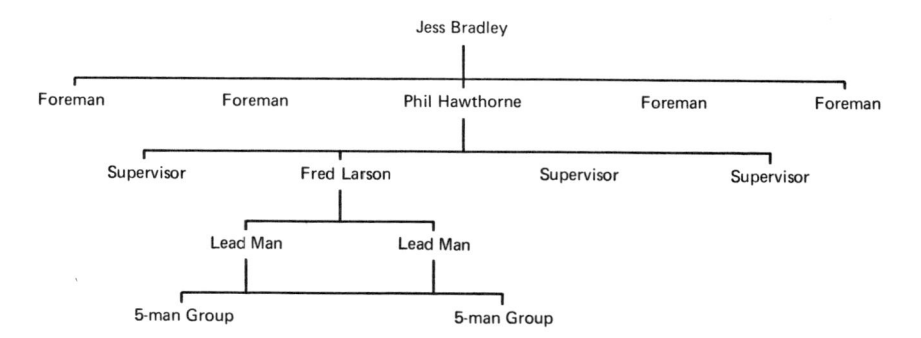

```
                            Jess Bradley
        ┌──────────┬────────────┼────────────┬──────────┐
     Foreman    Foreman    Phil Hawthorne  Foreman    Foreman
                    ┌──────────┼────────────┬──────────┐
                Supervisor  Fred Larson  Supervisor  Supervisor
                              ┌──────┴──────┐
                           Lead Man      Lead Man
                              │             │
                        ┌─────┴─────┬───────┘
                     5-man Group        5-man Group
```

THE ADJUSTMENT DEPARTMENT   CASE 24

After graduating from a small liberal arts college, Jerry Piatt accepted a position with a large merchandising organization which operated several hundred retail stores and strategically located mail order houses throughout the country. Attached to the mail order units were warehouses which held and distributed merchandise for the chain stores. Jerry chose to enter the mail order division of the firm rather than the retail store organization, and within six months he had completed the junior executive training program for college graduates. During the following three years he worked in several departments as an operating supervisor, transferring from one assignment to another as prescribed by the training supervisor in charge of the company's job rotation program for managers.

When a chain of promotions and transfers of personnel removed the assistant manager of the adjustment department, Jerry Piatt was selected for the vacancy. Jerry had acquired experience as a line supervisor in the mail opening and banking department, three different stock and order filling departments, the packing and shipping department and, finally, the merchandise exchange unit of the adjustment department. Although some of the older men in the division felt that Jerry was too young to act as the assistant manager of a major department, it was recognized by most of the management people that he had reorganized and improved the operations in the merchandise exchange unit. The adjustment of customer complaints had frequently been delayed because of loss or damage to the goods returned for credit. Jerry had developed a new system of identifying and storing returned merchandise and matching the returned goods with customers' complaints. His innovations had noticeably improved the overall adjustment service.

The adjustment department employed approximately 220 people, working as exchange clerks, returned goods handlers, adjusters, correspondents, typists, dictaphone operators, file clerks and miscellaneous clerical personnel. The department was organized into eight units, each directed by a supervisor reporting to the assistant manager. All employees in the department were women excepting the supervisor and twelve correspondents in the technical correspondence section, Jerry, and Mr. Swanson, the department manager.

The men in the technical correspondence section were engineers, or technical specialists, qualified to analyze customers' complaints and problems pertaining to electrical or mechanical equipment. Each man specialized in a line or merchandise group and was trained to find solutions to technical problems and to handle all correspondence with customers and suppliers related to these problems. Letters dictated by the technical correspondents were transcribed by the dictaphone operators in a special group within the central stenographic pool.

The supervisor of the technical correspondence unit, Milton Harvey, was a well qualified specialist with an engineering education and many years of experience in the mail order business. Although Mr. Harvey usually devoted considerable time to training new men for his department, he told Jerry that he considered the twelve correspondents under his supervision to be professional men who could work with little direction. Harvey usually went directly to Mr. Swanson, the department head, for assistance with his problems and, on several occasions, Harvey indicated to Jerry that he considered his position as technical correspondence supervisor to be more important than that of the assistant manager. Harvey always attended meetings of supervisors called by Mr. Swanson but he seldom attended those called by Jerry. Nevertheless, Mr. Swanson assigned Jerry the responsibility for the flow of work in the technical correspondence section, because requests for information from files, instructions to typists, and other services used by all correspondents involved employees under his supervision. Jerry was willing to adjust to this relationship with Milton Harvey, because he realized that most of the engineers in the technical correspondence unit were paid higher salaries than he received. Since Mr. Swanson had never prepared a formal organization chart, Jerry visualized the relationships within the department as shown in Figure 1.

Figure 1
The Adjustment Department

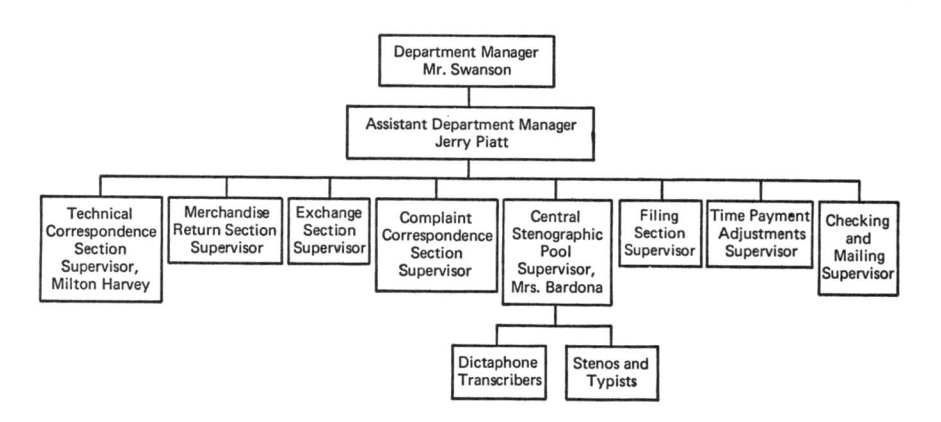

```
                        Department Manager
                          Mr. Swanson
                              |
                    Assistant Department Manager
                           Jerry Piatt
   _____|_____
   |          |         |         |         |        |        |          |
Technical  Merchandise Exchange Complaint  Central  Filing  Time Payment Checking
Correspondence Return  Section  Correspondence Stenographic Section Adjustments and
Section    Section   Supervisor Section    Pool     Supervisor Supervisor Mailing
Supervisor, Supervisor          Supervisor Supervisor,                   Supervisor
Milton Harvey                              Mrs. Bardona
                                              |
                                      _____|_____
                                      |               |
                                  Dictaphone      Stenos and
                                  Transcribers    Typists
```

After several months, Jerry Piatt was confronted with a developing personnel problem which seemed to have affected two or three units within the department. It concerned one of the dictaphone operators, Margie Thompson, and several of her friends. Jerry realized that the latest incident involving Margie called for a thorough review of the case and probably some specific action. In trying to decide what to do about Margie, Jerry reviewed the following facts:

Margie Thompson was considered by all supervisors to be a competent dictaphone operator, who did neat and efficient work, especially on technical and difficult correspondence. When transcribing routine letters, she usually produced above standard and earned bonus payments under the division's incentive wage payment plan.[1]

Margie was a personable and vivacious young lady, one of the most popular in the department. She frequently was the center of attraction among a small group of girls in the department who seemed to enjoy working together. In general, the members of this group did better than average work but frequently they had disagreements with their supervisor, Mrs. Bardona. Margie had had several open quarrels with Mrs. Bardona over work assignments, more than any of the other girls.

At the same time, Margie appeared anxious to please the manager and the assistant manager of the department. Jerry recalled one occasion while he was talking with Mrs. Bardona, Margie came to him and asked a routine question which could have been addressed to Mrs. Bardona. She had said, "Jerry, can you tell me what time the mail opening department goes home today?" to which Jerry quickly gave her the answer. When Margie had returned to her desk, Mrs. Bardona commented that Margie could have obtained the information from the daily record sheet on her desk. She also said that on numerous occasions she had told Margie and the other girls that they should address Jerry as "Mr. Piatt," even though all the men in the department did not do so. Mrs. Bardona felt that addressing Jerry as "Mr. Piatt" would contribute to a more formal atmosphere among the girls in the department.

Jerry also was aware that Margie Thompson frequently had differences of opinion and arguments with members of the technical correspondence unit, especially with the supervisor, Milton Harvey. Because of her recognized proficiency, these men often called upon her and two or three other girls for the typing of special letters and difficult technical reports. The girls usually took pride in being asked to do the most difficult work in the department but several, especially Margie, resented these requests when they interfered with work on routine and standardized correspondence which provided opportunities for extra compensation. Harvey was quick to criticize Margie for the occasional mistakes found in her technical correspondence typing. Margie resented this criticism and had engaged in several open arguments with Milton Harvey which disturbed other members of the department. After one especially stormy argument Harvey had complained to Mr. Swanson that the girls in the transcribing unit were not cooperative— they were "a bunch of prima donnas and Margie Thompson was the ring-leader of the lot!" Mr. Swanson had replied that he was sorry about the difficulties, but that the girls in that group were the best dictaphone operators in the entire company.

The latest incident implicating Margie Thompson was the result of her apparent failure to follow one of Mrs. Bardona's instructions. Early in the afternoon Mr. Swanson and Jerry had asked all supervisors to instruct correspondents and typists to go through the accumulated mail and make sure that all two- and three-day old

---

[1] In clerical activities in mail order houses, completion of form letters and dictated letters with a limited number of paragraphs constitute repetitive work which can be standardized and compensated for under an incentive wage plan.

letters from customers were answered before the end of the day. Requests of this type were frequently made in order to give special attention to customers' mail which had been delayed. When such instructions were given, it was Mrs. Bardona's practice to go down the aisle between the dictaphone operators, stopping at every four or five desks in order to speak to several girls at a time. In this instance she specifically asked the operators to go through their mail, promptly handle the older letters, and give to her any of the old correspondence which could not be completed during the day. She was later told by the supervisor in the adjoining unit that while in the employee lounge she had overheard Margie comment to several of the girls, "Who does that old battleaxe think she is? I've made quota today and I'm not going to bother with those tough cases." At the end of the day after all the operators had gone home, Mrs. Bardona brought to Jerry's desk the unfinished correspondence which she had collected from Margie's desk and the desks of four other girls whose desks were close to Margie's. It was obvious that neither Margie nor the other girls had endeavored to complete the older correspondence, and they had not turned it over to their supervisor.

Jerry pondered what course of action he should take.

THE GENERAL ELECTRIC COMPANY (A)— FROM CENTRALIZATION TO DECENTRALIZATION, 1878-1950'S

CASE 25

FIRST ORGANIZATION STRUCTURE[1]

The General Electric Company grew from the Edison Electric Light Company, which was organized in 1878 to develop Thomas A. Edison's incandescent lamp. The Edison Electric Light Company and seven other Edison companies were combined in 1889 into the Edison General Electric Company. In 1892 that company and the Thomson-Houston Company were combined to form the General Electric Company, with Charles A. Coffin as its first President and Thomas A. Edison as one of its directors. Thus, 1953 marked 75 years of electrical progress since Thomas A. Edison organized the first of the companies which became the General Electric Company, and 1952 marked the sixtieth anniversary of the Company's present corporate form.

In 1892, when General Electric was formed, the businesses of the predecessor companies were combined into a single business having an annual sales volume of $14 million. The new Company had a centralized organization structure consisting of five centralized functional operating departments: The Manufacturing and Electrical Department, the Selling Department, the Accounting Department, the Treasury Department, and the Law Department.

President Coffin, in January 1894, stated in the Company's Second Annual Report:

> ... Your Directors have been earnestly endeavoring to simplify your organization... At first your Board had little success in its efforts to centralize and simplify the organization, but the events of the last summer emphasized the necessity of radical changes so unmistakably as to secure the cooperation necessary to effect the desired results.
>
> ... The business management of the Company has been concentrated at its principal office at Schenectady and its whole organization has been greatly simplified. All accounts are kept there, and all sales and credits are supervised there. So far as practicable, your manufacturing business has been and will be concentrated at Schenectady, and the operations of its other factories are now directed from there. During the short time since this change was effected, many advantages have accrued to the Company from this CONCENTRATION of the Selling, Accounting, Manufacturing, and Engineering Departments of the Company...

[1] From General Electric Company, *Professional Management in General Electric* (New York: 1953). Used by permission.

Numerous vacancies ... have occurred in your official organization during the year. ... The SELECTIONS to fill such vacancies have, in every instance, been made in recognition of GENERAL MERIT and of FITNESS. ... This has resulted in a large saving of expense and increased efficiency.

For the Company's relatively small number of product lines, this centralized functional type of organization was effective and economical. It met the needs of the Company's business and the social-economic conditions of that time. The Company had only three plants—Schenectady, Lynn, and Harrison (Edison Lamp Works). Sales volume at that time, and for many years thereafter, was about the same as that of some of the Company's smaller product departments of today.

NEW FRONTIERS FOR PROFESSIONAL MANAGERS[2]

Up until 1939, the Company was able to operate efficiently under a highly centralized form of management. During World War II, however, General Electric began a period of almost explosive growth which caused its managers to question whether it might not be necessary to evolve new techniques of organizing and managing the Company ...

From the beginning of the study, it was apparent that the Company was going to require increasingly better planning, greater flexibility, and faster, more informed decisions than was possible under the highly centralized organization structure, which was suited for earlier and different conditions. Unless we could put the responsibility and authority for decision-making closer in each case to the scene of the problem, where complete understanding and prompt action are possible, the Company would not be able to compete with the hundreds of nimble competitors who were, as they say, able to turn on a dime.

In addition, General Electric faced the need to develop capable leaders for the future; the need for more friendly and cooperative relationships between managers and other employees; the need to stay ahead of competition in serving the customers; and the very human need to make the work of a manager at all echelons of the organization more manageable. The work had to be made more manageable so that it could be understood and carried out by people of normally available energy and intelligence, thus leaving no requirement for the so-called indispensable man. ...

Now, decentralization has different meanings for different people. The decicion to decentralize General Electric did not mean that it was decided to "break up the Company" into smaller pieces. This would be self-defeating, because it would lose to the public and to the Company those advantages that are the distinctive contribution of large enterprises: the ability to serve as a source of major innovations in the nation's economic life, creating new products, new industries, new employment, and new outlets for smaller businesses; the ability to energize

---

[2] From *New Frontiers for Professional Managers,* by Ralph J. Cordiner (McKinsey Foundation Lecture series, Columbia University). Copyright © 1956, McGraw-Hill Book Company. Used by permission. Note: In this section, Mr. Cordiner is personally describing the philosophy of decentralization as implemented at General Electric Company.

the flow of mass production and mass distribution; and the ability to provide a broad range of advanced technical capacity in order to produce the more complex products and systems of our times.

In General Electric, decentralization is a way of preserving and enhancing these contributions of the large enterprise, and at the same time achieving the flexibility and the "human touch" that are popularly associated with—though not always attained by—small organizations.

Under this concept, we have undertaken decentralization not only according to products, geography, and functional types of work. The most important aspect of the Company's philosophy is thorough decentralization of the responsibility and authority for making business decisions.

Here is the underlying logic. The share owners, through their Board of Directors, delegate to the President responsibility for the conduct of the whole business. The responsibility carries with it all the authority required to get the work done, except such authorities as are specifically withheld by the Board and the share owners. The total responsibility also carries with it full accountability for results. General Electric may be unique in that the Board of Directors has issued a position guide for the President, stating in detail his responsibility, authority, and accountability.

Now, the President is of course unable to do all the work himself, and so he delegates the responsibility for portions of the total work through organization channels to individuals who have the talents and knowledge required to do it. This is done by planning and building the work of the Company into an organization structure which consists of all the necessary positions and components required to do all the work in the most effective and efficient manner.

Each employee thus takes on responsibility for some part of the over-all Company work. Along with this responsibility, each position naturally carries with it full accountability for measured results, and all the necessary authority required for the position except those authorities that are specifically stated as withheld. Therefore each employee of the Company has, in his position, full responsibility, authority and accountability for a certain defined body of work and teamwork. Through teamwork he recognizes his relationships to the other employees who perform a share of the total work of the Company.

With this philosophy, General Electric achieves a community of purpose between leaders and their associates, and is able to attain that voluntary integration which is the hallmark of a free and decentralized enterprise...

Since philosophy is, by definition, a system of first principles, I should like to list for you ten principles which express General Electric's philosophy of decentralization.

1. Decentralization places authority to make decisions at points as near as possible where actions take place.
2. Decentralization is likely to get best over-all results by getting greatest and most directly applicable knowledge and most timely understanding actually into play on the greatest number of decisions.

3. Decentralization will work if real authority is delegated; and not if details then have to be reported, or, worse yet, if they have to be "checked" first.
4. Decentralization requires confidence that associates in decentralized positions will have the capacity to make sound decisions in the majority of cases; and such confidence starts at the executive level. Unless the President and all the other Officers have a deep personal conviction and an active desire to decentralize full decision-making responsibility and authority, actual decentralization will never take place. The Officers must set an example in the art of full delegation.
5. Decentralization requires understanding that the main role of staff or services is the rendering of assistance and advice to line operators through a relatively few experienced people, so that those making decisions can themselves make them correctly.
6. Decentralization requires realization that the natural aggregate of many individually sound decisions will be better for the business and for the public than centrally planned and controlled decisions.
7. Decentralization rests on the need to have general business objectives, organization structure, relationships, policies, and measurement known, understood, and followed; but realizing that definition of policies does not necessarily mean uniformity of methods of executing such policies in decentralized operations.
8. Decentralization can be achieved only when higher executives realize that authority genuinely delegated to lower echelons cannot, in fact, also be retained by them. We have, today, Officers and Managers who still believe in decentralization down to themselves and no further. By paying lip service to decentralization, but actually reviewing detailed work and decisions and continually "second-guessing" their associates, such Officers keep their organization in confusion and prevent the growth of self-reliant men.
9. Decentralization will work only if responsibility commensurate with decision-making authority is truly accepted and exercised at all levels.
10. Decentralization requires personnel policies based on measured performance, enforced standards, rewards for good performance, and removal for incapacity of poor performance.

THE GENERAL ELECTRIC COMPANY (B)—
PROBLEMS WITH DECENTRALIZATION, 1961[1]

In the midst of General Electric's highly-publicized anti-trust troubles[2] and its earnings slump, some G. E. executives are worrying more about another problem: Is G. E. too decentralized?

The giant electrical products manufacturer in the past decade has split up its operations into 113 departments, each with a large degree of autonomy. Critics both inside and outside the company claim this has led to internal strife, lack of cooperation among departments, frustration of top management's will, and an over-riding concern by some G. E. department managers for the good of their own units at the expense of the general welfare of the company. Some G. E. men argue that the company's high degree of decentralization made it easier for middle-level officials to engage in price-fixing conspiracies without the knowledge of top management.

G. E., however, claims it is still firmly commited to decentralization; top officials argue it is the only possible course for a company so big and diversified. G. E.'s sales, they note, have continued to rise under decentralization. Though profit margins aren't as large as they were in the years just before decentralization, they compare favorably with those of major competitors in a period when corporate profit margins generally are under pressure.

PROBLEMS OF "GIGANTICISM"

Perhaps a fair analysis would be that the most carefully worked out systems that management planners can devise turn out to have serious flaws when applied to a big organization, be it business or governmental. "Giganticism" seems to create certain problems which defy those who believe management can be reduced to anything like a science. . . .

G. E. first moved into decentralization to try to become as nimble as hundreds of smaller competitors. It decided it had to let men close to the market make as many day-to-day business decisions as possible. In the words of a company manual, each G. E. department is tailored as a business "a single manager can get his arms around." The average department rings up sales of $40 million a year.

---

[1] From "Company Officials Debate Merit of Its Decentralized System," by Stanley Penn and Ed Cony, *Wall Street Journal* (Chicago, March 22, 1961.) Copyright 1961. Dow Jones & Company, Inc. All rights reserved. Used by permission.
[2] General Electric Company and 28 other concerns were prosecuted and convicted for conspiracy to divide markets and fix prices in the heavy electrical equipment industry. (Only three of G. E.'s 21 divisions were involved.) A number of executives received heavy fines and jail sentences.

The department general manager has great responsibilities. He may hire and fire, set prices, decide on products he wants to push and shape his inventory as he wishes. His total compensation may run from $50,000 to $60,000 a year.

In return, he must account for his stewardship. He's judged largely on his profits. High profits bring rewards, substantial bonuses which he shares with his subordinates. Failure brings punishment; firing is a frequent penalty.

A step above the department manager in G. E.'s management hierarchy is the division manager. He guides a "family of related departments" or, in the words of one vice president of G. E., "he acts as a buffer between the departments and the executive office in New York." For example, under the wing of the Lamp Divisions general manager are six departments: Large Lamps, Lamp Glass, Lamp Metals and Components, Lamp Development Operation, Miniature Lamps and Photo Lamps. In all, there are 21 divisions.

Top management in New York retains ultimate power, of course. But the theory is that at this lofty level, executives are freed from many details of day-to-day operations and can concentrate on broad company policy and on long range planning.

The chief architect of this plan has been Ralph Cordiner, dynamic board chairman of G. E. During World War II, G. E.'s sales quadrupled reaching $1.5 billion in 1945. As G. E. continued to grow after the war, Mr. Cordiner and others became convinced the company was too big to run in a highly centralized fashion by executives working in "the G. E. tower" at 57 Lexington Avenue, in New York City.

G. E.'S EMPIRE

The G. E. empire is indeed a mighty one to manage. In the United States 167 plants bear the G. E. symbol; they are scattered through 29 states and 133 cities. Overseas, the sun never sets on G. E.'s foreign operations in 21 countries.

An industrial army of more than 250,000 draws paychecks from the corporation—to the tune of more than $1.8 billion a year. Sales of $4.2 billion last year placed G. E. fourth in the land among industrial concerns. It outsold such giants as Socony Mobil Oil Co., U. S. Steel Corp. and Chrysler Corp.

The firm's great diversity compounds its management problems. The company will sell you a 25-cent light bulb, a $15 million generator, an electric can opener, a synthetic diamond or a jet aircraft engine.

Mr. Cordiner has speculated publicly that G. E. may be the most diversified company in the world. In all, it turns out about 200,000 different products. The company confesses it can't give the precise number (is a pink fluorescent lamp a separate product from a yellow one?).

So complex was G. E.'s decentralization that it took about five years, 1951-55, to push through the bulk of it. Officially, no one at G. E. now will utter a harsh word against the program. "We consider decentralization a great source of strength, which builds high quality management," Mr. Cordiner declared recently.

Says Harold Smiddy, a G. E. Vice President who played a major role in decentralizing the company: "We believe the (decentralization) policy is sound and the approach workable." Mr. Smiddy heads G. E.'s Management Consultation Services, a unit which does "basic and applied research" in professional management and passes along the results of such research to G. E. managers. Mr. Smiddy's unit, among other things, tries to get department managers to do a better job, both for their departments and for the company as a whole.

"PROFITABLE INNOVATIONS"

As a result of decentralization, Mr. Smiddy says, G. E. today has "in all components more people with better understanding" of how to manage their business. "While many (G. E. managers) have made mistakes along the way, which more centralized controls might have prevented, they also have made countless and profitable innovations which central executives never would have conceived."

It is known, however, that Mr. Cordiner himself is privately something less than fully satisfied with decentralization. And he is inviting and listening to criticism of the system.

Several G. E. executives share the view that decentralization was partly responsible for the company's recent anti-trust difficulties. Says one G. E. man: "When you decentralize, each department general manager is measured by profits of his product. Before decentralization, when all types of turbine generators, for instance, were under one man, he could decide to let sales of 10,000-kilowatt units. But when you are decentralized, one man is being measured on sales of the bigger units. So you lose some flexibility. This increases the pressure to fix prices in order to maintain your profit."

In the recent anti-trust action, G. E. contended Mr. Cordiner and other members of top management knew nothing of the abuses. Government attorneys acknowledged they were not claiming that the G. E. board, the chairman or the president had any knowledge of the price-fixing conspiracies. . . .

MANY SEPARATE STAFFS

One tenet of decentralization is that each department, in order to operate as a business, should have all the tools or services available to an independent company. This has meant in practice that most departments have hired their own people to handle such staff assignments as finance, marketing, engineering, and public relations. G. E.'s directory of "Press Relations Personnel," for instance, runs to 26 pages.

Consider what happened in 1956 when G. E.'s Hotpoint division was decentralized into five product departments—laundry, refrigerators, television, ranges, kitchen appliances. The number of people in "finance" rose from 300 to about 520, according to an executive in the division at the time. A Hotpoint spokesman admits there was some increase but says financial personnel have dwindled again to "about 300" now.

One former department manager says: "When you get one of those lovely organization charts with all the little rectangles in it—for the staff positions—you tend to fill them up with people, whether you really need them or not."

Those who insist that G. E.'s decentralization went too far claim department managers tend to take only a short-range view of their operations. "The manager worries too much about his immediate profits," claims one G. E. man, "His view gets too narrow. He neglects to concentrate on new areas the company ought to be looking into."

THE GENERAL ELECTRIC COMPANY (C)—
THE EMPIRE THAT SUBDIVIDED, 1970[1]

General Electric Chairman and Chief Executive Officer Fred J. Borch takes a pragmatic approach toward running what is probably the world's most diversified industrial organization. "We've had diversity and we've had experience in organizing to cope with it."

The experience, frequently painful and often expensive, has been a continuing one. Smaller, less diversified companies that took the conglomerate route to growth have been able to build management structures and controls tailored to their needs. GE, by contrast, has had to handle new ventures with a management already strained by the complexities of running a diversified corporation.

Its performance over the past decade has followed the broad movements of the economy and has prompted critics to put GE in the category of a beleaguered colossus, sluggishly moving on its momentum rather than aggressively pushing ahead.

The company's answer to the problem, devised in the early 1950s, has been decentralization. Ralph J. Cordiner, then president, split it into some 100 autonomous departments, each with a profit responsibility and a business of its own.

Decentralization remains the strategy today. Borch, who has spent his entire business career with GE, is sticking to Cordiner's basic game plan and updating it to cope with the same problems that perplexed GE 20 years ago—size and complexity. Two years ago, Borch used Cordiner's tactic again and split GE into more manageable units. A current move that Borch terms "adaptive and evolutionary" involves the creation of top-level staff groups charged with long-range planning and an attempt to streamline day-to-day administrative chores that can be snarled in a bureaucratic maze.

Cordiner's objective was to get profit and loss responsibility to a level where managers could influence it rapidly. By the time Borch succeeded Cordiner as chief executive in December, 1963, GE's managers were comfortable with a structure composed of five general groups, 25 divisions, and some 110 departments. But from 1959 to 1963, sales were on a plateau of around $5-billion.

A sluggish economy and operating problems combined to put pressure on GE management in the early 1960s. Preoccupation with the electrical price-fixing antitrust suit had tightened the vise. As a result, any assessment of its organization structure got short shrift, as did ventures such as commercial jet engines, nuclear energy, and computers. Borch and then Chairman Gerald L. Phillippe pushed ahead in the new areas.

[1] Reprinted by permission from *Business Week,* October 17, 1970. Copyright 1970, by McGraw-Hill, Inc.

By 1967, the five groups, each with about $1.6-billion in volume—were almost as large as the entire company was in 1952. "The businesses," says Borch, "were getting too big. There are parameters on any job." Borch expanded the number of groups from five to 10, divisions from 25 to 50, and departments from 110 to 170. It involved a massive personnel shift, including eight new group executives.

With the new alignment in place, Borch says, "I realized I couldn't get my arms around 10 groups." This prompted his second major move of creating the President's Office. Three former group executives, Phillippe, and Borch comprised the President's Office. Their responsibility was overseeing the total corporation and laying strategies for GE. "We didn't want to assign anyone accountability for any group. The minute you do that you get advocacy and we were responsible for the whole company's operations. We wanted a review and challenge approach," says Borch.

The new structure was effective in January, 1968, but the sudden death of Phillippe in October forced another change. The three executive vice-presidents were elevated to vice-chairmen and elected to the board. And the group's name was changed to the Corporate Executive Office.

A further step Borch wanted to take at that time involved splitting up the staff functions at the headquarters level. But there were already too many people in new jobs as a result of the earlier reorganization to make such a move feasible.

By last June, the reshaping of the headquarters staff was accomplished. The Corporate Executive Staff advises the Corporate Executive Office on effective use of GE's resources and reviews long-range plans with the operating groups. The Corporate Administrative Staff coordinates functions ranging from accounting and legal operations to employee relations.

GE's latest move has been criticized as another example of over-organizing. Borch says the new structure allows GE to project "where we will be five years hence and how to get there and fill the gap in between. There are so many opportunities that it is a problem of priorities."

Generating cash to exploit opportunities in new areas will also be a top priority item. And its pullback from the computer business will, says Borch, "allow us to make capital investment in more of the other things. The computer business is a tremendous cash drain."

GE's problem-plagued attempt to crack the computer business is, in fact, often cited as evidence that big, institutionalized companies rarely succeed in new businesses where they encounter smaller and leaner competitors. But GE hung on for 14 years, and Borch insists the venture announced last May with Honeywell, Inc.—involving a new company that takes over the computer manufacturing and sales activities of both companies with Honeywell holding an 81½% interest—did not result from a moment of panic. "Investigation showed that in order to survive in the computer business, a merger was necessary," Borch says emphatically.

With the computer experience behind it, Borch is not letting GE get bogged down in postmortems. Rather, the management structure he has put in place, he says, means that GE can concentrate on new areas of growth to "get us off the GNP trend."

HILL CITY JUNIOR COLLEGE   CASE 26

Hill City Junior College was established in 1963. It grew rapidly, drawing students from communities and towns in the county of which Hill City is the county seat. Enrollment increased from 1800 to 3200 students in the five-year period following 1964, when Dr. Henry Palmer became president

"THE COLUMBIA CLIQUE"

Dr. Palmer had left a professorship at Columbia Teacher's College to take the post at Hill City Junior College. At the time of leaving Columbia, Dr. Palmer confided to close friends that he planned to return to Columbia after the Hill City program and its teaching-administrative staff had been reasonably well developed.

After two years at Hill City Junior College, Dr. Palmer obtained the services of George Motte, a former student and colleague at Columbia. Dr. Motte had completed his graduate work at Teachers College, earning the D.Ed. degree after several years of experience as a high school teacher and four years as an assistant professor at Columbia. He accepted the position as dean of instruction at Hill City in preference to an associate professorship at Columbia. During his three years in office as dean of instruction, three additional Teachers College men were brought to Hill City. One was Howard White, a former assistant professor; the other two were graduate students, George Teasdale and William Bower, who had not yet completed the requirements for the D.Ed. degree.

George Motte and Howard White had been graduate students together at Teachers College, and had been on the faculty at the same time. Soon after George Motte came to Hill City as dean of instruction, he invited Howard White to join his faculty. After some persuasion, Professor White came to Hill City as head of the social science department. He was given a salary higher than any other professor or division head in the school. In the year following his acceptance of the position at Hill City, Professor White employed his former student, George Teasdale, at the rank of associate professor. Mr. Teasdale had been an instructor at Teachers College and was involved in research for his doctoral dissertation.

During the negotiations for the employment of Mr. Teasdale, another graduate student who was working on the doctorate at Columbia applied for a student counselling position at Hill City. Eventually this man, William Bower, was employed as assistant dean of students. Bower was making a study of student-faculty relations as a part of his research for his doctorate. He considered the Hill City Junior College position as an opportunity to develop further his competence in this area. Although he agreed to remain at least two years in the position of assistant dean, it was understood that Bower would leave Hill City Junior College soon after he had earned his doctorate. At the time of their employment, George Motte and Howard White both were in their mid-thirties; the other young men, George Teasdale and William Bower were 28 and 29 years of age respectively.

Hill City Junior College was recognized as one of the better new junior colleges in the midwestern part of the United States. Dr. Palmer was in great demand as a speaker on educational topics and as a consultant to other communities interested in the junior college movement. With a great many demands upon his time, Dr. Palmer became concerned that a "gap" had developed between himself and the members of his college faculty. He had been told by Mr. Art Remke, the dean of students, that a number of faculty members complained that most of the administrative communications to the faculty came through the "Columbia clique." Mr. Remke frequently quoted to Dr. Palmer the remarks of Harry Holet, chairman of the natural science and mathematics department. Professor Holet had been with the college since its inception, having left a post as school superintendent in Hill City. At one time several members of the board of trustees had urged Dr. Palmer to promote Holet to the position of dean of instruction, but Palmer had procured George Motte for the post. Remke quoted Holet as saying, "No matter what Palmer has to say, it has the Columbia twist before it gets to the rest of us—and there's not much opportunity around here for anyone who hasn't been to Teachers College!"

The latest complaint from Professor Holet concerned the rank and salary being paid to Bert Brunswick, the assistant chairman of the natural science and mathematics department. Brunswick was 34 years of age; he had been employed to teach half-time and to assist Professor Holet with the administrative work in the department. Brunswick had come to Hill City from the State University where he had been an instructor of mathematics for six years and where he had done graduate work. He held an M.A. and had completed half of the classroom work for his doctorate. Brunswick expected to continue his academic work in summer school until he completed the work for another graduate degree. Apparently, he had reminded Professor Holet frequently that he was only an assistant professor and that his salary was probably much less than the salaries paid to the Columbia men who had been hired at higher ranks.

FACULTY PARTICIPATION

In an effort to improve relationships with the faculty, Dr. Palmer had developed a Professional Standards Committee. This committee was organized to consist of three faculty members from each department, one administrator from the business office, the two deans, and himself. The committee met monthly to discuss college problems of all kinds, although most of the discussions were concerned with academic matters. Each department head in the college arranged for an election in the spring of each year for the selection of the departmental representatives to serve on the committee. Even though this democratic procedure was used to obtain representation from the faculty, dissatisfaction with the Professional Standards Committee was expressed frequently. Occasionally faculty members referred to the committee as the "President's Debating Club."

With neither commendation nor interference from the administration of the college, several members of the faculty banded together and organized a Faculty Association. Membership in the Faculty Association was limited to members of the teaching faculty in the college, and an estimated 25 to 30 per cent of the teachers had been persuaded to join the association and pay the $5 annual dues. Occasionally, a committee from the Faculty Association obtained an interview with Dr. Palmer and Dean Motte to present suggestions or complaints which had been generated from discussions at the meetings of the association. In some instances, the administration was able to take action upon these suggestions and complaints, but at other times it was necessary for Dr. Palmer or Dean Motte to explain to the committee why action could not be taken as suggested. Frequently, Dr. Palmer or Dean Motte took the complaints or grievances from the Faculty Association Committee to meetings of the Professional Standards Committee for analysis and consideration. Dean Motte believed that all communications from the Faculty Association should be discussed at meetings of the Professional Standards Committee, but Dr. Palmer felt that this was not necessary.

STUDENT PARTICIPATION

Soon after the opening of the 1968 fall semester, four students called on Dr. Palmer and Dean Motte—informing them that they had organized and were officers of a chapter of Students for Democratic Society (SDS). The students claimed that their SDS chapter was interested in more democratic procedures for the establishment of campus policies which affected the students. The student group apparently had received organizational assistance from several graduate students from the State University approximately 100 miles away. The elected officers reported that interest in SDS and discussions on the Hill City campus were being created by asking the question, "Who makes policy for this college?" When asked about the size of the SDS organization, the officers said that there were 15 or 20 members in the chapter but rapid growth was expected. Dr. Palmer asked each of the four SDS officers who called on him if they wished to meet regularly with a member of the administration, or if they preferred to wait and bring complaints or suggestions to the administration when they considered something was wrong with college policies or programs. Three of the four students replied that they would prefer to meet regularly, at least once each month with one of the college administrators; but the fourth student said he preferred to have SDS make an occasional review of college policies at the convenience of the group and then subsequently take their complaints, grievances, or suggestions to the administration.

Dr. Palmer also asked the students representing the SDS if they had endeavored to work with the Student Council which had been elected from the student body during the first month of school. The chairman of the SDS group replied, "The Student Council is all right in its way, but the Students for Democratic Society feel that the Student Council collaborates too closely with the administration and does not really represent the interests of students."

WHO'S IN CHARGE HERE?

The next day following his meeting with the SDS representatives, Dr. Palmer received two communications from his staff (see following memoranda). He was not sure whether he should discuss these memos with his entire administrative staff, take them to the Professional Standards Committee, discuss them in open meeting with the faculty, or perhaps even discuss them with student groups. While he was considering the alternatives, George Motte entered his office. "George," said Dr. Palmer, "these reports you and Remke have sent me are indicative of more serious problems. It seems to me that everybody either has or wants to run the college in his own way. What in the world can we do to get these situations under control and manage this place more effectively? We've got to think this out and come up with some better alternatives!"

Hill City Junior College
Memo

> To: Dr. Palmer, President
>
> From: George Motte, Dean of Instruction
>
> Re: (1) Purchasing Procedure
>
> (2) Class Meeting Schedules

1. A very conscientious instructor ordered an item of instructional equipment (a typewriter) through the regular channels. The item was budgeted and approved and the order was referred to the purchasing agent for processing. During the purchasing operation, the purchasing agent was convinced that the same item of equipment manufactured by a competitive company was much superior to the item ordered by the teacher. Not being able to reach the teacher during the summer recess, an order was placed for the substitute item. When the item of equipment arrived at the campus, the instructor expressed extreme displeasure because the machine would not do the copy work that he desired. He threatened to resign. What procedures need to be followed in a case like this?

2. It has come to my attention that considerable discussion is being carried on among the faculty concerning the concept of academic freedom, and whether or not the rights implied by this concept extend to such areas as punctuality in meeting classes and the early dismissal of classes without prior notification of the Office of Instruction. Department chairmen report that a number of the members of the faculty are of the opinion that it is the prerogative of an instructor to be ten or fifteen minutes late to class, and that such behavior in no way detracts from the effectiveness of the classroom situation. Further, there are members of the staff who believe that academic freedom implies the right to dismiss a class at any time the instructor decides that this is desirable for educational purposes. It is my opinion that instructors should be considerate of their students by arriving

at the class on time, and by providing a full fifty minutes of instruction in accordance with the printed schedule. This is not a change from any previous policy, but rather a continuation of a policy that has been in effect. It has been assumed that such a responsibility was accepted by staff members as a matter of course.

At a regular meeting of department chairmen, it was recognized that confusion did exist on the part of the faculty with respect to the policy in this area. The chairmen turned to the question of how this policy could be brought to the attention of the faculty without causing an unpleasant reaction from conscientious faculty members. After considering a number of possible alternatives, which included having the matter handled by the chairmen who would attempt to identify those involved in the practice and discuss the situation with them, it was the consensus of the group that a brief memorandum should be prepared for distribution to the faculty and insertion in the faculty manual. The memorandum was duly prepared and after being approved by the dean of instruction was disseminated to the staff. The memorandum stated that faculty members were expected to meet their classes on time and to provde for the full period of instruction listed in the schedule of classes. Dismissals of classes were to occur only with the prior approval of the office of instruction.

A number of faculty members were concerned about the memorandum. At the meeting of the Faculty Association attended by approximately thirty of the eighty staff members of the college, a motion was introduced to criticize the office of instruction for issuing the memorandum. The motion failed to gain sufficient support and was withdrawn in favor of a substitute motion that simply stated that faculty members should have the right to determine the length of their classes. The substitute motion passed on a vote of 16 to 12, and the president of the Faculty Association placed this item on the agenda for faculty and staff meetings to be held the following month.

Hill City Junior College
Memo

        To: Dr. Palmer, President

        From: A. E. Remke, Dean of Students

        Re: (1) Athletics and (2) Newspaper Advertising

1. Our present program of intercollegiate athletics has evolved informally out of our intra-mural activities. Either formally or informally, we now have teams representing our school in basketball, baseball, track and swimming. An autonomous administrative pattern developed as a result of the autonomous nature of an intra-mural program. These informal procedures are no longer suitable.

As you know, the local YMCA has generously cooperated with us and has shared their facilities including the swimming pool for our limited program. There is no policy statement for our program; no college regulations or guidelines; and no operating procedures in the area of inter-collegiate athletics.

We are faced with problems relating to organizational responsibility and faculty involvement, schedule construction, recruiting, conference affiliation, budgeting, income from gate receipts, income from advertising, athletic scholarships, etc.

2. In March, a student representative from the school newspaper came to the Dean of Students and requested that the paper's staff be permitted to sell advertising space. The student was asked that he submit his proposal in writing giving suggested rates. He did so, and the matter was discussed with the Dean of Instruction.

The decision was made to permit the newspaper staff to initiate an advertising office and to test the feasibility of the program during the few remaining issues of the newspaper for the current academic year.

The matter was informally discussed in the Student Personnel Services Committee pending official consideration of the matter by the President's Office. Some preliminary information was to be collected by one of the deans pertaining to rates for advertising space, the organization structure of an advertising operation, and guidelines for the selection of advertising copy.

During the summer months, little was accomplished due to the absence of key administrative personnel. At the beginning of the fall semester, work continued on the project.

In the meantime, the final draft of the student activity budget was being considered by the President's Office. The budget was constructed on the assumption that newspaper advertising would be continued and the income derived would be applied to the student activity budget. This income item was deleted from the student activity budget by the President's Office with the comment that advertising should not be permitted in any student publications without specific approval by the President's Office. In order to encourage worthwhile student activity, it is suggested that this decision regarding advertising for the student newspaper be reconsidered.

Hill City Junior College 163

Hill City Junior College Organization Chart

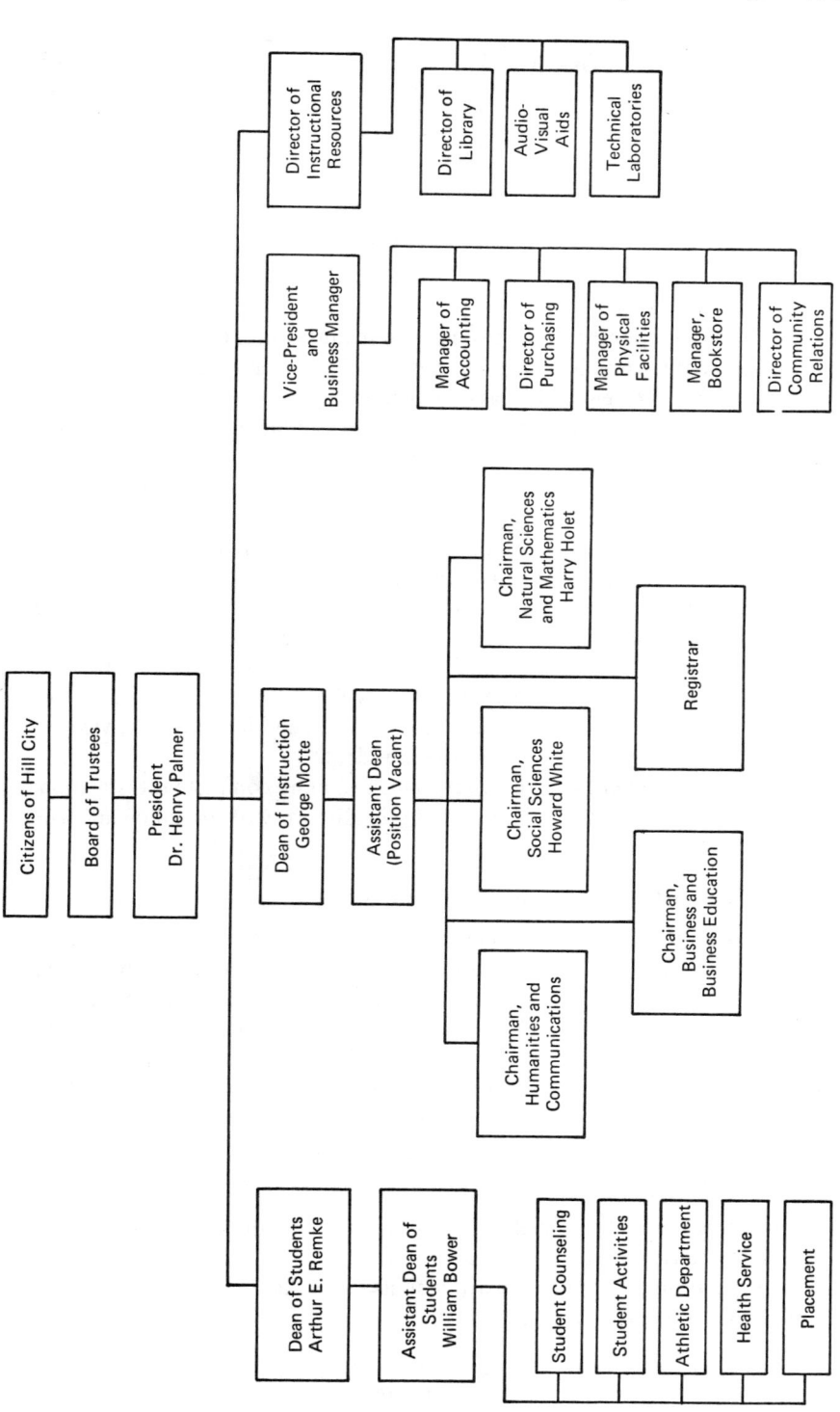

- Citizens of Hill City
- Board of Trustees
- President — Dr. Henry Palmer
  - Vice-President and Business Manager
    - Manager of Accounting
    - Director of Purchasing
    - Manager of Physical Facilities
    - Manager, Bookstore
    - Director of Community Relations
  - Director of Instructional Resources
    - Director of Library
    - Audio-Visual Aids
    - Technical Laboratories
  - Dean of Instruction — George Motte
    - Assistant Dean (Position Vacant)
      - Chairman, Humanities and Communications
      - Chairman, Business and Business Education
      - Chairman, Social Sciences — Howard White
      - Chairman, Natural Sciences and Mathematics — Harry Holet
    - Registrar
  - Dean of Students — Arthur E. Remke
    - Assistant Dean of Students — William Bower
      - Student Counseling
      - Student Activities
      - Athletic Department
      - Health Service
      - Placement

OSCAR METZ TOOL COMPANY   CASE 27

The Oscar Metz Tool Company is a closely held manufacturer of bottling and canning equipment located in a large midwestern city. It was organized in the early Twenties and in recent years has experienced rapid growth. The company hopes to double in size in the next ten years. At present Metz employs approximately 300 persons. It manufactures bottling and canning equipment to order. The entire management group takes great pride in the quality of their products and in the company in general.

The case writer was requested by the executive vice president to investigate the organizational structure of the manufacturing division of the company. A preliminary investigation revealed the following problems: (1) a tendency on the part of lower echelon managers to try to shift all possible decisions up to their superiors, (2) confusion on the part of most front-line supervisors regarding the functions and authority of the management levels above them and, (3) a tendency to bypass intermediate levels and to take problems and complaints to the vice president of manufacturing and even to the president.

Permission was granted the case writer to make a more complete investigation of the situation. This investigation resulted in the discovery of the following organizational problems:

THE ORGANIZATIONAL PROBLEM IN THE SHOP

The management group in manufacturing consisted of a vice-president of manufacturing, a shop superintendent, a night general supervisor, nine day supervisors, and four night supervisors. Although the manufacturing functions of the various supervisors are clearly defined and do not appear to offer a major problem, there are few clear-cut lines of authority. The shop superintendent believes that he reports to the president, but the vice-president of manufacturing believes that the shop superintendent reports to him. The shop superintendent believes that the nine day departmental supervisors report to him, but his opinion is not shared by many of the supervisors. They made the following comments:

1. The supervisor of the miscellaneous machining department says that he reports to the vice-president of manufacturing.
2. The supervisor of the lathe department also says that he reports to the vice-president of manufacturing.

Case prepared by Professor James C. Hodgetts of Memphis State University as a basis for class discussion. Reproduced by permission of the author.

164

3. The supervisor of the grinding department says he reports to the vice-president of manufacturing and to the miscellaneous machining supervisor.
4. The supervisor of the milling machine department says he reports to the production control manager and to the vice-president of manufacturing.
5. The supervisor of maintenance says that he reports to the shop superintendent and to the vice-president of manufacturing.
6. The supervisor of the drilling department says he reports to the shop superintendent and to the vice-president of manufacturing.
7. The supervisor of the tool and die room says he reports to the plant manager and to a minor degree to the chief engineer.
8. The supervisor of assembly says he reports to the president, vice-president of manufacturing and to the shop superintendent.

In summary it appears that only one of the nine day supervisors report entirely to the shop superintendent. Only three acknowledged a partial responsibility to him, and five did not even mention his name when asked who was their immediate boss. About the only undisputed authority the shop superintendent appears to have is in connection with the heat treat department, but he believes that he is in charge of the entire shop.

THE ORGANIZATIONAL PROBLEM IN PRODUCTION CONTROL

The production control manager says that he supervises the work of the shipping supervisor, the final inspection supervisor, and six clerks. Both the final inspection supervisor and the shipping supervisor say they report to both the production control manager and the vice-president of manufacturing. The milling machine supervisor says that he reports to the production control manager as well as to the plant manager. Other comments from the various production supervisors also indicate that the production control manager has some authority over them.

THE ORGANIZATION PROBLEM ON THE NIGHT SHIFT

Discussions with the four night supervisors, the night general supervisor, the vice-president of manufacturing, and the shop superintendent indicate differences of opinion relative to lines of authority on the night shift. The vice-president of manufacturing believes that the night general supervisor reports to him. So does the shop superintendent. The shop superintendent believes that the night general supervisor also reports to the president; but the night general supervisor says this is definitely not correct and that he reports to the vice-president of manufacturing. The vice-president of manufacturing believes that the night lathe supervisor reports to the day lathe supervisor but the night general supervisor does not believe a night lathe supervisor has been appointed but believes this should happen and that he should report to him. The person who believes that he is the night lathe supervisor says he reports to the night general supervisor. The vice-president of manufacturing believes the night supervisor of assembly reports to the day supervisors of both assembly and milling. However, the night supervisor of assembly says that he reports both to the day supervisor of assembly and to the night general supervisor. The night general supervisor says he reports to him. Both the night shipping supervisor and the night milling machine supervisor say they report to the vice-president of manufacturing, but the night general supervisor says that he is their immediate supervisor.

THE ALLEN COMPANY   CASE 28

EARLY HISTORY

The A. A. Allen Company was established in Middletown, Tennessee, in 1925 by the three Allen brothers, Amos, Joshua, and Benjamin. With funds left to them by their mother's family and money received from the sale of the family farm and its dairy herd, the brothers obtained an abandoned warehouse, purchased wood and metal working machinery and bench tools, and began the manufacture of lamps and lighting equipment.

With the help of relatives in Oregon City, the Allen brothers came in contact with a brilliant young man named Timothy Smith. Smith had acquired several patents in the electrical and lighting equipment field, but he lacked financial backing for his projects. He was persuaded to move to Middletown and join the new venture in a manufacturing partnership. In the newly formed firm, it was decided that the company's fortunes would be found in the manufacture of a high-grade line of table and floor-lighting fixtures. Smith proved to be an inventive genius and provided the Allen partnership with a considerable amount of technical "know-how." Although his fixture designs frequently lacked the beauty and esthetic appearance thought to be desirable by the Allen brothers, the firm's products were sold easily.

From the start, Benjamin Allen did most of the direct selling of the firm's products to stores in Atlanta, Nashville, and other cities. Smith and Joshua Allen were in charge of production, and Amos Allen assisted and coordinated work in all areas. After the first year of operation, a commercial artist was employed to work with Smith in both the design and production of an extensive line of table and floor lamps and lighting fixtures. The first production runs were small, but production and sales increased gradually and a reputation for quality products was established.

THE CORPORATION

By 1928 the firm was incorporated and had grown to the point where the original warehouse and an acquired three-story store building were inadequate. The store building was abandoned, and a more efficient two-story factory was built. The factory worked only one shift, employing fifty production workers; sixteen people worked in the office and four salesmen in the field. By this time, the Allen firm

Original version of this case contributed by William Schoppenhorst, Director of Management Development, Emerson Electric Co.

was one of the first lighting manufacturers in the United States to use fine grain wood in their products. The company was also well known for clever adaptations utilizing imported vases and globes for the bases of their lamps. It was known that some Allen fixtures were in the White House, and special order lamps were displayed prominently in the homes of many well-to-do people. The firm's quality production had been directed toward the market where price was not a significant factor and esthetic beauty and dependability were valued.

After the stock market crash of 1929 and during the ensuing depression, it was necessary for the company to review and reappraise its position and to consider the production of medium and low-priced products as well as luxury fixtures. Smith had developed a good understanding of the market, and he wanted the Allen Company to begin producing a low-priced but high-quality line of fixtures and lamps appealing to a larger market. Two of the Allen brothers did not agree with the philosophy which was required for the production of low-priced products, and a difference of opinion among the partners developed. This conflict was resolved when Joshua Allen and Timothy Smith purchased the interest of the other two Allen brothers, leaving the ownership and the management in the hands of Smith and one of the Allens.

Smith's idea to produce low- and moderately-priced but high-quality light fixtures was successful. One of the first products manufactured by the firm in quantity were student "study lamps." In the mid-1930's, the Allen Company organized and trained a sales and marketing team which proved to be highly successful in its new markets. Allen products were marketed from coast to coast, advertised in some of the leading magazines of the day as style setters, and the company sales increased greatly.

However, during World War II, the production of the Allen Company was shifted primarily to support the war effort. The firm maintained its reputation for producing high-quality products, with some of the company's regular lines being purchased and used in military installations. Government contracts for lighting equipment of various kinds resulted in the company doubling its production facilities. By improving truck dock facilities and generally improving its physical plant situation, the firm was left in an excellent position for civilian production when the war was over.

In the late 1940's, the Allen Company became associated in a marketing venture with a large chain of wholesale outlets. This organization provided an excellent method of marketing lighting fixtures which allowed the Allen Company to maintain a smaller sales staff than otherwise would be required. This reduction of overhead allowed the Allen Company to lower wholesale prices to their major distributors, who in turn accepted more and more of the Allen Company's products.

SECOND GENERATION MANAGEMENT

In 1950, John Smith, Timothy Smith's only son, completed requirements for an engineering degree at a nearby college and joined the Allen Company as a designer. Timothy Smith still remained an active member of the management organization, but he was showing less and less interest in the firm and more and more concern with his hobbies and sideline activities. J. B. Allen, Jr. was the only member of the Allen family still remaining in the management hierarchy, since his father, Joshua Allen, had died in 1947. J. B. Allen, Jr., had worked for the company for twenty years and since 1947 had carried the title of President of the Allen Company. Actually, he spent less than half of his time in Middletown working for the company. He maintained a home in Florida and had been married three times, his first two marriages ending in divorce

By 1958 John Smith was serving as plant superintendent. At about this time J. B. Allen, Jr., announced that he was interested in selling all of his stock in the Allen Company to anyone who was interested in purchasing it. Apparently, his increased debts caused by divorce settlements and alimony payments forced him to take this position. Unfortunately, Timothy Smith had recently relinquished some of his stock to a local bank which held loan papers and claims on some of his interesting but less profitable inventions and sideline activities. The outcome of this situation was that the owners of the Allen Company began to look for a larger corporation to acquire the firm, since the purchase price of between $7,000,000 and $8,000,000 did not appear to be available in the Middletown area.

THE MERGER

Both J. B. Allen, Jr., and Timothy Smith found that there were few individuals who understood the value of the Allen organization and who would pay a reasonable price for it. However, through the efforts of a law firm with offices in Nashville and Memphis, their investigations led to United Stores, Inc., a successfully diversified chain of department stores which was acquiring small manufacturing firms producing items marketable in their stores. This department store chain already had acquired a paint manufacturing firm, a toy manufacturer, and several bakeries. Large portions of the output of these manufacturing firms were sold in the company stores.

After a series of merger talks and some rather hard bargaining by Allen, Smith, and their lawyers, an agreement was reached. The Allen Company was sold to United Stores, Inc., with J. B. Allen, Jr., receiving approximately 57 per cent of the stock settlement and Timothy Smith receiving the remainder. Allen was elected to the board of directors of the "parent company" and was given the title of Divisional President of the Allen Division. Timothy Smith was made Vice-President and Plant Manager of the Allen Division.

Following a series of events which many of his friends considered to be unfortunate, Timothy Smith sold approximately two-thirds of his "parent company" stock when it was at a low point in the market. He then reinvested his proceeds from the stock sale in several unsuccessful experiments and part-time activities. For example, in the basement of his home he produced some rather ingenious products, a few of which were patentable, but none of which were successful commercially. Because of the mismanagement of his own funds and his problems as a manager, the parent company, United Stores, decided that Timothy Smith should retire two years early. Timothy Smith was agreeable to retirement, and he recommended that his son John be appointed Plant Manager of the Allen Division. This recommendation was accepted by the parent company.

For a number of years J. B. Allen, Jr., continued as President of the Allen Division, although he made only rare visits to the plant. John Smith became a successful manager and was given the title of divisional vice-president and plant manager. Under John Smith's management and with the help of the "parent company," the Allen Division prospered. The philosophy of the firm remained approximately the same, but its market penetration became stronger and sales increased. The parent company successfully injected some of its management philosophy and personnel into the operations of the Allen Division.

PERSONNEL AND ORGANIZATION

Early during the operation of the Allen Division as a subsidiary of United Stores, Mr. George Bracken was established by the parent organization as Treasurer and Controller of the Allen Division. In accordance with the policies of the parent organization, Bracken instigated a complete reorganization of the division's financial reporting procedures, and many new forms and systems were required. John Smith understood and accepted these changes, because he knew that the parent organization was interested in close financial control. There were times, however, when he appeared to be upset by Bracken who occasionally demonstrated an impatient and aggressive attitude. Under normal conditions, Bracken appeared to be an easygoing and likable person. Under duress and strain, however, Bracken became sullen and cold, threatening to make special reports to his former superiors in the home office. At times John Smith had difficulty in keeping his production manager, Pat Brown, and his sales manager, Clyde Hill, from reacting violently to Bracken's temperament. The production manager and the sales manager occasionally took exception to Bracken's methods and reacted slowly or not at all to Bracken's requests for cooperation.

The Allen Division was under John Smith's management when a local union made its first attempt to organize the production employees. In order to help the division oppose the union attempt, the "parent company" sent to Mr. Smith a bright, personable young industrial relations man, Bill Young, to help with management's strategy in the election campaign. Bill Young had acquired enough experience in union-management relations to do an excellent job in coordinating the plant's total efforts and to counsel the division's management and plant supervisors on what actions they should take during the organizing campaign. Through these efforts, directed by Bill Young, the union was defeated in a NLRB election by a margin of 131 to 73. This was an unusual achievement inasmuch as other manufacturing firms in the area had been unionized with little or no difficulty. John Smith was so pleased that he requested that Young be appointed the manager of employee relations on a permanent basis. The "parent company" agreed to this suggestion.

ORGANIZATIONAL RELATIONSHIPS

Bill Young was able to make a smooth transition and was accepted readily by most of the managers on John Smith's staff. He was looked upon with awe by most of the foremen and supervisors in the organization, and his pronouncements and suggestions were readily accepted. The one individual who did not completely accept the new manager of employee relations was Bracken, the treasurer and controller, the only other executive who had also been appointed by the home office. Upon occasion Bracken would openly defy Young's suggestions, and it would be necessary for Smith to intercede and settle the differences of opinion. As time went on, Smith had to settle more and more controversies, and he became less satisfied with the functioning of his staff.

Difficulties among management personnel apparently spread, and there also appeared to be considerable dissensions between Bill Young, Pat Brown, the production manager, and Frank Black, the longtime manager of quality control. Smith felt that there was too much bickering or playing "political games" in the organization. His staff meetings seemed to have two agendas: one he announced in advance and that was discussed superficially, and a "hidden" agenda that was voiced effectively in the undercurrents and innuendos in the managers' verbal interaction. In private discussions with Smith, various department heads criticized each other with considerable malice. This condition bothered Smith, and he felt it was affecting morale in some sections of the plant and possibly restricting production.

To further complicate organizational problems for Mr. Smith, the parent organization made a strong recommendation that Clyde Hill, the sales manager, be promoted to the level of assistant vice-president of marketing. United Stores felt that this move would enhance Mr. Hill's position in the marketing community and reward him for a job well done. On the surface Smith felt that this was a good move, because Hill had been effective and productive as sales manager, even though he was somewhat reserved and remote from the rest of the managers in his organization. Hill often had behaved as though production or plant problems had little connection with his sales activities. After considering the situation, Smith rejected the home office proposal and stated that the higher title for Hill would only increase the distance between Hill and other department heads. Smith reasoned that a difference in status for Hill would increase the possibility of additional conflicts and difficulties among the Allen Division management.

However, Smith's arguments were not accepted by the parent company, and Clyde Hill was promoted to the position of Assistant Vice-President of Marketing and Sales Manager for the Allen Division. While he still remained on Smith's staff, he was responsible also to the vice-president of sales in the parent organization. On the organization chart he appeared to be a member of the Allen organization; yet he also reported directly to the vice-president of sales in the United Stores hierarchy.

The relationship between Clyde Hill and the parent organization conveyed to John Smith the impression that the marketing and sales problems of the Allen

Division were removed from his responsibility. Nevertheless, Allen's market penetration was increasing and sales were improving continuously.

Partially as a consequence of the organizational changes, Smith maintained his closest working relationships with Pat Brown, manager of production, and Herb Hand, the day-shift superintendent and assistant production manager. These were old, experienced employees who had proven their worth to the organization and who were loyal to Smith. Smith also felt comfortable about his relationship with Frank Black, the manager of quality control, who had started employment with the company as an inspector fifteen years earlier.

In his position as manager of quality control, Frank Black maintained operating standards throughout the production facilities; in addition he provided staff assistance to both John Smith and Pat Brown. At times, Black was upset because his wife had a drinking problem which occasionally kept him off the job. This led further to a personality clash with Bill Young, the personnel manager, whom Black thought was trying to interfere with him by advising him on his personal family problems. Frequently, it was necessary for Smith to talk with Frank Black about being more understanding in working with Young and accepting some of the new "personnel procedures" which had been implemented in the company.

Smith had little trouble with Rus Reed, the traffic and receiving manager, who had joined the Allen Division about a year previous. Reed had graduated from the University of Tennessee in business administration and had worked for five years as a traffic manager at one of Allen's better competitors. It had been difficult to persuade Reed to move from the competitor to the Allen organization, but John Smith's promise of greater responsibility and more compensation had resulted in his move. However, Smith was concerned about the fact that Rus Reed's salary was almost as much as that of Clyde Hill, the assistant vice-president and sales manager. Smith felt that if this were known to the others, particularly to the "old-timers," a great deal of dissension in the organization would be created. Management salary administration had always been a confidential matter in the organization.

On one occasion there had been confusion in the handling of company mail which involved careless control of the sending of payroll records. Smith believed that a memorandum regarding Rus Reed's salary might have gotten into the hands of one of the other members of the staff. He was not sure, but some of the remarks made by Frank Black and Pat Brown had indicated that they "knew something they weren't talking about." There was also concern about the fact that Herb Hand, who had just completed his college degree in industrial engineering, was earning almost as much as Pat Brown, his supervisor, who had more than 10 years of additional experience with the company.

THE INCIDENT

While walking through the manufacturing plant, John Smith suffered a heart attack. He was immediately taken to the Middletown Hospital and put into intensive care. Two days after the heart attack, his physician and the specialist at the hospital reported that he would be incapacitated as far as work was concerned for at least nine months.

When the news of John Smith's hospitalization was circulated, J. B. Allen, Jr., announced that he would return from semi-retirement and play an active role in managing the Allen Division of United Stores, Inc. However, George Townsend, the Executive Vice-President in charge of Manufacturing of United Stores, notified Pat Brown that a manager from the home office would be sent to the Allen Division and would be in charge of all operations until further notice.

THE ASSIGNMENT

Steve Whitaker, a graduate mechanical engineer from Purdue University, had been with United Stores, Inc., or one of its subsidiaries for about fourteen years. He spent four years in the production department and two years as assistant sales manager with a paint company which was acquired by United. For about eight years, Whitaker had worked in the controller's division and as a staff assistant in the manufacturing division of the parent organization. During the previous eighteen months, he had been one of four special staff assistants to Mr. Townsend, the executive vice-president and director of manufacturing, and he enjoyed considerable success as an auditor and "trouble shooter."

Upon his return from a trip to several factories belonging to United Stores, Whitaker was called into Mr. Townsend's office and was told, "The company has a real problem. I would like to think that you could solve it for us. It could be the greatest opportunity you've ever had. The manager of our Allen Division has recently had a heart attack and the so-called president, J. B. Allen, who has been partially retired, thinks that he can come back to the company. We don't have much confidence in his ability to take charge, so we're telling him that it's too much of a job for one man. We are going to send him an experienced company manager. We'd like for you to go down there and take over. You probably remember John Smith, the manager who had the heart attack. He was beginning to have some problems with his organization, but we do believe that he has some very good men in the plant.

"There's another reason why you're needed down there and why this may be your greatest opportunity. Our acquisition boys are completing arrangements to take over another lighting fixture and lamp manufacturer, and most of this outfit's sales have been to mail order houses. This new company is in Atlanta, and it has had rather weak management and a poor sales organization. But its shop activities are good, and we plan to buy this outfit and integrate it into the Allen Division. If you will take this assignment, your first job will be to establish yourself as the real manager of the Allen organization, and then you could integrate this other plant into the division. As we see it, the present Allen production facilities can produce our higher quality products, and the new Atlanta plant could expand its mass production operations and produce our lower priced lines."

Steve Whitaker told Mr. Townsend that he had surveyed the Allen Division on three occasions, and he was quite familiar with the organization. He asked several questions about the move to Middletown, and then Mr. Townsend said, "Here is a chart of the Allen organization. I'd like for you to take a couple of days off, talk it over with your family, and tell me if you want to make this move. If you go down to Middletown you will be in complete charge—but you had better go along with J. B. Allen temporarily. We will advise you and help you from this office to the extent that you need it. Naturally, you will be expected to continue production of the division. Because J. B. Allen is on the board of United, you must be tactful; you should let him do what he wants to do, and let him help you if he can. You might even want to make him feel that you are helping him. However, in this emergency we will count on you running the division."

As he listened to these comments, Steve Whitaker became more and more interested. He stood up and said, "I can tell you now that this is very exciting news for me. I am almost positive that my answer is, 'yes, I'll go,' but I do want to go home and talk it over with my wife."

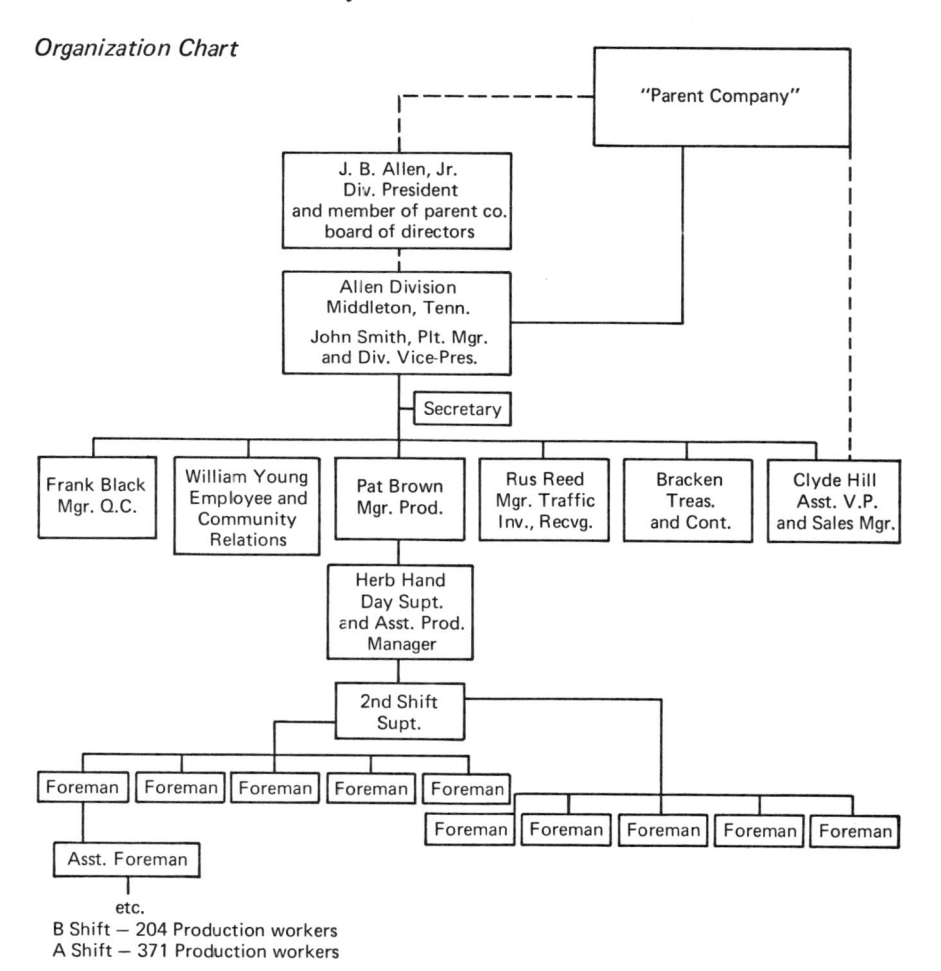

Organization Chart

```
                                    ┌──────────────────┐
                                    │  "Parent Company"│
                                    └──────────────────┘
                ┌──────────────────┐         │
                │ J. B. Allen, Jr. │         │
                │  Div. President  │─────────┤
                │and member of parent co.    │
                │ board of directors│        │
                └──────────────────┘         │
                         │                   │
                ┌──────────────────┐         │
                │ Allen Division   │         │
                │ Middleton, Tenn. │         │
                │John Smith, Plt. Mgr.│      │
                │and Div. Vice-Pres.│        │
                └──────────────────┘         │
                         │ ┌─Secretary       │
```

- Frank Black, Mgr. Q.C.
- William Young, Employee and Community Relations
- Pat Brown, Mgr. Prod.
- Rus Reed, Mgr. Traffic Inv., Recvg.
- Bracken, Treas. and Cont.
- Clyde Hill, Asst. V.P. and Sales Mgr.

Under Pat Brown:
- Herb Hand, Day Supt. and Asst. Prod. Manager
- 2nd Shift Supt.
- Foreman | Foreman | Foreman | Foreman | Foreman
- Foreman | Foreman | Foreman | Foreman | Foreman
- Asst. Foreman

etc.
B Shift — 204 Production workers
A Shift — 371 Production workers

PART FIVE

Frazer's Department Store (B)
Paragon Pulp & Paper Company, Ltd.
Simmons Retail Chain Store
Valley Metal Products Company
John Edwards
Petri Chemical Company (A) and (B)
Management Development at the Ford Motor Company
Incident in a Government Agency: The Unqualified Examiner

Selection and Development

The personnel selection and development functions of management are not separate activities, but are parts of a continuous process directly focusing on the acquisition and maintenance of human resources in the business concern. The selection and development of workers should not be isolated from other organizational processes, because all personnel management activities are part of a total system of organizational behavior. However, the cases in this section have been grouped together for sake of convenience and to emphasize the importance of the employment function. They are primarily concerned with the procurement, the training, and the development of people for the business enterprise.[1]

SELECTION

A firm's personnel policies in hiring employees are most critical. The success or failure of a firm hinges upon the skills and abilities of its management and operating personnel. It is necessary, therefore, to formulate policies and plans to obtain access to a supply of qualified people and to carefully choose from this supply those who can contribute most to the objectives of the organization.

The selection problems of personnel management are an interrelated, ordered series of problems. These are as follows:

---

[1] For a thorough discussion of selection and development processes see Wendell French, *The Personnel Management Process*, Second Edition (Boston: Houghton Mifflin Co., 1970).

1. What are the firm's manpower needs; what types of personnel are required and in what numbers?
2. What sources of labor supply can be used to obtain the necessary personnel? Are both inside and outside sources readily available?
3. What methods and promotions should be used to encourage the "right" people to seek employment with the firm?
4. What selection procedures should be used to decide which applicants to choose for what positions?[2]

The first of these problems primarily involves analyzing manpower needs. More and more companies recognize the importance of looking into future operating plans and carefully estimating the number and types of employee and managerial skills that will be needed, both for the present and for years to come. This forecasting includes considering such factors as the size and composition of the existing work force, the plan for company growth, the anticipated changes in operating technology, and projected turnover of personnel. With manpower planning of this magnitude, more accurate labor cost budgets and employment office schedules may be developed.

The second and third problems of selection are both part of the *recruitment* function. Many firms hold to a policy of "promotion from within," normally employing inexperienced and untrained people only for beginning jobs; others attempt to fill all or certain key positions by attracting competent and experienced personnel from other concerns. Regardless of these differing policies, at one time or another every firm must look to the labor market to fill job openings, and recruitment policies are formulated to attract qualified people. Many companies have recently increased their efforts to recruit graduates of schools and colleges. Representatives are sent to educational institutions of all kinds to describe employment opportunities in their firms and to interview interested prospective graduates. Today, the college recruiter is an important official within the personnel department of most large corporations.

Other sources of labor supply include employment agencies (private or state-operated) and newspaper advertisements. The agencies and the classified sections serve as major outlets through which firms announce job opportunities. Some firms use employment agencies, newspaper advertisements, and school recruiting simultaneously and continuously to attract sufficient job applicants to meet their employment needs. But the success of all these procedures is dependent upon the public image of the company as a good place to work. In many instances the word-of-mouth advertising of a firm's reputation is a major asset in interesting friends and relatives of employees to seek employment with the firm. The flow of applicants to the employment office is increased through aggressive recruiting methods, but in the long run the good-will developed in the community is a valuable asset for the employer. A reputation for quality products or services and

---

[2] George Strauss and Leonard R. Sayles, *Personnel: The Human Problems of Management*, Second Edition (Englewood Cliffs, N.J.: Prentice-Hall, Inc. 1967), pp. 449-485.

for sound personnel policies may be the principal reasons applicants seek employment with particular firms.

The fourth and final selection problem is determining the best-qualified individuals from among applicants who actually apply for work in the firm. Most selection techniques attempt to place people in positions for which they are educationally, technically, and personally suited by balancing the capacities and interests of workers with the requirements and opportunities of jobs.[3] Carefully prepared *job descriptions,* which describe the nature of duties and responsibilities involved in a job and *job specifications* which list the personnel attributes and skills required of the job holder, are valuable tools in the selection procedure. Job descriptions facilitate the preliminary screening of applicants by providing job information which can be easily compared with the personal information supplied by the applicant on the written application form. The *job interview* is usually the most important selection technique. Employment managers and other executives use the interview situation to study the individual applicant and to appraise his abilities and personal characteristics. Interviewing is not a precise technique, but the skillful interviewer is able to ascertain information about the interviewee which, when coupled with other selection criteria, is significant in the decision to accept or reject the applicant for employment. In brief, the objectives of the job interview are (1) to obtain information about the applicant, (2) to give information about the employer and the job opening, and (3) to make a new friend for the company.

Another selection technique that is frequently a part of the employment procedure is *personnel testing.* When administered to job applicants, tests attempt to measure certain traits or qualifications more objectively and more accurately than could be appraised in the interview. Their validity and reliability vary greatly with different tests and in different situations. They are most successful when test results are viewed as additional information to supplement the other criteria used for personnel selection and placement. Among the most useful tests for industrial employment work are certain achievement tests, mental ability (intelligence) and aptitude tests. Personality tests are sometimes used in an attempt to determine an individual's psychological make-up. They have been used primarily in evaluating candidates for management or professional positions, since a successful manager must be able to deal effectively with people. In general, however, the validity of personality testing in the industrial situation has been questioned. The complexity of individual human beings and the difficulty in isolating leadership traits indicate that personality tests have questionable validity in the selection of executives. On the other hand, personality tests are tools of the clinical psychologist, whose services can be of considerable value to the industrial employment office.

DEVELOPMENT

The development process is one which theoretically begins when an employee starts work with a firm and continues throughout his tenure of employment.

[3] See Stanley Sokolik, *The Personnel Process: Line and Staff Dimensions in Managing People at Work* (Scranton, Pa.: International Textbook Company, 1970), pp. 207-223.

Orientation training, the introduction of the worker to his job, formal and on-the-job training, job rotation and promotion, performance evaluation and correction, various skill training programs, and other factors are all part of the personnel development process.

The purpose of personnel training and development is for employees to acquire and maintain the necessary skills, capabilities, and personal capacities to more adequately contribute their services towards the fulfillment of objectives of the firm. One of these organizational goals is for workers to maximize their accomplishments and job satisfactions. Newly-hired employees need training to begin their work; older workers need training to keep them aware of the changing requirements of their jobs and to qualify them for transfers and promotions.

Training is also related to employee motivation. Employees who know and understand their jobs and who feel that management values them enough to prepare them for future assignments are more likely to demonstrate higher morale and greater interest in job performance.

The techniques and procedures for the training and development of workers in business and industry are diverse, and they are described in most personnel management textbooks. Personnel training is generally effective to the degree that it is tailored to fit the particular needs of the organization and the individuals being trained. Some training programs are designed to convert or change attitudes of employees towards a company point of view. These efforts are apt to fail unless employees are able to identify such a view with their own goals and their own set of experiences. Recent research has disclosed that there is often a basic conflict between the objectives and needs of a business organization and those of the individual worker. In this context, the training and development program can contribute to a lessening or a reconciliation of this conflict. Thus, a challenge and an opportunity is presented to every manager in working with each individual employee to make the employee better able to serve the firm while at the same time realizing a greater satisfaction of his individual needs and aspirations.

The area of management development and promotion has received considerable attention since World War II. The depression of the 1930's and the urgencies of a great war reduced the supply of business executives. After the war, however, business concerns found that their strength and growth depended upon capable management. Management capability includes a firm's capacity to secure and develop competent talented personnel who are able to step in and take over major responsibilities as other executives leave or retire. Again, many different types of management development programs are used. Some organizations have designed elaborate, formal programs in which selected managers are moved from job to job and are given specialized training to prepare for specific executive positions. Other concerns leave job rotation and the acquisition of experience to normal executive turnover. The employment, training, and development of carefully selected college graduates is a common procedure for the building of a management organization. Some companies, however, believe that management-development programs should not be confined to just a few key people, since this may overlook competent individuals deserving of higher positions. They believe that the most effective management-development program involves all levels of management.

For many companies, especially the larger ones, the executive development program has become an important part of overall management training. Some of these are "in-company" programs sponsored for the men within an organization by the company itself or by consultants. University programs or courses sponsored by professional associations for business executives are also popular, for they provide managers with the broadening experience of studying and exchanging ideas with experienced men from other companies and other industries. All of these activities indicate that top management places a high priority upon the development of its human resources. Executives appreciate opportunities to broaden their vision and improve their managerial skills. In addition, the dynamics of a progressive organization are accompanied by an atmosphere conducive to competition for promotions and healthy attitudes within the management organization.

FRAZER'S DEPARTMENT STORE (B)— A COLLEGE SENIOR VIEWS THE EMPLOYMENT PROCESS

CASE 29

Frazer's Department Store has approximately 800 employees and about 325 of them are sales people. The personnel department consists of Mr. Stone, the personnel manager; Mrs. Willoughby, the training supervisor; and four or five others whom I have not met. Mr. Stone is a very busy man. I was employed as a salesman in the men's furnishings department.

First, it is important to tell you of my attitude and my opinion of a job at Frazer's before my interview for employment. I had a very high regard for the store's merchandise, employee relations, and customer contacts. I also had the idea that as a college senior I was going to be treated on a higher level than other employees. I believed this, not because I thought myself superior to the other employees, but because of my college education and my previous retail training. I also believed that my store service would not only be a job, but something of an educational program in merchandising, publicity, personnel, and organization.

I had two interviews before I actually started my selling job. My first interview was with Mr. Stone. (Before the interview, I filled out an application blank which asked for details about my work experience and personal information.) I sat in the personnel office a few minutes waiting for Mr. Stone. When he walked in, he introduced himself to me in an uninterested and indifferent manner. (I hope I do not sound overcritical, but it is the truth.) We then proceeded to his office. He did not ask me to be seated, but after a few moments of hesitation I sat down. I expected him to start the conversation, so I remained silent while he looked over my application blank. After two or three minutes of silence he asked me a few questions about my previous employment. He then read my application blank again. Up to this time I had felt confident and relaxed, but because of the silence and Mr. Stone's seemingly indifferent attitude, I began to feel slightly nervous. He then interrupted the silence by saying, "At the present time there are no openings, but we will call you when we want you to start. You'd better wear a necktie when we call you back." I then said good-bye and left.

After being notified two weeks later that Frazer's had an opening for me, I received my second interview. I was interviewed by Mrs. Willoughby, who is an assistant to Mr. Stone. She is a charming, tactful, and courteous woman. Through-

---

Many colleges and universities are integrating work experiences and educational programs for certain students. Some of these programs, called "cooperative courses," provide that students work in industry for one term and then attend school the next. Other programs require students to work in business or industry for shorter periods of time. This case is a student report pertaining to his experience in a department store.

out the entire interview she seemed interested in my problems and questions, and she made me feel important and comfortable.

At the beginning of the interview, she told me of the different positions that were open and asked me which job I would prefer. It was this consideration which gave me a feeling of importance. We then agreed on the job best suited for me, and she courteously said good-bye. Because of Mrs. Willoughby, my attitude toward Frazer's again changed (for the better). Mrs. Willoughby made me a friend of the store.

The day after my final interview, Mrs. Willoughby, who is also in charge of training new employees, took me and two others into a conference room and started our training. The room was very comfortable; it was equipped with a round table, ash trays, and fairly comfortable chairs. We were allowed to smoke. She handed us a pamphlet on store rules and regulations which she explained, clarifying the policies and explaining why the rules were important.

After acquainting us with store regulations, she taught us how to write the different types of sales checks (charges, deliveries, cash sales, will-call, and C.O.D.). She used a good procedure in teaching us different transactions. Each of us was handed a sales book; she then took each kind of purchase, told us how to write it up, and then she wrote out an example and showed it to us. She then described another transaction, and we wrote it up independently, and she checked the final results. After going through each type of sale, she gave us a review and stressed the important points to remember. Before closing the session, Mrs. Willoughby told us that if we had any problems, we should "come up and see her" and she "would try to straighten them out."

During the entire session, Mrs. Willoughby appeared to be an excellent teacher and a charming individual. There is only one criticism I had about my centralized training, and that is I was not informed about the exact duties of my job. Apparently, Mrs. Willoughby did not give us much information about our jobs, because she expected our supervisors to do that.

After my training in the personnel department, Mrs. Willoughby took me to the men's furnishings department and introduced me to the floorwalker who seemed to be a courteous and respected person. He, in turn, introduced me to a salesman in my department, who showed me the stock and introduced me to some "tricks-of-the-trade." This initial introduction was brief and quite inadequate.

I wasn't introduced to the head of my department and, therefore, I did not know who my boss was. Besides not being introduced to my boss, I also wasn't introduced to any of the other salesmen. From the way some salesmen acted, I thought they resented my presence in the department.

Another inadequacy of my job introduction was the failure to inform me of the proper techniques of selling including wrapping packages and making change. I wasn't told exactly what was expected of me.

Numerous problems arose from these shortcomings. Before I learned who was my boss, a salesman told me to go eat lunch, which I did. When I came back, the boss of the department met me and was angry. Our relationship was complicated and disagreeable from the start.

Another problem arose from the improper introduction to my job. My boss saw me wrapping a package in what he thought was an incorrect way; nobody had told me the proper method. He reprimanded me, and then took his own time to teach me what he considered to be the proper method. Other salesmen wrap packages differently. This could have been avoided, if I had been taught correctly in the first place.

Since I wasn't told exactly what duties I was to perform, I had only a general idea of what was expected of me. During the period I worked in this specific department, I thought that the work I performed was adequate. After a few weeks on the job, however, I was notified that I was only doing an average amount of work and that they expected much more from me. I am positive that this episode could have been avoided if I had known exactly what was expected of me.

PARAGON PULP & PAPER COMPANY, LTD.

CASE 30

"Sure, we'll be glad to give you all the information you want on our personnel selection method. Why don't you talk to Bill Gilroy first, though. He's our office manager and the man who does the actual interviewing and evaluation."

John Humphrey was the manager of the newest of the Paragon Pulp & Paper Company's two Vancouver plants. The plant, which he had designed and now supervised, produced a heavy duty draft stock for use in making paper boxes and containers. The new plant had been in production about a year and a half.

Paragon Pulp & Paper maintained a standard personnel selection method at each of its plants. This method had been worked out by a management consulting firm, together with the company's industrial relations vice-president, a former Austrian who held degrees in psychology and law. Company management attributed a considerable portion of the company's low turnover rate, among the lowest in the industry, to its personnel selection method. Both John Humphrey and Bill Gilroy also felt that their success in attaining an efficient level of production six months ahead of schedule was due in large part to this method.

The formal paperwork required by this method of selecting plant personnel was comprised of three main parts: an application form, Exhibit 1; a test of reasoning ability called Progressive Matrices; and a patterned interview form, Exhibit 2. Evaluations resulting from these three sources and face-to-face contact were recorded on a summary form contained in Exhibit 3. Bill Gilroy, office manager, had spent three days at a course given by the management consulting firm to instruct potential users in the administration, application, and evaluation of this series of selection method.

The functions of the overall system, in Bill Gilroy's opinion, were (1) to determine, insofar as possible, an applicant's reasoning power, personal compatibility, and stability, and (2) on the basis of the final summary, to permit selection of the proper men for jobs in the plant.

Each step in the process served as a screening, which started when an applicant obtained an application form from the office receptionist and continued until a man had successfully completed the required one-month probationary period in the plant. This latter final screening was spelled out in the company's union agreement, the relevant article of which is contained in Exhibit 4. (For exhibits, see pages 190 through 202.)

Reprinted by the permission of the Faculty of Commerce, University of Alberta, Edmonton, Canada. Copyright, by the University of Alberta. All names, places, certain wage data, and dates disguised.

"You'd be surprised," said Bill Gilroy in describing the first screening, "but we've had people come in for a job who are obviously drunk. We don't waste much time in dealing with them. Similarly, we'll get applicants who might be what I call miscast—their social tendencies might be bad. This is the type that says in a loud voice to our receptionist, 'Get me the big boss—I don't want to speak to the office manager.' Finally there are the one-armed, the cripples, the paraplegics and so on. The physical requirements of the jobs we have to offer are beyond the abilities of this latter group. In most of these cases, I go out to the man and tell him at the present, there are no openings, but leave his name—we'll call him, he needn't call us—you know the routine."

The next step in the process required the filling out of the standard application form. Bill said, "We're looking for several things here, some general and some specific. As an example of the former, take the way a man fills out the form. You can tell if a man's careless and sloppy, or if he's ambitious enough to take a little care when he fills in the form. Basically, the application form gives me a brief look at the man before the interview. Take his date of birth—this gives me an idea of what job he can hold. What about his residence? If it's a fashionable address, what's he doing here? How long has he lived in the same place? This gives you an idea as to a man's stability. Of course, if he has been working in the construction field, I expect him to have moved around a lot. What kind of earnings does a man expect? If he wants $3.50 an hour, why? I'm going to offer him $1.96.

"Another thing I check for in the application form is the number of children a man has. If he's got too many, he's out. You can't support six or seven kids in Vancouver on monthly wages of $350, but a man's not going to make more than that when he starts with us. So he just couldn't do it without some other income; unrest and trouble would eventually result. I also find out in the interview what type of car a man has, because where we are, just outside the city, you really need a car. Of course, a man doesn't have to have a car, but it helps. To get back to the application form, I want to know how much education a man has had. We're not looking for men with university degrees, either. I've found that if a man with a degree applies for a job in our plant, getting that degree was probably the last constructive thing he did in his life. But if a man has been to trade school, or a business school, that's O. K.

"Then I take a look at a man's extra-curricular activities, if any, and especially at any offices he might have held. This gives you an idea of a man's initiative, and willingness, and desire to lead. Similarly, as far as a man's military service goes, I look for a man who was promoted—indicating some ambition. I begin to wonder about the man who went in and came out a private; professional privates, they call them.

"Finally, I look at a man's record of employment, on the back of the application form, especially the last five years. There are eight spaces, and if a man says that's not enough for five years (unless he's been in construction work) we don't want him. We seldom bother to check a man's references if it involves anything more than a phone call."

The next step in the selection procedure was the Progressive Matrices test. This test on which there was no time limit was comprised of five sections of twelve problems each.

Each section was progressively more difficult than the previous one. The test was designed to compare people with respect to their capacities for observation and clear thinking. It was "a test of a person's capacity at the time of the test to apprehend meaningless figures presented for his observation, see the relations between them, conceive the nature of the figure completing each system of relations presented, and by doing so, develop a systematic method of reasoning."

The scoring of this test involved two steps. First, each of the five sections was graded from 0 to 12, depending on the number right. Secondly, the five separate scores were added together to attain a final score. This score was then related to a scale divided into five parts, I, II, III, IV, and V, I representing the highest bracket, III the average and V the lowest. In addition, each score, whether I, II, etc., was given a "stability" rating, determined by a man's separate scores on the five parts. For example, the normal distribution for a total score equivalent to a III for a man aged 45 would be progressive scores on the five parts of 10, 8, 7, 7, 3. A man whose separate scores deviated from these norms by more than two in any one case (for example 10, 9, 4, 4, 3) was thereby considered erratic.

"We don't want the erratic type," Bill Gilroy commented, "and people can be erratic whether they're brilliant or not. Almost every time I've hired somebody whose Matrices' test result on two individual sections or more was off by more than two from the norm, thereby indicating he was erratic, there's been trouble. One example is a man whose test results showed him to be erratic—I hired him—and found out later he was an alcoholic—a highly excitable type. Another man, who was a fork truck driver in the plant, all of a sudden blew up at the plant superintendent one day, and we had to let him go. The funny thing is, though, he'd formed a social club among some of the fellows in the plant that collapsed when he left.

"Basically, with this test we're looking for men who can reason. Any one below a score of Grade III is automatically out with rare exceptions—and we fell flat on our face in every case. One good example involves a young woman who came to Vancouver from Edmonton, with her six-month old child. She told me she's left her husband, who was 20 to 25 years older than she, and who wasn't taking good care of her. She really needed a job. Even though she was Grade IV on the Matrices test, I gave her a job plus an advance in wages. She told me she felt she hadn't done her best on the test, so a couple of weeks later I let her take it again—and she barely made Grade III. Then she started being absent for sickness—either she was sick or the child was sick. Well, we reserve to let a person go if their absentee rate indicates that the work is adversely affecting their health, so I called her in and pointed that out to her. She was O. K. for two or three weeks, but then it was the same old story, so the plant supervisors were forced to release her.

"I've found that people who score Grade III on the Matrices test are the workers, while people with Grade II have the top jobs. Some of the men in Grade III appear stupid in the interview as a defense mechanism, but I've found this type often makes a good routine worker. Of course, you can't equate reasoning power alone with ambition, and the desire to take responsibility.

"We will take people with a score of Grade I, subject to their having the right background. They're too mentally active for the type of job we have here—they tend to ask questions that aren't necessary to get the job done. We have one man in the category. Similarly, because of our seniority clause, we're cutting down on the number of Grade II's we take. We can, if the senior man is not qualified to take the responsibility, jump him. We haven't had much trouble with this situation, however, because usually an unqualified, although senior, man will refuse the promotion."

The next step in the screening process for a job applicant involved the patterned interview conducted by Bill Gilroy, using the form shown in Exhibit 2. The interview ordinarily took 20 to 30 minutes, unless, as Bill said, "a man was frightened, reticent, or opposed." Each man, before the actual interview started, was assured that he did not have to answer any questions he did not want to. Bill felt, however, that any man who did not want to answer all questions directly was leaving himself open to indirect questioning to determine the necessary information.

"In the interview," Bill said, "I look for quite a few things, as you can see from the form. The main thing the questions bring out is a man's stability, and as far as his personal compatability goes, I get a good idea of that by the way he conducts himself in the interview, and then of course there's the thirty-day probationary period on the job. I'm always thinking of the summary sheet (Exhibit 3) as I go along.

"A man has to prove himself in the interview. If the man is obviously trying to gain sympathy from me, say by telling me about his aches and pains, I usually don't want him. This type of thing will carry over to the job. One question I think is pretty important is the one, 'When did you have your last drink?' Typically a man will hesitate a moment, and then remember the beer he had a few nights ago, and then he might mention the drink he had at his birthday party, or something like that. But when a man says, 'I had my last drink at 2 o'clock on such and such a day and year,' watch out! The man, 99 out of 100 times, is, or was, a confirmed alcoholic. Any man that can tell you to the minute the last time he had a drink is the worst risk from the alcoholic point of view.

"I deliberately hired two alcoholics not long ago. When they're sober, they'll work twice as hard as any one around them—to punish themselves. You can't put them on the line, because when they're out there will be a hole. Maintenance, stores, etc., are O. K. for this type. One of the two I hired had been a major league pitcher, and had owned his own furniture manufacturing outfit. I thought he'd be able to transfer his knowledge, but he couldn't do it; the job was too broad for him.

"Another thing I definitely look for is the man who is accident-prone. That's the only way I can think of saying it, but I don't like the expression. I check on health, car accidents, and the last accident on their former jobs. Of course, a man with too many accidents tries to hide it, but it usually always comes out.

"I also look for a smooth domestic life. It's almost a prerequisite. I like to see a good healthy home life too. For one thing, with poor health in the family, a man usually needs extra money. As far as our plant goes, we have voluntary medical service insurance with the cost carried by the workers, but no hospitalization insurance. Vancouver, the city, that is, has a plan that helps out there.

"We have some fringe benefits, but don't forget this plant is still growing and right now we can't afford to commit ourselves more to these expenditures. Take our wage spread—from a base rate of $1.96 up to $3.33. That $1.96 might be a little low, but we deliberately tried to start low in anticipation of union demands.

"Notice the questions about an applicant's financial situation. Here I'm looking for the man in the middle. You'd be surprised how many people come in here and tell me about the farm their father left them, from which they might be earning $6,000 a year. It's not hard to predict that these people aren't going to be the steadiest workers in the world. They just aren't hungry. On the other hand, we can't take people who are too hungry, with too many mouths to feed, as I mentioned before.

"Single girls on their own are especially bad. It's typical of them to say, in answer to my questions as to how much they need a month, 'Oh, I can live on $250 a month.' Then when I ask them about the payments on the coat they're wearing, and their car, rent, and so on, they'll say 'Oh, *gosh,* guess I can't live on a $250.' Eventually, they realize it will be tough for them to live on the wages that we pay."

The final step in the selection process required Bill Gilroy to fill out the Selection & Evaluation Summary form, as shown in Exhibit 3. Bill filled out this form from information and opinions he obtained from the application form, the Matrices test, and the patterned interview. Applicants were rated "Outstanding," "Good," "Marginal," or "Poor" in comparison with men actually working in the plant, and not against any outside standard. Bill explained that the ideal applicant would have a series of checkmarks distributed between the first three categories—from "Outstanding" to "Marginal." "We don't want a man with too many 'Poor' checks," Bill said, "but neither do we want a man who is the opposite—too outstanding. It just wouldn't work out."

"I first used this method," Bill said, "when we were just starting up. Another fellow from the company was helping me. Then last year, when we added a second shift, the other fellow and I had to hire another 60 men, and we had over 300 applicants. Ordinarily though, I'd say we reject about 65% of the people who apply for jobs. Right now, we're back to one shift, so we've got a backlog of men with experience on our seniority list that aren't working right now. The last six months, we've had about one or two applicants a month.

"Even though on two occasions we needed a lot of men in a relatively short time, I can think of only one instance where we hired a man who didn't pass through the selection procedure, and that was due to coincidence. A foreman called me up and said he needed a man on the line right away and at the same time a fellow was outside just starting to fill out his application form. He was out in the plant before the ink was dry."

"There are some men in the plant now that I wouldn't hire today. They're chiefly the ones in the 45-60 age bracket. They're able to reason, but they are not as alert physically as they should be. Older men sometimes lack that certain something that is necessary on production jobs requiring continual judgment.

"What we try to do, if possible, is give these men 'prestige' jobs though we have only a few. One example is our First-Aid man. Although he's on a low paying job, he gets a bonus—10¢ an hour—for his first-aid job. He's between the devil and the deep blue sea, which is where we want him. You see, we have a 4-cent spread between rates, and if this man were promoted up one notch, he realizes he'd probably lose the 10¢ bonus—in other words he'd be out 6¢. So he's happy right where he is.

"Sometimes you have people who hunger for authority. We occasionally put a man on the safety committee to satisfy his hunger. The union's the same way—they provide positions that have the prestige and authority.

"The important thing is to keep the plant operating efficiently," Bill concluded, "and if it is not operating all this red tape and all our records are meaningless. We are attempting to keep it going as efficiently as possible. The plant is the be-all and end-all."

Appendix:
Exhibits 1 through 4

Exhibit 1 *Paragon Pulp and Paper Co. Application for Employment*

Name_____ Date_____

(please print plainly)   Home Tel. No._____

Present address No._____ Street_____ City_____ Province_____ How long have you lived there?_____

Previous address No._____ Street_____ City_____ Province_____ How long did you live there?_____

Position applied for?_____ Earnings expected $_____

PERSONAL

Sex: ☐ M, ☐ F; Date of birth _____ 19___	☐ Single, ☐ Married, ☐ Separated	No. children_____ Their ages_____
Height ___ ft. ___ in. Weight ___ lbs.	☐ Engaged, ☐ Widowed, ☐ Divorced	No. other dependents_____ Ages_____
Are you a Can. citizen? ☐ Yes, ☐ No	Date of marriage_____	U.I.C. No._____

Do you: ☐ Own your home? ☐ Rent? ☐ Live with relatives? ☐ Board? ☐ Stay with friends? Other_____

(If you rent) What monthly rent do you pay? $_____ Do you own your furniture? ☐ Yes, ☐ No

Is your wife employed? ☐ No, ☐ Yes, part time, ☐ Yes, full time; What kind of work?_____ Her earnings $_____ per_____

Do you carry life insurance? ☐ No, ☐ Yes; Amount $_____

What physical defects do you have?_____

In case of emergency, notify_____ Name_____ Address_____ Phone_____

EDUCATION

Type of School	Name and Address of School	Courses Majored in	Check Last Year Completed				Graduate? Give Degrees	Last Year Attended
			5	6	7	8		
Elementary			1	2	3	4	☐ Yes, ☐ No	19
High School			1	2	3	4	☐ Yes, ☐ No	19
University			1	2	3	4		19
University			1	2	3	4		19
Graduate School			1	2	3	4		19
Business or Trade School			1	2	3	4		19
Corresp. or Night School			1	2	3	4		19

Scholastic standing in H. S.? _____ University? _____

EXTRACURRICULAR ACTIVITIES (athletics, clubs, etc.)
(Do not include military, racial, religious, or nationality groups)

In high school _____ In college _____

Offices held _____ Offices held _____

MILITARY SERVICE

Have you had Military Service? ☐ Yes, ☐ No; (If yes) Date enlisted _____ 19 _____

Which Service? _____ What branch of that Service? _____ Starting Rank _____

Date of discharge _____ 19 _____ Rank at discharge _____

Form No. OA-201

Copyright, 1959, The Dartnell Corporation, Chicago 40, Ill., Printed in U. S. A.
Developed by The McMurry Company

Exhibit 1 (continued)

WORK HISTORY

List below the names of all your employers, beginning with the most recent: a. Employer's Name b. Business Address	Kind of Business	Time Employed				Nature of Work	Starting Salary	Salary at Leaving	Reasons for Leaving	Name of Immediate Superior
		From		To						
		Mo.	Yr.	Mo.	Yr.					
1. a. b.										Name Title
2. a. b.										Name Title
3. a. b.										Name Title
4. a. b.										Name Title
5. a. b.										Name Title
6. a. b.										Name Title
7. a. b.										Name Title
8. a. b.										Name Title

Indicate by number _____ any of the above employers whom you do not wish us to contact. Why: _____

References (Not former employers or relatives)	Address	Phone Number
1.		
2.		
3.		

Are there any other experiences, skills, or qualifications which you feel would especially fit you for work with our Company? _____

If your application is considered favorably, on what date will you be available for work? _____ 19 ____ Signature _____

APPLICANT SHOULD NOT WRITE BELOW THIS LINE

Comments _____

Interviewer: _____

Selection and Development

Exhibit 2 *Patterned Interview (Short Form)*

Name_____ Sex: ☐ M, ☐ F; Date of Birth_____ Soc. Sec. No._____
Address_____   Check your State law as to discrimination because of age.

SUMMARY

Rating: | 1 | 2 | 3 | 4 | Comments:_____
(In making final rating, be sure to consider applicant's stability, industry, perseverance, loyalty, ability to get along with others, self-reliance, leadership, maturity, motivation; also, domestic situation and health.)

Interviewer:_____ Job Considered for:_____ Date_____

Why are you applying for work in this Company?_____ (Is his underlying reason a desire for prestige, security, or earnings?)

If you were hired, how long would it take you to get to work?_____ How would you do it?_____
                                                                    (Is there anything undesirable here?)

WORK EXPERIENCE. Cover all positions. This information is very important. Interviewer should record last position first. Every month since leaving school should be accounted for. Note military service in work record in continuity with jobs held since that time.

	LAST OR PRESENT POSITION	NEXT TO LAST POSITION	SECOND FROM LAST POSITION
Name of Company			
Address			
Dates of employment	From To	From To	From To
	(Do these dates check with his application?)		

Paragon Pulp & Paper Company, Ltd. 195

Nature of work		(Will his previous experience be helpful on this job?)
Starting salary		
Salary at leaving		(Has he made good work progress?) (General or merit increases?)
Was anything especially liked about the job?		(Has he been happy and contented in his work?)
Was there anything especially disliked?		(Were his dislikes justified?) (Is he chronically dissatisfied?)
Reasons for leaving		(Are his reasons for leaving reasonable and consistent?)

OTHER POSITIONS

Name of Company	Type of Work	Salary	Date Started	Date Left	Reasons for Leaving
	(Has he stayed in one line of work for the most part?)				
	(Has he gotten along well on his jobs?)				
	(Are his attitudes toward his employers loyal?)				
	(Was he interested in creative work? In work requiring activity?)				
	(Has he improved himself and his position?)				

Form No. OP-202

Copyright, 1964, The Dartnell Corporation, Chicago, Ill. 60640. Printed in U. S. A.
Developed by The McMurry Company

Exhibit 2 (continued)

How much unemployment
compensation have you drawn? _____ When? _____ Why? _____
(Does he depend on himself?)

How many weeks have you been
unemployed in the past five years? _____ How did you spend this time? _____
(Did conditions in his occupation justify this time? Did he use his time profitably?)

What accidents have
you had in recent years? _____ (Is he "accident-prone"? Any disabilities which will interfere with his work?)

SCHOOLING

How far did you go in school? Grade: 1 2 3 4 5 6 7 8   High School: 1 2 3 4   College: 1 2 3 4   Date of leaving school _____
(Is his schooling adequate for the job?)

If you did not graduate from
high school or college, why not? _____ Who paid for your schooling? _____ (Self-reliant?)
(Are his reasons for not finishing sound?)

What special training have you taken? _____
(Will this be helpful? Indications of perseverance? Industry?)

Extracurricular activities (exclude military,
racial, religious, nationality groups) _____ What offices did you hold in these groups? _____
(Did he get along well with others?)   (Indications of leadership?)

FAMILY BACKGROUND	FINANCIAL SITUATION	DOMESTIC AND SOCIAL SITUATION
Father living? _____ Mother living? _____ (Normal background?)	Own home: $ _____ Mortgage: $ _____ (Stability?)	Single? _____ Engaged? _____
Father's occupation _____	Rent House: $ _____ Apt.: $ _____	Married? _____ When? _____
Average earnings _____	Live with friends: $ _____ Relatives: $ _____	Widowed? _____ Divorced? _____
Number of brothers or sisters older _____ Younger _____ (Has he been babied?)	Own furniture _____ Number of Rooms _____	Ages of children _____
Financial aid to family _____	Cost of living per month $ _____ (Realistic?)	How do you and your wife get along? _____ (Motivation?) (Maturity?)

Paragon Pulp & Paper Company, Ltd.

Leisure time activities_____ (Habits of Industry?)	Any current debts?_____ (Mature financially?)	Recreation_____ (Maturity?)
Summer vacations_____ (Did he keep busy?)	Wages ever garnisheed?_____	Hobbies_____ (Will these help?)
Church activities_____ (Do not ask what church)	Ever need to borrow money?_____ (Judgment?)	Entertain at home?_____ (Get along well with others?)
Group activities_____ (Exclude military, racial, religious, and nationality groups)	Savings on last job $_____ Net Worth $_____	Group activities_____ (Exclude military, racial, religious, nationality groups)
Positions of leadership_____ (Leader?)	Wife employed?_____ Her earnings: $_____ (Effect on motivation?) Other income $_____	When did you have last drink?_____ (Sensible?) What types of people rub you the wrong way?_____ (Bias?)
How old when fully self-supporting?_____ (Self-Reliant?)	Life insurance $_____ Accident insurance $_____ (Is he provident?)	Ever arrested?_____ Charges_____ (Immaturity?)

HEALTH

What serious illnesses, operations, or accidents did you have as a child?_____ (Has he retained any infantile personality traits due to childhood illnesses?)

What illnesses, operations, or accidents have you had in recent years?_____ (Are his illnesses legitimate rather than indicating a desire to "enjoy ill health"?)

How much time have you lost from work because of illness during past year?_____ (Will he be able to do the job?)

How are your teeth?_____

Does anyone in your home suffer ill health?_____ (Are his wife, children, or family relatively healthy?)

Do you suffer from:
☐ Poor Eyesight
☐ Poor Hearing
☐ Rupture
☐ Rheumatism
☐ Asthma
☐ Heart Trouble
☐ Diabetes
☐ Ulcers
☐ Hay Fever
☐ Flat Feet
☐ Nervousness

ADDITIONAL INFORMATION:_____

Exhibit 3 Paragon Pulp & Paper Co. Selection and Evaluation Summary

Applicant's Name _____ Date _____ 19___.

Position Applied for _____ Job Class _____

	Rating on Each Factor	Out-standing	Good	Mar-ginal	Poor
"CAN DO" FACTORS	Appearance, manners				
	Availability for this work.				
	Education, as required by this job.				
	Intelligence, ability to learn, solve problems				
	Experience in this field.				
	Knowledge of the product.				
	Physical condition, health, energy.				
	CHARACTER TRAITS (Basic Habits)				
"WILL DO" FACTORS	STABILITY; maintaining same jobs and interests.				
	INDUSTRY; willingness to work				
	PERSEVERANCE; finishing what he starts. . .				
	ABILITY to get along with people.				
	LOYALTY; identifying with employer.				
	SELF-RELIANCE; standing on own feet, making own decisions				
	LEADERSHIP.				

MOTIVATION

INTEREST in this work . . . .
ECONOMIC NEED . . . .
NEED FOR RECOGNITION; personal status .
NEED TO EXCEL . . . .
NEED TO SERVE . . . .
NEED TO ACQUIRE . . . .

DEGREE OF EMOTIONAL MATURITY

Freedom from dependence . . . .
Regard for consequences . . . .
Capacity for self-discipline. . . . . .
Freedom from selfishness. . . . .
Freedom from show-off tendencies. . . .
Freedom from pleasure-mindedness. . . .
Freedom from destructive tendencies . .
Freedom from wishful thinking . . . . .

Important: Do not add or average these factors in making the Over-all Rating. Match the qualifications of the applicant against the requirements of the particular position for which he is being considered.

Strong Points for This Position _____

Weak Points for This Position _____

Over-all Rating: [1] [2] [3] [4] Recommendation to Employ: ☐ Yes ☐ No Rating by: _____

Exhibit 4
Paragon Pulp & Paper Company Limited
Article VIII—Seniority

Section 1:

The Company recognizes the principle of seniority, competency considered. In the application of seniority, it shall be determined firstly, by department, and secondly, by plant. Notwithstanding anything to the contrary contained in this Agreement, it shall be mutually agreed that all employees are hired on probation, the probationary period to continue for thirty (30) calendar days during which time they are to be considered temporary workers only. Upon completion of the probationary period, they shall be regarded as regular employees and shall then be entitled to Seniority, dated from the day on which they entered the Company's employ.

Section 2:

(a) Promotions shall be based on departmental seniority, competency considered, but must follow the lines of progression from job to job within the department.
(b) Any employee shall have the right to refuse promotion. However, in no case can departmental seniority be used to bypass any position in the line.
(c) Job openings will be held open for twenty-four (24) hours, during which time the employee eligible for promotion must make his intention known, as promotion may involve a change from swing shift to third shift and vice versa. In the event the eligible employee for the promotion refuses, other employees in the same category will be approached in order of their departmental seniority. Should no one in that category accept, the employees in next lower category of the department shall be approached in a similar manner. Should no one in the department accept the promotion, in such event the job will be posted for forty-eight (48) hours and in such case employees in other departments will be considered according to their plant seniority.

An employee who has entered a department in this manner shall be eligible for further progress in the new line of progression, subject only to longer departmental seniorities of other employees in the same bracket into which he has entered.

Section 3:

In the event of reduction of forces, the last person hired shall be the first released, subject to provisions as outlined in Section 1. The employees retained on the payroll will have the right to retain their jobs according to their departmental seniority. Those with insufficient departmental seniority to retain their jobs shall return to the job(s) previously held in the department and in such cases replace anyone holding such job with less departmental seniority. Those with insufficient departmental seniority to remain in the department will take the jobs opened up by those laid off. In case of re-establishment of forces, those "demoted" shall have first claim on their previously held jobs and in such event jobs will not be posted.

Section 4:

The Committee and the Company shall meet whenever necessary to discuss the basis of departments for seniority purposes.

Section 5:

It is hereby agreed that, when re-hiring, all employees laid off due to a seasonal shutdown or reduction in the working forces will be notified by telegram at least seven (7) days before re-start of operations and they shall be re-hired in the order of their plant seniority, provided that they reply to the telegram in the affirmative within ninety-six (96) hours of the telegram's being sent out, and appear for work not later than the end of the above-stated seven (7) day period. However, employees resident in Alberta, Saskatchewan or the Yukon Territory will be given one (1) additional day's time for reporting and any employee resident in any other Canadian Province or the United States will receive two (2) additional days' time for reporting. It is agreed that all employees shall, upon returning to employment within the required number of days of being notified by the Company, retain all seniority rights. It shall be the employees' responsibility to keep the Company informed of their address during lay-off.

Section 6:

It is agreed when hiring new employees, returned men with suitable qualifications shall have preference.

Section 7:

Any employee who is absent without leave for a period of more than three (3) consecutive working days, who cannot show just reason for such absence, shall forfeit all seniority rights. This shall not interfere with the Company's right to discharge for proper cause.

Section 8:

The Company shall supply to the bargaining agent, a complete seniority list every three (3) months. Said seniority list shall be immediately brought up to date in the event of a reduction of the working forces.

Section 9:

Weekend workers and others not desirous or available for regular employment will be regarded as casual employees, and will not accrue seniority.

Section 10:

Employees leaving the bargaining unit to assume supervisory duties shall, in the event of returning to the bargaining unit, retain that seniority which they held, at the time of leaving the bargaining unit.

SIMMONS RETAIL CHAIN STORE— SELECTION OF AN AUDITOR

CASE 31

Harry Jamison, the employment manager of the Simmons Retail Chain Store Company, returned to his office from a luncheon engagement with two assistant controllers where several important matters had been discussed. Among them was the company's expansion program, which included the establishment and acquisition of new stores throughout the southwestern part of the country. These changes, plus the normal amount of turnover, had greatly increased the need for additions to the company's accounting and internal auditing staffs.

Several of the traveling auditors had been promoted to more responsible positions, some were made regional controllers, and others were brought into the Chicago office as department heads. Two experienced men had retired during the past year, and four had left the company to take positions with other companies. As a result of these changes and difficulties in hiring new auditors as replacements, eight requisitions for either experienced accountants or auditors were in the employment office. It was desirable but not necessary that the auditors be certified public accountants.

The assistant controllers were convinced that ten years of accounting or auditing experience was necessary for an individual to qualify as a retail chain store auditor. Harry Jamison believed that it might be possible to employ college graduates with specialized training in accounting, place them on a planned job rotation program and develop them into auditors in five or six years. Simmons' policy, however, was to hire only experienced personnel, so Mr. Jamison usually sought auditors through newspaper advertisements and private employment agencies.

The pressing problem of the moment was to fill the immediate vacancies with qualified men. In recent years, Jamison had experienced extreme difficulty in hiring of new auditors. Part of the problem was that the starting salary paid to a new auditor was somewhat lower than the prevailing rate in the Chicago area (about $500 a year lower). Jamison believed, however, that most of the problem lay in the nature of the job itself. Simmons' auditors were required to travel extensively and to be away from their homes for long periods of time, sometimes several months. Qualified accountants with family responsibilities objected to the long absences from home, and often turned down positions at Simmons because of this problem. Several auditors had resigned in the past specifically because they disliked being away from their homes on extended assignments.

Harry reached into his pocket and pulled out a newspaper clipping which the chief controller, Mr. Griffin, had given to him. It was a section from the want ads and was heavily marked with pencil. It read:

> Wanted
>
> Position in accounting or auditing work by well qualified man with 25 years of financial experience with two corporations and one bank. Long service in responsible positions marred by one human error, an embezzlement. Interested in discussing employment with corporations executive needing the services of good accountant, controller or auditor. Single. Will travel. Box M-103.

The penciled notation indicated that Mr. Griffin was willing to talk to this man. However, Harry knew that Mr. Griffin was aware of the company's unwritten policy against hiring people with prison records. In addition, this applicant was probably in his late forties or early fifties, and the company seldom hired men over 40 years of age.

Just then the telephone rang. It was Mr. Griffin.

"Harry," said Mr. Griffin, "how about my requisitions for accountants and auditors? Look, boy, this thing is getting serious. We need men and fast."

Jamison answered, "Griff, I've been saying for years that we need to establish some type of policies or training program in regards to where, when, and how we're to get and keep qualified auditors. It's going to be a tough proposition to find eight experienced men right away."

"Maybe so," replied Mr. Griffin, "but the problem is that we need auditors today. I say, let's get whatever men we can get today and worry about the policies some other day when we can afford to think about them. Do you think we should talk to the guy in the want ad who has the prison record?"

For a moment, Jamison pondered what his reply should be.

VALLEY METAL PRODUCTS COMPANY   CASE 32

The resignation of Carl Caldwell, the 40-year-old production manager of the Valley Metal Products Company, and the promotion of the 33-year-old assistant production manager, Joe Bailey, to his job left the latter position open. Valley's manufacturing organization, which currently had somewhat more than 200 employees on its payroll, is charted in Exhibit 1. The company produced a limited line of vehicle parts, custom designed in a wide range of sizes, for a customer list of about 20 vehicle manufacturers.

Because Joe Bailey's education and experience did not qualify him fully to handle all aspects of Valley's production processes, his new assistant would have to fill in the gaps, be strong in the areas where Joe was weak. Both the president of the company, Mr. Ralph Preston, and Joe recognized this hard fact; and in jointly selecting the new assistant production manager planned to take it into account.

Caldwell, who had left Valley on short notice to accept a better job, had graduated from college as a mechanical engineer. During the next 18 years he had worked in a number of manufacturing plants, large and small, as product designer tooling engineer, mechanical superintendent, assistant production manager and production manager. During his 6 years with Valley Metals Products Company he had, as production manager, done an outstanding job of modernizing equipment and tooling, streamlining and improving production processes and methods, and cutting unit costs.

He was, however, a rugged individualist and had failed, in Mr Preston's judgment, to build up a strong supporting organization. He had been singularly unsuccessful, for example, in his selection of assistant production managers, except for Joe Bailey. Joe's four predecessors in the job had lasted only about a year each. The first, an "old-timer" foreman and shop superintendent with forty years of practical manufacturing experience had run off one night with one of the women employees, leaving a wife and three children behind. The second, also thoroughly competent in shop supervision, had developed a habit of sitting around the front office and acting like an executive more than Caldwell liked. The third, while extremely useful as a solver of tough new production problems and in the meeting of emergencies, had bullied his subordinates to the point where both foremen and union complained that he was unfair, inconsiderate and a liar. Occasionally he had disappeared for several days at a time and returned somewhat

From Austin Grimshaw and John Hennessey, *Organizational Behavior* (New York: McGraw-Hill Book Company, 1960). Used by permission.

the worse for wear. The last incident of this type had resulted in his dismissal. The fourth knew production well, but had been a poor administrator, spending most of his time bending over unruly machines or in the tool room making suggestions on new tooling design or tooling revisions. He had finally been transferred to the tool design office, where he was currently doing an excellent job.

Because Caldwell was unfit, by temperament, to cope with union representatives on contract negotiations and day-to-day grievances, Mr. Preston had taken over such matters himself, assisted by the personnel manager, Francis Dugan.

Everything considered, however, loss of Caldwell's services could not be considered as other than a serious blow to the company.

Joe Bailey had been with Valley Metal Products Company for 11 years, the last two as assistant production manager. He had come to Valley directly upon graduation from college, where he had majored in sociology and played varsity football. He served successively as shipping clerk, shipping room foreman, outside expediter and production control manager over a period of nine years. It was his habit, whenever emergency shipments had to be made to keep customers' production lines from shutting down, to help out on the final assembly line. He filled in wherever more manpower was needed and for as long as it was needed, sometimes putting in 16 to 18 hours at a stretch. The union had never protested, although on a number of occasions they had brought in grievances against working foremen.

Joe was by no means an extrovert but he did have an easy manner, a flair for listening, and an ability to form quick and lasting friendships. His associates at Valley Metal Products Company and the executives and supervisors he dealt with at suppliers' and customers' plants all liked, trusted and respected him. He organized, managed and was a star on Valley's softball and basketball teams. In Mr. Preston's opinion, he was probably the most universally popular member of management that Valley had ever had in its 15-year history.

When Carl Caldwell had suggested, two years earlier, that Joe be made assistant production manager, even though he was deficient in technical education and had no background as a machinist except what he had picked up from years of observation in the shop, Mr. Preston gave his enthusiastic approval. Carl and Joe made a good team throughout the next two years, getting along harmoniously together and dividing the work load on a common consent basis.

When Caldwell resigned, Mr. Preston had only two alternatives: take a chance on Joe Bailey or bring in a production manager from the outside. Joe, as he saw it, was the only man in the existing shop organization who had any chance of succeeding in the top production spot. If appointed, he would be pretty much on his own since Mr. Preston, himself a graduate mechanical engineer with years of experience as a machine tool salesman, would have to devote most of his time to sales, product development, and overall administration.

Mr. Preston decided to back Joe. He called him in, told him so, and listed the gaps in his background where he would need support. The two men agreed that Joe should continue in full charge of master scheduling, including all customer contacts on production and delivery problems. He had carried these duties over to his job as assistant production manager and now as production manager would still take primary responsibility for them. During the next few days Mr. Preston and Joe discussed at length the duties to be assigned to the new assistant production manager and appraised the background, the strengths and the weaknesses of 10 eligibles. This list included four production foremen, four non-production foremen, and two shop-office employees. Their tentative duty assignments and thumbnail histories and impressions of the 10 candidates follow:

DUTIES TO BE ASSIGNED TO ASSISTANT PRODUCTION MANAGER

1. Follow-up of production, to make sure that foremen are scheduling their daily production through the months in a manner which will permit meeting of monthly master schedules and delivery promises to customers.
2. Analysis and approval of labor requisitions submitted by foremen who wish to expand their workforces or replace workers.
3. Maintenance of quality at required levels.
4. Maintenance of plant, machines, and tooling in good working condition, available for production as needed.
5. Furnishing of technical assistance on production operations to foremen faced with difficult problems.
6. Reduction of operation costs by methods improvement.
7. Disciplining of workers with unsatisfactory output records.

LIST AND APPRAISAL OF ELIGIBLES
PRODUCTION FOREMEN

1. *Curry.* Heavy machining and assembly foreman. 32 years old. Supervised 50 workers. Came up through the department over a period of five years, the last three as foreman. Good record as a worker and as a supervisor, although both Mr. Preston and Carl Caldwell had been somewhat doubtful about his making the grade during his first two years as a foreman because he hated to crack down on his men. Had firmed up considerably in past year. Spent a lot of time outside working hours with men under him, fishing, playing cards, and drinking beer. Attractive personality and very popular with all shop and office personnel. Like all the other candidates had gone to high school but no further. Spent a month one summer at college, taking a special course in methods work, at company expenses. Reported to cronies that he had a wonderful time, particularly evenings.

2. *Waggoner.* Light machining and assembly foreman. 45 years old. Supervised 50 workers. Came up through the department, over a period of three years, the last two as a foreman. Demoted once because either unable or unwilling to handle discipline problems as management thought they should be. Previous industrial background had made him somewhat of an agitator, prior to his promotion to foreman. Got quite excited when he thought the management had given him the run-around or had failed to back him. Had no hesitation when it came to speaking his mind before and about his superiors in the organization. In the dumps frequently and had to be en-

couraged. Got very happy when praised for good performance. Well liked by his workers, even though he got a little tough with them now and then.

3. *Palmer.* Punch press and stampings assembly foreman. 52 years old. Hired as a foreman for the department four years previously, from the outside. Many years of punch press supervisory experience, but no machining experience. Supervised 25 workers. Often waylaid Mr. Preston on trips through shop to suggest possible improvements which he had seen elsewhere in previous jobs, such as better production controls, incentives, equipment. Sniped at other foremen's ability, knowledge. Hard to pin down when something went wrong, good at alibis, double talk. Kept his workers at arms' length, enforced discipline. Management had never heard any indications that workers did not consider him a good foreman.

4. *Ernst.* Night foreman. 35 years old. Supervised 25 machine, punch press and assembly workers. Came up through heavy machining and assembly department as a setup man over a period of four years, the last six months as foreman. Appeared to be easy-going but had shown good judgment and considerable ingenuity in settling problems arising on night shift when he was entirely on his own. Got along well with his workers. Trustworthy from management viewpoint, getting out rush jobs pretty much as required.

NON-PRODUCTION FOREMEN

5. *Cartwright.* General foreman, maintenance and tool room. 31 years old. Supervised maintenance and tool room foremen. Came up through the tool room over a period of five years. Promoted two years previously from hourly worker, over the head of the present tool room foreman, Dobie, as a result of ability shown while a member of the union bargaining committee. Aggressive, hard-bitten, ambitious, hard-working. Ready to tackle any problem of tooling, machine setup or maintenance, worked with his own hands until he mastered details of each machine, then delegated its maintenance to members of the maintenance crew. Workers considered him hard but fair, except for occasional flashes of temper. Blunt with everyone, including his superior in the organization, but ready to take the blame if in any way at fault. No production experience. Had attended methods course at college with heavy machining and assembly foreman, Curry, with whom he spent a lot of time outside working hours.

6. *Dobie.* Tool room foreman. 35 years old. Supervised 15 workers. Came up through the tool room over a period of eight years. No previous manufacturing experience. Had been foreman for three years. A good administrator, although workers under him claimed that several men in the department knew a lot more than he did about tool, fixture and die construction. Very easy-going, good natured, quiet. Avoided argument, readily accepted views of others.

7. *Stillman.* Maintenance foreman. 29 years old. Supervised 10 workers. Came up through the department, over a period of five years, the last one as foreman. Knew more about plant maintenance than about machine main-

tenance. Had trouble getting proper amount of work out of machine maintenance crew, two of whom were officials of the union and one of whom had hoped to become foreman. Hard worker, conscientious, showed signs of gradually overcoming rebellion against his authority. Union had twice asked for his removal, on the grounds that he rode too roughshod over the men, insisted that they do jobs requiring less skill than their classifications called for. Had fired one man on spur of the moment for insufficient cause, company had been forced to take him back or face unfair labor charge.

8. *Gould.* Inspection foreman. 55 years old. Supervised seven workers, on plant-wide basis. Knew machining, punch press, and assembly work thoroughly, although he had never been a production foreman. Able to advise workers turning out unacceptable quality what to do with their machines, fixtures, speeds, feeds, setups, to correct errors. Hired from outside as inspection foreman two years previously and had done excellent job of building up department and improving quality. A good supervisor, who let his workers know what he expected and made sure he got it. Did not hesitate to shut down machines, over protests of production foremen, when quality failure made it advisable.

SHOP-OFFICE EMPLOYEES

9. *Allen.* Trouble-shooter. 34 years old. Formerly foreman of light machining and assembly department, then promoted to shop-office for special assignments including trouble-shooting in customer's plants, filling in for foremen on vacation or sick, solution of bottleneck and high-cost operation problems, production chasing, etc. Hired from outside as a foreman, five years previously, transferred to shop office after three years. Also had attended special methods course, in summer prior to the year Curry and Cartwright had attended it. Plenty of backbone, got along well with shop and office personnel, although a little ill at ease with latter.

10. *Parkman.* Assistant to methods manager. 27 years old. Came up through the heavy machining and assembly department over a six-year-period and prior to existing appointment two years previously, had been its assistant foreman. Transferred to office because of technical competence. Had not as assistant foreman been entirely satisfactory in keeping worker output up, although his ability to schedule work seemed good. Proved to be an excellent methods man, because of understanding of equipment and ability to get along well with workers being studied. Owned a farm, on which he spent his non-working hours. Always left by the clock in order to get his farming done. Not too healthy, particularly when transferred to salary payroll.

Selection and Development

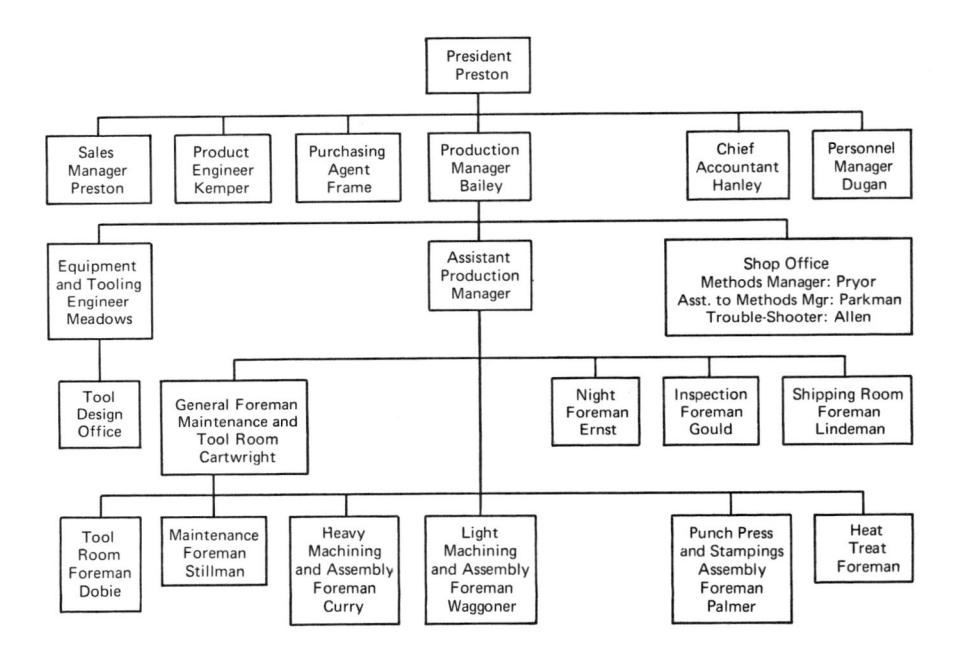

Exhibit 1
Valley Metal Products Co.
Partial Organization Chart, with Detail for Manufacturing Division

```
                                    President
                                     Preston
                                        |
   ┌────────────┬────────────┬──────────┴──────┬──────────────┬────────────┐
  Sales      Product     Purchasing       Production        Chief       Personnel
 Manager    Engineer       Agent            Manager      Accountant     Manager
 Preston    Kemper         Frame            Bailey         Hanley        Dugan
                                              |
             ┌────────────────────────────────┼────────────────────────────────┐
        Equipment                        Assistant                        Shop Office
       and Tooling                      Production                   Methods Manager: Pryor
         Engineer                         Manager               Asst. to Methods Mgr: Parkman
         Meadows                                                  Trouble-Shooter: Allen
             |                               |                              |
          Tool                               |                 ┌────────────┼────────────┐
         Design              General Foreman |               Night      Inspection   Shipping Room
         Office              Maintenance and |              Foreman      Foreman       Foreman
                              Tool Room      |               Ernst        Gould        Lindeman
                              Cartwright     |
             ┌──────────┬──────────┬─────────┼─────────┬──────────┬──────────┐
           Tool      Maintenance  Heavy     Light                Punch Press   Heat
           Room       Foreman    Machining Machining            and Stampings  Treat
          Foreman    Stillman   and Assembly and Assembly         Assembly   Foreman
           Dobie                 Foreman    Foreman               Foreman
                                  Curry     Waggoner              Palmer
```

JOHN EDWARDS   CASE 33

As soon as Peter Ravey, the Assistant Purchasing Agent of the Nustile Company, had announced the appointment of John Edwards to succeed Harry Wellman as Chief of the Pricing and Quotation Division, three other men in the division protested his promotion. At the suggestion of Edwards, Ravey decided to confer with each of the three disgruntled men the next day.

The Nustile Company was a large manufacturer of oil well equipment and also a distributor of oil well supplies made by other firms. The company's line of merchandise comprised several thousand items. Normally the company maintained active purchasing relations with about 500 of the 2,700 separate sources of oil well supplies or raw materials and parts for the equipment which the Nustile Company manufactured. The company sold not only within the United States but also in many foreign countries.

The purchasing department, which employed 44 persons, was under the general supervision of Sam Brown, vice president in charge of sales and purchasing, and under the immediate supervision of Ray Kirby, head of the department and the purchasing agent of the company, who was assisted by Ravey. The department was divided into five divisions one of which was the pricing and quotation division. Exhibit 1 gives the detailed organization of this division and shows its relationship to the other divisions and the top executive.

The principal functions of the pricing and quotation divisions were (a) to check the costs of raw materials and purchased parts used in the manufacture of equipment and to determine whether the company was obtaining good buys in terms of quality and price, (b) to negotiate for the best prices and quality on the purchased supplies used for resale, (c) to examine cost data on manufacturing and recommend to a merchandising committee consisting of the vice president in charge of sales and purchasing, the purchasing agent, and the sales manager, prices for equipment to be sold in various markets of the world, and (d) to recommend resale prices on supplies to this same merchandising committee.

The work of the pricing and quotations division under Wellman's direction had been divided among Edwards, Allison, Truman, and Fleck. Until the promo-

---

Case prepared by Professors Edmund P. Learned and George F. F. Lombard of the Harvard Graduate School of Business Administration and appears in John D. Glover and Ralph M. Hower, *The Administrator,* (Homewood, Illinois: Richard D. Irwin, Inc., 1963). Case material of the Harvard Graduate School of Business Administration is prepared as a basis for class discussions. Cases are not designed to present illustrations of either effective or ineffective handling of administrative problems. Copyright © 1947 by the President and Fellows of Harvard College. Reproduced by permission.

Nustile Co.
Partial Organization Chart, Sales and Purchasing Department

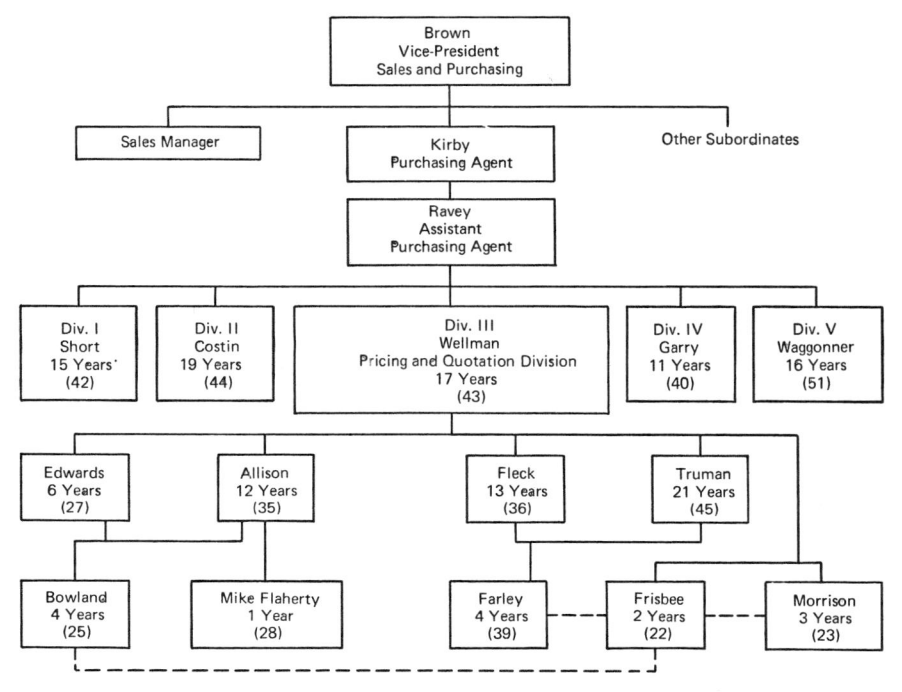

```
                    Brown
                 Vice-President
              Sales and Purchasing
    ┌───────────────┬───────────────────┐
 Sales Manager    Kirby          Other Subordinates
              Purchasing Agent
                    │
                  Ravey
                 Assistant
              Purchasing Agent
    ┌────────┬────────┬────────┬────────┐
  Div. I   Div. II   Div. III  Div. IV  Div. V
  Short    Costin    Wellman   Garry    Waggonner
 15 Years' 19 Years  Pricing and  11 Years  16 Years
  (42)     (44)    Quotation Division (40)   (51)
                   17 Years
                    (43)
    ┌────────┬────────────┬────────┐
 Edwards  Allison      Fleck    Truman
 6 Years  12 Years    13 Years  21 Years
  (27)     (35)        (36)     (45)
    │        │           │        │
 Bowland  Mike Flaherty Farley  Frisbee  Morrison
 4 Years   1 Year      4 Years  2 Years  3 Years
  (25)     (28)        (39)     (22)     (23)
```

Organization breakdown given for pricing and quotation division only. Total strength of the purchasing department—44 employees.

Note: Employees' service with the company is shown immediately under their names. Figures in parentheses ( ) give ages of employees. The dotted line from Miss Frisbee to the other girls denotes an unofficial advisory and supervisory capacity.

tion of Edwards, relations between these men had, in Edwards' opinion, been harmonious.

Allison had always been considered an excellent worker by Wellman. A high school graduate, he was 35 years old, and had had 12 years' experience with the company. He did not talk much to anyone while at work, although he was always agreeable and everyone in the department liked him. According to Wellman, he had not expressed a desire to progress far in the organization. Wellman had attributed this lack of ambition to the fact that Allison had a monthly income for life equal to his salary from the Nustile Company.

Truman was the oldest man in the pricing and quotation division and next oldest in the purchasing department. He was 45 years old, had a college education, and had been married many years. He and Allison were good friends and usually lunched together. Truman's work in the pricing and quotation division was highly specialized.

Fleck was a conscientious, efficient worker, good at detail work. He was 36 years old, a college graduate, and had been with the company for 13 years. He had been married nearly two years. At times he was considered by his associates to be sour and hard to get along with, and Wellman had heard him remark a number of times that he did not want to go higher in the organization because it would bring him too much responsibility.

The men in the pricing and quotation division were aided by four girls who performed secretarial and routine services. Miss Frisbee and Miss Morrison helped the division chief, Miss Bowland worked for Edwards and Allison, and Miss Farley for Fleck and Truman. Miss Frisbee advised the other three girls and acted as an informal supervisor. The girls were considered very good workers and were popular with the employees of the entire purchasing department. The only exception was when there were occasional clashes between Fleck and Miss Bowland. Often they did not speak to each other (except when necessary) for days at a time. Miss Bowland was a high-strung girl but was a good worker and everyone got along with her except Fleck.

The rise of John Edwards in the company had been fairly rapid. When he graduated from college six years before, he came to work for the company in a purely routine capacity in the purchasing department. He worked under Mr. Garry's direction learning both about the concerns from which the company regularly and occasionally made purchases and about the thousands of items sold by the company. Garry and Ravey considered Edwards an ambitious and willing worker who was well liked by his fellow employees. After two years in this division Edwards was transferred to the pricing and quotation division. This division had relationships with most of the manufacturing and selling departments of the company.

Six months after Edwards started in the pricing and quotation division, he was interviewed by Wellman, the manager, who expressed satisfaction with his work. He stated that he was looking for someone to understudy his job so as to be able to step into it whenever he himself might earn a promotion. Wellman said that he had often mentioned this idea to the others in the division but had never succeeded in interesting one of the other men in such a possibility. Wellman laid out a two-year program of training for Edwards which was designed to give him experience in all aspects of work in the division, its relations to other division chiefs within the purchasing department, and with other departments of the company. The other men in the pricing and quotation division knew Edwards was getting this training, but they indicated, he felt, that in their opinion he was wasting his time. Even though they teased him about the training, Edwards spent much of his spare time learning about the work and procedures of this division, and was able to get the help of nearly everyone in solving new problems when they arose.

Six years after joining the company and four years after his transfer to the pricing and quotation division, Edwards was promoted to chief of the division to succeed Wellman. Wellman had an opportunity to go to the head office of the company on short notice. Before departing he recommended Edwards as his successor. Brown at first thought that Edwards was too young and had insufficient experience for the job. Both Wellman and Ravey insisted that Edwards could handle the work and that he was well qualified by his training for the vacancy. The vice president, with Kirby's concurrence, put through an order promoting Edwards to the chief of the pricing and quotation division.

Peter Ravey arranged to have Allison, Fleck, and Truman come to his office together at which time he announced to them Brown's approval of the appointment of John Edwards to succeed Wellman as Chief of the Pricing and Quotation Division. Each of the three men expressed disapproval of the move. This reaction surprised Ravey, but because of an urgent engagement he felt unable to discuss the matter further at that time. He told them that he would think about it. That evening Ravey telephoned Edwards and reported what had happened during the conference with the three men. This conversation concluded with a suggestion from Edwards that Ravey confer with each of the three men the next day.

PETRI CHEMICAL COMPANY (A)— THE PROMOTION OF KENNETH ROGERS

CASE 34

The Petri Chemical Company is a large manufacturer of industrial chemicals. Its principal operations are conducted in the Lafayette and Cartier plants which are located in a large manufacturing center in the Midwest. At the time of this case, annual sales amounted to approximately 35 million dollars. Petri employed approximately 1000 production, 100 maintenance, and 400 clerical, sales, and executive personnel at the two plants which are situated about one mile apart.

The company has the reputation for being an excellent employer. The company selects its employees very carefully; management devotes considerable attention to encouraging and aiding individuals to advance to the highest levels that their ability and interests permit. Further, management prides itself in its policies and practices of fair treatment and good leadership for everyone from the president to the janitor! While production and maintenance workers belong to a union, it is an independent union with which the company has enjoyed a very good working relationship for many years. The company has never had a strike over either wages or the administration and interpretation of the collective agreement.

THE MAINTENANCE DEPARTMENT

The maintenance department of the Lafayette plant is made up of seven craft groups, each under the supervision of a foreman. The organization of the department is as shown on the following page.

The union had been placing heavy pressure upon the company to eliminate the practice of having managerial personnel perform work normally performed by members of the union. Also, it strongly objected to the practice of having members of the union assume temporary supervision over men in the craft group in the absence of the foreman. The union had negotiated the following contractual clause with the company:

ARTICLE VI

No member of management shall perform non-supervisory manual work normally performed by personnel under his supervision. This shall not prevent management personnel from instructing employees, or from operating new or revised equipment or processes, or from performing such work in an emergency or for experimental purposes.

The employer agrees to replace supervisory personnel who are absent because of vacation, illness, etc., with other managerial personnel.

THE PROMOTION OF KENNETH ROGERS

On Friday, August 31, Jim Counce, foreman of the carpenter shop in the Lafayette Plant of the Petri Chemical Company, retired. On Monday, September 3, Kenneth Rogers, foreman of the riggers, assumed supervisory responsibilities over the carpenters.

George Barnes, maintenance department superintendent, had been looking for a successor to Counce since the middle of July. Barnes finally had decided to place Kenneth Rogers over the carpenter shop, so on Saturday morning, September 1, Barnes posted an announcement of Rogers' appointment on the bulletin board. No one in the carpenter shop worked on Saturday. Barnes made no previous announcement of the appointment because, "I did not want to hurt Jim's feelings I was afraid that if I asked him about his successor, or announced his successor, before he left, he would think that we were glad to be rid of him."

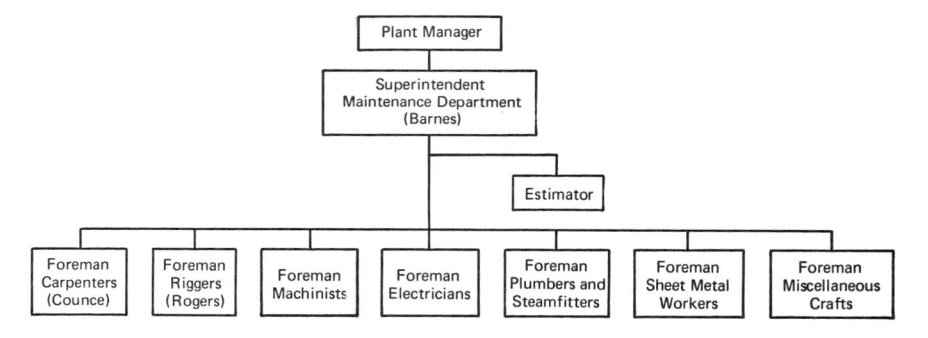

```
                        Plant Manager
                              |
                       Superintendent
                    Maintenance Department
                           (Barnes)
                              |
                          Estimator
                              |
   ┌─────────┬─────────┬─────────┬─────────┬─────────┬─────────┐
 Foreman   Foreman   Foreman   Foreman   Foreman   Foreman   Foreman
Carpenters Riggers  Machinists Electricians Plumbers and Sheet Metal Miscellaneous
 (Counce)  (Rogers)                       Steamfitters  Workers      Crafts
```

Jim Counce had worked for Petri for twenty-seven years, and he had been the foreman of the carpenter shop in the Lafayette plant for the last eleven years of that time. He supervised nine skilled carpenters. Counce, too, was a skilled craftsman, who not only knew carpentry, but who also knew how to set up and repair the power woodworking machine, sharpen saws, and service other equipment. Since his supervisory duties did not require his full time, he spent about one-third of his time working alongside his men.

Rogers, the new foreman over the carpenters, was forty-five years old, and he had had three years of high school. Prior to coming to Petri, Rogers was a skilled bricklayer. Rogers had worked at Petri for nine years, during the last five years of which he was foreman over the riggers. (Riggers at Petri do such work as to move heavy machines and equipment, erect structural iron work, and build concrete roads, floors, and walls.) Mr. Barnes expected Rogers to continue to supervise his crew of about fifteen riggers, in addition to supervising the carpenter shop. The riggers were located in the same building as the carpenters, and Rogers' office adjoined the carpenter shop.

Rogers was considered to be one of the best maintenance foremen in the entire company. His crew was enlarged as it was discovered that he could supervise several projects simultaneously with no loss in efficiency. He was well liked by his crew who always seemed to continue working at high efficiency, even "when the boss wasn't around."

He was very quiet and seldom spoke up in the maintenance department meetings. He never raised his voice, even in correcting a member of his crew.

Rogers liked to delegate responsibility to his men; he solicited the ideas of the men; and he often permitted them to do the job their way, if he was convinced that they preferred their methods to his.

CANDIDATES FOR THE POSITION OF FOREMAN

Although Barnes had selected Rogers to be the new foreman, three other candidates considered themselves to be qualified. According to several executives, Robert Mangrum seriously considered himself a candidate for the position of foreman in the carpenter shop. Mangrum was sixty-two years of age and had worked at Petri for twenty-one years. He had more seniority than any other carpenter. About eight years ago, he was transferred to the maintenance shop of the Cartier plant located a few blocks from the Lafayette plant in preparation for promotion to the position of foreman of the maintenance department in the Cartier plant. Shortly after he was transferred, however, a physical examination showed that working conditions in the Cartier plant would be injurious to his health. He was then transferred back to the Lafayette plant. Mangrum expected to be promoted when Jim Counce retired.

Both Counce and a member of the personnel department had agreed that Mangrum was very capable. However, they also felt that he pushed the difficult and unpleasant jobs off on other carpenters whenever possible. They reported that he did not do as much of the work as he was capable of doing, and that he did not work as hard as most of the other carpenters.

A member of the personnel department stated that, "The other carpenters do not like Mangrum. "They would not tolerate him as their foreman." One carpenter commented on Mangrum, "What do you think of a —— like that? He spent two days cutting a hole in a roof that should have taken five hours—and then asked for a helper." Counce had stated that Mangrum was very seniority conscious.

Joe Emery also showed interest in being promoted when Jim Counce retired. In fact, when Mangrum was transferred back into the carpenter shop and announced that he expected to get the next promotion, Emery went to Mr. Barnes to protest. Emery obtained assurance from Barnes that Mangrum was not in line for the job, and that he (Emery) was considered the most likely prospect.

Emery was forty-seven years of age and a widower. He had worked at Petri for nineteen years. Emery was considered by all of his associates to be the best carpenter in the shop. He was regularly assigned all the cabinet work that had to be done. While the other carpenters liked cabinet work, they recognized the superior craftsmanship of Emery, and they did not resent the assignment of cabinet work to him. Emery was both respected and well-liked by the other carpenters. A representative of the personnel department described him as "very neat, courteous, efficient, and businesslike. He would make a good lead man or foreman."

Although Wilbur Schuh was a third possible candidate for the foreman's job, Mr. Barnes had not seriously considered him for the position. Schuh was the union steward, forty-four years of age, and had worked for Petri for eleven years. He was liked by the other carpenters, but according to one executive, "Schuh is very outspoken and aggressive. At times he does not use good judgment in talking with his foreman and department head."

The other carpenters were not considered eligible for promotion at this time.

THE MONDAY MORNING MEETING

On Monday morning, the first work day following the posting of the notice of Rogers' appointment by Barnes, the carpenters congregated in the shop at the start of the shift waiting for the new foreman to appear. As Rogers and Barnes walked into the shop, Al Blount, the oldest carpenter in the shop, asked, "I want to know why a carpenter wasn't promoted to be our boss?" Before either Barnes or Rogers could reply, Mangrum exploded, "Who is going to change the jointer blades? If you think that I would run the jointer with Rogers making the setups, you're crazy! Besides, who is going to sharpen the saw blades around here?" Schuh joined in, "This is a lot of stuff. The men aren't going to stand for it. You can't treat us this way and expect us to take it. I'm filing a grievance in protest!"

PETRI CHEMICAL COMPANY (B)—
THE CASE OF HARRY THURMAN

THE GRIEVANCE

Robert Campbell, a foreman in the packing department of Petri Chemical Company, was walking through the department when Harry Thurman, a stock picker and department union shop steward, stopped him.

THURMAN: Campbell, I'm filing a grievance today, since I didn't get that promotion to stock clerk. I've been at Petri for 18 years, and I've worked in packing for 14 years. I can do the work in this department as well as anybody else. It's not fair to promote Bill Hendricks instead of me. Hendricks has only been here eight years. What does it take to get a promotion in this place? I think that I should get either a checker's or a stock clerk's job. Besides, the union contract says that when a man has the ability, seniority counts.

CAMPBELL: Harry, I considered the matter carefully, and I decided that you didn't have the ability to do the Stock Clerk's job. Hendricks was the next highest man in seniority, and he does have the ability. That's why he got the job when it came open.

THURMAN: What in the hell do you mean, I don't have the ability? I've done the Stock Clerk's job many times in the past. You've never told me before that I couldn't handle it. It was my understanding that I'd get the next promotion in the department, since I have the highest seniority. This is a hell of a time to tell me that I don't have ability to do what I've already done before.

CAMPBELL: Nevertheless, that was my decision.

THURMAN: You may think it's your decision now, but when the union gets through with you and your boss, you may think about it differently.

With that Thurman walked away, and Robert Campbell wondered what his next move should be.

BACKGROUND INFORMATION

The packing department of Petri Chemical Company packaged bulk chemicals into small containers, stored the packaged chemicals, and filled and shipped customer orders. Robert Campbell supervised the section which both stored the packaged items, and filled and shipped customer orders.

Stock clerks were responsible for maintaining an adequate inventory of each item in stock. When a stock clerk noticed that a particular item had reached a predetermined minimum inventory, he filled out a work order which authorized the packaging sections to package more of that item. He also placed the various chemicals into their proper bins or storage areas and was further responsible for arranging stock so that the oldest stock would be shipped out first.

Stock pickers filled customer orders by passing through the aisles with a cart and placing the amount of each item listed on the invoice in the cart. Stock pickers were supposed to check each item against the invoice by both the stock number and product name.

Invoices were checked against the physical items by a *checker* to insure absolute accuracy of the order prior to the packing of the order by the *packagers*.

Campbell insisted that orders be filled accurately. Errors in filling orders made the Petri Company liable for damage claims from customers. Petri had developed an excellent reputation for both quality and reliability. Errors would result in serious losses to good will.

Stock clerk and checker were considered the most important positions in determining the accuracy with which orders were filled. These jobs received 32 cents an hour more base pay than did stock pickers and packers—($3.42 vs. $3.10).

All employees in the packing department were compensated according to the Gantt task-and-bonus incentive plan. Under this plan, a standard time allowance was computed for each task performed in the department. Completion of work within the standard time allowance enabled the employee to earn a 25 per cent bonus. Hence, each employee had a strong incentive to complete his tasks within the time allowed.

At this time, Harry Thurman was 41 years of age, and married. He had completed two years of high school. Robert Campbell, the foreman, had worked in the packing department for seven years. He was promoted to the position of foreman about eight years ago.

Thurman had performed various duties in the packing department, including that of stock clerk when the regular stock clerks were on vacation. Campbell considered Thurman to be unsatisfactory as a stock clerk. According to Campbell, Thurman made too many errors in placing stock in the stock bins. Such errors slowed up the stock pickers and caused them to make errors in filling orders.

Also, on several of these occasions Thurman had been unable to meet the standard times allowed for shelving stock. In order not to lose his bonus, he made up several work orders authorizing the packaging sections to prepare more stock of the items indicated on the work orders. He did this even though the supply of these items had not reached the minimum established for reorder. By making up several of these work orders, Thurman was able to build up ample time credits to enable him to make his bonus. The effect of this practice was to upset production in the packaging sections and to build up excessive inventories of the items.

Harry Thurman also previously held the position of vault man. In this capacity, he was in charge of a locked vault containing valuable stock items. By his own admission he was unqualified to hold this position. He made many errors in filling orders from stock, and he was unable to keep accurate control over inventories. He attributed some of his difficulties to poor vision. Robert Campbell believed that some of Thurman's difficulties in shelving and picking stock were a result of his defective vision. Campbell also felt that Thurman made more errors on his present job of stock picking than those other stock pickers. While these errors were serious, the checkers often were able to catch them. Checkers knew that orders filled by Thurman often contained errors. As a consequence, they gave special attention to checking orders which he had prepared. However, no records were kept concerning the number of errors for which Thurman was responsible.

Campbell believed that Harry Thurman lacked the ability and dependability necessary to be either a stock clerk or a checker. He further noted that Thurman was frequently absent from his work. In the previous year, he had been absent 20 days, offering illness as his reason for his frequent absence.

THE MEETING

Several days later, Robert Campbell was asked to meet with Mr. Ralph Compton, the personnel department supervisor, to discuss the grievance filed by the plant union on behalf of Harry Thurman.

COMPTON: Bob, in looking over Harry Thurman's employee record file, I noticed that his work performance has usually been rated average. I see no mentions of discussions with him concerning unsatisfactory work. How was it that you passed him up for the Stock Clerk position?

CAMPBELL: Look, Ralph, I know and so does everybody else in the department that Thurman shouldn't get the Stock Clerk's job. He makes too damn many errors. I can't produce any records to prove it, but I know what I'm talking about. Isn't my evaluation enough when it comes to choosing the man most qualified for promotion?

COMPTON: It should be, Bob, but Thurman claims in his grievance that he's entitled to a chance at the Stock Clerk's job based on his seniority and past performance in the department. Here's what the contract says about it.

Mr. Compton showed Mr. Campbell Article V, Section 6, of the union contract, which provided that:

> In filling vacancies or making promotions within a department or classification (except supervisory jobs) the Employer shall give preference to the employee having the greatest seniority in that department, provided, however, that ability and merit are equal. Any claims of personal prejudice or of discrimination for Union activity may be subject to grievance procedure.

CAMPBELL: Well, Ralph, what do you suggest I should do? I know I'm right. If I have to give Thurman the Stock Clerk's job, I'm going to have more trouble with departmental performance than I've ever had before.

MANAGEMENT DEVELOPMENT AT THE FORD MOTOR COMPANY

CASE 35

"Ladies and gentlemen, I have three books . . . a green book . . . a black book . . . and a brown book.

"Later on I'll tell you what's in them—or at least some of what's in them—because I think they may help you understand just how important management development is to Ford Motor Company and to any other company which hopes to survive in a competitive market.

"I suspect most of you already are pretty well sold on the value of management development or you wouldn't be attending this particular session. For those of you who have some doubts about its value, I warn you I shall use whatever powers of persuasion I have to alter your thinking.

"Our key managers at Ford Motor Company, and at the Ford Division which I head, have no more important job than the development of other managerial talent. We rate management development on a par with product development. A strong product is essential, of course; but no product is strong enough to carry a weak management team. In fact, no company can have a consistently strong product line unless it first has a strong management team.

"At Ford Motor Company we speak from direct experience on this subject. When Henry Ford II became chief executive officer of our company at the end of World War II, it was losing nine million dollars a month and was short of everything but rundown plants and obsolete products.

"At the root of the trouble was a shortage of capable management. A handful of top executives was responsible for top-staff policy and planning functions as well as daily operations. Many good managers had been forced out of the company. Those who remained were, for the most part, locked in place with no chance to develop.

"Henry Ford II realized that his first job was to mold a strong management team—and he did it. He persuaded outstanding men from other companies to take on top management duties at the company and to develop their own successors. He brought in a group of 10 young U. S. Air Force officers whose wartime accomplishments in military management offered promise that they might be equally successful in the automobile business. One of them—Arjay Miller—now is president

---

Text of remarks by L. A. Iacocca, who at the time of this address was Ford Motor Company vice president and Ford Division general manager, at a meeting of the 13th CIOS International Management Conference at the New York Hilton Hotel, New York, N. Y., Thursday, September 19, 1963. Reprinted by permission.

of the company. Another—Robert McNamara—was president before he resigned to become Secretary of Defense.[1]

"Mr. Ford also brought back able men who had left the company, and sought out men within the company who could be developed and promoted.

"It took the company until 1949 to develop a new product line, but well before then the new management team had put the company back on its feet financially. By 1953 the company had spent more than a billion dollars for expansion and modernization—and had done it entirely out of earnings!

"It was products that made possible the spending of that billion dollars. But it was management skills that developed the products and effective means of merchandising them.

"I mention our company's postwar resurgence not to boast—although we're mighty proud of it—but to stress the extreme importance of the management function and to explain why the company is so determined never to let the caliber of its management team decline again. Once was nearly too often.

"There is very little danger that we will repeat our mistake. From Henry Ford II on down, every member of Ford management is sold on the value of management development and accepts it as a key part of his job. It is as built-in at Ford as styling and engineering and selling.

"I think the best way to tell you how we go about the job of management development at Ford is to cite some specific examples. First, though, let me set the stage for you.

"We have at Ford Motor Company at the present time about 71-hundred management positions, out of a total of 312-thousand employes worldwide. These managers work at 86 locations in 26 states of the U. S. A., and in 29 other countries of the free world.

"Obviously, with as big an operation as ours, we have two tremendous problems in remaining well-managed: we must replace those managers we lose through retirement, death, resignation or other contingency, and we must find additional management talent to meet the added requirements generated by new products, growth, expansion and reorganization.

"The answer to these problems is, of course, management training in depth. At Ford we have a very specific objective: two replacements for each key position in the company—one fully qualified to step in tomorrow morning if need be, the other to be ready within two years.

"How do we accomplish this? That's where the three books come in. They contain both the guidelines to what we're trying to accomplish, and the record of how well we're going.

"Here's the first book—the Green Book. It's called "Ford Motor Company Management Development—Appraisal of Performance, Promotability and Potential." It is on the desk of every one of our managers, and it is well-thumbed. It's

---

[1] *Editors' Note:* Since this address was given by Mr. Iacocca, Mr. Miller has left the Ford Motor Company and Mr. McNamara has become head of the World Bank. Mr. Iacocca has since become President of Ford Motor Company.

a detailed guide to a system of annual personnel appraisals which are the foundation of our management-development program.

"Let me read you just two paragraphs from the Green Book. (I might add that any manager who can read these two paragraphs without realizing their importance to his own future welfare—as well as that of his subordinates—would do well to look for work elsewhere.)

"Here's what they say:

> The continuing success of the Ford Motor Company will depend largely upon the availability of highly qualified personnel in the essential areas of managerial, technical and professional skills.
>
> It is the policy of this company that every manager and supervisor is responsible for stimulating increasingly high performance of personnel in their present positions, and for developing subordinates who are competent, in every respect, to assume the duties and responsibilities of their superiors and of other key positions within the organization. *Moreover,* the performance of Ford Motor Company's managerial and supervisory ranks will be judged in direct proportion to their ability to select and develop such personnel.

"The Green Book goes on to spell out rules for appraising each of the employes on whom management-development records are kept. These are employes who have been selected as potential managers on the basis of their performance either with our own company, or with another company prior to joining Ford.

"The formal appraisal rates an employe as to (1) how he is doing on the job; (2) what higher job he is qualified for either now or later; (3) how much ultimate potential he has; (4) what plans have been made for his development, and (5) who his replacements would be.

"Performance ratings on current work are expressed as outstanding, excellent, satisfactory plus, satisfactory, satisfactory minus, or unsatisfactory. Both "outstanding" and "unsatisfactory" ratings are rare; to be "outstanding" an employe must be little short of perfect, while the individual who would wind up with an "unsatisfactory" rating in most cases wouldn't reach the appraisal level in the first place.

"The second book—the Black Book—is also on the desk of every Ford manager charged with appraising his subordinates. It contains detailed records on each one of his employes covered by the management-development plan—his personal history, education, experience with Ford, experience outside the company, and assessments of his performance in his present job, his qualifications for promotion either immediately or within two years, and his ultimate potential. Plus, of course, that all-important rating.

"I have my own black book. It contains exhaustive profiles on each of the 107 executives who make up the top management of Ford Division. It is updated constantly, because we shift our management people from job to job at planned intervals to give them the broadest possible experience and to maximize the number of areas in which to test their capabilities. You'd be surprised how good a salesman you can make of an engineer, or how good a product-planner you can make of a finance man!

"As I've indicated, this Black Book does a lot more than assess a man on the basis of his present performance. More importantly, it tells where he can go from here. *Most* importantly, it describes what plans we have for getting him there—assuming our assessment of him turns out to be correct.

"Let me give you an example. Here's a young man 33 years old. He has a bachelor of arts degree in economics and mathematics, and a master of business administration degree in finance. He started with Ford as a financial analyst five years ago after two years as credit manager for another company.

"He was spotted immediately as a comer—and has justified our assessment since. He was named a supervisor after only five months on the job, since has held three managerial positions of increasing importance in the controller's office, and now is manager of a key department in the general sales office.

"Our plans for him? To move him to the field sales organization, probably as a district sales manager, in 1965; make him a regional sales manager in 1967; move him back to the general office in a different and more important capacity in 1969, and groom him as a possible assistant divisional general manager by 1972 and a general manager by 1973 or 1974.

"These, as I say, are our present plans. They could change. We might divert him into product planning. He could go back into finance, as a divisional controller. We might lose him to the corporate Finance Staff, where he could ultimately become company controller, or vice president-finance.

"Here's another high-potential candidate. This man is 43 years old, has bachelor's and master's degrees in business administration, and joined the company 11 years ago after varied service as a purchasing agent, accountant and cost engineer. He has spent most of his Ford Division career in product planning. Under our 10-year development program, he has the potential to become divisional head of his specialty by 1965, general parts and service manager in 1968, an assistant general manager in 1971, and a division general manager in 1973. It's also considered possible that he could move into a corporate job as head of the central product planning office, or perhaps as general manager of a basic manufacturing division.

"One thing is certain: if we don't develop men with this kind of potential—and pay them what they're worth in the process—we stand a good chance of losing them. These men *expect* us to provide them with opportunities to develop. If we don't, we have no defense whatsoever if they accept better offers elsewhere.

"We'd be pretty *inept* not to develop these men to the limit of both their ability and ours. We get maximum return on our investment in an outstanding employe, only when we get him into the biggest job he is capable of handling.

"An important part of the record on each man listed in my Black Book is his compensation profile. This traces his progress in salary, bonuses, and possibly even stock options. It notes what key executives for whom the man has worked have had to say about him. Their verbatim comments are included, and these are compared with the man's compensation to see if his bosses—to use a rather direct

American phrase—put their money where their mouths were. If his compensation hasn't kept pace with his job progress, or hasn't been consistent with management's evaluation of him and his potential, questions are asked and second looks are taken—at both the individual and his superiors!

"You'll recall my reading from the Green Book that a Ford manager's own performance is judged importantly on how good a job he does in developing the people under him. In determining promotions, and salary increases, and bonuses, I myself give a great deal of weight to the kind of job the person being considered has done in the management-development area. I reason that if he is effective in this field, he *understands* the job of managing and appreciates its importance. Because of this, he is important to the future success of our division and our company.

"Incidentally, I had our Industrial Relations experts do a special study of the 107 profiles in my Black Book recently and they came up with some interesting statistics.

"For example, the average age of the top 107 executives in our division is 45. Five are under 35 and only 14 are over 55; more than 75 per cent of them are under 50. They have an average of 16 years with the company; only two have less than five years' Ford service, and 10 have 30 years or more with the company.

"What these figures say is that essentially we are a young division, management-wise. Because we are young, we can expect that we're going to have to feed talent into other company components—and that comes right back to the importance of our management-development efforts.

"Incidentally, in further analyzing our top 107 executives, we determined that 76.6 per cent of them are rated as still promotable within the division. Of the remaining 23.4 per cent, some have reached the top of their potential, and others simply have no better jobs to go to within the division. Many of these 23.4 per cent, however, are promotable to other components of the company.

"This point brings us to our third book—the Brown Book. In this book, I keep records on the top 65 or 70 of the 107 divisional executives listed in my Black Book. Once a year I discuss the performance and potential of each of these 65 managers with Henry Ford II and other members of the company's Executive Office—A. R. Miller, president, and C. H. Patterson, executive vice president. I spend literally hours with these men discussing the contributions I think my divisional executives can make to the long-range welfare of the company. The Brown Book contains individual profiles on these men. It also reviews the division's long-range management needs . . . anticipated losses from retirements, deaths and resignations . . . and major areas of replacement strength. And, it details progress made by the division in management development since the last meeting with Mr. Ford.

"If there is anything Mr. Ford emphasizes in these annual reviews, it is his insistence that there be free and constant interchange of talent among the various company components. He expects that our division—as well as every other major segment of Ford Motor Company—will consider it has an obligation to help develop talent to be used wherever it is needed—whether it's in Ford Division headquarters in Dearborn . . . or a stamping plant in Buffalo . . . or the Ford of Britain works in Dagenham, England . . . or a sales office in Los Angeles . . . or our new ball-bearing plant in Puerto Rico. We are running a business—a big business. The welfare of our 312-thousand employes around the world . . . of our 18,500 dealers or holders of selling agreements and their tens of thousands of employes throughout the Free World . . . and of our more than 301,000 stockholders in Ford U. S. and its affiliates abroad, transcends that of any individual or any single company component.

"I'd like to go back for a moment now to what we consider the real key to success of the management-development program at Ford. That is the individual personnel appraisal.

"I emphasize the word "individual." It applies to both companies and people. No matter how much you formalize the theory and elaborate the practice, management development remains an inexact science. And, the pattern that emerges for one company will not necessarily fit any *other* company. As a matter of fact, it probably won't fit the *same* company very long.

"This is simply because . . . in dealing with management development . . . we are dealing with people—and people rarely fit a common mold. Moreover, we are looking for *exceptional* people—people with that rare quality of leadership that makes them stand out from the crowd. The very differences that distinguish them, dictate a large amount of *individual* handling.

"Our appraisal system affords just that kind of handling. Each employe within the system is rated individually on his performance and potential, and given a chance to develop his potential to the utmost. In addition to being assigned jobs that test his versatility and adaptability, he is given a chance to broaden himself through formal education at company expense. We help our people obtain fellowships—such as the year-long Sloan Fellowships at Massachusetts Institute of Technology. In certain cases we sponsor their attendance at university development courses such as the ones at Harvard Business School and similar institutions. We conduct college graduate training programs . . . and enroll particularly promising candidates in special problem-solving courses which give us an added insight into their management potential. We urge our employes to take advantage of a continuing-education plan under which the company pays tuition and fees for those wanting to pursue job-related studies at nearby schools on their own time. In one of our largest Ford Division components—the Product Engineering Office—26 per cent of *all* employes—not just those included in the management-appraisal program—are enrolled in such courses.

"An important feature of our appraisal program is that it provides two-way communication. Each employe has a personal interview with his superior. He is told what development plans we have for him. His written appraisal is discussed with him, and he is invited to submit comments which are entered as part of his management-development record.

"And, people in the program take advantage of this opportunity. Most of them promise efforts to correct areas of weakness, and many suggest changes in assignment to make more effective use of their own experience and potential. These suggestions are given serious consideration in duty changes.

"I believe the success of any management-development program is in direct proportion to the freedom with which people can be moved around in the organization. To provide that freedom, many deep-rooted attitudes around a company may need to be changed.

"For example, you may have a manager who hoards talent. He prides himself on having a strong staff and an efficient office. Rather than recommend his good people for promotion, he holds onto them until they either lose their initiative, or get discouraged and start looking elsewhere.

"Or, there may be the *independent* manager, who doesn't want to admit he needs help. He'd rather promote a weak man from his own bailiwick to fill a vacancy, than call on another department which has surplus talent it would like to relocate.

"Then there's the softhearted manager who lets deadwood block the path for more promising men on their way up.

"If it is made sufficiently clear that managers are going to be judged by the quantity and quality of the managerial talent they produce—as we do at Ford—then I think these managers will see the light. Either that, or they themselves will have to be removed as deadwood. The hoarder will start pushing his people instead of holding them back. The self-sufficient manager will realize that his only hope of sending good material out of his office, is to bring good material *in*. And, the softhearted one will have to come to the same reluctant conclusion as the rest of us—that managing involves *de*motions as well as *pro*motions. It may be rough on the man being demoted, but, in the long run, is it fair to prevent the other man from progressing? And, when you get right down to it, is it really fair to keep a man in a position he can't handle, and in which therefore he can only become very frustrated?

"No management-development program is perfect. Certainly ours isn't at Ford. But the important point is that we have one—and that it's working. The value of a well-planned, well-executed, systematic program of management development is that it reduces the element of chance. It provides a system of controls and checkpoints. It substitutes careful thinking for hunch-plays. It helps keep the whole organization aware of the need for developing new management talent. It coordinates the development efforts toward one common goal, instead of many separate, and perhaps conflicting goals.

"Ladies and gentlemen, the strength of tomorrow's executive talent is something no company can afford to gamble on. Management development is the insurance policy on the team that will be running the business when the present managers are gone.

"I'd like to close by quoting a recent statement by Henry Ford II. He said:

> Executive talent is the most important asset we have. It doesn't appear on our balance sheet, but it will have more important effects on our progress, our profits and the price of our stock, than any other asset we possess or can acquire. Nor is this asset an expensive one to acquire. It's a bargain-buy every day of the year, a low-cost risk with a high-return potential. If you will give as much thought to the acquisition and development of men with top-management potential as you do to planning a plant or a product, nothing can stop this company.

"Thank you."

INCIDENT IN A GOVERNMENT AGENCY: THE UNQUALIFIED EXAMINER

CASE 36

INTRODUCTION

Albert Grumm, the case writer of this incident, first was employed by the Federal Deposit Insurance Corporation, Sixtieth District, Division of Examination, as a trainee assistant bank examiner.[1] As a prerequisite to being hired, he was required to possess a college degree or have equivalent banking experience and to pass the Federal Service Entrance Examination with a grade of at least 80 per cent. His initial grade service level was a grade six, which was maintained for a probationary period of six months. Under FDIC policy, if sufficient progress was made at the end of six months, a grade seven was granted.

During the first six months and a subsequent period of several months, Albert Grumm was rotated from assignment to assignment within the four-state area encompassed by the Sixtieth District, each assignment lasting from six weeks to three months. At the end of approximately one year, having made sufficient progress, he was promoted to the level of senior assistant examiner, grade nine, and assigned to the Metro City subdistrict.

Like all trainees, Albert Grumm's progress was determined in part by periodic progress reports which were completed by his immediate supervisors, usually the bank examiner in charge of the FDIC subdistrict where he was assigned. These reports graded men on the basis of their abilities to perform the work, cooperation and helpfulness, and several other factors. Various factors were given ratings of unsatisfactory, satisfactory, or excellent. The progress report was reviewed with the subordinate before being submitted to the Sixtieth District office and on to Washington.

Within eighteen months after receiving a grade nine, a senior assistant examiner was expected to be prepared to go before a board of examiners in the Washington office to take a proficiency examination which revealed his knowledge and familiarity with FDIC rules and regulations, banking laws, and which indicated his ability to evaluate overall asset condition and management of a bank. If he passed the proficiency examination, he was promoted to a grade eleven with the title of bank examiner. In this position, he was given charge of a group of assistant examiners and was responsible for completing reports of examination.

ORDINARY HIRING POLICY

The standard hiring policy of the FDIC had been to hire primarily college graduates, generally with a business degree. To be eligible, the applicant had to take the

[1] All names and specific locations within the FDIC disguised.

Federal Service Entrance Examination and achieve a score of at least 80 per cent. All applicants taking the Federal Service Entrance Examination with a score of at least 70 per cent had their names placed on the Federal Job Register. From this list, the various government agencies who hired through the Civil Service Commission selected prospective job candidates according to grade criteria established for their particular agency. The Federal Deposit Insurance Corporation was one of many agencies hiring through the Civil Service Commission. Based on its required qualifying score, background of the applicant, and a personal interview with a representative of the Federal Deposit Insurance Corporation, an applicant was accepted or rejected.

NEW HIRING POLICY

Beginning in July of 1966, a new recruiting approach was begun in order to attract more qualified personnel. This approach consisted of an attractively designed brochure which was mailed to banks throughout the country. This brochure was designed to attract experienced bank officers; the new policy was to offer starting positions with the Federal Deposit Insurance Corporations at grade nine depending on experience, and at grade eleven if even more banking experience was possessed. The only qualifications for these positions were that sufficient banking experience in an officer position be possessed, and that the applicant obtain a passing grade of 80 per cent on the Federal Service Entrance Examination. Sufficient banking experience in some cases consisted of twenty years as assistant cashier or cashier, or some other title of relative importance in commercial banking. In many cases, men employed under this new policy were war veterans, and as such they were given an additional ten points on the score they received in taking the Federal Service Entrance Examination. This meant that a man could receive a true score of 70 per cent on the examination, but because he was a war veteran, he received ten additional points which gave him 80 per cent and made him eligible for the position.

This new policy of attracting qualified personnel was carried on simultaneously with the standard hiring policy previously discussed. Under the new policy, a man hired at a grade nine level was expected, as under the standard policy, to be prepared to take the proficiency examination after eighteen months as a grade nine in order to advance to the position of bank examiner, grade eleven. A man hired at grade eleven under the new policy was expected to be able to assume the supervisory and examination responsibilities of an examiner after only a short period of training.

Thus, the new policy did not in essence conflict with the standard policy previously in use. When the new policy was announced, there was at first some grumbling among the younger men who had been with the organization for a year or more at a grade seven level, because they feared that older men starting at a level higher than their own would lessen their own chances for advancement. In the case to follow as reported by Albert Grumm, this turned out to be a real problem which caused a substantial amount of stress within the FDIC subdistrict located in Metro City.

RESULTS OF NEW HIRING POLICY

In the latter part of 1966, two men were brought into the Metro City subdistrict, both having been hired under the new policy at a grade level nine. Both men had considerable previous banking experience. One was a World War II veteran, a high school graduate, who had been in charge of the installment loan department of a bank with approximately fifty million dollars total assets, having achieved this position after twenty years of service with the bank. This man, Harold Smith, was forty-two years of age, married, and he had a twenty-year-old daughter. The other man, Charlie Jones, was thirty-two years old, married and the father of two small children. He had three years of college; after six years of employment with a bank with total assets of eight million dollars, he had attained the position of cashier, holding this position when employed by the Federal Deposit Insurance Corporation. Both these men, upon entering on duty with the subdistrict, had previously spent approximately two months in small rural subdistricts familiarizing themselves with examination policies and procedures.

Charlie Jones caught on very quickly, and almost immediately upon being assigned to the Metro City subdistrict was able to assume responsibility for completion of the detailed aspects of examinations as required by the grade nine job description.

Harold Smith, on the other hand, experienced much difficulty in completing even the most routine work required of a senior assistant examiner, grade nine. Whereas he should have been able to assume responsibility for assigning work to junior assistant examiners and seeing that all the detailed aspects of examinations were completed, he was unable to complete tasks which junior assistant examiners ordinarily completed.

This led to much resentment on the part of the grade seven junior assistants, since they were forced to pick up the slack created by the inability of Harold Smith to perform his duties. The resentment was not only due to Smith's inability to perform his duties, but also because he was a grade nine and received a considerably higher salary for work which grade seven performed. Further resentment was created, because Smith as a grade nine would have to be promoted, according to policy, to grade eleven before any of the men below him could advance to that position.

The men of grade level seven began to feel frustrated because of Smith's inability to learn the necessary skills required for his job. At first the junior assistants as well as the senior assistants already assigned to the Metro City subdistrict made considerable effort to help Smith overcome his deficiencies. They took special pains to explain various facets of the job to him, and they let him repeat each detail of a job as often as he wished. Yet, Smith still was unable to perform on his own without close guidance and supervision. When the bank examiner in charge of the Metro City subdistrict began to question the other men on Smith's progress, they at first covered up for him, making statements such as, "He is a little slow," but they thought he would "begin making some progress in the near future." After several months, it became obvious that Smith was totally unable to perform the duties required by his grade level; he had made little, if any, progress since being assigned to the Metro City subdistrict.

When the Sixtieth District Office sent out the periodic performance forms for Smith to the bank examiner in charge of the Metro City subdistrict, the examiner called the other grade nine senior assistants in to discuss Smith's progress. The appraisal forms rate a man as "unsatisfactory," "satisfactory," or "excellent" on several factors such as ability to perform the work, leadership, and so forth. A rating of at least "satisfactory" is required on each factor before a man is considered eligible for promotion. After consultation with each of his other senior assistant examiners, the bank examiner rated Smith "unsatisfactory" on almost every factor, and in addition, he attached a special letter to the appraisal form recommending that Smith be transferred for a period of time to a rural subdistrict where the work would be less demanding and the opportunity for him to gain the necessary skills would be easier.

The bank examiner discussed this decision and the "unsatisfactory" ratings with Smith. Smith acknowledged his difficulties in learning the job, and he agreed that his opportunity to learn would be greater in a less demanding work situation. Smith stated that on several occasions in the past he had indicated he was reluctant to come to Metro City in the beginning. Smith apparently had hoped that when he was hired he would be allowed to remain near his home in another state.

Several weeks after the performance appraisal form was submitted to the district office, Smith was assigned temporarily to a rural subdistrict (in a town about a hundred miles from Metro City) where he was the only assistant examiner.

After a period of several weeks, Smith returned to Metro City. While apparently he had performed somewhat better in the rural subdistrict, reports indicated that he had made little overall improvement while there. After several weeks back in Metro City, he still was unable to perform noticeably better than before.

The bank examiner in charge of the Metro City subdistrict pondered what he should do next in this situation.

PART SIX

Ten Women at the Employment Office
Melba Moore
Sarah Jones
The Reluctant Employee
The Leadership Skills Conference for Supervisors
Willis B. Johnson
A Problem of Tardiness
The "Fixed" Election

Equal Opportunity Employment

DISCRIMINATION—A MAJOR AND PERVASIVE PROBLEM

All major institutions in our society hold to the ideal of equal opportunity employment, although in the past employment and promotion practices have fallen far short of our professed ideals. During the past decade, however, almost all major institutions and organizations have undertaken to bring practice into closer alignment with the ideals and values of our society.

Discrimination in the employment, development, and promotion of people is as old as recorded history. It has been both overtly and covertly incorporated into all of our economic, political, social, and religious institutions. Race, color, religion, nationality, sex, and age have been the bases for various types of segregation and discrimination through the ages.

Racial discrimination against blacks occupied most of our attention during the decade of the 1960's. On the other hand, Jews have long felt the sting of anti-Semitic prejudices in hiring and promotion practices in organizations, both public and private. Catholics and many Protestant sects have been, from time to time, in one place or another, the objects of social and employment discrimination. Persons of Polish, Slovak, Italian, Irish, Chinese, Mexican, Puerto Rican and other nationalities have been subjected to discrimination. The Indian American, the original "American," has been subjected to very severe discrimination and segregation. Age has been an important basis for discrimination in our society. The aged, and not-so-aged, have been denied employment and advancement opportunities without regard to ability to perform the work. Sex most recently has been recognized as a major basis for discrimination in employment and career advancement. Women have entered our labor market in increasing numbers and are pressing for abolition of the old concepts of "woman's work" and "woman's place."

On the surface, equal opportunity employment should be relatively easy to achieve. The enactment of the Civil Rights Act of 1964 and the Employment Act of 1967, accompanied by supporting statements of policy from business, government, political, educational, and other organizations, should have brought quick and complete compliance. Good intentions are not enough. Discrimination is deeply imbedded in our culture. It permeates all our institutions. Its bases are recorded in centuries of laws, policies, practices, attitudes, and human relationships.

For example, the concept of the role and place of women in family and community life dates back to the era of the early man. From these early roles we developed many stereotypes about women which are not valid. In some religious organizations women are not permitted to vote on matters of doctrine, policy, or practice. They find it most difficult, if not impossible, to become members of the clergy; and only rarely do they occupy important positions in church hierarchy.

Discrimination in employment and promotion is only one small part of the total pattern of discrimination which encompasses all human relationships in our social system. It is very difficult to change one part of a highly interrelated system unless the other parts are changed also. Thus, business organizations will find it difficult to implement equal opportunity employment policies and programs unless the educational system is better able to motivate minority youth to learn skills and knowledge useful on the job. On the other hand, it is difficult to motivate minority youth to learn skills which they do not believe they will be given the opportunity to use. It will be difficult to convince them that their newly acquired skills will be used until they see members of their race actually employing those skills on the job and being given the opportunity to grow and advance on their merits.

Some forms of discrimination on the job are overt. The labor unions in the construction industry have frustrated most efforts on the part of the federal government to voluntarily integrate the construction industry. Union members make no attempt to conceal their fears about job security. They also fear loss of control over their unions. Further, they look upon their craft and their union with considerable pride; their trade and union represent not only a livelihood but also a set of social relationships and a way of life which they fear will be upset by admission to their union of substantial numbers of minority workers.

Much discrimination is covert—and even unconscious. The minority worker always fears that he may not be privy to the discussions which occur and the decisions which are made on the golf course, at the private club, or at social affairs attended only by whites. A black vice-president of a large company commented, "I've never been invited to any social function hosted by any other vice-president or the president of our company." He feared that he and his family were being omitted from the social activities of his peers because he was black. When asked whether or not the other executives mixed socially off the job, he expressed his second fear—he did not feel sufficiently "in the know" in the organization to be certain one way or the other. In other words, he did not feel confident that he was genuinely accepted either within or without the organization. Another black put it somewhat differently, "If you are a black, you can never feel confident that you are denied or offered an opportunity because of your lack or possession of the necessary qualifications—it may have also been denied or offered you because of your color. A white can feel, or assume, that he lost or won the opportunity on the basis of his merit, but a black never knows whether it was merit or color which lost or won the opportunity for him."

Sometimes discrimination is viewed as a process in which white Anglo-Saxon Protestants (WASPs) subtly and not-so-subtly discriminate against all other groups. Minority groups, however, have their own "pecking orders." Until recently, for instance, blacks occupied the lowest positions, both social and economic, in New York City. But, by now, the influx of hundreds of thousands of poor, uneducated Puerto Ricans has transferred the dubious distinction of being "low man on the totem pole" from blacks to Puerto Ricans. We also have many recorded instances of discrimination and segregation in hiring and promotion in organizations based upon religion and ethnic origins.[1]

Blacks

Blacks constitute the largest single identifiable minority group in the United States. As of 1970, they numbered about 22.7 million persons or 12.8 per cent of the total population.[2] They have been the object of unusually severe discrimination in our society, and for them assimiliation has been most difficult. As one educated black put it, "I returned to my high school reunion recently. I learned that my Polish, Italian and Jewish classmates had, in one way or another, made themselves more assimilable by changing their names and through cosmetic surgery, but I was as black as ever." Blacks have long protested their exclusion from the social, political, and economic life of our nation. It was in the spring of 1963 on the streets of Birmingham that Martin Luther King charted a new course not only for the blacks in that city but also for our country. Since that time, our country has been wrestling with the problem of bringing minority people, especially blacks, into the mainstream of our life. Business institutions were the first to feel the impact of this new thrust. Now, however, almost every institution in our society is being confronted with this problem—probably the greatest social problem of this century.

---

[1] Orvis Collins, "Ethnic Behavior in Industry: Sponsorship and Rejection in a New England Factory," *American Journal of Sociology* (Vol. 51, January 1946), pp. 293-298. Also see Andrew M. Greeley, *Why Can't They Be Like Us?* (New York: E. P. Dutton and Co., Inc., 1971), especially, Ch. 5, "Ethnic Group Competition."
[2] U. S. Department of Commerce, Current Population Reports, Series P-25, No. 441, March 19, 1970. *Estimates of the Population of the U. S. by Age, Race, and Sex: July 1, 1969* (Washington: U. S. Government Printing Office).

Most people in our society achieve and maintain both their economic position and social status largely through employment in business and by accepting and participating in the activities of business organizations. Middle-class status is associated in large measure with employment in business institutions. Unfortunately, black and other minority Americans in the past either have not found business to be an attractive career choice or have been frustrated in their efforts to achieve economic and social status via this route. Therefore, business institutions have not produced a substantial black American middle class; rather, this has been produced by the professions of teaching, medicine, dentistry, law, the ministry, and small proprietorships. Or, as one black prospective Master of Business Administration student phrased it during a meeting with young white business executives, "My folks said, 'Son, you have only two choices, to teach or to preach.' Not until a representative of the Consortium for Graduate Study in Management talked to me about the opportunities which exist in business had I given serious consideration to a managerial career in business. I majored in sociology, but I am most happy that I have chosen business for my career. This is my golden opportunity, and I can assure you that I am going to give it everything I've got!" The Negro middle class in our society will not reach its full potential until such time as blacks can freely and openly compete on an equal basis with whites for responsible positions in business institutions.

The task of equal employment opportunity exists at all levels of work. A massive attack on the problem has already been made to get blacks and other minorities onto payrolls. It is not enough, however, for minority people to obtain jobs. They must also be able to train for and occupy jobs which utilize them according to their ability, interests, and drives.[3] Thus, there is a pressing need to recruit able blacks into management positions in business. This has not been easy. Business has not been perceived by blacks as an attractive career choice. Further, the more able the individual, the less attractive business has appeared to him. Some companies, such as IBM, Standard Oil Company (N.J.), R. J. Reynolds Industries, General Foods, First National City Bank of New York, to name a few, have been very aggressively recruiting and developing minority people for responsible positions in management. Two groups of graduate schools have formed consortiums, the purpose of which is to hasten the entry of minorities into management positions in business. The Consortium for Graduate Study in Management and the Council for Graduate Opportunity in Management Education (COGME) have been actively recruiting elite minority men and women for their graduate schools of business.[4]

[3] James S. Spain, "A Modest Proposal for the Abatement of Corporate Racism," *The MBA* (Vol. 4, No. 7, April 1970), pp. 16-25.
[4] The Consortium for Graduate Study in Management was formed in 1966 for the purpose of hastening the entry of minorities into management positions in business via the MBA route. The Consortium is composed of Indiana University, the University of Rochester, the University of Southern California, Washington University, and the University of Wisconsin. The Council for Graduate Opportunity in Management Education was formed in 1968 to achieve somewhat the same purpose. COGME is composed of the University of California, Berkeley; Carnegie-Mellon University; the University of Chicago; Columbia University; Cornell University; Dartmouth College; Harvard University; Massachusetts Institute of Technology; the University of Pennsylvania; and Stanford University.

Equal opportunity employment is related to black entrepreneurship. There are few blacks and other minority business leaders in our society. Those who manage businesses are typically limited to the small "mom and pop" type of corner grocery or dry cleaning establishment. Many government agencies, as well as private organizations, currently are promoting minority entrepreneurship. They are facing great difficulties because of a lack of managerial talent.

Most top level executives in organizations have held these positions through many years of successful decision-making and problem-solving at lower levels in organizations. Vice-presidents are not produced quickly. The equal employment opportunity endeavors in our society have not been going on long enough to recruit large numbers of elite minority people and provide them with the necessary learning experiences which will enable them to manage successfully their own enterprises. Entrepreneurship, at best, is risky. Entrepreneurship for an inexperienced minority manager typically spells disaster.[5] There is an urgent need to recruit the best and most able minority men and women into business careers.

Spanish Surnamed Americans

"Spanish surnamed Americans" typically means Puerto Ricans, Mexican Americans, and Cubans. They constitute three distinct groups having somewhat different problems and characteristics. The Cubans, starting in 1966, came to America to escape the Fidel Castro regime in Cuba. Most are recent arrivals, numbering about 565,000.[6] Typically, they represent the educated professional and managerial class of Cuba. They have brought with them a strong tradition and proud heritage, and most possess usable and needed skills in our society. Many of them are bilingual, and almost all of them were able to make a quick and successful adaptation to our society.[7] A prominent Mexican American leader in the United States, in discussing Spanish surnamed minorities, dismissed the Cubans with the statement, "They need no assistance. As a matter of fact, they treat us no better than the Anglos."

Mexican Americans consider the United States to be their home. They point to the fact that they founded Santa Fe eleven years before the Pilgrims arrived in America, and that their ancestry antedates that of almost every American. The matter is more complex, however, for Mexican Americans immigrated to the United States at different times and for different reasons. Estimates as to the number of Mexican Americans who have settled in the United States vary from five to seven and one-half million.[8] Many of the arrivals during the last decade came illegally, and no accurate account of their number exists. Those who have

---

[5] Current literature lists many examples of this problem. See: Theodore M. Cross, *Black Capitalism* (New York: Atheneum, 1969); "Black Car Dealers Struggle to Exist," *Business Week* (April 10, 1971), pp. 54-56; Andrew F. Brimmer and Henry S. Terrell, "The Economic Potential of Black Capitalism," a paper presented at the 82nd Annual Meeting of the American Economic Association, New York, December 29, 1969.
[6] U. S. Department of Commerce, Current Population Reports, Series P-20, No. 195, February 20, 1970, *Spanish American Population: November 1969* (Washington: U. S. Government Printing Office).
[7] "How the Immigrants Made It in Miami," *Business Week* (May 1, 1971), pp. 88-89.
[8] Current Population Reports, Series P-20, *op. cit.*; "The Chicanos Campaign for a Better Deal," *Business Week* (May 29, 1971), pp. 48-53.

immigrated since 1911 represent the poor, unskilled, and uneducated who sought relief from the poverty and overcrowded conditions in Mexico. They are concentrated mainly in California, New Mexico, Arizona, Colorado, and Texas. They constitute some 27 per cent of the total population of New Mexico and 23 per cent of that of Texas. They consider themselves to be more "disadvantaged" than blacks. They point to the fact that blacks share a common language and religion with whites and lack a foreign cultural heritage with which to identify. On the other hand, Mexican Americans think of themselves as being culturally far different from either whites or other minorities. Typically, they think of themselves as being linguistically different. They speak Spanish for the most part, and they think Spanish. They also have a different religion and different value system. Mexican Americans are part Spanish and part Indian. In fact, they sometimes talk about their "Indianness."[9]

Approximately one and one-half million Puerto Ricans now live in the United States.[10] They are concentrated in the Northeast, with almost one million living in New York City. They represent the poor, uneducated, and unskilled Puerto Ricans. On the other hand, they also represent a group of people who tore up their roots and moved far away to a strange land in order that they might have a better life. They represent probably the poorest, most unskilled, and least educated minority group. They are looked down upon by blacks and whites alike. The language and cultural barriers for them, as for the Mexican American, are very great.

Indian Americans

Indian Americans living on or near reservations now number approximately 827,000.[11] This minority has been an object of neglect, persecution, and social ostracism since the coming of the white man.[12] The Indians have never adapted to our culture, and we have sometimes deliberately and sometimes unwittingly prevented them from developing on their own. They tend to live on reservations, except for those who have intermarried and become assimilated into our society. By and large, the reservations which they occupy have not been suited to the

---

[9] U. S. Commission on Civil Rights, Clearinghouse Publication No. 19, May 1970, *Stranger In One's Land* (Washington: U. S. Government Printing Office), pp. 1-9; Inter-Agency Committee on Mexican American Affairs, *The Mexican American*, Testimony Presented at the Cabinet Committee Hearings on Mexican American Affairs, El Paso, Texas, October 26-28, 1967 (Washington: U. S. Government Printing Office, 1968).
[10] Current Population Reports, Series P-20, *op. cit.*
[11] Bureau of Indian Affairs, Statistics Division, *Preliminary 1970 Census Counts of American Indians and Alaska Natives,* unpublished data from the 1970 Census supplied by Bureau of Census (March, 1971), p. 2.
[12] Harold E. Fey, "America's Most Oppressed Minority," *The Christian Century* (January 20, 1971), pp. 65-68; Mark E. Yudof, "Federal Money for Indians in Public Schools: Where Does It Go?," *Harvard Graduate School of Education Association Bulletin* (Vol. XV, No. 2, Spring 1971), pp. 1-7; Lyndon B. Johnson, "The Forgotten American," President's Message to the Congress on Goals and Programs for the American Indian, March 6, 1968, *Indian Record,* March 1968 (Washington: U. S. Government Printing Office); Harold E. Fey and d'Arcy McNickle, *Indians and Other Americans; Two Ways of Life Met* (New York: Harper and Brothers, 1959).

development of modern industry. Indians have not learned the skills needed in modern society, nor have they been very successful in carrying on the important values and ideals of their culture. Also they have lost by and large the important skills associated with their own culture. The educational attainment of Indians has been much lower than that of whites or blacks.

The Indian is faced with the dilemma of having to obtain the type of education and learn the type of skills which will enable him to succeed in the broader society, while at the same time maintaining familial and tribal cultural ties which provide him with a feeling of pride and a sense of self-identity.

Women

Women constituted 37 per cent of our civilian labor force in 1969.[13] While women have continued to represent an increasing portion of our total labor force during the past half century, the most significant development has been the large increase in the number of employed married women. Of the 29.9 million employed women in 1969, 19.1 million were married.[14] There are many reasons for this change in modern society, beginning with the turn of the twentieth century. First of all, it is now considered appropriate and proper for women to work. Second, labor-saving devices and modern methods of food preparation make it possible for women to perform household tasks in much less time than formerly. Third, women are better educated than ever before. New vistas have been opened to them. They see the challenges which exist in society, and they want to participate in them. Household chores and rearing children do not provide adequate challenge for many. Fourth, women are bearing children earlier in their life and are spacing them in such a manner that they are able to return to work at a rather young age—after only a few years' absence from the labor market. Fifth, the demarcation between "men's work" and "women's work" has become blurred. Not only is it considered appropriate for women to work in an office, but men also now consider it appropriate for males to prepare meals, do housework, and engage in other activities which a few decades ago were considered beneath their dignity and a denial of their maleness. Finally, society needs the talents and skills which women possess. We can no longer afford the luxury of relegating women only to the performance of menial tasks either at home or in the factory and office.

The women's liberation movement has been developing for a long time. It goes far beyond employment; but discrimination in the hiring and promotion of women has been one of the principle targets of the women's liberation movement. In essence, women are saying that they want to make more decisions for themselves concerning their lives and careers. They want to be accepted and treated as indi-

---

[13] U. S. Department of Labor, Bureau of Labor Statistics, "Employment Status of the Institutional Population, By Sex and Race, 1950 to 1970," *Employment and Earnings* (Washington, D. C.: U. S. Government Printing Office, 1970).
[14] U. S. Department of Labor, Bureau of Labor Statistics, "Marital Status of Women in the Civilian Labor Force: 1940 to 1969," *Special Labor Force Reports* (Washington, D. C.: U. S. Government Printing Office).

viduals. They seek opportunities based upon their abilities and interests and not upon their sex.[15] The Civil Rights Act of 1964 has clearly stated that employers must not discriminate on the basis of sex, just as they must not discriminate on the basis of color, race, or religion.

Age and Equal Opportunity Employment

It has been a common practice in our society to discriminate against the hiring and promotion of people after they reach some arbitrary age.[16] In some societies, people acquire more stature and prestige with age. Ours, however, generally has concluded that the infirmities which are associated with advanced age somehow disqualify people from useful employment at a rather early age.

Further, age has been an important criterion for eliminating people from the work force on the theory that there are too many people in the labor force to do the work which society needs to have done! As a result of this, we find organizations establishing arbitrary age limits for the hiring and promotion of people. Executives over age 40 have found it difficult to find new employment. In fact, they have found it so difficult that they have formed organizations to aid them in their job-seeking activities. Many government and private organizations and agencies require retirement at some arbitrary age, typically 65. Many collective agreements negotiated by unions and employers provide for this type of compulsory retirement. Age carries with it certain disabilities. On the other hand, these do not affect all people at the same time in the same way. It is as unreasonable to stereotype persons on the basis of age as it is to stereotype them on the basis of sex, color, race, religion, or ethnic ancestry.

BUSINESS ORGANIZATIONS AS SOCIAL SYSTEMS[17]

Business organizations, like all organizations, are social systems; in any social system, the members are tied together by many subtle and delicate interpersonal relationships. We commonly examine business organizations as primarily economic institutions; in this context, we attempt to understand the relationships which exist among the people in a business by examining the organization chart. Charts do tell us something about the way those who develop the charts believe the organization functions and the way they think it ought to function. However, in reality, charts tell us very little about power, communication channels, decision channels, functional relationships and the socio-emotional feelings which people have toward each other. The organization chart tells very little about the leadership philosophy, about the style and attitudes of those who hold formal leadership

---

15 See: Elizabeth Janeway, *Man's World, Woman's Place* (New York: Morrow, 1971); Betty Friedan, *The Feminine Mystique* (New York: W. W. Norton and Co., Inc., 1963); Caroline Bird, *Born Female*, Revised Edition (New York: David McKay Co., Inc., 1968); Ishbel Ross, *Sons of Adam, Daughters of Eve* (New York: Harper and Row Publishers, 1969).
16 Jim Hyatt, "Prohibition on Age Bias in Employment Proves Difficult to Enforce," *Wall Street Journal* (Vol. 51, No. 171, June 16, 1971).
17 This section is based substantially upon an address by Sterling H. Schoen, "New Opportunities and New Challenges for Negroes in Business," *American Pharmaceutical Manufacturers Association*, Personnel Section, Washington, D. C.: April 24, 1969.

positions, or about the social climate of the organization and the expectations of its members.

The social structure of an organization has a very great impact upon the new employee and his probable success in it. It is especially important in determining the readiness with which he will be accepted. It is also important in determining whether or not he will be stimulated to give his best to the organization, and whether or not he will be provided with learning experiences which will enable him to utilize fully his abilities and rise up through the organization to the point where his responsibilities match his capabilities.

Most of the things people learn about their jobs, they learn from their supervisor and from their colleagues. Much of their "education" is unplanned and informal. People qualify for higher positions in a variety of ways. First of all, they qualify by being given and accepting assignments outside their regular work. Second, they qualify by learning their present job well and mastering it. Third, they qualify by receiving formal training, i.e., by attending management development programs of one sort or another. Finally, they qualify by asking questions and learning from others through a variety of informal contacts.

The state of race relations and the patterns of segregation and discrimination, which have existed in our country, have tended to exclude minority persons from many learning experiences. This is true in all types of organizations. For example, a supervisor tends to think of those people with whom he has associated most and whom he knows best when he selects subordinates for special assignments and for special formal and informal training programs. This supervisor typically is white. He has developed more intimate relationships with whites in his organization than with minority people for various reasons: their cultural backgrounds, interests and experiences tend to be more similar; they feel more comfortable in each others' presence; and they share more time with each other, both on and off the job.

Further, informal groups tend to be made up of individuals who possess similar values, beliefs, sentiments—and color. As a consequence, minority employees tend to be excluded from many valuable unplanned, informal learning opportunities which occur in organizations. When the time approaches for a promotion, the superior, first of all, tends to think about those individuals whom he knows best. This includes people to whom he has given assignments and people with whom he has associated and likes. Since the minority organizational member tends to receive fewer learning experiences and is more likely to be excluded from many informal learning opportunities than his white counterpart, it is very likely that he will be passed over when promotions occur. After all, the superior will promote those individuals in whom he has confidence, whom he knows, and whom he also knows would have obtained the best training for the position to be filled.

The need to satisfy the equal opportunity employment guidelines developed by government agencies and feelings of guilt on the part of some executives frequently have led to the selection and promotion of less qualified or unqualified minority persons. Thus, complaints are made that minority people "plateau out" after two or three minor promotions at lower levels in the organization. Decisions made at these lower levels do not "make or break the organization."

Typically, people at lower levels are responsible for coordinating and communicating within and between groups. Their decisions are minor, and control systems within the organization prevent them from inflicting serious damage upon the total organization. Organizations look more closely at the qualifications of people promoted to higher levels in their organization where they expect managers to assume responsibility for important decisions which affect the profits of the organization. An exception to this occurs in instances where a minority person is deliberately promoted to a high-level position but is given few responsibilities, because his presence is desired primarily for the image he will provide for the organization.

All of this is reinforced by off-the-job situations. Since business organizations are social institutions, the members associate on many occasions with one another off the job. This applies not only to the business-related contacts off the job, but more importantly to the contacts which occur in the country club, the poker game, the golf match, and so forth.

Wives of executives play an important role in determining the careers of their husbands. Wives, like their husbands, tend to associate with others with whom they feel comfortable and whose values, beliefs, and sentiments they believe to be similar to their own. Since husbands and wives talk with each other about business, it is expected that wives have some influence over the relationships which occur on the job. Yet, if wives of black executives are excluded from the social activities of wives of their white counterparts, they are not "in the know." It thus becomes difficult for them to enter into comfortable social relationships on occasions when husbands and wives come together in off-the-job organizational, social, and business activities.

When we review the history of race relations, it is reasonable to say that blacks and other racial and ethnic minorities operate under a handicap with respect to their interpersonal relationships with whites in organizations. This occurs for a variety of reasons. First, there is the matter of out-and-out prejudice or racial bias. Second, there is the problem of the minority member entering the comfortable closely-knit "in-group." These small groups in organizations are made up of whites who see minority persons as being very "different." They tend to resist attempts on the part of these "outsiders" to break into their groups. If minority people make overtures toward entering these groups, they are looked upon as being pushy or aggressive; yet, the successful executive in any kind of organization—business, education, government—tends to be the outgoing individual who does not hesitate to make overt gestures toward meeting and working with people and seeking out work assignments. Third, many whites feel that their organizations are practicing reverse discrimination and are allowing minority persons to advance more rapidly than comparable whites. Finally, whites tend to fear that their social and economic position will be lessened by the presence of minority people, especially if they look upon them as being "unqualified."

Thus, when we consider organization-related activities, it is likely that the minority executive will tend to be restricted from sources of information which are potentially valuable to his career. He will also be shortchanged when it comes to those organization-related, but off-the-job situations in which matters pertaining to the organization and his job are discussed incidentally. Further, in the case of extra-organizational activities, his spouse, parents, and children also will be deprived of the socialization and educational processes which provide an understanding of the nature of the executive's work, obligations, and frustrations. There is a great danger that failure to become involved in extra-organizational activities will prevent the development within the family of commitments, understanding, and empathy, which are necessary to provide a home environment supportive of the executive's rigorous work schedule and possibly even absence from home for prolonged periods. The success or failure of any executive in large measure depends upon the understanding, empathy, and support which he receives from his spouse and children.

What does this mean to the organization which employs talented and ambitious young minority persons? It means that it is not enough to provide the new employee with a job, an office, and a salary. The organization must take active steps to insure that the minority manager obtains appropriate learning experiences. The superior can insure this in a variety of ways, such as making sure that the minority person receives a fair share of the special assignments, that he is invited to participate in conferences within the organization, that he is considered for enrollment in management development conferences sponsored by universities and business associations, and that he is invited to those informal activities over which the superior has control within the organization. These things are not adequate, however, for the minority manager still may miss out on the learning experiences which occur as a result of friendly relationships which exist within his peer group in the organization. The superior must be prepared to deal with prejudice and bias, even though it is virtually impossible to legislate anyone's attitudes and state of mind. He must attempt to allay the fears of other white executives, and he must take steps to educate them as to their responsibilities. There are many specific things which he might do to bring about good interpersonal relationships in the organization; common sense and a little thought will indicate what most of these things should entail.

The white executive also needs to be aware of the fact that social organizations, such as businesses, function 24 hours a day in the sense that it is impossible to disassociate work life from home life. He must be prepared to bring the entire minority family into the organization in the same way that the entire white family is involved in the organization. Again, this is not easy, but common sense, thought, and empathy for the feelings of other human beings will carry the executive a long way in dealing with these problems.

SUMMARY

Achievement of equal opportunity employment is a necessary objective for our society. While progress is being made in this direction, it will not be easy to achieve equal opportunity employment in our complex and highly inter-related social systems without comparable related measures being taken in various parts of each system. Discrimination on the basis of color, race, ethnic ancestry, sex, and age, permeates almost all aspects of our social, political, economic, and religious institutions.

Business organizations are social organizations. Minority employees experience the same kinds of problems in making their way in business organizations that they experience in making their way in other types of organizations and in the entire social system. White executives who tend to be in the superior positions in these organizations have a special responsibility to make the organization more open to new minority workers who differ from other employees on the basis of race, religion, ethnic ancestry, sex, and age. It is they who will determine whether or not minority people will have the opportunity to achieve their full potential and whether or not the organization will obtain the full benefit of their interests, abilities, and drives.

TEN WOMEN AT THE EMPLOYMENT OFFICE   CASE 37

A group of black women gathered at a church in Hillsborough, North Carolina, on the morning of September 2, 1965. They agreed to visit various plants in the town, seeking employment. They planned to return to the church later and file complaints against the companies which did not offer them employment.

That morning Dorothy Mead, Roberta Seay, Anna Teesdale, Bea D. Beasley, Tandy Jones, Laura Beasley, Caroline Jackson, Minnie Johnson, Josie Washington, and Emma Jean Torrence[1] made applications at a mill known as the Eno plant of the Cone Mills Corporation. They filled out the application forms and provided all information required by the company. Anna Teesdale and Tandy Jones were the only two applicants in the group who had telephones. Both included their telephone numbers in the information provided to the company.

They were then interviewed, two or more at a time, by the personnel manager. None of the ladies had ever worked at a textile plant before nor had relatives or close friends working at the plant. One of them was already employed and one had never held a job.

When they met again at the church, Minnie Johnson and Anna Teesdale reported to the group that they were interviewed by the personnel manager at the same time. They said that the personnel manager told them that the Eno plant did not employ black females.[2]

Near the beginning of November, a vacancy occurred in the Eno plant for which at least one of the ladies was qualified. No one in the group was contacted by the company and an inexperienced white female was given the job. It was on March 17, 1966, that the first black female was employed at the plant. She was not a member of the above group. In August of that year, another vacancy occurred. When no experienced person was located to take the job, one of the women who was a member of the group was hired.

Near the end of November in 1965, the women who had applied at the Eno plant had filed charges with the Equal Employment Opportunity Commission. On June 24, 1966, after reviewing the charges, the commission reported that it found reasonable cause to believe that Tandy Jones, Josie Washington, Caroline Jackson, Dorothy Mead, Minnie Johnson, and Laura Beasley had not been considered for employment at the Eno plant because of their race.

[1] All names disguised.

[2] At a subsequent legal proceeding on the case, the women reiterated their charge that the personnel manager told them that the Eno plant did not employ black females. The personnel manager stated that he did not remember the question being asked, but said that it was true that no black females had ever been employed at the plant.

Almost two months later, on August 19, 1966, each of these ladies received a letter from Kenneth F. Holber, the acting director of compliance for the commission. The letter stated that due to the heavy workload of the commission it had been impossible to undertake or to conclude conciliation efforts. He suggested that they file a civil action in the appropriate federal district court. Dorothy Mead, Josie Washington, and Laura Beasley took his advice and filed on September 19, 1966.

BACKGROUND

Cone Mills Corporation

The Cone Mills Corporation has its principal corporation office and place of business in Greensboro, North Carolina. Other mills, facilities, and offices are maintained by Cone Mills throughout the state of North Carolina. One of the manufacturing plants, the Eno plant, is located in Hillsborough. This plant manufactures griege (unfinished) goods.

In 1961, John Bagwill, who was the Vice-president for industrial relations at Cone Mills at that time, asked for a review of Cone's hiring policies with regard to the number of blacks employed. He was provided a series of directives which had been sent to the plant managers. In April of 1963, Mr. Bagwill placed these directives in Cone Mills' personnel policy manual. One of the policies was that the applicant's ability to perform the job should be *the* factor considered when hiring. In addition, it was stated that this factor should be considered with no reference to race, creed, color or national origin. When two or more applicants each could meet the ability criterion for a particular vacancy, the manual established the following priorities for selection among the candidates:

(a) Laid-off employees
(b) Former employees
(c) Persons residing in or near the communities in which Cone Mills plants are located.

Written hiring procedures applicable at the Eno plant were as follows:

(a) The applicant fills out an application form, is interviewed by the personnel manager, and is given aptitude and visual tests.
(b) The applicant's work history is investigated, and if found satisfactory, the applicant is interviewed further.
(c) Applicants found satisfactory are then given a physical examination.
(d) Applicants satisfying all such requirements, including the physical examination, are offered employment.

During the summer of 1965, shortly before the Civil Rights Act of 1964 was to go into effect, officials at Cone Mills held a meeting with all plant managers and reviewed the provisions of the act, as well as company policy.

Eno Plant

Prior to and following July 2, 1965, it was the custom at the Eno plant to accept applications from all applicants, whether a vacancy existed or not. However, applications were not accepted during the last week of each July when the plant closed for vacations. Also, during a period of a week or so in June of 1965, applications were not accepted. A notice to this effect was placed on the door of the plant during those occasions.

All applicants at the Eno plant were asked to complete an application form and then were interviewed by the personnel manager in order to review the applicant's work history. The personnel manager also determined in the interview whether the applicant was a former employee, whether he resided nearby, and/or was a friend or relative of someone presently employed at the plant. The interview was conducted even if a vacancy did not exist.

If there was a vacancy, the supervisor of the department in which the vacancy existed typically interviewed the applicant. If the supervisor found the applicant satisfactory, the applicant was given a physical examination. If he passed the physical examination, he was hired.

If the applicant was not offered a job at the time he made his application, the application was placed at the top of a stack of previously filed applications in the personnel office. Applicants for work at the Eno plant were required to renew their application every two weeks to indicate to the personnel manager that they were still seeking employment. When an application was renewed, the renewal date was recorded and the application was placed on top of the stack. If it was not renewed within approximately two weeks, the application remained on the bottom of the stack. Applications which had not been renewed were filed alphabetically every two to four weeks. If the application was renewed at some later date, the renewal date was noted and the application again was placed on top of the stack.

If a vacancy for which no one applied personally developed, the personnel manager reviewed current applications for a qualified prospect. If the name of a qualified applicant was on file, he was contacted by telephone, postcard, or one of the references he provided on his application form. If the applicant passed the physical examination, he was offered the job. Inexperienced applicants were considered only if no experienced applicants could be found. Vacancies at the Eno plant generally were filled in one or two days.

The plant manager at the Eno plant gave first priority to applicants with experience. Second in order of priorities was an applicant who had a relative employed at the plant. An applicant who had a close friend working at the plant was next. The last priority was the residence of the applicant.

While no applicant was asked to state his race on the application form, he was required to list the schools which he had attended. Before 1965, the race of the applicant usually could be determined from this information, since the schools in Orange County were segregated at that time.

Certain jobs at the Eno plant were classified as "male" jobs because of their physical requirements. Other jobs, such as spinner, spool tender, quiller operator, and battery filler, which were not so physically demanding, were considered "female" jobs.

The Eno plant was virtually the only manufacturing plant in the Hillsborough area offering industrial employment.

Employment Statistics

As of July 2, 1965, there were 346 persons employed at the Eno plant, 310 white and 35 black. Between this date and November 1, 1966, 167 persons were employed. Of these, 85 were white males, 53 were black males, 22 were white females, and 7 were black females. (Prior to the beginning of 1965, no black females had filed applications at the plant.)

POSITION OF THE PLAINTIFFS

The plaintiffs charged that they had been denied employment by Cone Mills at the Eno plant on September 2, 1965, because of their race. They contended that the company's policy on giving priorities in hiring to former employees and close friends of existing employees discriminated against black females. In support of their complaint, they stated that they had not been informed of the company policy that applications for employment had to be renewed every two weeks in order for them to remain active. The plaintiffs demanded that they be offered employment by the company and that back pay should be awarded them for the time that they would have worked if the company had not discriminated against them. They further demanded that the company stop discriminating against black females.

POSITION OF THE COMPANY

The company contended that its hiring policies were neither outwardly nor inherently discriminatory with respect to black females. It was further argued that the lack of black female applicants prior to 1965 was a result of their lack of interest. The company claimed that the plaintiffs' suit should be dismissed in its entirety.

APPENDIX

Section 703 (a) of the Civil Rights Act of 1964, 42 U.S.C. 2000e-2 (a) provides:

> (a) It shall be an unlawful employment practice for an employer—
> (1) to fail or refuse to hire or to discharge any individual, or otherwise to discriminate against any individual with respect to his compensation, terms, conditions or privileges of employment, because of such individual's race, color, religion, sex, or national origin; or
> (2) to limit, segregate, or classify his employees in any way which would deprive or tend to deprive any individual of employment opportunities or otherwise adversely affect his status as an employee, because of such individual's race, color, religion, sex, or national origin.

Section 706 (g) of the Civil Rights Act of 1964, 42 U.S.C. 2000e-5(g) provides:

> (g) If the court finds that the respondent has intentionally engaged in or is intentionally engaging in an unlawful employment practice charged in the

complaint, the court may enjoin the respondent from engaging in such unlawful employment practice, and order such affirmative action as may be appropriate, which may include reinstatement or hiring of employees, with or without back pay (Payable by the employer, employment agency, or labor organization, as the case may be, responsible for the unlawful employment practice). Interim earnings or amounts earnable with reasonable diligence by the person or persons discriminated against shall operate to reduce the back pay otherwise allowable. No order of the court shall require the admission or reinstatement of an individual as a member of a union or the hiring, reinstatement, or promotion of an individual as an employee, or the payment to him of any back pay, if such individual was refused admission, suspended, or expelled or was refused employment or advancement or was suspended or discharged for any reason other than discrimination on account of race, color, religion, sex or national origin or in violation of section 2000e-3 (a) of this title.

MELBA MOORE CASE 38

The Global United Manufacturing Company employs over 1500 people in its headquarters in Cleveland, Ohio. The company has several government contracts and thus is subjected annually to an equal employment opportunity compliance review conducted by a federal agency. The company has an affirmative action program to implement its policy of equal employment opportunity. The government's compliance staff has found the company's affirmative action program to be comprehensive and the company to be serious in its attempts to correct any deficiencies uncovered by the review.

The purchasing department of Global United is responsible for ordering all manufacturing materials, office supplies, and services. The department is headed by the chief purchasing agent, Pete Wilson. Reporting to Pete are five supervisors, each having responsibility for purchasing different types of goods and services. Each supervisor has a staff of several buyers, a stenographer, and a typist.

Most of the buyers are college graduates or have a college background with equivalent experience. The buyers are considered to be semiprofessional employees and are given considerable leeway in their purchasing decisions. The buyers must exercise considerable tact in dealing with the many salesmen who call on Global.

Under the provisions of the company's affirmative action program (and as required by various governmental orders), all major suppliers and subcontractors must certify that they are equal employment opportunity employers and that they have an affirmative action program. The purchasing department is responsible for seeing that the necessary certifications are received from each supplier and subcontractor.

However, over the years the purchasing department itself had employed only a few blacks, and as of July, 1970, no blacks were employed in the purchasing department. During the annual compliance review in February, 1970, the EEO (Equal Employment Opportunity) compliance staff pointed out that Global was deficient in not employing any blacks in its purchasing department. Pete Wilson and the five supervisors reporting to him agreed that they would make a special effort to employ a black buyer.

In August, 1970, Melba Moore began her employment with Global as a clerk-typist in the purchasing department, thus becoming the only black in the department. She had attended a junior college in Cleveland and had studied several

Case contributed by John R. Hundley, III, Instructor, University College Division, Washington University. All names disguised.

courses in business administration. After a year and a half of college, Melba left school due to marriage. Upon leaving college, Melba went to work as a clerk-typist in the accounting department of a chemical company headquartered in Cleveland. Melba worked for the chemical company for three years before leaving due to pregnancy.

When her son, Jeff, reached age one, Melba decided to re-enter the labor market and again assist in earning the family income. Melba's husband, Bob, was employed as a marketing representative by a major oil company and was assigned to a territory in the Ohio area. Although Bob earned a fairly good income, both Bob and Melba wanted to save enough money to purchase a home.

During her first several months on the job, Melba performed in an outstanding manner. She learned her job quickly and reached a high output level as a typist. Melba formed cordial relationships with the other employees in the purchasing department, and she was very pleasant with the salesmen who called on Global.

In January, 1971, one of the buyers under supervisor Tom Schmitt left Global to accept a position with another company. After discussion of possible ways to fill the vacant buyer's position, Pete Wilson and Tom Schmitt decided to offer the promotion to Melba. Melba accepted the promotion and was moved under Tom Schmitt's supervision. The company was pleased that it had been able to upgrade a black employee to fill this semiprofessional position. Melba thus became one of the few blacks to occupy a comparable position in the company, although the company did employ many blacks in lower occupational jobs.

However, after several months as a buyer, Melba began to complain to Tom Schmitt about discriminatory actions on the part of other members of the department. Melba cited examples of not receiving phone messages or copies of departmental memoranda on several occasions. She also mentioned an incident where one of the typists refused to do her work because another buyer had already given her some work. Melba further stated that she felt certain supervisors in other departments were biased.

Tom talked with Melba for several hours, advising her that these incidents should "be taken for what they are and no more—irritations that cannot be avoided in the business world." Tom advised Melba that even Pete Wilson didn't receive all of his phone messages, and that this was not necessarily a subtle form of discrimination on the part of her co-workers. Melba told Tom that these incidents were attempts "to remind me that I'm the least important person in the department." Melba further stated, "I'm not important here, so if I'm out a day or so, my work won't suffer—someone else will do it or it'll wait."

After Melba became a buyer, her attendance began to slip. During a six month period, Melba missed fifteen days. On each occasion Melba had seemingly good reasons for being absent, but this amount of absence was far more than customary in the purchasing department.

Melba was shaken by the following incident. She invited several of her co-workers to a "home decorating" party over a weekend. A representative of a home decorating firm planned to display his merchandise and provide Melba with a commission on any merchandise sold as a result of the party. None of the men or women working for Tom Schmitt whom Melba invited attended the party. One of the buyers said he planned a trip on that date. Another buyer became ill several days prior to the party and was unable to attend. A stenographer in the unit decided not to attend since she did not know anyone else attending the party. Even though several employees of the company attended the party, Melba was disturbed that no one from the purchasing department attended. She made it a point to tell Tom Schmitt about this experience on Monday morning, and she commented that, "This shows again that the whites in this department are against me and don't care about my feelings."

In previous discussions of problems in relationships with co-workers, Melba usually had reacted negatively toward Tom's advice. No amount of reassurance or personal counseling had convinced Melba that her beliefs were without foundation. Tom wondered what action, if any, he should take regarding the latest incident.

SARAH JONES   CASE 39

INTRODUCTION

At 2:00 p.m., on July 15, 1969, Mrs. Sarah Jones[1] was discharged by the Singer Controls Company of America, Motor Division, located at Jacksonville, Arkansas, for violation of shop rule number 15, "Fighting or incitement for fighting shall be cause for discharge."

On July 18, 1969 the union, Local 1000, United Automobile Workers of America, filed a grievance demanding that Miss Jones be reinstated with full back pay and stating that:

> Miss Jones feels that the other girl was just as much to blame as she was and that both should have the same discipline. Miss Jones says that she has been here two years and 11 months, and she knows other cases of fighting and they were not discharged. She thinks one company rule should stand for all.

The company denied the grievance on July 24, 1969, and the union immediately filed another grievance which alleged that Miss Jones "was being discriminated against." The grievance ultimately was submitted to arbitration for final settlement.

BACKGROUND

The Singer Controls Company of America, Motor Divison, employed Miss Sarah Jones, a black woman, as a production operator on the internal motor assembly line on August 18, 1966. Miss Jones continued in that position for almost three years when she was discharged by the company for striking a fellow employee.

Miss Jones had experienced difficulties in her relationship with some of her associates on the job during the year prior to her discharge. On March 12, 1969, and again on April 3, 1969, she spoke with management protesting that her fellow employees were "making fun of her body odor and were holding their noses as they passed her work station." She complained that their behavior made her nervous. She visited her physician, Dr. B. D. Smith in Little Rock on March 31 for advice regarding a possible body odor problem. He assured her that she had no such problem and prescribed medication for her nervous condition, recommending that she drink considerable quantities of liquids.

---

[1] Case adapted from a published arbitration case in *Labor Arbitration Reports*. Used by permission of the Bureau of National Affairs, Inc. All names disguised.

Miss Jones spoke with one of her white co-workers, Betty Thompson, about the way she was being treated by other employees in her work area. She told Betty that she felt that their behavior was very uncomplimentary and that they were making fun of her because she was black.

As a result of Miss Jones' personal complaints to several company officials, the general foreman, James Thurston, conducted a personal survey of the employees in her work area. Thurston reported to his superiors that he found no indication of the situation about which Miss Jones was complaining.

Hedda Johnson, a representative on the union bargaining committee, later met with Sarah about her allegations. Miss Johnson informed Sarah that she could not find anyone who thought that there was a problem and told Sarah that "we thought she was imagining some of this." Miss Jones later met again with company officials and during the course of the meeting threatened to sue the company. Personnel manager Rex Tupper told her that she would be fired if she continued to complain about her problems with her associates in the area. After this meeting with company officials, Miss Jones left the plant for about two hours, and it required union intervention to get the company to allow her to return to work without further disciplinary action.

The Incident

The incident occurred at about 2:00 p.m. on a very hot summer day, July 15, 1969. The facts of the incident were not clear, and the parties gave conflicting testimony.

The company summarized the incident as follows:

> Miss Jones, a production operator on internal motor assembly, was seated diagonally across from Jane Barber, an inspector. There was general discussion by the employees on this production line concerning the afternoon heat, which was unusually high. Jane Barber said to Miss Jones, "Are you hot, too?" Miss Jones, without warning hit Jane on the right temple with her fist, and followed with other blows. Jane stated that, although she did not fall, she was in fact hit hard enough so that she blacked out and was unconscious on her feet. The foreman sent Miss Jones to personnel and followed with Jane. Jane who was taken by surprise and did not even attempt to defend herself, was calmed down and after it was determined she was all right, returned to work.

The union summarized the incident somewhat differently:

> Right after lunch . . . Mrs. Barber remarked to Miss Jones that she (Barber) was hot, and that her deodorant was beginning to fail. Miss Jones asked Mrs. Barber about the kind of deodorant she used. Mrs. Barber replied, "The question is, what kind of deodorant do *you* use?" Later in the afternoon, she was, according to Mrs. Barber's testimony, discussing the temperature in the plant with some of the employees on the assembly line. Barber testified that she asked Miss Jones if she also was hot. Miss Jones affirmatively

replied and inquired whether Mrs. Barber meant that there was anything unique or significant about her (Miss Jones) being hot.

Miss Jones testified that Mrs. Barber then began to laugh and continued after Miss Jones inquired why she was doing so. Miss Jones admitted that she then lost her temper and spontaneously struck out at Mrs. Barber with the back of her hand.

The only person who witnessed the altercation, Mrs. Lucille Harrison, stated that she was only a few feet away from Mrs. Barber and Miss Jones, that there was only one blow, and that it was a kind of backhand gesture. Mrs. Harrison also reported that she saw Mrs. Barber laugh in response to Miss Jones' inquiry about what Mrs. Barber meant by asking her if she was hot.

Foreman John Mercer stated that when he escorted Mrs. Barber to first aid immediately after the incident, she said that she didn't know what happened. Mrs. Barber's subsequent written report of the altercation, however, was as follows:

> I asked Miss Jones if she was hot, too. I did not do this to irritate her or upset her. I continued to work and the next thing I knew I was hit on the right temple by her fist. I didn't see her hit me. I just felt it, although the next blows felt like they were hitting a numb spot. I didn't fall but when I was conscious again, I was yelling.

UNION POSITION

The union contended that events leading to the discharge incident caused Miss Jones to become quite sensitive to comments and actions by her associates involving subtle, but overt, derogatory racial overtones.

The union argued that the mere occurrence of an altercation on company premises did not justify discharge of one of the participants without reference to all the circumstances surrounding the dispute. Miss Jones had been unduly harassed

Miss Jones was very disturbed by, and resentful of, what she considered to be crude and unkind remarks by her fellow workers reflecting disparagingly on her race. It was therefore understandable that Miss Jones finally became very angry and lost her self-control when Mrs. Barber tauntingly laughed in response to Miss Jones' inquiry as to whether her being hot implied anything different from any other employee's being hot in the same situation.

In conclusion, the union argued that the conduct of Miss Jones did not warrant the ultimate punishment of summary discharge, and that the provocation was sufficient to rescind the company's decision to discharge her.

COMPANY POSITION

Personnel Manager Rex Tupper expressed the judgment that the discharge of Miss Jones was consistent with plant practice, and that he would take similar action again if similar circumstances arose.

The company stated its position in the following quotation from its brief submitted to the arbitrator:

The testimony of Jane Barber, the struck employee, indicates she was hit without warning, hard enough to be unconscious and was hit more than once...

(Miss Jones) had upset the efficiency of operations at least three times with the pursual of a discrimination complex. None of her accusations were ignored or treated lightly and none, including the last one, were justified...

It is obvious that the company cannot employ people who cannot control themselves, or decide individually when they are justified in hitting other employees depending on their mood of the day...

It is curious that (Miss Jones), who believes the employees and the company are discriminating against her, would want to return to work for a wage difference of $6.00 a week, much of which must be consumed in transportation costs.[2]

The company concluded that Miss Jones was discharged for cause and asked the arbitrator to deny Miss Jones' claim for reinstatement with full back pay.

APPENDIX

Pertinent Contract Provisions:

Article II

Managements' Rights

Section 2: Subject to the terms of this Agreement the right to promote, demote, discharge or discipline for cause; and to maintain discipline and efficiency of employees is the sole responsibility of the Company. Should any employee or the Union be aggrieved by Company action in applying the above, he shall have recourse through the grievance procedure as provided in this Agreement.

Article VI

Seniority

Section 26: LOSS OF SENIORITY
Loss of Seniority and removal of an employee's name from the seniority list will be in the event that:

(a) The employee is discharged for just cause.

---

[2] After her discharge on July 15, 1969, Miss Jones worked for about two weeks at the University of Arkansas Medical Center. After October, 1969, she was employed by Linen and Drapery Service, Inc., where she earned $64 per week, about $6.00 less than she was paid at the Singer Controls Company.

THE RELUCTANT EMPLOYEE   CASE 40

INTRODUCTION

On the morning of May 17, 1969, Jane Souther,[1] floor supervisor of the first shift at the Enka, North Carolina plant of the American Enka Corporation, discovered that Sandra Lyons, a new black employee, had inserted several spools in machine 15 incorrectly. In the attempt to correct the situation, the problem escalated to the point where Mr. Hopkins, acting foreman, asked Miss Lyons to return to machine 15 to correct her error. Miss Lyons persistently refused, whereupon Mr. Hopkins discharged her.

Local 2598 of the United Textile Workers, which represented employees at the plant, filed a grievance on behalf of Miss Lyons protesting the discharge. The grievance eventually was carried to arbitration. In its grievance, the union requested that Sandra Lyons be reinstated with full seniority and back pay.

BACKGROUND

On February 3, 1969, Miss Sandra Lyons, a young black high school graduate with no industrial experience, was employed by the American Enka Corporation. Her first two weeks on the job were devoted to a two-week training program on the first shift. Upon completion of her training, she was assigned the A shift in "Nylon Draw-twisting." She worked in that department for about three months, completing her probationary period in early May.

Previously the Enka Corporation had employed blacks only in menial positions—as janitors and maids. But in 1963, the company became "an equal opportunity employer" and began to employ and recruit black employees. Of the 3500 workers, 155 were black, and they were dispersed throughout most departments. Both management and the union had worked together to establish non-discriminatory policies and practices.

At the time of the incident leading to her discharge, Miss Lyons was working on a doffing board[2] with Mrs. Ewbank and Mrs. Simpson, two long-term white employees of the company. The three women worked closely together, rotating specific duties as they moved from one machine to another, racking spools of yarn onto spindles.

---

[1] Case adapted from a published arbitration case in *Labor Arbitration Reports,* Used by permission of the Bureau of National Affairs, Inc. All names disguised.
[2] Doffing board—a machine that is used to transfer carded (combed) fibers from the cylinder and then prepared for conversion into sliver (continuous strands of twisted fibers).

258 *Equal Opportunity Employment*

Mrs. Jane Souther, the floor supervisor, discovered on the morning of May 17 that a mistake was made on machine 15. The mistake involved the insertion of from some 20 spools in machine 15 in a clockwise manner instead of a counterclockwise manner. Mrs. Souther discovered that Miss Lyons had worked on machine 15 and was responsible for the mistake. She told Miss Lyons that she should correct her mistake and warned her to "watch it next time."

A short time later Miss Gibson, the area supervisor, came to Miss Lyons to tell her that after completing work on the machine she was currently loading, she was to return to machine 15 to help several other girls who already were in the process of correcting her mistake. At first Miss Lyons agreed to do so, but after conferring with her two teammates, she changed her mind and refused to return. When Miss Lyons persisted in her refusal, Miss Gibson insisted that they go to see Mr. Harold Hopkins, acting shift foreman.

On their way to Mr. Hopkins' office, they met him in the plant. Mrs. Gibson related the situation to Mr. Hopkins, who then requested Miss Lyons to return to machine 15 to correct her mistake. When Miss Lyons refused, Mr. Hopkins asked clerical worker Dot Peoples to listen in on the discussion. Mr. Hopkins several times asked Miss Lyons to return to machine 15. Miss Lyons persistently refused. The verbal argument between the two attracted other employees to the scene. At this point, Mr. Hopkins asked Miss Lyons if she knew what her refusal meant, and she replied "No." Mr. Hopkins then informed her that it meant her dismissal. At this time, Miss Lyons flew into a rage and accused Mr. Hopkins and the gathering crowd of being prejudiced. She let loose upon him a barrage of "foul" language. Mr. Hopkins thereupon told Miss Lyons to leave the premises and not to return until further notice. A short time later, Miss Lyons went into Mr. Hopkins' office, threw in her scissors and other equipment, and then left the plant.

UNION POSITION

The union conceded that Miss Lyons did make the mistake, but maintained that the company's behavior was discriminatory and needlessly provocative, leading Miss Lyons to become belligerent and uncooperative. The union contended that new employees customarily depend upon the counsel and example of senior fellow employees. Miss Lyons, a new employee, had at first agreed to return to machine 15 to correct her mistake, but then after consulting with her two senior fellow workers, she decided not to go. Being black and new on the job, Miss Lyons was concerned about the attitudes of the other workers, and she did not want to cause their wrath by directly ignoring their advice.

Miss Lyons contended that she was told by her two fellow employees that, in all their years of employment, they had never been asked to go back to correct such mistakes, and they had not seen any other employee return to correct a similar mistake. Furthermore, their schedule was such that it did not permit employees to return and correct mistakes. Miss Lyons believed that she was asked to return because she was black.

Finally, due to some previous difficulties with the company and especially with Mr. Hopkins, Miss Lyons believed that she was being discriminated against. Miss

Lyons stated that on a number of occasions, Mr. Hopkins had called her into his office to reprimand her, and that on one instance, she had an argument with him over her being late. Further, Miss Lyons stated that Mrs. Souther "hollered" at her about her work. Miss Lyons previously had filed two grievances against Mrs. Souther, one of which was still pending at the time of her discharge.

The union contended that Mr. Hopkins provoked a number of grievances, that he was prejudiced against blacks, and that he showed it in his treatment of Miss Lyons. For example, it was customary that the employees be reprimanded in the privacy of the supervisor's office. But in the case of Miss Lyons, Mr. Hopkins did not follow this rule, thereby causing undue attention to himself and Miss Lyons in front of the other employees. He discussed their differences in the shop, repeatedly asking her in a voice which rose higher and higher whether or not she was going back. The tone of voice and reddened face indicated anger to Miss Lyons and the crowd of spectators.

The union pleaded that Miss Lyons was a young black girl with no previous industrial experience, and that she thought she was being unduly discriminated against by being asked to do something which her fellow employees said that she did not have to do and which normally they did not do either. The union further pleaded that Miss Lyons regretted her outburst, and that usually she was a quiet and diligent worker. Her outburst reflected her sincere belief that Mr. Hopkins was harassing her because she was black. The union contended that discrimination did appear on the first supervisory level in this case, even though it was against company policy. The union requested that Miss Lyons be reinstated on another shift with full seniority and back pay.

COMPANY POSITION

The company contended that there was no discrimination in this case, and that Miss Lyons was discharged because she persistently refused to follow instructions, and because she made a verbal attack upon a supervisor.

The company claimed that Miss Lyons was a marginal worker, and that her attitude showed that she was "disinterested" in her work. The company stated that it was customary for a new employee to go through a probationary period, and that, during her probationary period, Miss Lyons was teamed with different employees, some of whom complained about her work.

On March 11, Mr. Hopkins called Miss Lyons to his office and discussed her work attitude, informing her that he had observed her slow progress and her apparent lack of motivation. At that time, he also specifically discussed her repeated practice of reporting in late. In fact, on March 11, she reported in for her 3:30 p.m. shift at 3:38 p.m., arriving at her work place at 4:10 p.m., so late that she had to be relieved.

On May 2, at the end of Miss Lyons' probationary period, management reviewed her case. Management decided to retain her even though she fell below minimum standards, because management felt her to be intelligent and capable if she could be motivated. However, a comment was placed in her personnel folder warning her that she must improve, and that her progress would be reviewed in 45 to 60 days.

The company contended that it was company policy to have an employee return and correct a mistake on a machine, and that such action was good training and not punishment for the employee. The company cited several incidents in which Mr. Hopkins or another foreman had sent workers back to correct their mistakes. Mr. Hopkins reported that Bruce Beaver, a fellow foreman, had sent three operators back and that he, himself, had sent employee Sandra Wells back. Mr. Hopkins was reluctant to name any more employees he sent back to correct mistakes, since doing so might embarass them or get them into trouble. Mr. Hopkins and Miss Gibson both stated that although a worker's job was almost 90 per cent complete, if a mistake was made early in the job, the worker usually was ordered to return to correct that mistake, since company policy was to get the job done correctly.

Miss Gibson added that it was not unusual for a worker to return to correct a mistake, and she cited the case of Maxine Dillingham, and of Elizabeth Harp, a black woman who was no longer with the company, to substantiate this fact.

Mr. Hopkins insisted that he was not discriminating against blacks, and that he had always gotten along well with them. He insisted that he did not raise his voice when asking Miss Lyons five times to return, and that he did not show any anger at Miss Lyons' persistent refusal. Miss Gibson contended that Mr. Hopkins was very calm; she substantiated what Mr. Hopkins stated to the effect that Miss Lyons fell into a verbal rage and started shouting curses at Mr. Hopkins during the incident in question.

The company argued that it did not spend money to hire minority workers only to discharge them discriminatorily. The company contended that Miss Lyons was discharged due to her persistent refusal to accept a direct order and her verbal attack against a supervisor.

THE LEADERSHIP SKILLS CONFERENCE FOR SUPERVISORS

CASE 41

The first session of the two-day conference had broken up at 9:30 p.m. and the participants had walked down the hill to the recreation hall, where they were enjoying a late evening snack and were chatting informally about the conference and generally becoming better acquainted with one another. The two conference leaders, Dr. Wendell Smith and Albert Hathaway, had spent the last ten minutes in the conference hall making last-minute revisions in the schedule for the following day.* Hathaway remained behind to set up his visual aids, and Smith started out the door to join the others. As he walked out into the night, one of the conference members, Tony Dombroski, dashed up to him excitedly and demanded: "You've got to move that guy who you put in my room with me! I don't mind working with niggers, but I'll be damned if I'll live with them. Either you move him or I'm going home."

Dombroski was visibly agitated. He made several exaggerated gestures as he spoke; he spoke in a loud tone of voice and in a rapid manner.

Smith asked him: "Who is the individual who has been assigned to that room with you?"

"Greene. Harris Greene is his name."

"Have you met him?"

"No. He is the fellow who arrived late. We had almost finished eating when he walked into the dining room. You have to get him out of there! I have already talked with Mr. Cristman (Harold Cristman, manager of the conference center). He told me to see you. What do you intend to do? Either he moves or I leave."

"Why don't you wait in the office while I find out what the situation is from Cristman? I'll be with you in a few minutes."

Smith found Cristman walking up from the recreation hall.

"Harold, what's the story on Dombroski and Greene? Dombroski is really wild."

Cristman recounted the conversation with Dombroski which had taken place before a small group of the conference participants. Dombroski had made the same demands to the conference manager and had also threatened to leave the conference.

THE CONFERENCE

The two-day conference on the development of leadership skills for supervisors had enrolled 28 participants, five of whom were female. Most of the members

* All names disguised.

worked in industry, although three were from hospitals, two were employed in a local welfare agency, and two occupied supervisory positions in a large university library. The educational background of the participants varied widely. Three had completed only grammar school; twelve were high school graduates; four had completed one to three years of college; nine were college graduates, two of whom held advanced college degrees. The conference participants ranged in age from 21-50 years, although most of them were 25-35 years old.

The conference was sponsored by Washington University and it was held at Windhaven, the university's residential conference center, located in the foothills of the Ozarks about 50 miles from St. Louis.

The February 1969 conference ran from Thursday evening until Saturday noon. Participants arrived late in the afternoon. The Thursday program was preceded by a brief "social hour" and dinner. The Saturday sessions were followed by lunch and a brief closing ceremony, which included awarding certificates of attendance. The conference schedule was rigorous, although coffee breaks and a lengthy open period had been built into the schedule to stimulate discussion and interaction among the participants and between them and the conference leaders.

Windhaven offers an idyllic environment for a conference. The cottages and other buildings are hidden in a woody hillside overlooking a small brook and distant wooded hills. Accommodations are excellent in every respect: the food is delicious and the cottages are new and electrically heated in the winter and air-conditioned in the summer. Participants are housed in one-story cottages, each containing four double rooms with private baths. (See Appendix, page 264, for a rough sketch of the conference center.)

UNIVERSITY POLICY AND CONFERENCE REGISTRATION PROCEDURES

The university holds to a strict policy of nondiscrimination in every aspect of employment and admission of students.

The conference was publicized by mailing the conference program to a selected list of business and other organizations throughout the midwestern United States. Persons wishing to attend the conference returned a registration form attached to the announcement. The manager of the center assigned registrants to rooms in the order of their application to the conference. If two or more registrations were received from one company, each registrant was assigned to a different room in order to promote interaction among the conference members. On occasion two participants from the same company, after arrival at the center, would request to be reassigned so that they could share the same room. If they persisted in their desire to share a room after being advised of the method of making room assignments, the manager of the center asked them to work it out with their current partners and then report their new locations to him.

TONY DOMBROSKI

Tony Dombroski, at age 45, was a general foreman at XYZ Industries. He had been with the company for 15 years, having started as a laborer in the drop forging department. He obtained an eighth grade education which was cut short at the death of his father. He was married and the father of six children, the oldest of whom was 18 years of age. The Dombroskis lived in the near south side of the city in a neighborhood that is largely Polish. They owned their modest home, free of any mortgage.

The company was a major manufacturer of heavy machinery. It is listed among the *Fortune* 500 largest industrial companies in the United States. It has plants throughout the major cities of the country and employs about 35,000 people.

The local plant employs about 1,500 at full production. Employment at the plant undergoes wide swings, following the peaks and valleys of the business cycle. The company employs large numbers of unskilled and semi-skilled workers who are drawn from the Negro, Polish, and Italian populations of the metropolitan area. Negroes have been the last to be hired and the first to be laid off; hence, few possess substantial seniority. They occupy the lower level jobs in the plant.

HAROLD GREENE

Greene was a foreman with the Acme Plastics Company. He had worked for the company for three years in various clerical and production positions in the plant. He was promoted to the position of foreman in the shipping department about six months prior to attending the conference. He was the first black man the company ever had promoted to a managerial position. The company debated Greene's promotion for several weeks. However, he was the unanimous choice of the plant superintendent, the personnel director, and the vice president for production.

The company employs approximately 600 people, about 50 of whom are blacks. Blacks occupy lower level positions in production and clerical jobs. Greene supervised 15 workers, five of whom were black.

Greene was 26 years of age. He had graduated four years previously from Central College, an institution which was classified as a "predominantly Negro college." He was married and had two children. His company is located in one of the newer suburbs of the city. He lived in a suburb about two miles from the plant.

He was the only black enrolled in the conference.

THURSDAY EVENING

Smith learned from Cristman that all of the rooms normally assigned to conference members were fully occupied. The only vacant room was in the office, which contained two small bedrooms used by the manager and other university personnel who frequently visit the center. Cristman occupied one bedroom; the other was vacant; no one was expected to visit from St. Louis.

Cristman expressed great reluctance to make a decision. He was inexperienced and new to the university. He felt that he didn't know university policy; he feared that he might "precipitate a riot" by doing the wrong thing; and he was fearful that an incorrect decision might cost him his job.

Smith saw that Cristman obviously was immobilized by the situation. He also felt that it demanded immediate action and that there was no one else at hand who might do this.

Appendix: Windhaven Parking Lot

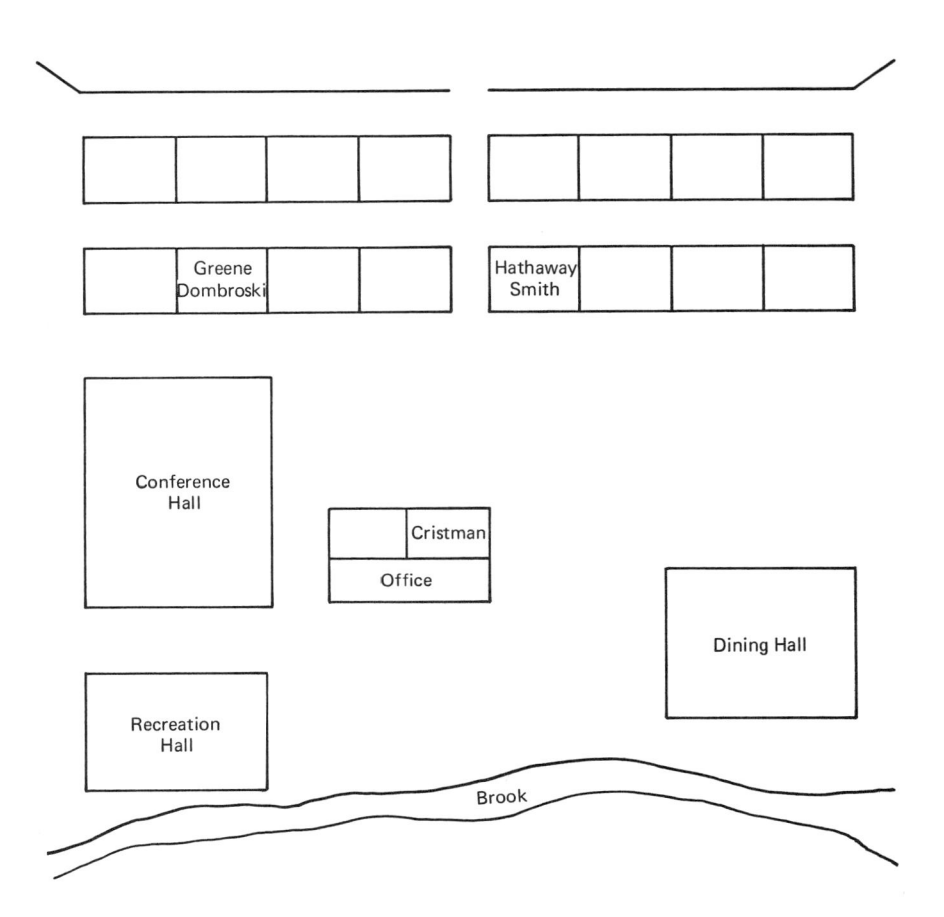

WILLIS B. JOHNSON   CASE 42

"Why aren't you sweeping the floors or operating an elevator—where you belong?" These words uttered by Ivory Washington, one of his black subordinates, worried Willis B. Johnson, who recently had been promoted to a position as supervisor. The thought that other black employees might resent his obtaining a management position had disturbed him ever since he entered the management training program. Although no one had called him an "Uncle Tom," to his face, Willis knew that many of his friends thought this of him. The allegation that he held a job which was not appropriate for a black man strengthened his apprehensions.

Willis B. Johnson, or "W.B." as he preferred to be called, graduated from Fisk University in Nashville, Tennessee, majoring in business education. Upon graduation, "W.B." started his career as a vocational counselor in the youth training center of a poverty program agency located in the inner city of his hometown, Midwestern City. After a year and a half as a vocational counselor, "W.B." decided to seek a job in private industry offering the opportunity for advancement.

"W.B." was employed by a public utility in Midwestern City as a management trainee assigned to the billing department. After a year and a half in several clerical positions in the billing department, "W.B." was promoted and became an assistant manager of the billing department with supervisory responsibility over thirty clerks. Of these thirty clerks, eight were blacks. Recently "W.B." moved with his wife and daughter into a new home in a suburban location.

The utility company is an equal employment opportunity employer and has an affirmative action program on file with a federal compliance agency. One of the goals of the utility's affirmative action program is to increase the number of blacks in management positions. "W.B." was one of the first blacks in the utility to attain a management position.

The personnel department had received several complaints from blacks about "W.B."'s tendency to set higher standards for black employees under his supervision than for white employees. "W.B." indicated that the charges were not valid. He stated: "I let everyone set their own pace. It's like a horse race, in that some employees are going to come out ahead of others. I reward the ones who come out in front. That's my job."

The manager of the billing department, Roland Scott, was of the opinion that "W.B." treated black and white workers alike Mr. Scott evaluated "W.B."'s

Case contributed by John R. Hundley, III, Instructor, University College Division, Washington University. All names disguised.

overall performance as very good and was of the opinion that one of "W.B."'s strengths was fairness in dealing with employees.

This most recent comment was not the only occasion on which black employees had made derogatory remarks to "W.B." about being a black supervisor. On two other occasions, black employees with whom he had good rapport had advised "W.B." that the "other black employees in the section don't believe that they receive the same treatment as whites." These previous incidents had involved the grapevine rather than a direct verbal confrontation. Away from the job, several of his former black acquaintances in the inner city had provided a verbal confrontation by indicating to "W.B." that he had "sold out to the establishment."

On the job, "W.B." had been approached directly by Ivory Washington who began her employment in the billing department at an entry level clerical position. Over a period of five years, Ivory had advanced through a series of promotions to one of the highest level clerical positions in the department.

Ivory's job was very complex, involving the adjustment of billing records based upon the system which was in effect at the time an error originally was made. The billing system had undergone a transition from a manual to a computerized system. During this transition, a number of intermediate systems had been in use. Ivory was one of the few people in the department who understood the various intermediate systems and methods of adjusting records which occurred under each. Ivory occasionally tried to put down "W.B." with her knowledge of adjustments to the billing system by asking him questions to which she knew he would not know the answers. She once asked "W.B.": "How do you expect to know in a few months what it took me five years to learn?"

Ivory was an extremely ambitious young woman. On several occasions, she had complained to the personnel department about being passed over for promotions into management level positions. Roland Scott had passed over Ivory for promotion to a first-line supervisory position on several occasions. Both the personnel department and Roland Scott agreed that Ivory lacked the tact and interpersonal skills needed in a supervisory position. Willis Johnson decided that the time had come for some response or action on his part, but he pondered what it should be. At least, he was anxious to have a good reply to Ivory Washington's next insinuation.

A PROBLEM OF TARDINESS   CASE 43

Lloyd Dauten was foreman of the assembly department of a large manufacturing company. Most of the time Dauten supervised about fifteen assembly line workers. All of the employees in the department were white with the exception of George Douglas.

Douglas was a black, 36 years old, who was a widower with six small children. He had worked in the company for about two years, since he had changed jobs and moved to the city following the death of his wife. Douglas was considered to be a very good worker, one of the best in the department, but he was perennially tardy for work in the morning. Lloyd Dauten had discussed the problem of tardiness with Douglas numerous times. Dauten had pointed out to Douglas that his tardiness was detrimental to the departmental operation, but Douglas nevertheless consistently was tardy, often several times a week. Douglas stated that he made every effort to be at work on time, but he just didn't seem to be able to make it because of the problem of his children. Douglas stated that getting six children off to school and to the baby sitter made it impossible for him to get to work by 7:30 a.m.

Douglas had stated to Dauten that he worked harder than anyone else in the department, and that he stayed over late in the afternoon and early evening to make up whatever time he lost in the mornings. There was little question in Dauten's mind that George Douglas did work as hard as anyone else in the department. Since the assembly operation was on an individual rather than a group process basis, the actual departmental production usually did not suffer too much from this situation. However, Lloyd Dauten was becoming concerned about Douglas' tardiness, since it did create occasional problems with rush orders, and there were some rumblings of discontent among the white employees in the department.

One Tuesday morning, George Douglas' tardiness was holding up a specific assembly job which was supposed to be finished by noon of that day. It was already 8:45 a.m., and regardless of how hard Douglas might work later during the morning, it would be difficult to finish the job by noon, since the production material had to dry out for several hours before leaving the department. Dauten might have assigned this particular assembly operation to some other worker in the department, but he felt that Douglas was the most qualified man to do this particular job. Dauten also was worried that if Douglas would not come in at all

Case contributed by Dr. Theo Haimann, Professor of Management Sciences, St. Louis University. All names disguised.

or come in quite late, the entire production schedule of the department might be in a very difficult situation for the day.

As this was going through Dauten's mind, he overheard a conversation among several workers at one of the work stations. Since the discussion was quite loud and the workers made no effort to conceal it, Dauten felt sure that the workers deliberately were trying to have him hear what they had on their minds. The general nature of the conversation focused around statements such as the following: "Why should a black guy like Douglas get any preferred treatment around here? He's always late, and the boss doesn't do a damm thing about it. Just because he's black, he's getting favors like he's something special."

At 9:30 a.m., Douglas arrived on the job and reported to Lloyd Dauten. Said Douglas: "I'm sorry boss, but I had a special sickness problem with my three-year-old daughter that had to be taken care of. I should have called you, but I forgot about it in all the turmoil at home. I'll work extra hard to make up the time, even through my lunch hour, and make up the rest at the end of the day. You can always count on me." With that, Douglas headed toward his work station.

Foreman Dauten knew that he had to do something to correct this situation. It was beginning to get out of hand, but he didn't know exactly what his action should be, and he pondered his next move.

THE "FIXED" ELECTION   CASE 44

INTRODUCTION

Pankoff Steel Company operates a nationwide chain of steel warehouses, with 24 plants in the United States and two in foreign countries. At the time of this case, the Victor warehouse, located in a large metropolitan area, was the third largest of the Pankoff chain with some 130 employees. The Victor plant was divided into two sections, an office and a large steel warehouse. The office had approximately 70 employees, 17 of which were female; its primary function was to accept and process customer orders for any of a comprehensive line of steel products and to forward the requisitions to the warehouse, where they were filled and trucked to the desired locations.

The office was divided into the following departments:

1. Inside Sales Departments. The outside salesmen received orders, and phoned or mailed them to the inside sales people for processing.
2. Engineering Department. Orders for non-stock items were forwarded to the engineering department for detailed analysis concerning fabricating techniques.
3. Credit Department. Upon receipt, all orders were forwarded to this department for an estimate of cost and credit check.
4. Inventory Control Department. This group maintained an adequate inventory of each of the stock products, balancing purchases and sales.
5. Shipping and Routing Department. Established delivery dates and routing for all customer orders.
6. Billing and Pricing Department.
7. Also, miscellaneous jobs—mailroom employees, file girls, switchboard operators, and a receptionist.

The Victor plant manager, Bob Allison, was 63 years old and had been with Pankoff Steel for 33 years. Allison had served as plant manager at the Victor plant for fifteen years. He was well liked by the entire staff, and he knew most of the office employees by name.

Joe Parker served in the capacity of office manager. Parker had been transferred from another plant to assume this position about 10 years previously. He, too, was well liked by the majority of office personnel.

Tom Cahill was the newest member of the management team, having been transferred in from a West Coast branch three years ago. Tom served in the capacity of personnel manager for the entire Victor branch. Cahill was not well liked by the

Exhibit 1 *Organization Chart for Victor Plant*

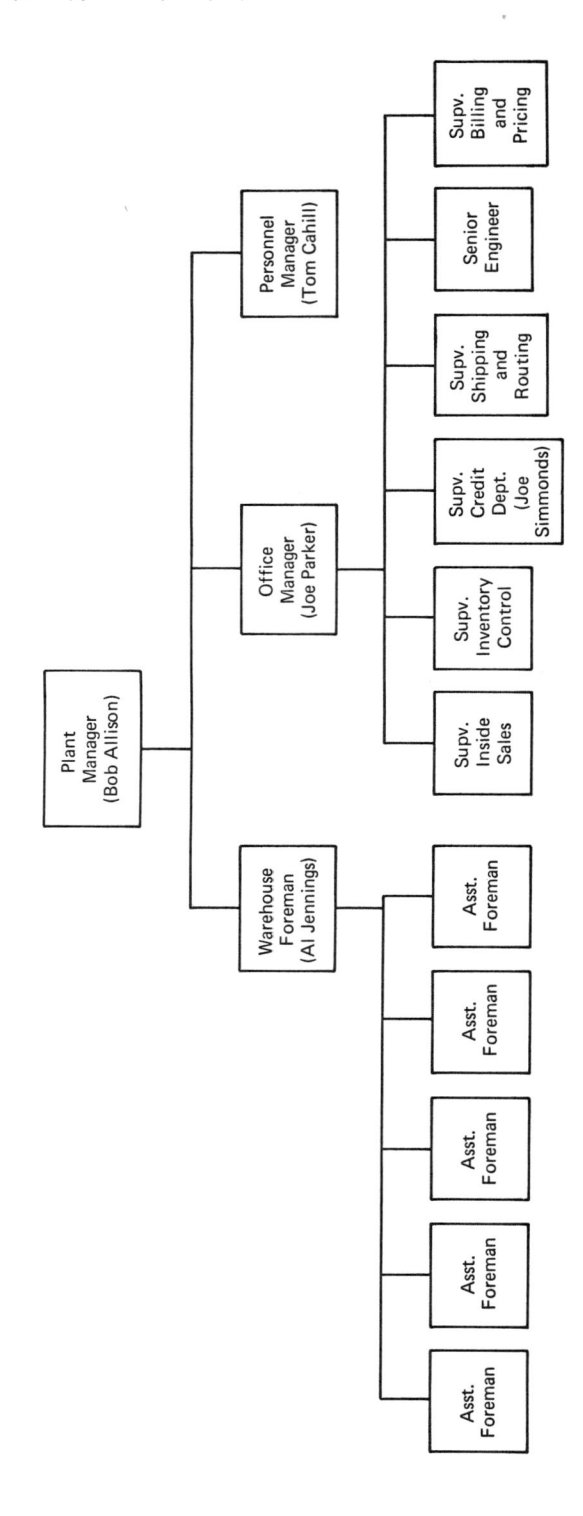

majority of the office people; many office personnel claimed that he assumed a "superior attitude" when speaking to them. Nevertheless, a good working relationship was maintained. (See Exhibit 1 for organization chart.)

THE SITUATION

Although the warehouse force of about sixty men was 90 per cent black, the office group had remained entirely white. Bob Allison had been approached by members of the NAACP in 1967 about the lack of black employees in the office. At that time, Bob advised the delegation that so far he had not received any black applicants who were qualified for jobs, but he would consider any who might be suitable in the future. After this visit, Bob Allison heard no more from that organization, and the incident soon was forgotten.

However, about two years later, a credit department girl gave three months notice of her resignation due to pregnancy, and Tom Cahill was asked to hire a replacement. Shortly thereafter, Cahill received a call from the local Urban League office, asking about employment possibilities for blacks. Cahill agreed to interview any qualified applicant recommended by the organization.

Barbara Harris, a black girl, was hired the following week to be trained by June Davis, who would be leaving in six weeks. Her job was to receive all orders from the inside sales people, figure the approximate weight and type of material, estimate costs, and check the customers' credit standing. This desk was kept exceptionally busy with a large volume of orders to be processed each day.

Barbara was 21 years of age. She had graduated from high school before joining a large electrical firm as a typist and comptometer operator. She appeared quite intelligent, and she was well recommended by her previous employer. Her reason for resigning her previous job was listed as "inadequate pay and limited possibility of advancement."

Barbara was accepted by most members of the office staff, although prejudiced attitudes were known to exist among several of the male employees. Barbara was well liked by the office girls, and she readily absorbed the training given by June Davis. At the time of June's departure, Barbara was progressing quite well.

Six months later, the office mail girl resigned, and a replacement was sought. A second black girl, Pat Bussam, was hired after recommendation by the Urban League. Pat was 18 years old, and she was beginning her first job after graduation from high school.

The two black girls, Barbara and Pat, immediately became good friends, and began spending lunch time and coffee breaks together. After several months passed, it appeared to the other office girls that the two seemed to show a certain resentment toward their associates. On several occasions, when other employees received raises or promotions to better jobs, the black girls openly stated their belief that they were being discriminated against. These statements were not brought directly to the office manager, but they reached all sections of the office through the informal grapevine. In addition, Barbara had not continued to progress on her job, and her male supervisor had talked to her on several occasions about her slow pace of work output. Her supervisor believed that the frequent overtime being expended by Barbara and another credit girl was not really necessary. Wanda Smith, the second credit girl, complained frequently to her supervisor that Barbara was not processing her share of customer orders. A growing resentment toward Barbara appeared evident on the part of some of the other office employees.

THE CREDIT UNION ELECTION

About this time, the Victor plant was approached with the idea of forming an employee credit union within the plant. An employee vote was taken, and the idea was approved. The company then contracted with an independent outside credit union to set up a "chapter" at the Victor plant. In order to form and organize the Victor Credit Union chapter, the outside firm asked that three employees be selected to an advisory board of directors to help process and censor loan requests from members within the company. The plant manager, Bob Allison, sent out a memorandum to all employees to the effect that anyone interested in holding these positions should submit his or her name, so that employees could choose the three by secret ballot. Barbara entered her name as a candidate. However, in the plantwide voting which ultimately took place, Barbara was beaten out by three white male candidates, all employees in the office section of the plant. At the urging of Pat Bussam, Barbara asked Joe Parker, the office manager, for a recount of the votes, claiming that the election was "fixed." Joe contacted Tom Cahill who explained that the ballots had been counted by himself, a representative of the outside credit union firm, and three department supervisors; the ballots had been destroyed after counting. Tom and Joe assured Barbara that they had no reason to "fix" the election, and they offered to make available the record tally of ballots received per candidate. Barbara declined to accept, stating that she firmly believed she was being discriminated against because of her sex and race. She also said that with the high percentage of blacks working in the Victor plant, it was discriminatory not to have a black person on the credit union advisory board of directors.

Word of this incident spread rapidly around the plant. Most of the office employees were resentful toward the two girls, but the black plant employees were definitely on their side and angry about the situation. Many of the black plant employees believed that their votes for Barbara had not been counted, although it was not clear exactly how many black employees actually had voted in the election.

About one week later, Joe Parker, Tom Cahill, Al Jennings, the warehouse foreman, and Joe Simmonds, Barbara's supervisor, received a call from Bob Allison, asking that they report to his office immediately. Mr. Allison explained that he had received a call from the Urban League office, asking an appointment to discuss a discrimination charge made by the two black girls of the firm. In addition, Allison was concerned over the racial trouble that appeared to be developing among the black plant employees. Allison asked that each man review his relationship with the two girls—including the handling of the election—and review the plant situation in general. They were to report to his office at 9:00 a.m. the next day to discuss what action, if any, should be taken.

PART SEVEN

Novac Company
Petri Chemical Company (C)
Boynton Department Store
The Filmore Electric Company (A)
The Superintendent's Vacation Pay
Jones Manufacturing Company
The Kaiser Steel Long-Range Sharing Plan
Charges of Discrimination Among the Library Staff
The Engineering Department Salary Administration Plan

Compensating the Workforce

Wage and salary administration is one of the most critical areas of a firm's total personnel program. Since wages and salaries usually constitute a major part of a firm's total costs, they must be administered properly for a firm to avoid a competitive disadvantage. At the same time, wage and salary administration is concerned with fundamental needs and goals of people. Monetary compensation is a means of satisfying basic physical and biological needs and also an indirect means of satisfying social and ego needs such as self-respect and recognition.

Wage and salary administration is usually considered a specialized personnel function. However, as with other aspects of personnel management, the development of sound wage and salary policies and their administration is an interrelated process of complex considerations, as illustrated by the following discussion.

OBJECTIVES

A soundly conceived and administered wage and salary program should result in the attainment of the following objectives:

1. Attracting and retaining an adequate number of qualified employees to perform the work of the organization.
2. Avoiding payment of rates for jobs and rates to individuals higher than the supply and demand situation requires (unless a firm establishes a deliberate policy to pay more).

3. Establishing a compensation system in which rates will reflect the relative difficulty and worth of each job.
4. Adjusting individual salaries according to individual performance.
5. Adjusting job rates and individual rates whenever significant changes in market rates, job content, or personal performance occur.
6. Determining the combination of cash wage payments and non-cash wage supplements which will provide the firm with the maximum amount of labor services for any specified cost which may be incurred.
7. Stimulating individuals to give their maximum effort on their present jobs, and providing an incentive for them to prepare themselves for promotion and transfer where their abilities make this feasible.

The attainment of these objectives thus depends upon a firm's ability to implement a compensation program consistent with the firm's external and internal conditions.

GENERAL LEVELS

General wage and salary levels are the first factor in wage and salary administration with which the manager must be concerned. If wages are too low, it may be difficult for a firm to attract and retain competent workers and to stimulate them to give their maximum effort. If wages are too high, a firm may find it difficult to compete in the product market.

What determines general salary and wage levels? **Competition,** the demand for workers and the supply of workers in a particular labor market at a particular time, is the major determinant. Other important factors include the following:

1. The financial condition of the firm, i.e., its ability to pay;
2. Cost of living and other general economic conditions;
3. Governmental wage and hour regulation;
4. The type of firm, its objectives in recruitment, selection, and employee turnover;
5. The presence or absence of labor unions.

Cost of living and ability to pay are rather vague wage and salary determinants. When the cost of living is rising, employees argue that they should receive wage increases in order to maintain a proper standard of living. When the cost of living declines, employees do not use this as a basis for securing wage increases. If the cost of living declines, employers advocate that wages should be reduced or held constant. Similarly, if a company's profits are large, workers argue that larger earnings justify increased wages. When profits are small or nonexistent, the company uses this to seek decreases or stabilize labor costs.

Since both cost of living and ability to pay can be manipulated as wage determinants, the manager should keep in mind that competition is a primary determinant to guide general wage policy. A firm must endeavor to pay employees wages and salaries which first of all are comparable to those paid by other firms for similar skills and positions.

Market rates for specific labor services are determined by *wage surveys.* Employers exchange information about wage rates in order to learn the competitive wage rates being paid in the local labor market for similar job classifications. Wage surveys are initiated by large companies, employers' associations, and by organizations, such as local Chambers of Commerce. Periodic wage surveys are helpful guides in determining a firm's general level of employee compensation. However, great care should be exercised in the interpretation of wage survey information, since job conditions in one company are rarely identical to those existing in other firms.

WAGE AND SALARY RELATIONSHIPS INTERNAL TO THE FIRM

A firm's general level of wages and salaries must be subjected to frequent periodic reviews and adjustment. This is also true for a firm's internal wage and salary structure, the second major element in wage policy. Personnel administrators should recognize that unjustified wage inequities among employees in the same firm or work group are apt to contribute to employee complaints and dissatisfaction, foster conditions which can detract from efficient work performance, and cause high employee turnover.

Job evaluation helps a manager to appraise the value of each job in relation to other jobs in his company. Because of unique products, processes, personalities, location, historical development, and so forth, each company is organizationally somewhat different from every other company. Some jobs are peculiar to each company, even in the same industry, and consequently, they possess no market rate. Job evaluation helps to solve this problem by providing a standardized and systematic procedure for determining the relative worth of each job in the organization. Basically, it involves comparing jobs whose market rates are known with jobs whose market rates are not known and through this comparison arriving at a proper wage for the job whose rate is not known.

Before jobs can be fairly evaluated, it is first necessary to ascertain the duties and the requirements which each job demands of an employee. *Job analysis* is the function of carefully studying and analyzing each job in the organization. The written report of each study is commonly called the *job description* and *job specification.* The job description essentially involves a listing and statement of the principal employee duties and responsibilities or working conditions associated with each job. Job specification is a written statement of the demands in terms of skills, knowledge, abilities, interests, and personal attributes which the job makes upon the individual who performs it.

Thus, job evaluation is a measuring device which leads to the proper determination of the values of jobs. There are four basic techniques for job evaluation:

1. Ranking, the comparing of one job against another;
2. Classification, comparing a job against an "objective" scale and placing it in its proper category or classification;
3. Point rating; and

4. Factor comparison, which involves complex forms of the ranking and classification techniques.

A brief description of the ranking and point rating techniques follows:

Ranking Method

Ranking is the simplest method of job evaluation, since the job evaluator uses the job descriptions and merely compares one job with another. For example, assume that as a result of a salary survey, the following monthly rates were found to be the "market rates" for the indicated positions:

Secretary	$525
Stenographer	475
Billing Machine Operator	425
Typist	380
File Clerk	340

It is not necessary to utilize job evaluation to determine the rates for these positions, since the "market" indicated the appropriate rates. Assume further that the firm has a unique position called a "check stub sorter." Other companies either do not perform this work or perform it differently. In order to compensate equitably the individuals performing the work, the evaluator can systematically compare the position of check stub sorter with each of the other positions. For example, after careful study the job might be evaluated as being worth more than that of typist but less than that of billing machine operator. The rate thus would be established somewhere between $380 and $425, and more careful evaluation would indicate exactly the appropriate location of this position in the job hierarchy

Point Rating Method

The point rating method, like the *factor comparison method,* assumes that there are a number of factors whose presence or absence should account for the greater or lesser value of each job in a job family, such as the clerical job family indicated above. Among the more common factors usually rated by point evaluation are education, basic skills or training, physical effort, mental effort, responsibility, and working conditions required for performance on the job.[1]

An "objective" measuring scale with numerical values attached to each of a number of degrees on the scale is developed for each factor. Arbitrary values for the various degrees of each factor are established in this scale, which is accepted as a standard "measuring stick." The scale is weighted with additional points for the changing increment of degrees of each factor. Each job position is evaluated, one factor at a time, against the scale for each factor. This provides a point value for each factor and a total point value is determined for each position. This rating

---

[1] See the job evaluation plan for salaried employees prepared by the National Electric Manufacturers Association or the American Association for Industrial Management. For a detailed description of the mechanics of point rating and factor comparison, see Dale Beach, *Personnel: The Management of People at Work,* Second Edition, (New York: MacMillan Company, 1970), pp. 667-675. The "Jones Manufacturing Company" Case in this section describes one method of equating point values to monetary values by statistical methodology.

is not a perfectly accurate procedure, since the rater must use a degree of subjective, arbitrary judgment in his analysis. Detailed studies and observations may bring greater objectivity to the rater's judgment concerning how each factor should be weighted for a particular job. When a committee instead of a single rater makes the evaluations, a "pooled judgment" is obtained which may result in more rational wage scales.

The point value for each position having a market rate then is plotted on a scatter diagram against the present wage or salary rate for the position. A wage curve or wage trend line is calculated and drawn to the "best fit" of the plotted data. The appropriate rate for a check stub sorter described earlier would be established by evaluating the position according to the point rating method and then determining the appropriate rate from the trend line. On this scatter diagram job positions which lie too far above the line are considered paid in excess of their worth; conversely, jobs which lie more than a reasonable distance below the line are interpreted as underpaid. Sound administration dictates that the organization should adjust its rate structure to bring all compensation rates in alignment with wage rate ranges or labor grades established by this trend line.

This adjustment process may take considerable time, especially for jobs whose wage rates are currently far above the rate at which they have been evaluated. It is necessary that jobs be periodically re-evaluated to ensure that changes in job content are properly rated and compensated. At the same time, periodic reviews of how key jobs compare with wage rates for comparable work in other industries will aid in maintaining a satisfactory general as well as internal wage structure

In job evaluation most firms use the point rating process to develop job classes or labor grades instead of determining a separate wage rate for each individual job. This procedure results in a structure of job classes. The entire wage scale usually contains ten to fifteen classes with each class including all jobs within a range of fifteen or twenty point values. Wage rate ranges can be developed for each job class or labor grade to establish minimum and maximum rates. An individual job holder may progress from the minimum rate in his labor grade to the maximum rate on the basis of seniority or merit. Employee evaluation is used to appraise the performance and behavior of an employee in order to reward him according to efficiency and productivity.

Policy Considerations

No matter how sophisticated or carefully constructed, a job evaluation program will not provide the answers to all the wage and salary problems of an individual firm. Many internal and external considerations which may obscure the objectivity of a job evaluation program enter into the situation. For example, conditions in the labor market may force a firm to pay higher wage rates than indicated by job evaluation in order to attract and retain certain types of skilled workers or specially qualified workers. If a labor union represents the work force, union representatives may be reluctant to accept any downward adjustments in wage rates as indicated by job evaluation. Some labor unions actively oppose job evaluation procedures, so that a firm may be forced to use job evaluation only as a guide in its wage negotiations with a union. In recent years, however, many unions are recognizing job evaluation as an effective management tool which basically is fair to employees.

Job evaluation is more complex in compensation plans for managerial, professional, and technically-trained employees such as engineers and scientists. In these positions it becomes difficult to separate the individual from the job. Managers presumably should be paid in proportion to the value of their managerial contributions to the company. This includes many "unmeasurable" attributes such as the ability to make sound decisions, supervisory skills, and the results of managerial leadership in terms of increased profits or reduced costs. For professional and technical people, particularly those engaged in research and engineering projects, it is virtually impossible to obtain direct measurements of productivity and individual contributions to company objectives. The establishment of salary ranges (or salary grades) for managerial and technically-trained people is usually based upon estimates of what must be paid to attract and keep competent top personnel. The administration of salaries paid to individuals affected by salary ranges should include careful estimates of each individual's worth and contributions to the firm.

MERIT RATING
EMPLOYEE PERFORMANCE APPRAISAL

The company that has determined the value of each job in its organization and established a wage or salary range for the compensation of workers in each position should try to pay a "fair day's wage for a fair day's work" by considering the quality of the performance of each individual worker. Obviously, higher rates in each salary range should be paid to the superior workers, and lower rates in each salary range should be paid to marginal or poor performers. Systematic procedures for employee evaluations are called "merit rating plans," "employee performance appraisal systems," "performance evaluations," and the like. Regardless of its name, the purpose of such a plan is to perform one of management's most difficult tasks, namely, the fair appraisal of human effort.

Among the many systems which have been developed for this activity are the following:

1. *Graphic Rating Scale.* Sometimes called the "chart system," this approach lists a number of traits or characteristics (productivity, accuracy, loyalty, reliability, cooperativeness, and so forth) and permits a superior or rater to indicate on a graduated scale the degree to which a worker displays each trait. Up to twelve or fifteen traits are used in some rating scales, but most procedures include the three basic appraisal factors, quantity of output, quality of output, and cooperation with others.
2. *Man-to-Man and Rank Order Systems.* The ratings of employees in groups or departments may be determined by comparing the performance of each worker with that of each of the others in his group. The rater simply ranks his employees on over-all job performance or on separate traits which

measure accomplishment one trait at a time. An employee's evaluation is represented by his rank in the group. For some purposes, this form of ranking is adequate.

3. *Forced Distribution Systems.* This system aims at avoiding the problem created when raters place most of their workers in the same category, (i.e., some rating most workers "average," some rating most workers "good," "excellent," etc.) In its simplest form, the forced distribution rating procedure evaluates the employees in a group on their "present-job performance." Considering each individual in comparison to others in his group, he is rated on a scale which places him in the upper 10 per cent, the next 10 per cent, etc. down to the lowest 10 per cent, forcing a distribution of all workers' performance from the poorest, the lowest decimal, through average up to the upper 10 per cent, the best in the group.

4. *Miscellaneous Systems.* Many ingenious schemes have been developed and used for appraising job performance of workers. Sometimes "check-lists" of traits or questions about behavior are used with the rater indicating the trait or statement which best describes the performance of the worker. Some organizations use group appraisal systems, interviews, written descriptions (essay style), and other means of obtaining evaluations of how workers perform on their job. The literature in the fields of psychology and management provides many results of research and experimentation on this subject.

Judgments regarding the capabilities and the reliability of workers must be made frequently by managers and supervisors. Both formally and informally, it is necessary for planners of operations to understand and depend upon the work of trustworthy employees. Consequently, systems for appraisal of worker performance have a variety of purposes and uses. Among the uses of employee ratings are:

1. *Promotions*—to provide management with objective and fair appraisals of employees' abilities, so that the best qualified workers are promoted to the better positions.
2. *Transfers, Layoffs and Discharges*—to provide necessary information which may be utilized when organizational changes and reduction in the working force are necessary.
3. *Wage or Salary Increases*—to provide a basis for giving employees wage or salary increases on the basis of merit. Usually, the higher rates in the salary range for any position are given to workers who perform their duties well— better than average. Many rating plans provide for a periodic salary or wage review for each employee with the performance rating being made at the same time. For non-union employees, most companies make these reviews and ratings at least once each year.
4. *Employee Counseling*—to provide a situation for the worker to discuss the appraisal of his work performance with his supervisor. Most companies either require or strongly suggest that the supervisor discusses the rating of performance with each worker. The intention of this discussion is to strengthen communications, letting each worker know "how he stands" with his im-

mediate superior. Often referred to as a "counseling interview," a discussion of his appraisal should help the employee understand his own strengths and weaknesses and provide him with suggestions for further development and progress. Although many supervisors find it difficult to conduct these "reviews" with employees, they are important procedures for developing and maintaining good employee relations, particularly when compensation is tied closely to the performance ratings.

WAGE-PAYMENT METHODS

Wage-payment methods are another major facet of wage and salary administration. Employees can be paid either on the basis of the time that they work or the output that they produce. Time wage systems are preferable and are most applicable when:

1. Employees have little or no control over output, and there is no direct relationship between employee effort and output.
2. Units of output are difficult to distinguish and measure.
3. Quality considerations are important and inspection is difficult.
4. Delays are frequent, beyond the control of the individual, and unpredictable

Incentive piece rate, or compensation plans based on output are preferable when.

1. Employees have control over output, and a direct relationship between effort and output exists.
2. Units of output can be measured.
3. Quality is not so important as quantity, or if quality is important, it can be readily measured and controlled.
4. The job is standardized, the flow of work is regular, and delays are few or predictable.
5. It is important that direct unit labor costs be accurately known and before production is undertaken.

All incentive or "piece rate" systems pay employees for actual results compared to anticipated results or a standard. The standard itself must be determined accurately and the results must be measured accurately.

Work simplification and standardization of work methods are the first steps in establishing an incentive system. Once the proper method for performing a job has been determined, time-study experts measure the work content of the job and establish quantity standards. Certain difficulties occur in the process of measuring. One difficulty is determining the rate and the level of effort at which the employee is working. Another is the determination of proper time allowances for the worker's personal needs, fatigue, and unavoidable delay. Time-study technicians also consider the amount of effort required to perform a job and the amount of effort expended by a timed employee.

After setting the output standard for the job, the incentive rate per unit of output is primarily determined by (1) the rate that should be paid for the job as determined by a wage survey or by job evaluation; and (2) the output standard as established by time study or some other means. For example, if the evaluated rate of the job of a machine operator is $3.50 per hour and the output standard is 350 pieces per hour, the rate per piece will be $\frac{3.50}{350}$ = $ .01. If either the evaluated rate for the job or the output standard should change, the rate paid per piece will also change.

Managers often assume that a wage incentive system can solve many of the major problems associated with employee work performance. By providing employees with an opportunity to earn bonus payments over some established rate, an incentive plan theoretically can add motivation and interest to otherwise routine jobs. Managers usually feel that incentive plans automatically will bring higher production and that possibly lower total costs per unit of output will result. However, many human relations problems may arise in establishing and administering an incentive system. It is not only essential that the incentive system *be* technically fair, but also that employees *believe* that it is fair. Unless workers believe that time standards are reasonable, they will probably not accept them and may attempt to prove by their performance that standards are unfair.

Wage-incentive plans should be clear to the average worker, so that he can readily understand how his wages are calculated in relation to his output. In addition, fair procedures for introducing rates on new jobs and changing rates on old jobs whose nature has changed should be established, so that workers do not fear changes and become suspicious of management intentions. Workers' fears of management-imposed speedups and tightening of piece rates can be serious obstacles to the proper functioning of an incentive plan. Where a labor union is present, management must expect and be willing to negotiate union challenges and grievances concerning the incentive plan.

In addition to incentive plans for individual workers, some companies use group or plant-wide incentive programs. Included in this category are profit-sharing plans, which are being increasingly introduced by many companies. The basic premise of group incentive plans is that employees will be motivated to increase their productivity and efficiency if they have a personal stake in the overall results of their work group or firm. Also, it is felt that these plans may promote teamwork and a cooperative spirit among work groups, which in turn will improve employee interest in jobs and improve morale.

WAGE AND SALARY SUPPLEMENTS

Supplements, often described as "fringe benefits," constitute the final important facet of wage and salary administration. These supplements take many forms. Some are considered to be payments for time not worked or deferred compensation or insurance, while others are in the category of monetary incentives.

1. Nonproduction awards and bonuses:
    Suggestion awards
    Profit sharing
    Service bonus

Christmas bonus
Safety awards
2. Payments for time not worked:
Holidays with pay
Jury duty time
Lunch periods
Rest periods
Sick leave
Religious holidays
Vacations
Severance pay
Voting time
Military service allowance
Time spent on grievances and contract negotiations
3. Extra compensation for time worked:
Overtime premiums
Shift premiums
Shift-in pay
Holiday premiums
4. Payments for or contributions toward employee security:
Accident and disability insurance
Life insurance
Hospitalization insurance
Medical and surgical insurance
Unemployment compensation
Supplements to unemployment compensation
Workmen's compensation
U.S. Government—Old Age and Survivors Insurance
Employee thrift plans
Employee stock purchase plans
Pensions
5. Employee services:
Cafeteria
Athletic teams and recreational programs
Housing
Stores
Educational scholarships and loans
Free meals
Special counseling services
   Income tax
   Legal aid
   Retirement
Transportation
Parking facilities

For most progressive companies, the cost of employee "fringe" benefits is twenty to forty per cent of the total employee compensation bill, and the long-term trend indicates that this proportion is likely to become even higher.

Profit sharing has received a special place among wage supplements in the United States. Advocates of profit sharing believe that employees will work harder, waste less, and become better representatives of the company if they receive some of the profits of the business.

The requirements for a successful profit-sharing plan are:

1. Favorable employer-employee relations resulting in high morale.
2. Wage levels in the company equal to or superior to that prevailing in the industry or area.
3. The company must enjoy large, stable profits which it is willing to share liberally with employees.
4. Employees must possess a real feeling of participation and partnership in the success of the company.

The record of profit sharing in the United States has not been entirely successful because the mortality rate of such plans has been high. The uncertainty and irregularity of company profits over long periods of time have resulted in the abandonment of both profit-sharing and stock-option plans by some companies.

Some employers believe that companies should not be expected to provide extensive employee benefits and services beyond the programs required by law. These employers contend that "welfare" programs are not the legitimate concern of a business organization and that "welfare" is essentially a matter for individual and public, not management, attention. At the other extreme are those employers who view employee "fringe" benefits as being good policy and worth the costs in terms of buying employee appreciation and company loyalty. This viewpoint suggests that employees will be more satisfied on their jobs and less apt to seek employment elsewhere if they can be closely tied to the company and relieved of concern for future security by an attractive package of "fringe" benefits.

A sounder and more realistic point of view is one which considers employee benefits and services to be just one part of the total personnel program. Such benefits should not be considered as frills, handouts, or tied to expectations of employee loyalty. Rather, they should be planned and administered from the standpoint of their contribution to the total personnel program. Employee benefits tailored to help meet the needs, anticipations, and expectations of workers as human beings can contribute to the effectiveness of organizational performance by fostering a positive influence upon the employee's sense of security, health, and work place morale.

NOVAC COMPANY CASE 45

Mr. A. M. Nolan, vice president of manufacturing of the Novac Company, Inc., was confronted with the problem of reappraising his organization's policies in the face of increased expansion. Increasing demands for his company's products in a greatly expanding market required continuous growth to meet competition. To meet this problem, he was considering the use of wage incentives as a means of increasing production and maintaining the company's earnings.

The company had begun during the 1930's with the development of an automatic pressure-valve control for fish aquariums. Dr. Putney, a professor, became interested in the company when he acquired one of these pressure valves for his aquarium as a gift from one of his aides, who was related to the inventor. This act was one of many links in the chain of circumstances which resulted in the development and growth of the company. Dr. Putney could see many possibilities in the application of this product for medical and surgical devices, and he was able to influence a neighbor of his, Mr. Mangini, to invest sufficient money to finance a new manufacturing company. The company was incorporated, and the serious work of manufacturing valves was begun. New uses for both industrial and military applications soon developed, and the original main products became minor items. The main output of the company became concentrated on the pressure-valve itself. However, a small part of the present production, one of which the company was justly proud, was the section which had developed equipment for use in physical therapy.

By the time of this case, the organization had grown from fewer than a dozen employees to over 700, with sales representatives all over the United States, in Canada, and Europe (see Exhibit 1).

Mr. R. G. Stevenson, executive vice president, in a report published in the company's newspaper, said: "No successful business can stand still and even if we were to grow at the rate of 10 per cent a year, we would be falling behind our competition and losing our place in the industry. We are projecting a growth rate this year of approximately 20 per cent and are consummating plans for five-year periods which are designed to fortify our position and improve earnings, which is in the direction of providing additional opportunity, security, and regard for all of us. Periods of growth are very expensive, and considerable investment and even temporary sacrifices of earnings have to be made ahead of the day when the real

---

Case prepared by Professor Justin C. Cronin, Assistant Dean, College of Business Administration, Boston College. Used by permission. All names and certain data disguised.

returns are experienced. Therefore, it will be difficult to sustain our past earning position during the initial phase of expansion."

The principal product utilized a unique patented principle. Each product was tailored to meet the specific needs of the user and while many basic components were common to many lines, each order presented special engineering considerations. Because of the design of these controls, there was little or no market for them as consumer goods.

The production process for the manufacturing of these extremely sensitive controls was carried on under rather difficult conditions. Operations were housed in an old three-story wooden factory building which required the location of all the heavy machinery in the basement. An example of the crowded conditions that existed was the necessity of cutting strip stock in half in order to feed it into the punch presses. Two hundred items of the company's product line accounted for approximately 80 per cent of the sales. A typical product had 88 separate operations ranging from hand operations to a 20-ton press operation. Testing varied from visual checks to an X-ray inspection. (See Exhibit 2).

Exhibit 1
Novac Company: "Staff and Indirect Labor"

Department	No. of Employees
Engineering and Research	85
Production Control	19
Standards	3
Methods Engineering	40
Purchasing	7
Personnel	9
Accounting	39
Sales (including sales engineers)	88
Quality Control	38
Maintenance	40
Tool Room	20
Executive Officers	12
Factory (supervisory, clerical, and so forth)	53

* See Exhibit 4 for "Direct Labor" force by departments.

Exhibit 2
Novac Company: Examples of Some of the Typical Machines and Equipment Used in Manufacturing

Automatic Lathes	20-Ton Punch Press
5-ton Punch Press	Double Torch Solder
Degreaser	Thread Roller
Tumbler	Snow Tapper
Capper Plating Equipment	Thomson Welder
Production Lathes	Induction Brazer
Broaching Equipment	Stanley Buffer
4-Ton Press	Artos Cutter
Auto-Drill Press	X-ray Equipment
Miller	Resistance Brazer

Plus special machines, tools and equipment made by the company.
Note: Does not include tool room machines and equipment.

Ever since its incorporation, the Novac Company had enjoyed the reputation of being a "fair dealer" with its employees. The company had followed a policy of filling newly created jobs or positions left vacant by advancement from within the company whenever possible. To aid in carrying out this policy, notices were posted on the bulletin boards and in the employees' paper telling of available positions. As part of the basic philosophy of the company, the employees shared in "the fruits of their labor" through the company's profit sharing plan. Quarterly payments to employees were computed on gross pay. In very few quarters had the company failed to show a profit, and the percentage distributed to employees had fluctuated from 17.8 per cent down to 2.04 per cent.

The two types of business were the industrial products, which correlated with the growth of the nation's capital equipment market, and the military, which fluctuated with the aircraft defense budget. Mr. A. R. Williams of the market research department felt that while there was increasing competition, especially in the military, the wide product line of Novac and the widely spread application of uses of the product made the demand for it fairly stable. Usually a user requested the product after he had designed his equipment; this meant that the product had to be adapted to its particular location in the machine. Changes in the method of attaching the control to the equipment resulted in additional engineering and methods work, and many of the designs might never be produced again. As a result, an extremely large proportion of the orders were for single units or nonstandard items. While General Electric, Honeywell, and similar large companies were competitors, no one company competed on all lines. However, competition required the company to maintain a constant search for new applications for its product to increase the breadth of growth as well as penetration of new markets.

The standards section was approximately 10 years old. It had been set up to aid in the establishment of rates and to perform the duties listed in Exhibit 3. At the present time, the time study group was under the production control supervisor. Although formerly they had been under the methods department, the groups had been separated to insure greater control. Mr. McCall, senior standards engineer, headed the group which consisted of himself and two standards engineers. One of the time study engineers spent three-quarters of his time evaluating suggestions of employees received through the company's suggestion system. The other worked almost exclusively on the establishment of standard time data for the methods department rate estimator. No time studies were taken by the standards section without a request from the methods department, the cost department, the departmental foreman, or an order from the methods department to establish standard data. The rates, set by time study, might or might not be accepted by the methods engineers, since they could use estimated rates. In reality, the section acted as a service group for the methods department rather than for the factory as a whole. Mr. McCall estimated that the standards section would require seven more time study men at approximately $10,000 per man to establish a wage incentive system. One clerk also would be required at $5,000, with additional clerical work performed by the time clerks set up in the various departments by the cost department. Time studies were made with an elemental breakdown, and all were taken through use of the snap-back method. The average time was used as the selected time, and 100 per cent was considered normal for rating:

$$\text{Average Time} \times \text{Rating Factor} = \text{Normal Time}$$
$$\text{Normal Time} + \text{Allowances} = \text{Standard Time per Piece}$$
$$\text{Standard Time} \times 1/60 \times 100 = \text{Standard Hours/Hundred}$$

Exhibit 3
Novac Company: Duties of Standards Department

1. Set standards as requested.
2. Compile standard data formulas, charts, and tables.
3. Aid in applying operational analysis (motion economy and work simplification) methods, tools, and cost reduction possibilities..
4. Aid in administration of suggestion system.
5. Aid in plant layout practices and methods analysis.
6. Aid in acquiring good inspection and quality control habits.
7. Write job descriptions.
8. Recommend improvements in process and equipment.
9. Make comparisons of alternate with existing methods.
10. Inform tool design of handling times required by typical fixtures.
11. Work with those employees on measured jobs until expectancy was reached.
12. Act as advisor, not instructor or supervisor, on any plant problem affecting labor standards, costs, estimates, or methods and any related phase of industrial application to which the standards department was referred as a "fact finding group."

The methods department was headed by Mr. Grayson, chief methods engineer, and was responsible for the method of performing all operations within the factory. This group made out the route sheets which contained the sequence of operations, the machines and equipment and rate of time required to perform the operation. All rates on the route sheet were expressed in hours per hundred sets or units. If an operation had not been time studied, the methods engineer set estimated rates on the work sheet, using standard data, if available, or from his experience. This group also was in charge of the design and manufacture of all tools and equipment used as well as the layout of the work area. Any deviation from the route sheet by the shop foreman was required to be reported to the methods engineer for his approval and for revision of the rate. Mr. Grayson believed that the shop was operating far below normal efficiency, with the machining shops about 80 per cent efficient and the assembly departments as low as 60-70 per cent. He felt that on the whole over 20 per cent savings could result if a wage incentive plan were set up. Of equal importance would be the savings of improved operating efficiency of the indirect labor and better control over operations and costs.

The cost department was in the process of setting up a new direct costing system, which they hoped would give them more usable data than their present system. Costing always had been somewhat of a problem due to the large number of small special orders which required special engineering. Much of the trouble with the cost setup was caused by the estimated rates which became a basis for the submitting of bid prices. While price was not as important as quality and service, they reported that they had lost some contracts to the military on price.

Mr. Morgan, presently head of the production control department, had wide experience as a time study engineer before coming to the Novac Company. While he had worked in companies that employed wage incentive systems with great success, he was not convinced that any such system would work here. Almost a third of Novac's orders were for single items with special engineering changes—a situation which, he believed, did not lend itself to a wage incentive system. The company's policy always had been to accept any order, and they had built up a special reputation in the market as being able to meet the needs of the industry. No order was too small for them to consider. Such a service, it was thought, would lead to additional orders. The basic product alone had thousands of different combinations, and one unit had 576 different application combinations.

Twelve foremen were in charge of the manufacturing departments under Mr. Dolan, the factory superintendent. Their average service with the company exceeded 10 years and they took personal pride in the accomplishments of the company. Twenty-five members of the company, including nine foremen, had completed a course in motion and time study under one of the plant's training programs. Many cost reductions resulted from the employees' suggestion system which was encouraged by the foremen, and during the past year 276 suggestions had been received and 34 per cent accepted. For an acceptable suggestion, the employee was paid one-half of the first year's saving after tooling costs.

During the preceding year, the personnel department had interviewed approximately 2,000 individuals in order to secure 307 employees. This ratio of approximately 1:7 was necessary because applicants lacked the necessary qualifications to meet the job requirements. During the same period, 197 left for various reasons. It was felt that the company paid wages equal to those in the area (Exhibit 4) and that the additional benefits were equally as good as any in the area. The employees had seven paid holidays, two weeks' vacation with pay after one year's service, three weeks' vacation with pay after five years' service, an insurance plan, and a

Exhibit 4
Novac Company: "Direct Labor"

Department	Hourly Rate	Number of Employees
Automatic Lathes	$3.90	12
Lathes & Presses	3.55	20
General Machine	3.30	34
Assembly—"A"	3.15	63
Assembly—"B"	3.05	61
Electronic Assembly	3.05	18
Short Order	3.65	17
Calibration	3.05	12
Plating	3.30	3
Shipping	3.05	6

tuition assistance program, in which the company paid 75 per cent of the cost of tuition and books for those employees who wished to further their education consistent with their job duties and responsibilities. Thirty-three employees were taking advantage of this program and were working on all levels from trade school up to and including advanced degrees in engineering and business administration. They also participated in a cooperative program with a nearby university and had four young men in electrical and mechanical engineering, alternately working 10 weeks and going to school for 10 weeks. The employees had an association which sponsored the company cafeteria and athletic and social events. While this group had been successful in the past, it was having difficulty at present in attracting and keeping its members, and the officers were considering whether or not it should be continued.

None of the company's production workers were unionized. As with most companies in this line of business, the company faced a shortage of scientific, engineering, technical, and secretarial personnel in the area, and the difficulty of attracting applicants with the necessary qualifications to fill existing openings. This tightening of the labor market also was reflected in securing other workers, and each succeeding year presented the personnel department with greater difficulty in meeting the company's labor requirements. The director of personnel felt that since the company was paying wages which, with the profit sharing, were equal to or exceeded the area wages, wage incentives would not be attractive to the workers. He also felt that wage incentives could lead to disputes over rates and that these disputes could lead to grievances and trouble.

Mr. Nolan believed that additional information was needed before he could reach a decision as to wage incentives, and he was considering hiring a consultant to further investigate the matter

PETRI CHEMICAL COMPANY (C)
THE CASE OF TOM MOXLEY

CASE 46

Tom Moxley was 19 years old and had worked for Petri Chemical Company for nine months as a laboratory technician. Tom was considered by his supervisor to be intelligent and dependable. He looked for additional work when he completed the assignments given him, and his work was satisfactory in almost every way. His supervisor stated that Tom's only real fault was that he worked too rapidly on occasion, which sometimes led to errors. However, these had never been serious, and the supervisor thought of Tom as an outstanding employee.

In general, Tom liked his work, and he was enthusiastic about it. He felt that his job might serve as a stepping-stone to promotion. In order to prepare himself for such an eventuality, Tom had enrolled in the night division at Midwestern University. At this time, Tom was taking two courses paid for at his own expense—algebra and chemistry.

Previously Tom Moxley had been employed by a large food store where he had earned $115 per week. His starting salary as a laboratory technician at Petri was $450 per month, but he took the position because he felt it offered him more opportunities for advancement. After six months, Tom complained to his supervisor that he felt that his salary was inadequate and that he should receive an increase in salary. His supervisor recommended that Tom be given an increase. After due consideration by the plant superintendent, Tom was granted an increase of $30 per month. Tom was dissatisfied with the size of the increase, feeling that it should have been at least $40. Shortly thereafter he received a $25 per month "adjustment," as did all other laboratory technicians (in line with an "across-the-board" company increase in wages and salaries). Tom was dissatisfied with this increase also. He felt that his outstanding work was not being considered by the company, and considered it unfair that several other laboratory technicians, who were not nearly so industrious and competent, had received the same increase.

Tom was very unhappy about his salary and had several discussions with his supervisor about the matter. On one occasion he told his supervisor that other firms were paying $30 to $50 per month more for comparable work. When the supervisor expressed disbelief, Tom produced several advertisements from the local newspaper offering higher salaries. The supervisor suggested that Tom investigate these positions very carefully, because often these positions involved night work or very undesirable working conditions. On another occasion Tom told his supervisor that his fiancee was prodding him to look for a higher-paying

All names, places, and certain wage data disguised.

job, and that she was earning more in her clerical position at a local bank than he was at Petri Chemical Company.

The supervisor was very fond of Tom Moxley and tried to soothe his feelings over wages as much as possible. He told Tom to be patient, and that "sooner or later" he would "take care of him." He even offered to help Tom with his studies, should he run into difficulties.

Tom also was aggravated by the fact that:

1. Overtime in the plant was virtually non-existent (usually only one or two days per month at time and one-half);
2. He expected to be transferred to a new ore processing plant when it was completed in several months, and his costs of transportation to the new plant would be higher, since it was further from his home;
3. Advertisements regularly appeared in the newspaper offering laboratory technicians $525 per month, plus more for experience.

In addition, Tom realized that chemical operators, porters, and dishwashers received higher salaries than he, although he never complained about this to his supervisor. Published union wage scales for these positions were as follows: chemical operators made from $3.50 to $3.85 per hour; based on an average of 175 hours per month, this ranged from about $612 to $674 per month. Porters and dishwashers received from $2.95 to $3.15 which on the same basis came to about $516 to $551 per month. Tom's supervisor knew that the salary classification for laboratory technicians ranged from $450 to $725 per month, but this was confidential information for supervisors only. These ranges had been adjusted upwards each year after a contract was settled with the plant union (which represented hourly paid production and maintenance workers). Whenever hourly wage rates were increased, across-the-board increases were granted to laboratory technicians, non-exempt salaried employees, and foremen who were not in the union. The amounts were usually the monthly equivalent of the cents-per-hour increase negotiated with the union.

Tom's supervisor decided that he should discuss the matter with the plant superintendent again. He told the superintendent that Tom Moxley could perform about three-fourths of the work normally performed by a college-trained chemist, and that the group of which Tom was a part was shorthanded. Further, he stated that the company should make every effort not to lose Tom, and that unless something could be done, Tom would quit shortly after the move to the new plant.

The plant superintendent told the supervisor to talk again to Tom, to point out to him the long-run advantages of working for Petri and to promise Tom that he would receive the consideration of management in regards to a fair adjustment of his wages.

BOYNTON DEPARTMENT STORE— THE RELUCTANT SALES CLERK

CASE 47

The Boynton Department Store is located in a large midwestern city. Its sales exceed 30 million dollars per year. The management of the store is considered by others in the industry to be very progressive, and personnel policies of the store are considered to be among the best in the area. Selection and training policies and procedures are thorough. Salaries are among the highest in retail organizations in the Midwest.

Sales personnel compensation is based upon a base salary plus an incentive system, known as "quota-bonus." Under the quota-bonus plan, each salesman is allocated a sales quota for the week; the quota is determined by the minimum amount of sales considered reasonable for a normally qualified salesman in each department for the week in question. The sales person earns a commission on all sales in excess of the quota for the week.

In the Men's Furnishing's Department the basic weekly salary paid to each salesman is $125 and the bonus is three per cent above quota. A salesman whose quota for the week would be $1,000, and who sold $1,500 of merchandise would receive $125 plus (3% x $500.00 = $45.00) or $170.00 for the week.

One day in June, the following incident occurred. John Roberts, supervisor of men's furnishings, had noticed that his sales people were not keeping stock correctly. In particular, salesmen were very careless about returning stock to display cases and bins. Roberts felt this must be done in order to prevent damage to merchandise, to enable the sales people to save time in showing merchandise to customers, and to enable the sales people to make a more effective presentation of merchandise. At that time George Kennedy, one of the top-selling salesmen in the department, walked past. Roberts stopped Kennedy and the following discussion took place within hearing and viewing distance of several sales people and customers:

ROBERTS: George, I want you to get these shirts back in stock and the counters straightened up as soon as possible.

KENNEDY: I'm busy filling a telephone order. I have no time. Besides, what about Bill (a new stock clerk who has been in the department only three months) or Frank (a college graduate who has been temporarily assigned to the department as a part of a management training program) doing that? I haven't seen them killing themselves lately.

ROBERTS: Look here, George, I'm running this department. When I want your advice, I'll ask for it.

KENNEDY: Well, I'm not going to do it. My job is to sell, not rearrange stock. What difference does it make anyway?

ROBERTS: If that is the way you feel about it, you can either spend the rest of the day straightening up the stock room, or go home for the rest of the day and think about it.[1] You know that stock must be kept in order. (In a heated tone of voice.) It's about time you clerks learn who is in charge of this department.

George Kennedy has been employed as a salesman at Boynton's for the past five years. Among the salesmen in the department, George's sales record has consistently been at or near the top. His disciplinary record has been excellent.

Simplified Organization Chart
Boynton Department Store

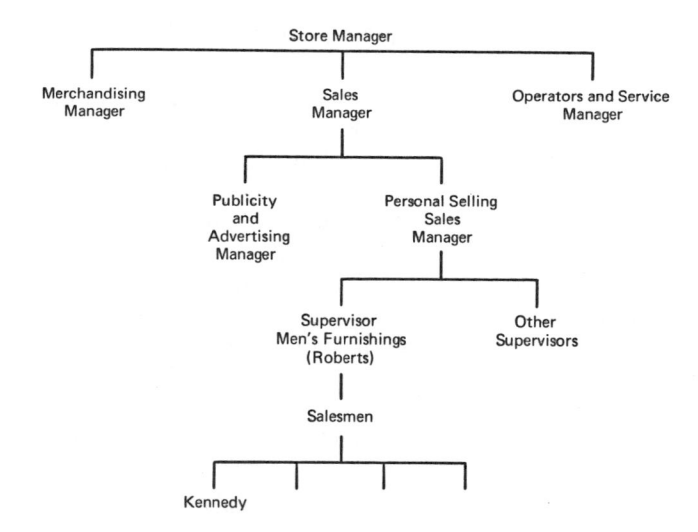

```
                         Store Manager
         ┌───────────────────┼───────────────────┐
   Merchandising           Sales           Operators and Service
     Manager              Manager                Manager
                    ┌────────┴────────┐
               Publicity         Personal Selling
                 and                 Sales
              Advertising           Manager
               Manager
                             ┌────────┴────────┐
                         Supervisor           Other
                       Men's Furnishings    Supervisors
                          (Roberts)
                              │
                          Salesmen
                    ┌─────┬───┴───┬─────┐
                 Kennedy
```

---

[1] The amount of space available for display in the Men's Furnishing Department is rather limited; therefore, the department maintains a small stockroom adjacent to the department. Sales personnel replenish stock from the stockroom as needed. The task of keeping the stockroom orderly is usually assigned to the junior salesman in the department

THE FILMORE ELECTRIC COMPANY (A)   CASE 48
THE MACHINE SHOP

George Whitmore, an experienced machinist for the Filmore Electric Company, had worked in the machine shop many years without an accident. About 9:30 one Monday morning he appeared at the door of the combination shop office and supply room with an injury. His hand was wrapped in a dirty handkerchief and was bleeding badly. "Say, Bill, where's that first aid kit? I nicked my finger a while ago—need some stuff to wrap it up in," he said to the foreman, Bill Webster.

"Well, I never thought it could happen to you, George. Let me see it! Oh, never mind—go up to the Doc's office—Miss Jordan can fix you up. I haven't sent her any business yet this morning," replied Bill the foreman.

"Takes too long up there. Just give me that first aid box. I'll wrap it up and go back to work."

"Okay, but let me take a look. Sometimes those cuts are worse than you think," and Bill stepped towards a cabinet to get the first aid kit.

George began to unwrap the handkerchief but was still trying to keep it partially covered and stop the bleeding by holding the base of the injured finger. Bill stepped back from the cabinet and was preparing to use the gauze when he stopped suddenly saying, "Hell's fire, George, that finger's really bleeding. Keep hold of it and go on up to medical."

"Naw, I don't want to do that, Bill. Dab it with that red stuff and tie it up for me," he asked.

"No, George, you know the rules—anything worse than a scratch has to be reported and treated upstairs. Besides that finger's almost cut to the bone."

"But Bill, I don't want to go up there," objected George.

"You've got to George—it's an order. Get up there before you bleed to death. Go on, maybe I'm saving your life or something," he said laughingly.

"Well, if you insist, I will—but I don't want to. Now don't do anything about the work at my machine. I'll be right back and take care of it," and somewhat grudgingly George strode off to the stairway still clutching his hand.

The incident was almost forgotten by Bill until Miss Jordan, the nurse, called about 10:15 a.m. She reported that she had done the best she could for George's finger, but she was insisting that he wait and see the doctor. A stitch or two might be taken in the wound. The doctor was due in the office any minute, but sometimes it was 10:30 or 11:00 o'clock before he arrived. George didn't want to wait, but had been persuaded to do so. He had asked her to tell Bill not to bother the work at his machine, as he'd take care of it as soon as he got back.

Bill thought it was a little strange that George, who'd never seemed to complain about any rules or regulations, was reluctant to visit the medical department. It was odd, too, that he seemed worried about the work at his machine. But the nurse had indicated that he wasn't hurt too badly so it would work out all right.

A short while later, Bill was walking down the aisle and passed the cylindrical grinding department. He noticed George's machine standing idle. Another grinder, Sid Stone, saw Bill and asked, "How's George, Bill? He sure got a nasty cut!"

"He's all right, Sid, but the Doc may take a couple of stitches in his finger. If he's not back before long I'd like to get Mike over here on his machine. Mike's crying his eyes out to get on a grinder since he spelled you guys during vacations." And with this remark Bill looked around the department. He spotted a tote pan under the bench beside George's machine. He gave it a kick with his foot—said "ouch" and then pulled it out into the aisle. "What's this doing under here, Sid? These shafts have a Saturday schedule for grinding. Must be four dozen here."

"I don't know, Bill. George put them there, I think," replied Sid.

Walking away from the grinding department, Bill thought that it was unusual for George to be as much as an hour's work behind schedule. All the operators in cylindrical grinding were on piece rate—they all made good bonus earnings, especially George, and the dispatcher would seldom permit a Saturday schedule on a batch of work carried over until Monday. These considerations left his mind as he thought of dependable George. He could always count on George. Everything would be taken care of unless he was sent home by the doctor. He would check on that after lunch.

Other matters absorbed his attention during the remainder of the morning and Bill didn't plan on checking with George until lunch time. Upon returning to his desk from the cafeteria he found this note written hurriedly in pencil:

> Bill—Sid tells me you found that tote pan under my grinder. You probably found out I counted that on last week's production. I'm sorry, because I haven't done it very often. This finger throbs like blazes and I don't feel good. I'm going home and I'll talk to you later.
>
> George

Bill began to realize that George had cheated on the previous week's bonus earnings. He was sitting and thinking about it, trying to analyze the situation when Sid Stone appeared at his door. "I've been watching for you, Bill. George came back awhile before lunch. I told him you'd been around and found those Saturday shafts. He was really pretty sick and went on home. I hopped on those shafts and finished them up. They're back on schedule."

"That's good Sid. But won't you be behind today?"

"No, I'd like to talk to you, Bill. Those lousy rates are getting us all down. The whole damned time study department has studied our jobs—and it seems to get worse every time they come around. You've got George hooked—and I want you to know that once in a while we all do what he did. We try to keep our bonus about the same each week, but you can go to town with rotors and you get behind on shafts. George got stuck Saturday and last week's report shows he finished 'em Saturday. He would have cleaned 'em up this morning if he hadn't cut his finger. I was on rotors and I had half a pan done Saturday that I didn't report. We keep our sheet about even. I guess we're all wrong, and maybe it's good you found out. Why don't you give us all a dime raise and throw out this damn piece rate system. Think of the fancy engineer's salaries the company'd save. I don't see how you can do anything about George when we all do it."

"O.K., Sid, I'll have to think this thing over. Are you speaking for all the grinders or just for yourself?"

"Well, at lunch the boys told me to see you. Everyone was there except the newer men. We decided that you couldn't do much about George if you knew we were all doing it," and with that Sid walked away.

"Say, Sid," called Bill, bringing him back, "send Tom Horton over to see me."

"Oh, no, Bill, don't tell that guy about this! He still wants to be our boss—and we can't stand him. If he plays the big shot around us much more, we'll run him clear out of grinders," complained Sid.

"All right, he's not your boss, but maybe I need a foreman over there. You and George both turned the job down, and Tom has gotten to be a pretty good set-up man. He's willing to set-up and break-in new men. I'm not making Tom an assistant foreman yet, but maybe I've got to do something," explained Bill.

"We get along pretty good, Bill. We like you for a boss. Unless George wants the job, I don't think we need anyone. Let Tom have the set-ups and training, but for God's sake don't make me take orders from him. Do you really want to see him?" asked Sid.

"Yes, I do. Send him over," said Bill.

A short while later Tom Horton, a skilled mechanic, came to Bill's office. Tom was younger and had several years less service with the company than George or Sid. "You want to see me, Bill?" he asked.

"Yea, Tom—what do you know about George's injury this morning and the work on his machine?"

"I know the whole story, Bill, and I'm sorry George cut his finger. But it's about time you found something like that pan of shafts. I guess you knew about the boys adjusting their weekly reports on Saturdays, didn't you?" asked Tom.

"No, I didn't know about it, Tom. Why didn't you tell me?" queried Bill.

"Why, didn't I tell you? How do you get that way—I'm not supposed to report everything that goes on around here and besides, I thought you probably knew. Anyway I'm not an assistant foreman, so I don't have any say over those guys."

"No, you're not an assistant but you are the set-up man for everyone but the old-timers—and you break in new people on grinders and engine lathes . . ." said Bill.

"Yea, I'm just a set-up man, but I haven't any real say. If I was assistant foreman, like Pete on the punch presses, a lot of things would be different," complained Tom.

"We went all through that last year, Tom, and we set up four assistant foremen—punch presses, drill presses, lathes and screw machines—but we decided that everybody else would report directly to me," stated Bill.

"Oh yea, and you yourself counted 56 men that you boss. You said it was too many ... and I've been studying up on that. I know it's too many ... fellows in the front office told me so."

"Well, Tom, I just can't go through that again now. You know that Sid and George and the other boys don't want you as a boss now. Maybe later it'll be different. But I want to get this bonus report business settled," said Bill. "Sid says the standards are no good. Rates on shafts are too tight and rotors are too loose. What do you think?"

"Well, I really think Sid is just an old fox. The rates are probably too loose on both shafts and rotors. He sits there all day long, taking it easy, making a big bonus. And he turns in a bonus report that fills his pocket. When the time study man comes around to change the rate he slows down to where you'd think he was dead. There's nothing I can do about it—they even get the new men to acting that way. They all do it, and poor old George gets caught and a sore finger to boot. Hell, I don't want to be the boss of a crazy gang like that!" and with that outburst Tom stomped out of the office.

Bill continued to sit at his desk and consider the problems in the grinding department. He wondered if he had been right in talking to Tom Horton. The shop really did need better supervision. Maybe Tom could supervise the bench work—eighteen or twenty of those fellows on broaching, filing and hand jobs and half of them "horsing around" all the time. But putting Tom over there would take him off of machines. Tom was a good set-up man. Suddenly Bill stood up and left the office, saying to himself, "I'm going to talk to Anderson about these problems. He's superintendent around here—let him worry some for me. I've got four assistant foremen, but forty or fifty guys yell at me all the time. I need two or three more supervisors just for insulation. Wonder what the supe will say about George and those rates on the grinding machine?"

THE SUPERINTENDENT'S VACATION PAY

CASE 49

The telephone rang in the office of Dr. John Marshall, Professor of Personnel Management at Sherwood University.

MARSHALL: Hello, this is Professor Marshall.

PETERMAN: Dr. Marshall, this is Bill Peterman. You and I met last year at the Public School Educators' Conference at the University. If you remember, I'm chairman of the Board of Education of our city's public school system.

MARSHALL: Oh, yes, Mr. Peterman. It's nice to hear from you again. What can I do for you?

PETERMAN: Well, Professor, I've really got a problem, and I thought you might be able to give me some advice. You see, Mr. George Whitaker, our superintendent of schools, recently resigned and we discussed the problem at the meeting of our Board of Education last night.

MARSHALL: I doubt that I know any likely candidates to help you out, Mr. Peterman.

PETERMAN: Oh, no, that's not our immediate problem, Professor. What we've got is something directly concerned with Mr. Whitaker, and our board has to reach a decision on it as soon as possible.

Let me give you the background of what we're concerned about. Mr. Whitaker has been our superintendent of schools for about eight years. He is one of the finest men I have ever known. He is well respected as an educational administrator, and he did an outstanding job as our superintendent. His salary was $24,000 annually, and he was worth every penny of it.

Well, he was just appointed to the presidency of Bay State University, which is quite an honor, and it reflects well upon our school system. We were happy to release him from his contract with us, so that he could accept the appointment effective March 1.

Mr. Whitaker's contract with our school system was a twelve-month contract, which allowed for thirty days of vacation and extended from August 1 of last year to July 30 of this year. What puzzles us is what we should do about a payment request which Whitaker turned in to the treasurer of our school system. Whitaker wants us to pay him seven-twelfths (7/12) of one month's pay to cover the vacation time he feels he has earned since last August. He's turned in a request for 7/12's of $2,000, or about $1,170.

Last night at the meeting of the Board of Education several members were extremely unhappy that Whitaker would turn in such a payment request. They felt that it was ridiculous for Whitaker to expect us to pick up the tab for his vacation, when he hadn't fulfilled the conditions of his contract. But other members thought that the board should pay the $1,170 on the grounds that Whitaker had "earned" and was entitled to 7/12's of a year's vacation, even if he did resign in the middle of his contract.

Regardless, all members of the board were unhappy that Whitaker, as a top salaried school official, would even turn in such a request, since they didn't think it was fitting for a superintendent at his salary level to be so mercenary, particularly under the circumstances of his leaving.

MARSHALL: Have you any policy with respect to such matters?

PETERMAN: No, we don't. Something like this seldom occurs. We just weren't prepared for this. However, last year we discharged a clerical employee in our printing department. We first did not pay her any accumulated vacation allowance. However, so many people complained about it, that we finally paid her the equivalent of 10 days' pay for the five months which she worked into the annual vacation period.

MARSHALL: You still haven't told me what you would like me to do, Mr. Peterman. Do you want me to advise you on what action you should take?

PETERMAN: Well, yes and no, Dr. Marshall. When the problem came to a vote last night, the board voted 5-4 to turn down the vacation pay request. But right after the vote was taken, some of the board members began having second thoughts about the decision. We don't want to be accused of being penny-pinchers, if Whitaker really is entitled to the vacation money. I suggested that we should contact several authorities in industry and at the university to get their opinions, and then reconsider the matter at the next board meeting. So, that's why I called you today, Professor; would you be willing to offer your view as to what we should do?

MARSHALL: Well, frankly, Mr. Peterman, I'm not exactly sure myself. Let me think the problem over a little while, and I'll call you back later today.

JONES MANUFACTURING COMPANY CASE 50

JOB EVALUATION WAGE SURVEY PROBLEM

The management of the Jones Manufacturing Company was in the process of installing a job evaluation program in the machine shop, based on a widely published job rating plan. This program was an attempt to establish more consistent relationships between the hourly rates for the various occupations and generally to improve the company's overall wage structure.

Occupational descriptions were prepared for all the different jobs in the machine shop, and an Evaluation Committee assigned point ratings to them in accordance with the rating plan.[1] The Evaluation Committee consisted of supervisors from the machine shop plus several staff personnel from the company's personnel department. It then became necessary to establish a point-to-money conversion curve for determining the actual monetary job values or labor-grade rate ranges. Out of all the jobs evaluated, the actual hourly rates for thirteen were considered by the committee as properly representing current and undisputed hourly rates. It was decided, therefore, to base the intraplant wage survey on these thirteen *key* jobs, and to establish the conversion curve from this survey. After this conversion curve had been established, the hourly rates for the balance of the jobs could be determined from the various point-values assigned by the committee. As a result of the survey, the table on the following page shows the job names, the point ratings assigned by the committee, and the actual hourly rates being paid at the time of this case for these various occupations.

Instructions to Students to Solve This Problem

1. On regular linear coordinate paper (8½ x 11) plot the point ratings as the independent (X) variable along the eleven-inch side of the paper, and the corresponding hourly rates as the dependent (Y) variable along the 8½-inch side of the paper. Start both scales from zero in the lower left hand corner, and allow one-half inch for each 25 points and each 50 cents. Since the money values are "actual" hourly rates, the points will not fall on a smooth curve; therefore, a "line of average relationship" must be determined.

Case contributed by Professor H. Barrett Rogers, Professor of Industrial Management, School of Business, Northwestern University. Certain wage data revised.
[1] For an excellent discussion of a typical point rating process, see Michael Jucius, *Personnel Management* 7th Ed. (Homewood, Ill.: Richard D. Irwin, Inc., 1971), pp. 344-351.

Job Ratings

Job No.	Job	Point Rating	Actual Hourly Rate
1	Automatic Screw Machine Operator	275	$3.75
2	Bench Lathe Operator	241	3.54
3	Bench Work—(Filing and Assembly)	164	2.67
4	Casting Grinder and Polisher	209	3.63
5	Drill Press Operator	224	2.96
6	Milling Machine Operator	311	3.88
7	Machine Operator (Tool Room)	311	4.44
8	Punch Press Operator	271	3.72
9	Soldering	216	2.85
10	Stores Clerk	205	2.83
11	Tool Crib Attendant	246	3.54
12	Tool Maker	381	4.41
13	Turret Lathe Operator	331	4.14

If this wage curve were to include the entire range of wages and salaries, from the lowest grade of common labor to high executive salaries, the line of average relationship would take the form of an upward curve, with a gradually increasing slope as the point values increased; but the actual direct labor wages in the typical factory represents only a relatively small range, and for this smaller range, a linear or straight line approximation is satisfactory for practical application. The general equation for a straight line is:

$$Y = a + bX$$

where Y is the monetary hourly rate which corresponds to any specific point value X. The Method of Least Squares should be used in finding the mathematical equation of this line. To do this, first the table below should be filled in. Slide rule accuracy is acceptable.

The table values then should be substituted into the following equations which are to be solved simultaneously to find the values (a) and (b).

Equation (1): $(\Sigma Y) = aN + b(\Sigma X)$
Equation (2): $(\Sigma XY) = a(\Sigma X) + b(\Sigma X^2)$

Job No.	(X) Point Rate	(Y) Hourly Rate	(X × Y)	(X²)
1	275	3.75	( )	( )
2	241	3.54	( )	( )
3	164	2.67	( )	( )
4	209	3.63	( )	( )
5	224	2.96	( )	( )
6	311	3.88	( )	( )
7	311	4.44	( )	( )
8	271	3.72	( )	( )
9	216	2.85	( )	( )
10	205	2.83	( )	( )
11	246	3.54	( )	( )
12	381	4.41	( )	( )
13	331	4.14	( )	( )
Totals (N=13)	( ) (ΣX)	( ) (ΣY)	( ) (ΣXY)	( ) (ΣX^2)

Submit your calculations with this problem.

Using the values of (a) and (b) thus calculated, write the equation for the straight line wage curve:

Equation (3): Hourly Rates = (a) + (b) x Point Value,

showing your calculated values in place of (a) and (b).

Substitute point values of (100) and (300) into Equation (3) and calculate the corresponding Hourly Rates. Plot these two points on the graph and draw a straight line through them, extending the line until it intersects the (Y) axis. This intersection should agree with the (a) value. Show Equation (3) on the graph.

2. Using this equation, determine the rate range for each labor grade by calculating the minimum and maximum monetary hourly rates* for the corresponding minimum and maximum point values for each of the ten labor grades, and fill in the table below, showing the hourly rates to the nearest one-tenth of a cent.

3. Calculate equations for rate range "limit" lines. The upper limit line should be 10% above the "mean" line represented by equation (3), and this limit line equation may be calculated from the (a) and (b) values in equation (3).

Upper Limit Rate = 1.10(a) + 1.10(b) Point Value.

Grade	Point Range Minimum	Point Range Maximum	Hourly Rate Range Minimum*	Hourly Rate Range Maximum*
10	162	183	( )	( )
9	184	205	( )	( )
8	206	227	( )	( )
7	228	249	( )	( )
6	250	271	( )	( )
5	272	293	( )	( )
4	294	315	( )	( )
3	316	337	( )	( )
2	338	359	( )	( )
1	360	381	( )	( )

The lower limit line should be 10% below the "mean" line, and its equation may be calculated as

Lower Limit Rate = .90(a) + .90(b) Point Value

Draw these limit lines (dotted) on the graph and show their equations.

Next, construct "rectangles" on the graph to show the entire rate range for each of the labor grades. To construct the "rectangles," do the following: Starting from the lowest rate, corresponding to the minimum point value of a grade, draw a horizontal line across the grade, *left* to *right*. This lowest rate (on the lower limit line) becomes the "Base" rate for the grade. Starting from the highest rate on the upper limit line, corresponding to the maximum point value of the grade, draw a horizontal line across the grade, *right* to *left*. Although varying with differing point spreads for the several grades, this method of constructing the rectangles automatically gives roughly two-thirds overlap of the rate ranges for consecutive

---

* Note: Since the least squares equation describes an "average" trend-line through the scatter-diagram of actual rates, this trend-line is equivalent to an "arithmetic mean." The calculated minimum and maximum rates are thus "minimum-mean rates" and "maximum-mean rates" for the respective labor grades.

grades. (Smaller overlaps can be achieved through arbitrary policy decisions.) Each labor grade thus will have a rate range in which the maximum rate is roughly 25% to 30% higher than the minimum (or Base) rate.

4. In the following table, for each occupation number check whether the present rate is inside or outside the established rate range as indicated by the rectangles. Calculate the theoretically correct hourly rate for each job by substituting the job point rating into the hourly rate equation (3). Then show the difference between the theoretically correct rate and the actual rate now being paid, and in front of each "difference" indicate by a (+) or (−) respectively whether the present base rate should be raised or lowered to bring it into line.

5. Write up an outline of instructions for making any adjustments which you consider necessary at the present time or which may develop in the future in regard to base rates which are, or may become, out of line. Submit your outline with the rest of the problem.

Job No.	Rate Within Rate Range	Rate Outside Rate Range	Point Rating	Present Actual Rate	Theoretically Correct Rate From Equation	Amount Difference (+) or (−)
1	( )	( )	275	$3.75	( )	( )
2	( )	( )	241	3.54	( )	( )
3	( )	( )	164	2.67	( )	( )
4	( )	( )	209	3.63	( )	( )
5	( )	( )	224	2.96	( )	( )
6	( )	( )	311	3.88	( )	( )
7	( )	( )	311	4.44	( )	( )
8	( )	( )	271	3.72	( )	( )
9	( )	( )	216	2.85	( )	( )
10	( )	( )	205	2.83	( )	( )
11	( )	( )	246	3.54	( )	( )
12	( )	( )	381	4.41	( )	( )
13	( )	( )	331	4.14	( )	( )

THE WAREHOUSE SITUATION

Soon after the job evaluation program was installed at the Jones Company Machine Shop, the warehouse foreman, Al Raymond, called at the personnel office asking for help about a report he had received from the Evaluation Committee. The Evaluation Committee subsequently had studied the jobs in the warehouse department, along with Al Raymond, and had assigned point values to the various warehouse jobs as a first step in bringing these jobs into proper alignment with the overall company compensation program.

Raymond stated that in the past he had received numerous complaints about wage rates in his department. "It's not my fault these rates are all fouled up. I've only been foreman for two years—and we've always had this mess!" With this comment, Raymond presented to the personnel director the data which he had received from the Evaluation Committee.

"Okay," said Raymond, "I know something should be done to get some of these rates in line, but what? Frankly, I don't trust these point values anymore than I do the whole damn evaluation program!"

Warehouse Department

Jobs	Point Values	Average Present Wage
Foreman (management)		$825.00 per month
Assistant Foreman (non-management)	400	$4.75 per hour
Lift Truck Operator	206	$3.85 per hour
Shipping Clerk	315	$3.10 per hour
Stockman	246	$2.60 per hour
Loaders	175	$2.25 per hour

THE KAISER STEEL
LONG-RANGE SHARING PLAN

CASE 51

In the winter of 1962, the Kaiser Steel Corporation and the United Steelworkers of America announced a contractual plan to share cost savings created by technological changes and increases in worker productivity. This case consists of two parts: (A) a summary of the original Kaiser long-range sharing plan, and (B) three articles reporting upon the experiences of Kaiser Steel Corporation under this plan from 1963 through 1967.

KAISER LONG RANGE SHARING PLAN[1]
EFFECTIVE MARCH 1, 1963

Summary

This plan, developed by the tripartite Long Range Committee, is designed to achieve equitable sharing of the company's progress among the company, employees, and the public. It also is intended to promote stability of employment and to permit necessary expansion. It covers all company employees at Fontana, Calif., who are represented by the Steelworkers.

The plan provides for monthly sharing with employees of all savings in the use of materials and supplies and from increased productivity. The standards to be used in measuring gains are based on actual performance at various operating levels in 1961. However, the standards for material and supply costs are to be increased or decreased to reflect changes in the Bureau of Labor Statistics Wholesale Price Index; those for labor costs are to be adjusted to reflect changes in the BLS Consumer Price Index.

Each month gains are to be calculated by comparing actual labor, material, and supply costs per finished ton of steel with the standards. Capital expenditures made to reduce product cost on existing facilities are to be deducted from the gains so computed, in an amount equal to the lesser of one third of the actual reduction in cost or one sixtieth of the capital expenditure.

Employees' share of the dollar gains is 32.5 percent of the total. Part of this may be used by agreement of the parties to improve existing benefits or to introduce new ones (reduced hours of work is mentioned as an example). The rest is distributed among employees in cash by means of a stated formula. Individual shares are part of the regular rate but are not considered in computing incentive earnings.

[1] Reprinted by permission from The Bureau of National Affairs, Inc., *Labor Policy and Practice* (Personnel Management Special Supplement No. 29), 1963.

Incentives—A principal aim of the plan is to do away with incentive rates over a period of time. The company is not to establish new incentives or to apply existing incentives to employees not already covered by them. The elimination of existing incentives may come about in either of two ways:

1. After the sharing plan has been in effect for 60 days, employees under an existing incentive plan may decide by majority vote to give up the incentive and participate in the sharing plan.
2. Employees in a unit covered by an incentive plan may decide, by majority vote, to accept a company offer of a lump-sum payment equal to about 2½ years' incentive earnings. In that event, the incentive will be eliminated, and the employees will participate in the sharing plan on an adjusted basis. If the offer is rejected, the employees will continue on incentive and will not participate in the sharing plan.

After the sharing plan has been in effect for two years, employees who have not been offered lump-sum settlements will nevertheless participate in the sharing plan on an adjusted basis, while continuing to work on an incentive basis.

Minimum Guarantee—If it turns out that in any year the ratio of actual labor cost to actual total cost was less than the ratio of standard labor cost to standard total cost, the company will pay into employees' gross share the amount necessary to bring the actual ratio up to the standard ratio. This is a cost to the company and is not to be charged against future employee sharing-plan earnings.

Employees also are guaranteed wage and benefit adjustments equal to those agreed to in negotiations between the union and the major basic steel producers. Such adjustments, other than those becoming effective within six months of the plan's effective date, are to be charged against a "wage and benefit reserve" established out of the money due employees under the plan. But if there is any deficit, the company will make it up.

Employment Guarantee—Employees are accorded protection against loss of employment opportunity because of technological change, new or improved work methods, or any other change in operations not resulting from a decrease in man-hour requirements caused by a decrease in finished steel production, or a change in product or production requirements. (Provision already is made for loss of employment opportunity because of changed production or production requirements under the existing supplemental unemployment benefit plan and the collective bargaining agreement.)

Two plant-wide employment reserves are established, one for production and maintenance employees and the other for clerical and technical employees. Employees with at least 26 weeks' service who otherwise would be laid off because of technological change or new or improved work methods are to be placed in the employment reserve. Employees in the reserve may be assigned by management to work anywhere in the plant, subject to certain restrictions. A maximum size is placed on the employment reserves to limit the company's obligation.

Employees whose earnings opportunities suffer because of technological changes or new or improved work methods receive "displacement differentials" equal to the difference between the old and new rates. These continue for 52 weeks or until an employee is offered work at the old rate of pay.

Disputes—Disputes relating to the application of the sharing plan, or to compliance with it, are subject to the regular grievance and arbitration procedures. Disputes relating to the interpretation or meaning of the plan are to be referred to the Long Range Committee for disposition.

Term—The plan is to remain in effect initially for four years, subject to annual review and revision by the parties. It is subject to renewal for additional four terms. Its installation on March 1, 1963, is conditional upon ratification by the local unions.

FRUITS OF KAISER PLAN TASTE SWEET TO ALL[2]

Last winter the Kaiser Steel Corporation and the United Steelworkers announced a radically different labor contract, a scheme to share the cost savings created by technological advances and the workers' own efforts.

The key feature of the long-range sharing plan is a complex formula that matches each month's material, labor, and supply costs against a 1961 base. Kaiser distributes 32.5% of whatever has been saved to its 4,800 participating employees in Fontana, California.

To date, the monthly bonuses have averaged $80—almost the equivalent of a $20 weekly pay increase. If they continue at present rates, each worker's share will add up to $1,000 in a year; Kaiser will pay out more than $4-million in "the fruits"—local slang for the bonuses' original, grandiloquent title, "the fruits of progress."

Although Eastern steel executives have expressed alarm at the price, Kaiser officials are inclined to view it as a bargain. They're plucking fruits of their own, they say. They believe that workers' cost-cutting efforts made a direct contribution to the company's return to black ink in the second quarter of 1963, after a first-quarter loss of about $1.4 million and a 1962 loss of $5.2 million.

"We pay no more through the sharing plan than most steel companies pay for incentive plans alone," says E. E. Trefethen, Jr., vice-chairman of Kaiser Steel's board and executive vice-president of Kaiser Industries Corp. "And the plan is doing what it's supposed to do—reduce costs. There's been a 180-degree switch in our cost trend and worker attitude."

The Kaiser plan inspires worker cooperation more effectively than standard profit-sharing plans—another Fontana executive says—because workers feel they can't do much to increase profits, which are tied to management decisions, but understand how their efforts influence production costs.

On their own, Kaiser overhead crane crews that once discarded a 300-ft. length of cable when it snapped, now retrieve the two pieces and carefully parcel out 50-ft. lengths for smaller, mobile cranes. That's a saving of $50 or $60 per 50-ft. cable. A machine shop crew hoards old nuts and bolts. Train switchings on the 90 miles of in-plant trackage have increased 10%—saving railroad switching charges. Sick leave among clerical employees has dropped 15%. Grievances have dropped from a range of 60 to 90 a month down to 20 to 30.

[2] Reprinted from the September 21, 1963 issue of *Business Week* by special permission. Copyrighted © 1963 by McGraw-Hill, Inc.

Of course, only a portion of the $5.6 million cost savings calculated in the first five months can be traced directly to worker effort. Much, perhaps most, stems from more efficient machinery, lower cost of raw materials such as ferromanganese and scrap iron, and figure-juggling that tries to account for changes in wholesale steel prices and cost-of-living tallies since 1961.

But that was the idea, Kaiser officials say: to find a way for workers to share in the fruits of technology and, in return, to benefit from their greater willingness to accept change and their more efficient work habits. The cumulative effect of these intangibles shows up in the monthly figures, the company officials say.

Another novel aspect of the Kaiser plan has remained untested so far, because rising production has kept the full work force on the job. This is the labor reserve pool made up of workers displaced by technology. Displaced workers would be assured first call on new jobs and, in the meantime, would draw a substantial portion of their former pay.

The Kaiser plan of rewarding cost-cutting on a plant-wide basis differs sharply from the usual practice of the steel industry, which typically pays bonuses based on hundreds of separate individual incentive plans, all geared to higher unit production. Perhaps 70% to 80% of all production and maintenance workers employed by steel companies participate in such plans.

Even at Kaiser, 40% of the work force is still on incentive—since a switchover to the new plan is voluntary for each worker. Naturally, the holdout group consists of those who have been doing best under the old arrangement. Their bonuses have averaged 30%, compared to the 16% to 25% of the cost-savings "fruits."

Though the company cannot compel a switch, it expects most of the holdouts to transfer voluntarily to the new plan as the payoff increases. One USW prediction is that it will double by the end of the four-year contract. Kaiser can also offer certain lures, such as the lump sum equal to more than a year's bonus paid out when a worker switches.

Rewarding cost consciousness makes more sense than rewarding higher output, since the latter may be achieved without regard to efficiency or costs, Kaiser executives believe.

Moreover—and this is a point that interests even those steel companies that insist the Kaiser plan was custom-tailored for a specific company and wouldn't work for them—it substitutes a group incentive for the old individual incentives. This is important to steel, one of many industries that are moving into an age of increasing mechanization and automation, when the contribution of the individual is hard to measure.

Kaiser salesmen also note that the ban against strikes on money matters during the four-year life of the contract makes an excellent point with strike-conscious steel customers. USW negotiators traded the no-strike guarantee for assurance that Kaiser workers would receive all benefits won from Big Steel regardless of the success of the Kaiser plan.

The sharing plan is an outgrowth of Kaiser's celebrated go-it-alone decision during the 116-day steel strike of 1959. Kaiser saw room for negotiation, couldn't persuade the rest of the industry, and broke ranks to sign separately. The settlement created a company-union-public committee to work out a new kind of labor contract. The resulting long-range sharing plan is believed to reflect the independent thinking of Edgar F. Kaiser, Kaiser Steel chairman and a maverick among orthodox steel producers.

ANOTHER PROGRESS REPORT[3]

In a comprehensive appraisal of Kaiser Steel's Long-Range Sharing Plan, Mr. C. A. MacIlvaine, the company's treasurer, reported that cash payments and set-aside provisions under the plan for the period March through December, 1963, amounted to approximately $3.5 million. Despite this large outlay, Kaiser's net earnings for 1963 were $11.3 million, compared with a loss of $5.2 million in 1962, Mr. MacIlvaine noted.

Main credit for the sharp earnings rise, he said, had to be attributed to a massive improvement in manufacturing costs—costs of finished steel products during the second quarter of 1963, for example, were approximately $12.50 a ton below the average for 1962, after allowing for the sharing plan costs for both hourly and salaried employees.

In fact, Mr. MacIlvaine said, the early results of the plan have been far better than anyone had really hoped for. As evidence of the marked improvement in labor-management relations at the plant level, he cited the fact that whereas in 1961 there was a backlog of over 500 grievances that had bogged down and were headed for arbitration, at the present time there are only about 70 grievances in process, few, if any, of which are expected to reach the final stage of the grievance procedure.

Both the workers themselves and their union representatives appear to be making a genuine effort to make the plan go, Mr. MacIlvaine added. The men naturally have been elated by the size of the payouts to date, which over the 10-month period have averaged 46 cents per hour, or 18 per cent of the standard hourly wage rates. Soon after the plan was installed, informal groups started to get together for brainstorming sessions in search of new savings ideas. During the past three months, these "savings committees" (which now number 169) have submitted 729 savings suggestions, of which 85 per cent have already been approved, while the remainder are still under consideration.

It was, of course, far too early as yet to draw any hard and fast conclusions about the ultimate success of the plan for Kaiser Steel, let alone its possible applicability to other organizations, Mr. MacIlvaine conceded. Nevertheless, the plan had undoubtedly started off well, and management was satisfied that a strong basis has been established on which to proceed for the future.

[3] Reprinted from *Personnel* (March-April, 1964), pp. 5–6, by the permission of the American Management Association.

NEW SLICES FOR KAISER'S MELON?[4]

A year of decision opened this week for the Kaiser Steel–United Steelworkers long-range sharing plan.

Unlike conventional profit-sharing, which gives workers some percentage of company profits, the Kaiser-USW formula shares with workers money saved by efforts to cut costs of labor and materials. Widely hailed, it has been copied only once.

Under the plan, company or union may call it quits anytime this year on four months' notice. According to prophets at plant headquarters in Fontana, Calif., and union headquarters in Pittsburgh, neither will, although both probably will propose changes in an arrangement that both regard as a qualified success.

The Kaiser plan followed the company's withdrawal from the industrywide bargaining group during the marathon steel strike of 1959. Kaiser signed a separate union agreement, putting aside for committee action a thorny work rules dispute that had triggered the strike. A tripartite committee was directed to create a plan "for equitable sharing of the fruits of the company's progress." Its aim was to promote stable employment and give workers a stake in increased productivity and labor-cost savings.

Kaiser had its reasons for breaking away from industry tradition. Not only was its chairman, Edgar Kaiser, known as an industrial liberal, but the company had just completed a major expansion that saddled it with high fixed debt. It needed to get back to work and to open the door to changed work practices that would take advantage of new technology. It wanted to curb an incentive system that it felt had spawned inequities and inefficiencies.

After two years of study, Dr. George Taylor of the University of Pennsylvania and his committee laid out the long-range sharing plan. It went into effect in March, 1963.

	1963-1964	1964-1965	1965-1966	1966-1967 [to date]
Average share per hour worked	53¢	39¢	46¢	77¢
Average annual cash payout	$810	$434	$319	$567

Data: Kaiser Steel Corp.–United Steelworkers

The plan calls for Kaiser to give one-third of its savings in labor and material costs to workers in the form of monthly cash payouts as well as payments to a wage and fringe benefits reserve fund. This fund pays for wage increases and fringe benefits won by USW in its negotiations with the steel industry. Savings are computed on a 1961 base under a complicated formula that averages some changes over six months to prevent sharp fluctuations.

In four years, the plan has distributed $10.8-million in "fruits"—Fontana talk for the monthly cash pay-outs. Another $8.2-million has gone into the wage and

---

[4] Reprinted from *Business Week*, March 4, 1967, by special permission. Copyright 1967, by McGraw-Hill, Inc.

benefit reserve fund. The plan also contains protections against layoffs stemming from automation, but these have seen little use during a boom period.

The plan unquestionably has achieved one major goal, the elimination of plant work stoppages. The Kaiser-USW contract terminates 60 days after the union reaches agreement with the basic steel industry, when Kaiser automatically matches industry terms. Presumably Kaiser workers never will have any reason to call an official strike. And wild-cat walkouts carry their own penalties in lower cost savings.

When Fontana had its first wild-cat strike in four years last December, the Sharing Plan News, published by the Kaiser-USW plan, told workers what they had lost, by their 32-hour quickie. Their monthly pay-outs dropped because of the delayed production, the publication said, and future payouts could be affected if customers lose faith in Kaiser's ability to guarantee delivery. That's an important point. Kaiser depends partly on its delivery record—excellent since the plan started—for dominance of the southwestern market.

Currently, the plan's biggest problem is the low level of recent monthly payouts; the latest averaged $21. To the company, this indicates that only limited increases in operating efficiency are being achieved; to the union, it means that members are going to complain—a depressing prospect with local union elections coming in June.

Both sides are inclined to blame the computation formula, which has been changed several times before in the course of annual reviews. Neither side will talk about the changes it wants this time when major revisions are in order. However, company-union subcommittee members are meeting, and the results probably will be ready for Taylor and his committee in May.

I. The Union

Worker complaints about the sharing plan—aggravated by the local union politics that flourish in Fontana—center on the portion of cost savings that goes into the wage and benefit reserve. The reserve was increased by $387,000 in the latest monthly contribution, while $123,000 went out in cash payouts. Obviously, the fund needs the extra money to pay for increased gains in USW-steel industry contracts.

"The fund takes it all now," says James Vezie, president of the 7,000-man local of production and maintenance workers. Vezie is pushing a change in the formula that would require the company itself to pay two-thirds of the gains won in basic steel industry contracts, with only one-third coming from the wage and benefit reserve. Such an arrangement, say company spokesmen, "would probably break us."

George Siroli, a USW representative who formerly headed Local 2869, agrees that the amount of cost savings earmarked to cover industry-wide gains creates a problem. "We'll have to out-produce what the fund absorbs in order to have a sharing plan," he says.

Union members also complain that workers who dropped their incentive plans to join the sharing plan wound up losing money.

Originally, the plan sought to end the incentive system by placing all new workers in the sharing plan; workers already on incentives had an option to switch. But morale suffered, especially in the plan's second and third years when payouts dropped. Junior employees found themselves earning far less than older men who did the same job but were still on incentive.

Last year—as a result of the annual review—some 400 workers in key production units were put back on "modified" incentive plans. The differential between their earnings and those of old-time incentive-plan workers went into the sharing plan, and payouts promptly increased. "We realized we couldn't eliminate incentives overnight," says Frank Polara, one of USW's three members on the tripartite committee. "We backtracked a little, but we haven't abandoned the original plan. Now we're moving toward a narrowing of the differential between incentive and non-incentive earnings."

Workers on incentive made up 42% of the labor force when the plan began, 25% in 1965, and 30% today. The industry average is 70%.

In USW's view, Kaiser workers don't realize the plan's real value because its most important provision—the employment security guarantee—hasn't been tested. "No more than 4 or 5 men at a time have been affected by technology changes or reduction in job class," Siroli says. "When there's 30 or 40 at a time, then they'll appreciate it."

Some industry observers predict that the USW's suggestions for plan revisions will be in the area of employment security—perhaps to protect workers laid off for any reason, rather than just for technological reasons.

II. The Company

A Kaiser official comments that the plan hasn't lived up to original expectations, but it's a lot better than conditions and practices in effect earlier. On the plus side, he lists cost savings, stable company-union relations, and a decrease in incentive grievances. Above-average labor costs are a liability, "but who knows how much worse they might have been if we had had any more expensive stoppages at the plant."

The company is disappointed that the plan hasn't helped reduce the work force on old machinery and processes as it has on the new. "I guess it goes against the union's basic philosophy," a spokesman says. "The union, after all, is made up of dues-paying members."

Over-all, though, the company hasn't done badly in this respect. While production has risen steeply—from 2.2-million tons in 1961 to 2.8-million last year, in raw steel alone—the work force has risen only from 8,080 to 8,800.

Kaiser officials also stress that savings in materials and supply costs have outpaced labor cost savings during the past four years.

Company and union officials agree that the plan has released a flood of cost-saving suggestions—more than 5,000, of which 3,500 were accepted. They also agree that it was unfortunate psychologically that payouts started on such a high level—$810 per employee the first year. This sharpened the contrast when they dropped.

Company officials believe they may have erred in attempting to get the plan off to a good start by paring costs drastically between 1961—when the agreement was signed—and 1963—when it went into effect. Workers had two years of accumulated cost savings awaiting them.

Since, on balance, both company and union feel they're benefited from the plan, why hasn't it been duplicated more widely? Only one other steel company—the Alan Wood Steel Co. of Conshohaken, Pa.—has established a similar plan. The answer seems to be that Kaiser and Alan Wood have certain features that larger companies lack.

A cost savings plan works best, USW believes, in a single-plant company on the verge of installing new processes, a company that wants operating efficiencies and to eliminate incentives.

The union thinks it would be impossible to draft a workable plan for a large, multi-plant steel company with many varieties of incentive plans. While the large company probably could afford inefficiencies that would be too much for a small company to swallow, it probably couldn't afford the high cost of guaranteeing income of technologically displaced workers—and this is at the core of the union's interest in the plan.

And USW isn't pushing the plan elsewhere. "We wouldn't try to sell it to anybody," says Polara. "If a company were interested, it would have to approach us."

CHARGES OF DISCRIMINATION AMONG THE LIBRARY STAFF

CASE 52

Art Tipton, Personnel Director of Midwest University, had just finished reading and signing a letter which he was sending to an employee on campus. As he sealed the letter, he pondered on the events which had occurred leading to this situation.

THE NEGRO SUPERVISOR'S LETTER

On June 7, 1969, Mr. Tipton had received the following letter from Carol Parker, a Negro supervisor in the main campus library.

June 6, 1969

Mr. Art Tipton
Personnel Director
Midwest University

Dear Sir:

I, Carol Parker, Negro supervisor at Main Campus Library, in the Card Preparation Division have a serious problem. I have approached my Chief, Mrs. Smith; the Library Administrative Assistant, Miss Caldwell; and the Associate Director of the Library, Mr. Peebles, with no satisfactory results.

My problem is, I feel that there is racial discrimination at Main Campus Library. One of my employees, Jean Rohs, (white) has been employed by Midwest University for seven months and has received twice as much for this year in raises as I have. She also presently makes thirty-five dollars a month more than Annie Waldron, a Negro employee in the same division, who had been employed eleven months at one time and left to have a baby. She returned to work on July 1, 1968, almost four months before Mrs. Rohs, who began on October 28, 1968.

Mrs. Waldron has also had occasion to take over when I was out on vacation several times. Mrs. Laclede, junior cataloger, assisted her on several occasions, but there were times Annie kept things going alone, yet Annie Waldron never was considered for a promotion.

I have been under the impression that raises were granted with merit. Merit as defined by Mr. Webster is "something deserving reward, praise, or gratitude; a reward of honor given for praiseworthy qualities or conduct." In my opinion, merit consists of dependability and the quantity and quality of work produced. If statistics mean anything, Jean Rohs quantity and quality of work does not surpass mine.

When I approached the management people at Main Campus Library with the situation, I only asked for justification for this large raise, which I did not receive. I never brought race into the issue. Miss Caldwell said that raises were based upon merit, but yet no one attempted to show me where Jean merited anymore than Annie Waldron or me. Mr. Peebles' reply was that there was nothing he could do at this time. Miss Caldwell stated that she could neither admit or deny the raises, but I know that Jean received a twenty dollar raise in January (I received fifteen), and she received *forty dollars* on her May check and my raise for July is *fifteen dollars*. I asked for an explanation and I got none.

I, myself, could think of no justification for the differences in raises, when I am supervisor and she is under my supervision.

The only conclusion that I could draw after receiving no answer from my superiors, was that I am Black and she is white. Maybe I am wrong, but as long as I receive no clear-cut answer, I will believe this.

I had thought of approaching the NAACP with this matter to see what they thought, but I felt I should approach the Personnel Office, before I go to outsiders.

I would appreciate your looking into this matter and I'm sure Mrs. Waldron would also.

Respectfully submitted,
Carol Parker (signed)
Carol Parker

The Personnel Director's Reply

After investigating the situation thoroughly, Art Tipton invited Carol Parker to his office for a discussion of the complaint. His letter to Mrs. Parker summarized the essence of that conversation.

June 13, 1969

Personal and Confidential

Mrs. Carol Parker
Main Campus
Box 1123

Subject: Your letter of June 6, 1969

Dear Mrs. Parker:

Thanks again for coming over and talking with me yesterday afternoon. I think it helped both of us to better understand the total situation.

As promised, I have analyzed the salary patterns for you and Jean Rohs; see graph enclosed. Let me make some observations based on what I think this graph shows:

1. You have made unusually rapid progress since joining the Library staff.

I complimented you on this yesterday. Going from $275 per month to

$445 per month in three years is a 62% improvement, an average of over 20% in raises per year.

2. You and Jean both showed fast-learning ability (you mentioned to me that Jean had caught on quickly), and this showed up early in the graph Notice that you and Jean both received a 19% raise in one 6-month period. Perhaps you didn't realize this, since it occurred in your case back in the first half of 1967.
3. Salary increases for clerical personnel in the metropolitan area have been going up, on the average, between 3½% and 5½% per *year* the past three years. The increases given *all* members of your department have considerably exceeded these averages, reflecting our concerted effort to upgrade our rates to competitive levels and thereby help to attract and retain good employees.
4. Our general policy is to maintain about a 10-15% salary differential between our supervisors and the *best* employee salary in the group. Your salary exceeds Jean Rohs' salary by $70 a month, or about 18% higher.

As mentioned in our talk, I am not particularly "happy" about your knowing detailed salary information on someone else; not because I think there are awkward or unjustifiable rates, but because a sharing of each other's salary information can easily lead to misunderstandings without knowing all the factors management tries to consider in setting salaries at equitable levels.

Anyway, I encouraged you to stay in your present supervisory position at least until the operational changes taking place in your department are completed. You said you will think about it—and I'm assuming that means "yes" for now.

Your openness in letting me know of your concerns after you discussed them with Library management was much appreciated by me. If I might be able to help further, I hope you will let me know.

Sincerely,

Arthur Tipton (signed)
Arthur Tipton
Director of Personnel

Encl. graph included

UNIVERSITY POLICY AND THE FUTURE

Art Tipton decided to review the University Policy statements concerning employee problems and discrimination. The following statements were included in the *University's Policies and Procedures Manual for Non-Academic Employees;*

Item 19b: Problem Handling

Employees who wish to question some treatment, procedure, or policy are encouraged to speak up. A procedure for handling such questions is available and in use, as follows:

Salary Patterns

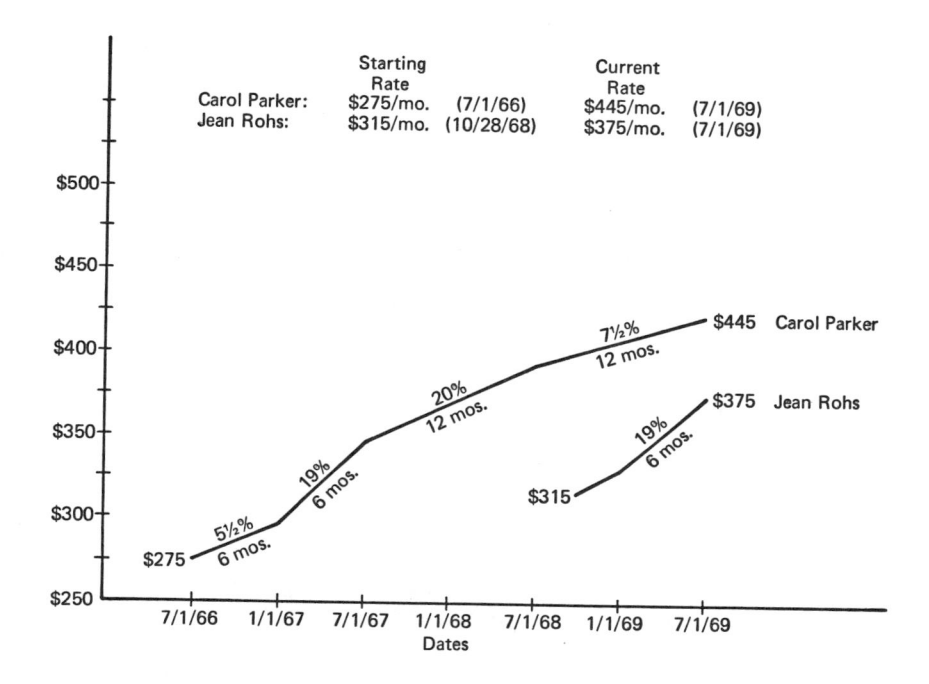

	Starting Rate		Current Rate	
Carol Parker:	$275/mo.	(7/1/66)	$445/mo.	(7/1/69)
Jean Rohs:	$315/mo.	(10/28/68)	$375/mo.	(7/1/69)

[Graph showing salary progression from 7/1/66 to 7/1/69. Carol Parker: $275 → 5½%/6 mos. → 19%/6 mos. → 20%/12 mos. → 7½%/12 mos. → $445. Jean Rohs: $315 → 19%/6 mos. → $375.]

1. Discuss with immediate supervisor.
2. If more satisfaction is desired, discuss with the Department Head.
3. Further appeal may be made to the Director of Personnel for a final reply. The "Problem" should be explained in writing at this stage, and a formal reply in writing will be given after thorough study of all facts. The Personnel Office is available at any time to discuss with any employee questions or misunderstandings he may have.

Item 20 - Equal Job Opportunity

Midwest University believes that the selection, training, and advancement of employees should be based on merit. The University is committed to a policy of nondiscrimination in the treatment of employees or applicants as regards age, race, color, religion, sex, or national origin.

Mr. Tipton wondered whether his letter to Mrs. Parker would close this particular incident. But he also wondered what actions, if any, he could take to prevent similar problems. As a staff personnel director, Mr. Tipton had no direct authority over any of the management people in other divisions of Midwest University. Yet, Mr. Tipton knew that university employee policies were ignored or poorly administered by some line supervisors. Further, there was no labor union on the campus, but several rumors had been circulating recently that a representative of the Office Employees Union had been distributing literature among the library employees.

THE ENGINEERING DEPARTMENT SALARY ADMINISTRATION PLAN

CASE 53

INTRODUCTION

The Majestic Corporation is a large chemical company with many plant locations. The Rockville plant is one of the company's largest. The plant produces a wide variety of chemical products and employs over 2,000 people. It also houses Majestic's applied and developmental research laboratories and pilot plants.

The engineering department at Rockville consists of approximately 100 people in the department supervised by seven engineering supervisors reporting to the chief engineer. Engineers in the department are in special functional groups such as mechanical design, instrument and electrical design, corrosion, pollution abatement, materials handling, and computer technology. Other engineers specialize in various production processes—performing chemical engineering work to improve existing processes and using the functional groups as various projects demand. At the time of this case, about half of the engineers had less than five years experience at Rockville; the other half possessed experience up to 35 years with the company. About 70 engineers were performing professional engineering work in the department; the remaining 30 were supervisors, technicians, secretaries, and higher level specialists.

SALARY ADMINISTRATION POLICY

Majestic has a well formulated salary administration plan. Each year, corporate headquarters allocates a "raise budget" to each plant, and the plant personnel department coordinates allocation of available raise funds. Each raise budget is expressed as a percent of existing salaries and is thus a constraint on the total amount of raises granted in one year in any plant.

Company policy states that the raise granted an engineering employee depends upon the following factors:

1. *Present performance level.*[1]
   a. Excellent—Maximum of 10%
   b. Above Adequate Plus—Maximum of 8%
   c. Above Adequate—Maximum of 7%
   d. Above Adequate Minus—Maximum of 6%
   e. Adequate—Maximum of 5%
   f. Below Adequate—No raise permitted

[1] The performance ratings of "excellent," "above adequate plus," and so forth, are overall ratings given by each supervisor to subordinates annually as part of a systematic company-wide merit rating system. See Part Seven Introduction for a discussion of merit rating.

2. *Employee's present salary in relation to the guide-rate for his job level.* In the case of engineering jobs (for which progressive job titles exist, such as assistant engineer, engineer, senior engineer and so forth), there is a single curve as a guide-rate at each performance level relative to the number of years since the employee received his baccalaureate degree. The curves slope upward from zero years experience to 20 years experience and then level out. (See Figure 1 for salary curves for "engineers." Similar curves have been developed for each of the other engineering job categories within the company. These curves are periodically revised and updated to reflect current conditions.)

Figure 1

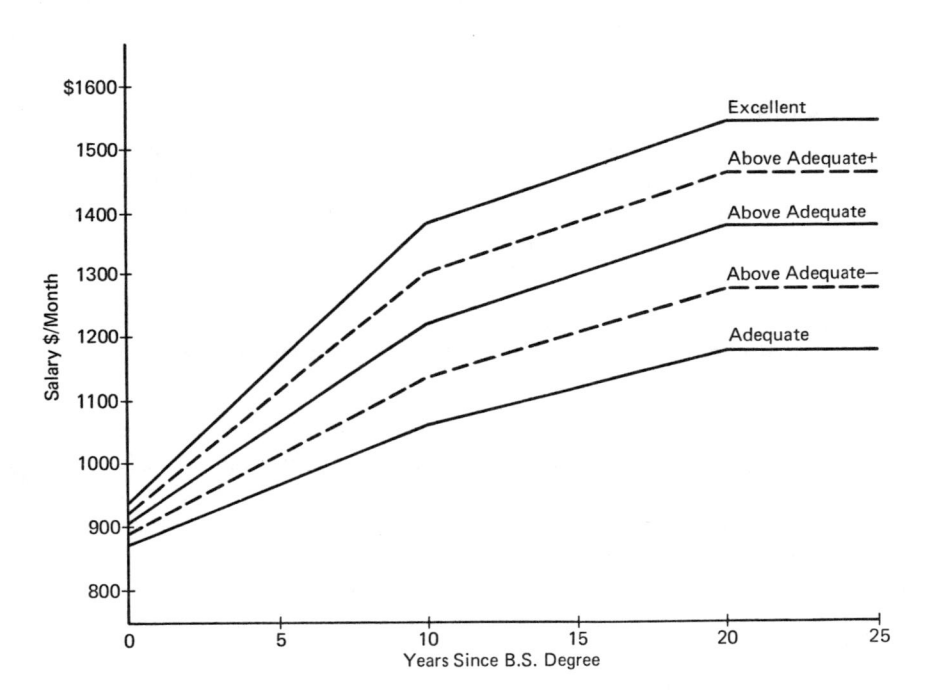

3. *Availability of raise budget.* This is expressed as a per cent of total plant salaries at the beginning of the year.
4. *Raise Frequency.* Newly hired employees can be given a raise after six months with Majestic and thereafter no more frequently than every 11 months. The policy guide-line for raise frequency is:
   a. Excellent—11 to 12 months
   b. Above Adequate Plus—12 to 13 months
   c. Above Adequate—12 to 14 months
   d. Above Adequate Minus—13 to 15 months
   e. Adequate—15 to 18 months

5. *Promotional Adjustment.* Upon promotion to a higher level job, a person can be given an additional raise of up to 15% if necessary to bring his salary in line with the higher level salary curve. This is not generally applied to the promotion from assistant engineer to engineer or to senior engineer.

All of these policy guide-lines can be altered, if a very strong case can be made by a supervisor for doing so. Seldom, however, is permission granted by higher management for deviation from the guide lines.

In addition, each year, supervisors must furnish a "potential for promotion" rating to the personnel department for each employee. The scale here is excellent, good, fair, and limited.[2] These ratings are forwarded to the salary administrator in the personnel department; but according to policy, the "potential for promotion" rating is not supposed to influence salary administration. The potential ratings are used for organizational planning and for developing training programs for employees.

MECHANICS OF SALARY ADMINISTRATION

About March of each year, each engineering supervisor in the plant prepares a salary raise plan for his employees for the following year. For example, initial planning of 1972 raises was done in March, 1971. Each individual plan is reviewed with the salary administrator in personnel who negotiates some adjustments in order to:

1. assure equity among various plant groups;
2. assure that planned increases will be within the plant raise budget;
3. assure that no one is overlooked.

The engineering supervisors also review their raise plan with the chief engineer to be sure that he concurs with their decisions. The salary administrator usually "keeps" a small reserve of raise money to cover exceptional performance improvements and new employees who are not on the plan. There is seldom any major problem using up the entire plant raise budget. A few January raises can be moved up to December or vice versa to do the fine tuning.

THE SITUATION

Tom Green, one of the engineering supervisors, had just returned from a review of his next year's salary plan with personnel and stepped into John Benson's office. Benson was a fellow engineering supervisor. Tom closed the door.

TOM: You know those personnel types are a real slippery bunch of so and so's.

JOHN: Oh, what have they done now?

TOM: I've just returned from reviewing next year's salary plan with Jim Hays (the personnel department salary administrator), and he wants to pass out the raises based on the ratings which I assigned my men for potential, rather than on the ratings I assigned them for present job performance.

[2] To be discussed in more detail later in the case.

JOHN: Did Hays really say that?

TOM: No, I just concluded that from the adjustments he recommended. He was constantly pushing raises up for the new kids we've hired out of college the past few years that we have rated excellent on potential, but only so-so on present performance. Jim says we don't have to worry about these guys getting too high on the salary curve, because they will probably be promoted to higher level jobs in a few years anyway. Of course, this doesn't leave much raise budget for our real good performers that have reached their ultimate level of advancement.

JOHN: I know what you mean. Mike Jones just transferred into my group last year, and he is about $200 below where his excellent performance and 30 years experience should put him. I don't know what we would do around here without engineers like Mike. The sad part is that Mike will be retiring in about seven or eight years, and his pension will be based on his last five year's salary. I feel I've got to get his salary in line within a year or two.

TOM: Too bad his former bosses didn't go to bat for Mike.

JOHN: I really think that the personnel office is working pretty hard to do a good job of salary administration. Generally, I think they are pretty fair. The trouble is that there is just not enough raise money to do everything we would like to do.

During the subsequent discussion, Tom Green and John Benson reached the conclusion that an employee's present performance was measured reasonably by the annual performance appraisal system, but that the potential rating was extremely subjective. Personnel never really had defined what it meant by "excellent potential" for advancement, and company policy was supposed to be that the potential ratings were not to influence salary administration anyway. The chief engineer had attempted to fill the departmental vacuum by providing the following guide-lines to his engineering supervisors.

Engineering Department Guidelines for Potential Rating
Potential Rating

	Criteria
Excellent	Expect person to advance two job levels in five years.
Good	Expect person to advance one level in five years.
Fair	Person may or may not advance one level in the next five years.
Limited	Expect person definitely will not move beyond his present level.

The Majestic Company has the dual advancement route whereby a person can move up the managerial ladder, or he may advance by the technological route from "senior engineer" to "engineering specialist," "senior engineering specialist," "technologist," and "advanced technologist." Majestic attempts to make pay and status for top technological jobs equal to top managerial jobs. The above criteria are applied to either managerial or technical advancement.

Both Green and Benson concluded that the potential rating was still too highly subjective, and they pondered what they could do in order to better implement the current salary plan and/or suggest changes in the overall salary administration policy for their department.

PART EIGHT

On Organizing a Labor Union
The Olympic Corporation (A) and (B)
The Forsythe Chemical Company
Beaver Glass Company Limited
Filmore Electric Company (B)
Petri Chemical Company (D)

Employee Representation: the Role of the Labor Union

Labor unions in the United States represent over nineteen million employees or roughly one-fifth of the total American labor force. Organizationally, more than 70,000 separate local union groups are affiliated with over 200 national and international unions, and most of these are further combined into the central federation for the labor movement, the American Federation of Labor-Congress of Industrial Organizations (A. F. L.-C. I. O.).

Despite the magnitude and the influence of the organized labor movement, labor unions remain as one of the most controversial and misunderstood segments of our society. People tend to judge labor unions on the basis of prejudices and emotions, rather than upon an objective evaluation of labor-management issues and of the roles which unions perform in industry. Some administrators in the field of personnel management consider labor unions as "evils," which are only to be tolerated and dealt with accordingly. However, modern personnel philosophy suggests that labor unions are but one major facet of the general problem of employee representation. This philosophy looks upon a labor union as a complex legal, economic, political, and social institution which must be studied and understood by management as part of a total system of dynamic behavioral processes. A manager who looks at labor unions from this perspective is more apt to be able to channel his individual relationships with labor unions towards a more satisfactory attainment of his company's objectives.

HISTORICAL PERSPECTIVE OF THE LABOR MOVEMENT

Even a brief overview concerning the historical development of the labor movement in the United States offers insights which can be of considerable significance in a manager's understanding of labor unions. In colonial times and during most of the first half of the 19th century, worker organizations were primarily limited to local craft guilds—such as shoemakers, carpenters, bakers, and tailors. Legally, the courts early held (1806) that any combination of workers to withhold labor in order to force higher wages was an "illegal conspiracy." This decision was liberalized in 1842 by the "illegal purpose" interpretation, which held that the mere withholding of labor by an organized group was not in itself illegal. However, the courts would consider the "purpose" and "means" used by labor unions in determining the legality of a union's actions.

The prevailing managerial and legal climate continued seriously to restrict the organization and effectiveness of the labor movement throughout the remainder of the nineteenth century and into the early twentieth century. Employers often resorted to tactics such as the *injunction,* a court order which could be easily obtained to force an end to union strike actions, and the *"yellow-dog" contract,* a device by which workers were forced to sign an agreement that they would not join a labor union as a condition of employment. The use of hired "armies" and federal and state troops to disburse striking workers characterized the most bitter union-management battles of this era.

The labor movement itself represented a conflicting heterogeneity of interests which also impeded its progress. The first attempt at amalgamation of the movement into a united front was the Knights of Labor organization founded in 1869. This organization was succeeded by the American Federation of Labor (1886), which chose to unite loosely only the craft unions and to avoid organization of unskilled and semi-skilled workers. A public fear of labor unions was generated by the "radical" elements of the movement, principally the Socialists and the International Workers of the World (I. W. W.). Whereas the Socialists advocated a peaceful change of the free-enterprise system, the I. W. W. (which largely was an organization of textile workers) sought a rapid—if necessary, violent—change in the system, and it was often considered to be in league with the Communists in this country. Both of these elements were at their peak in the years immediately prior to World War I.

During the 1920's, organized labor consisted primarily of the American Federation of Labor craft unions. These were years of unprecedented prosperity during which time the total membership of unions dropped from nearly four million members to approximately three and a half million members—despite the addition of millions of workers into the national labor force. Management of many companies combated the growth of unions by establishing "company unions," usually called "employee representation plans." These employer-sponsored organizations enabled workers to have a voice in matters related to their job situations, but they seldom provided for organized or collective action. Many workers had an implicit confidence in management's ability to provide for their welfare; they could see no real need to join an outside labor union. Under these conditions management saw itself as a paternalistic overseer of its employees' destinies.

But the market crash of 1929 and the ensuing deep depression years of the 1930's changed this picture completely. As millions of workers lost their jobs, a great disillusionment with management practice entered the minds of American workers. The advent of federal labor legislation favorable to union organization was accompanied by a flocking of workers into the ranks of unions. A separate amalgamation of industrial unions—the Congress of Industrial Organizations (C. I. O.)—concentrated its efforts upon organization of unskilled and semi-skilled workers in the mass production industries. By the end of the decade, union membership had swelled to almost ten millions, and this continued to increase to more than fifteen million members by the end of World War II.

The Federal labor laws which most contributed to this dramatic growth in unionism were the Norris-La Guardia Act of 1932 and the National Labor Relations (Wagner) Act of 1935. The former strictly limited the use of the court injunction in labor disputes and made unenforceable the "yellow-dog" agreements between workers and employers. The Wagner Act was the most sweeping labor legislation ever enacted. It extended Federal government protection to cover a union's right to organize workers and to bargain collectively with employers. Its premise was that workers needed union organization as protection from an inequality of bargaining power. Employees were granted "the right of self-organization, to form, join, or assist labor organizations, to bargain collectively through representatives of their own choosing, and to engage in other concerted activities, for the purpose of collective bargaining, or other mutual aid or protection."[1] Employers were forbidden to interfere with the establishment or the administration of unions, to discriminate against union members, and to refuse to bargain collectively with chosen representatives of employees. These and other activities were designated as unfair labor practices. The National Labor Relations Board was established as the principal administrator of provisions of the law.

Many employers nevertheless resisted efforts of their workers to organize. During the 1930's, unions devoted as much or more of their efforts towards gaining management recognition and acceptance as they did towards achievement of economic objectives. A number of bitter strikes, particularly in the automotive industry, centered upon the issue of union recognition. While labor unions were seeking recognition and growth, employers felt that their freedoms of speech and action were being curtailed by legislation and its administration by the National Labor Relations Board.

A rash of strike activity immediately following World War II, coupled with a growing demand from management interests that certain provisions of the Wagner Act should be changed, led to passage of the Labor-Management Relations Act (Taft-Hartley) in 1947. Technically an amendment to the Wagner Act, this act attempted to curb certain union abuses that had come into practice by listing a series of unfair labor practices for unions. Employers' rights in dealing with union

[1] Section 7, Labor-Management Relations Act as amended.

situations were more explicitly stated. Several provisions of the Act were designed to protect the individual worker who might not want to join a labor union. Other important provisions of the Act covered aspects related to internal practices of labor unions, union security agreements, and governmental procedures in event of strikes considered to be national emergencies. Although various amendments to the Taft-Hartley Act have since been added, it remains today as the principal labor legislation which governs the union-management collective bargaining process.

In 1959, the Labor Management Reporting and Disclosure Act was passed by Congress to further regulate the internal affairs of labor unions. This Act had its origin in a series of Congressional investigations which disclosed numerous corrupt practices existing in certain labor organizations.

THE LABOR MOVEMENT TODAY

With years of struggle to gain legal status and employer recognition behind them, labor leaders concentrated their post-World War II efforts upon achievement of economic objectives. In terms of wages and fringe benefits, the average American worker today is by far the highest paid worker in the world, and credit for this prosperity is partially attributed to the existence and activities of strong and powerful labor unions. Management interests claim that unions today are too powerful, and that union demands have contributed to an inflationary wage-price spiral.

But the economic success of the labor movement has been accompanied by the presence of new problems which labor leaders currently face. As union members have become increasingly satisfied economically, many have lost the fervent zeal for union activity which they displayed in days of economic strain. Wholesale changes in the composition of the labor force have taken place. White collar workers and technically trained personnel have been entering the labor force at an increasing rate, while the numbers of blue-collar workers have been declining due primarily to the impact of automation and technological change. Unionism has traditionally had little appeal to the white-collar and technical workers. For these and other reasons, total union membership in the United States has grown very little since the late 1950's; as a percentage of the total labor force, union membership actually has declined.

The labor movement also has continued to suffer from problems of internal strife. Although labor leaders succeeded in bringing about a unification of the separate A. F. L. and C. I. O. organizations into the combined A. F. L.-C. I. O. in 1955, the former craft and industrial union antagonisms still exist. Inter-union jurisdictional and representational competition is keen, since each union is sensitive to the need for retaining and adding to its membership rolls. In addition, some labor unions have been severely criticized for their inability (or unwillingness) to rid themselves of undesirable leadership elements and to eliminate practices which discriminate against minority groups in employment and union circumstances.

Some writers feel that the problems posed by our complex and inter-dependent industrial society, technology and automation, unemployment, civil rights, even the international situation—all of these are of such a magnitude as to be beyond the scope of traditional union-management collective bargaining. These writers point to the increasing role being played by government as the third or public party in many industrial disputes. Another development is the establishment of pre-bargaining, union-management committees in several industries. These committees meet on a periodic basis in order to explore problem areas and to seek possible areas of agreement. It is possible that both the role of government and of these types of joint committees will be expanded, and that the use of strikes as a labor weapon may be limited somewhat in future years.

THE MANAGER AND THE LOCAL UNION RELATIONSHIP

The typical manager deals with a labor union at a local plant or firm level, where the union-management relationship is narrowed to an intensely interpersonal as well as institutional basis. The manager must periodically meet with union officers and shop stewards to discuss employee grievances. The presence of the union represents a regulating force of which the manager must always be cognizant. Union leaders are quick to challenge management decisions which affect their memberships. At contract time, the manager meets to bargain with union representatives. The manager is acutely aware that the possibility of strike action may pose a threat to his company's operations, and that whatever contractual agreements are decided upon must be based upon careful consideration of many factors.

In this type of atmosphere, it is important for the manager to maintain a clear perspective as to why his workers are represented by a labor union. Many managers maintain that workers are mere captives of unions, forced to join and pay dues against their will because of union security agreements. These managers consider union leaders to be "strong-armed politicians," who rise to union leadership positions through power tactics and because of membership apathy. Although there may be some truth to these allegations, a manager who holds to such a view (without foundation) has limited his perspective and range of alternatives in dealing with a union. Managers who regard unions in this vein are apt to engage in power struggles, a relationship fraught with strife and misunderstandings which is not likely to be satisfactory to either management or employees.

Modern personnel philosophy suggests that labor unions fulfill a sociopsychological need of workers, which managers too often overlook. The union provides a collective mechanism by which workers hope to gain some control over their economic situation. It provides a means of communication to management by which employee grievances and complaints may be aired. In many instances workers look to their unions for collective security and economic progress, since they doubt that management will be concerned about employee welfare unless pressed for it by the union. This is particularly true of older workers, who remember the early years of labor's long struggle for recognition and collective bargaining rights. Some unionists feel that their organizations also provide a means by which workers can "strike back" at the business system which places them at routine, monotonous jobs; the union provides a restoration of collective dignity to the otherwise insignificant individual employee.

Managers lament that these attitudes exist among union members, but it is important to recognize that these beliefs stem from an industrial system in a democratic society, where some form of employee representation is probably a necessity. Managers who recognize that labor unions in part are a socio-psychological response to the industrial environment will be more willing to accept the union as representing the legitimate interests of the employees.

Modern personnel philosophy also suggests that a manager should not consider his relationship with a labor union to be an entity isolated to the environment of the local plant or firm. Rather a manager must view a union from a perspective that is cognizant of labor's past, present, and predicated future. Union demands and activities should be studied and understood as part of a continuing process both internal and external to the immediate situation of the local plant or firm. For example, a union's demands for increased job security for its members should be studied with an awareness of the technological currents affecting the labor movement throughout the country, as well as in light of the impact of such demands upon the particular company involved.

The manager must possess objective knowledge and understanding of many other related aspects, which will have an important bearing upon his relationship with the union. He must recognize the union as a political institution in which the leaders seek to hold their positions by "getting more" for the membership. He must understand the legal position of the union and his company's obligations under labor law to bargain in "good faith" with union representatives. He must be astute in labor contract interpretation and administration. Concomitant to all of these, he must learn to accept union leaders as acknowledged spokesmen for the employees, supplementing and strengthening other channels of communication within the organization. With this attitude of participation, policies may be formulated which build a working relationship with the union.[2]

The manager who understands and accepts the role of the labor union in his company has not assured himself of a satisfactory union-management relationship. A broad managerial perspective, however, is one which is conducive to a managerial approach to the union that can be mutually beneficial. Research studies in industrial relations indicate that union-management relationships based upon mutual respect, understanding, and fair dealing are more apt to lead to the constructive solution of mutual problems. The manager who keeps open the lines of communication and information-sharing to the union usually finds union leaders appreciative and more responsive to working with management—rather than against management. In essence, the presence of a labor union in a company requires that the personnel management job be adapted to fit the institutional and personal needs of the union and its membership.[3]

---

[2] See Ross Stagner and Hjalmar Rosen, *Psychology of Union-Management Relations* (Belmont, Calif.: Wadsworth Publishing Co., 1965).
[3] For a decisional approach to case analysis in union-management relationships, see Sterling Schoen and Raymond Hilgert, *Cases in Collective Bargaining and Industrial Relations. A Decisional Approach* (Homewood, Ill.: Richard D. Irwin, 1969).

ON ORGANIZING A LABOR UNION— AN INTERVIEW WITH A UNION OFFICIAL

CASE 54

As part of an industrial relations research project supervised by the School of Business of Washington University, an interview was conducted by a Washington University researcher with a high-ranking official of a major labor union located in the St. Louis, Missouri, area. This particular interview focused on questions pertaining to the union's successful approach to organizing workers in previously unorganized plants and businesses. The answers provided by the union official— an articulate spokesman who preferred not to be identified in a published summary of the interview—were candid and informative.

An edited summary of the interview is presented here partly for its informative value, and also as the basis for a discussion on the issue of union organizational efforts.

THE INTERVIEW

RESEARCHER: How does your union locate companies to organize?

UNION OFFICIAL: Usually, someone comes to us from the company and tells us that there might be a good chance to organize their plant. Almost without exception, the workers are unhappy—about their pay, their benefits, security, or they're just plain unhappy about management's way of doing things.

RESEARCHER: What kind of plants are best for you to organize?

UNION OFFICIAL: Those that are economical for us to organize. If the plant is too small, it may not be worth our time and effort. As a rule we'll try to organize any and all kinds of firms as long as it's economical, as long as it's worth the cost.

RESEARCHER: What other general factors do you take into consideration when looking for plants to organize?

UNION OFFICIAL: We have to consider the political attitude of the state toward unions, how strong labor sentiments are in the firm and community, and what kind of strategy would be best in trying to organize the plant. In the South, right-to-work laws make it more difficult for us, since they favor management's efforts to weaken the union's position.

RESEARCHER: How does a union try to organize a plant?

UNION OFFICIAL: There are several ways to do this. Sometimes we can go to an employer and persuade him to cooperate with us in organizing his plant. This type of agreement is called "Top Down" organizing. We nudge the employer

Case adapted from an article by Raymond L. Hilgert, "On Organizing a Labor Union," published in *Northwest Business Management* (Fall 1965), pp. 21-23.

by telling him that we'll get his workers anyway, so he may want to cooperate with us in return for some future favors. You shouldn't assume that an employer never wants a union. The nonunion workers might be getting a lower wage, but their productivity is so low that it's hurting the business. The employer might encourage a union which will increase the wages, but which will work with him to make the workers more productive.

The more usual approach to organizing a plant is called "Bottom Up" organizing. Instead of organizing a plant from the employer down, we organize the employees themselves. This, of course, is the major type of organizing. It is a means of taking on the boss by force, using economic and social pressures, and winning an NLRB election.

RESEARCHER: What are some of the tricks of the trade that organizers use to organize a plant?

UNION OFFICIAL: Let me give you an example of this. George Matthew,[1] one of our professional organizers from Chicago, was sent to Fort Worth, Texas, with the mission to organize a plant of about 100 workers. So, he dressed up—a business suit, white shirt, shined shoes, and a fancy hat—and visited the Fort Worth Chamber of Commerce. There he obtained information on the prevailing labor climate. Then Matty changed clothes, put on an old cowboy hat, cowboy pants, and boots, put a pencil in his shirt pocket, and went over to organize the plant. Well, he spent five or six months there. He worked with the leaders of the plant-drive to get out information on the union and on plant issues. He made and distributed leaflets at eight in the morning and four in the afternoon; he made home calls, met people at the taverns—any way he could get them to sign union cards. I might add that he was quite successful. The workers voted for the union, partly because the plant management had been pressuring the people to be against the union.

RESEARCHER: How does management pressure people to be against the union?

UNION OFFICIAL: Sometimes a stupid employer will start firing or threatening employees. All this does is to build up the anger of many more men in the plant. These antagonized workers become afraid that they'll be fired next, so they look to the union for help. Of course, we can go to the Labor Board to get the jobs back for workers who were fired for union activities. It's against the law for an employer to discriminate against union people. It often happens that management will fight the union by offering the workers higher wages. Sometimes management sends letters to the workers implying that wage increases will be given if the people will reject the union, but the letters don't explicitly state this. Legally, management can't threaten employees, but they do it in subtle ways. For example, they might say dirty things about unions in general—pass out books by writers who slander unions and union leaders. More often than not, these tactics backfire against management. It makes the people angry to have management tell them that they're not smart enough to make up their own minds about the union.

[1] Name disguised.

Our organizers play this to the hilt in working out strategies to get workers to sign union cards.

RESEARCHER: What is the basic purpose of a union which you relate to the workers?

UNION OFFICIAL: The final measurement of a union's worth is what it can do for the people. Unless we can offer the people something in return for their monthly dues, we haven't a chance. But as I said earlier, usually someone in the plant has come to us first. He tells us pay is low, management is unfair, workers are afraid for their jobs. Our organizer must convince workers that the union can help get higher pay, benefits, job security, and a voice through a grievance system. You know, I really think it doesn't make a lot of difference what the organizer does or says. If a group of workers want a union, then they'll vote for the union despite mistakes of the union organizer. After all, really our best organizers aren't on the union payroll anyway. They're the employers; management organizes the sentiments of the workers for or against a union long before the union ever comes on the scene. If it weren't for the fact that managements are careless in so many ways, our union organizers wouldn't get to first base.

RESEARCHER: Do you have summary views of the organizing problem?

UNION OFFICIAL: Organizing is done to reach a balance. This means a balancing of rights and earnings with the proper working unit. People's lives are not personal property, and an employer must realize this or run into trouble. Usually, the small businessman is the worst example of this type. He tends to be egocentric and domineering. He thinks that all he has to do is pay the people a wage and they will do what he wants. He hates even the slightest talk of a union in his plant, and he will fight with all his might to keep one out because he doesn't want his precious rights being challenged. He's only kidding himself. Unions don't just happen in a plant; they're caused. And it's management, not the unions, which cause them.

THE OLYMPIC CORPORATION (A) CASE 55

INTRODUCTION

Plant 37 of the Olympic Corporation is a large can manufacturing plant located in a midwestern metropolitan area. The plant produces cans to serve a number of large food and beverage plants located in the same area. About 700 workers in the plant are represented by Local 1213, United Industrial Workers Union, A.F.L.-C.I.O.

The history of local union-management relationships during the plant's fifteen years of operation was one that both management and the union had described as "good." Only one strike had occurred at the plant; this was about eight years ago in a national company contractual wage dispute. In general, local plant management felt that the local union's past leadership had been fairly reasonable in its demands and grievance processing.

Most of the jobs in the plant were classified as unskilled or semi-skilled. The pay scales were considered to be above average for the type of work involved, and at the time of this case, wages and fringe benefits did not constitute a major issue in union-management relationships, since wages and benefits were negotiated nationally.

Local 1213 of the United Industrial Union was led by its local president, Dan Maurice, who by occupation was a low paid janitor in the plant. A management representative described Maurice in the following terms: "He seems driven by a desire for status. His ego was considerably inflated by his election to presidency of the union. He has a rebellious nature, having rebelled against his family, previous employers, and school. He even dropped out of school before completing the 8th grade." At the same time, however, Maurice's first two-year term of office as union president was one which had been relatively satisfactory to plant management. Maurice had demonstrated a reasonable approach to plant problems, and he was considered by management to be "easy to talk to."

Although most workers in the plant usually appeared to be disinterested in union affairs, the recent election of union officers was one of the most "spirited" which management officials had observed in recent years. Mr. Maurice won re-election to the union presidency for a second two-year term only several months previously in a closely contested election. His principal opposition had come from a faction of employees in the assembly department of the plant, a faction which management considered to represent the most militant, anti-company element.

All names disguised.

Several pre-election posters on union bulletin boards had accused Maurice of having "gone soft" with management and not "fighting hard enough for our rights." Plant management felt that Maurice's recent actions reflected a desire on his part to "prove" to the membership that he had not become soft as a union leader.

For several weeks immediately prior to Friday, October 6, Mr. Maurice had displayed considerable impatience with management concerning a list of union grievances and complaints. Mr. Maurice insisted that he might have to call a strike in order for the union to "get all of our problems out on the table." The union president contended that management was stalling in its handling of eight union grievances concerning disciplinary, contractual, and personal matters. Mr. Tom Harper, plant personnel supervisor, told Maurice that management was trying to expedite the grievances as fast as possible, but that several involved policy matters which had to be discussed and resolved with officials of the company at its headquarters office.

Two September incidents involving the union president also were indicative of his apparent growing resentment towards plant management at this time. In one, Maurice became involved in a loud, bitter argument with a supervisor in the quality control department, who had refused to man the department for Saturday work in accordance with the demands of Mr. Maurice. In another incident, Maurice dared a maintenance department supervisor to suspend a union shop steward who had been accused of "loafing on the job." This dare was taken up by the supervisor, who proceeded to suspend the union steward. However, the plant manager, Mr. Robert Palmer, recognized this incident to be trouble-in-the-making, and the union steward was reinstated 30 minutes later. It was management's feeling that Mr. Maurice tried to incite a walkout over this incident, but was overruled by his membership.

THE WORK STOPPAGE

At 3:00 P.M. on Friday, October 6, Mr. Maurice told Mr. Al Whitworth, press department foreman, that the press operator on Presses 8A, 9A, 11A, and 12A was being subjected to a safety hazard. Presses 8A through 12A are in line with a metal platform (fourteen inches from floor) placed in front of them to facilitate feeding operations of metal goods parts. These presses are normally all "fed" by one individual, since one hopper load will run approximately thirty minutes and "feeding" time is approximately five minutes per machine. Press #10A had been turned around so that the platform continuity had been broken. In order for the operator to go from 8A and 9A to 11A and 12A, he had to step from the fourteen-inch platform, walk approximately ten feet, and step up on the platform again. This, Maurice said, constituted a safety hazard. Mr. Whitworth stated that he considered the situation somewhat inconvenient, but not unsafe.

Mr. Whitworth returned to his department office, and learned that his day foreman had started construction of a platform to fill the gap on the previous day, but construction had stopped because of a shortage of manpower and materials. Mr. Whitworth, therefore, told his night foreman, Mr. Sam Gore, to temporarily "double-man the presses" in question so that one man could stay on each side of the gap. Mr. Whitworth called Mr. Joe McCarthy, the union shop steward in the press department, and Mr. Bob Mueller, union steward in the assembly department, to his office. He informed them that he did not think the present situation was unsafe, but that he would temporarily "double-man" the presses anyway. Both shop stewards were present when Mr. Whitworth again repeated his manning instructions to his night foreman, Mr. Gore. At 4:50 P.M., Mr. Gore began an inventory check to determine which machine should be shut down to supply the extra man. After checking the inventory, he found that the operators he wanted to contact concerning the manning procedure were absent on their scheduled rest period in the cafeteria.

About 5:00 p.m., Mr. Whitworth noticed that press lines near his office were not operating. He asked one employee why he wasn't working, and the employee said, "The union told me not to." Mr. Gore, returned from his unsuccessful manning attempt at 5:10 p.m. and found that the press department was completely shut down. In all, about 50 workers in the department had stopped working, and all equipment was turned off.

Mr. Whitworth immediately called Mr. Tom Harper, the plant personnel supervisor, by telephone at his home. Mr. Harper advised the foreman to tell both union shop stewards that any employee not returning to work immediately would be suspended. This was done, and shortly after the stewards had returned to the plant floor, department operations resumed suddenly as though a signal had been given. The work stoppage had lasted approximately 38 minutes.

Mr. Harper arrived at the plant at 5:50 p.m., and while talking to the press department foreman and the two shop stewards, Mr. Maurice came into the plant meeting unexpectedly. Maurice had officially been off work for over two hours. Mr. Harper asked McCarthy why press department operations had stopped. Mr. McCarthy said, "On orders from higher up. We're not working under unsafe conditions!" Mr. Harper then asked Mueller if he had orders, and Mr. Maurice immediately answered "No" for Mr. Mueller. Maurice later said, "They were my orders," but he would not say what his orders had been. The meeting was adjourned and the two shop stewards went back to work.

At 6:30 p.m., the plant manager, Mr. Robert Palmer, arrived at the plant. Mr. Harper had called Mr. Palmer earlier, but Mr. Palmer had been unable to get to the plant sooner.

Mr. Harper and Mr. Palmer began an investigation of the stoppage, which included interviews with Al Whitworth and Sam Gore, but not with any of the union representatives. In studying the contractual agreement between the company and union, they re-read Article 15 of the contract which stated as follows:

> The Union agrees that there will be no strikes of any type for any cause during the life of this Agreement.
>
> The Company agrees that there will be no lockout.
>
> If, during the life of this Agreement, any employees engage in any strike of any kind, stoppages of work or slowdowns, the International Officers,

Local Officers, and paid representatives of the Union will cooperate with the Company in ending such occurrence and returning the employees to work.

Employees who engage in any of these acts may be discharged or disciplined by the Company but shall have recourse to the Grievance Procedure provided for in Article XIII of this Agreement.

"Do you know what this means, Tom?" said Mr. Palmer. "We could legally fire the whole damn department if we wanted to."

"The way things have been going lately," replied Harper, "that's what's needed to shake things up around here. Do you know that Al and Sam estimate that with all of the things going on, we lost over an hour and a half production time? And if my figures are correct, that comes out to a dollar production loss of about $15,000."

"Well, Tom," said Mr. Palmer, "what do we do? It's 9:30 p.m. and getting late. Should we go home and sleep on it, or do you think we should take action now? Maybe we just ought to forget about the whole mess and get that platform fixed up before they decide to shut us down again. We're already way behind in production orders, and we can't afford any more lost time."

Harper replied, "I don't know, boss. It looks to me like this whole thing was all set up regardless of what we would do with the platform problem in the press department. A show of strength is involved, and I think we have to do something to show that they can't pull off stunts like this whenever they want to."

THE OLYMPIC CORPORATION (B)

After considerable discussion, Mr. Palmer and Mr. Harper finally reached a decision. They decided that the three union leaders involved—Maurice, McCarthy, and Mueller—should be suspended indefinitely.

Mr. Maurice was located in the plant drinking coffee in the plant cafeteria with other union workers. Maurice was asked to come to the plant manager's office by Mr. Harper. About the same time Mr. Whitworth informed stewards McCarthy and Mueller to leave their jobs and report to the plant manager's office.

It was 10:00 p.m. when Mr. Palmer informed the three men of his decision. "Boys, you're all suspended from your jobs until further notice. We'll let you know next week where we go from here." The three union men said nothing as they left Mr. Palmer's office.

At about 10:15 p.m., Mr. Palmer was preparing to go home, when Mr. Harper excitedly entered his office.

"Well, boss, I guess we did it now. They're shutting down the whole plant!"

Both men hurried to the plant floor, where it was apparent that a full-scale walkout was in process. From all departments in the plant, workers were shutting off their machines and leaving the plant. Mr. Palmer and Mr. Harper pleaded with a number of workers not to participate in an unauthorized walkout, but their pleas were unheeded. With the exception of the foremen, the management men, and plant guards, the entire plant was emptied of workers in less than a half hour.

Production had been scheduled for Saturday, October 7. However, members of the United Industrial Union did not work, and pickets were patrolling the sidewalks surrounding the plant.

Mr. Palmer contacted Mr. F. A. Schulte, an International Union representative for the area, on Saturday morning. Mr. Schulte apparently had not heard all the details of the situation, but he could not understand why the three union men had been suspended since the press department had gone back to work after the 38-minute stoppage. Mr. Schulte wanted the suspensions lifted; then he would see what he could do about getting the men back to work.

Mr. Palmer told Mr. Schulte that he could not overlook a 38-minute work stoppage, and that the employees must return to work before he would discuss the suspensions.

The walkout remained in effect on the first shift of Monday, October 9, Mr. Palmer and Mr. Harper had arranged to meet Mr. Schulte in the latter's office to

All names disguised.

again talk over the situation. They again demanded that the employees return to work before any discussion of the suspensions could begin. At this meeting, Mr. Schulte was more cooperative and said that the employees would be ordered back to work. His order was carried out, and normal plant operations were resumed on the second shift of the same day, Monday, October 9.

A hearing was scheduled at the plant on Thursday, October 12, to allow management and union to present their views. The meeting was attended by Mr. Harper and Mr. Palmer for the company and by Mr. Maurice, Mr. McCarthy, Mr. Mueller, and Mr. Schulte for the union. In addition, each side had an observer taking notes. At this meeting, all union representatives denied having led the walkout. Maurice denied that he gave "orders" for the walkout. McCarthy denied having said that he "acted on orders from higher up." They both insisted that the only orders given were the usual ones left by Maurice when he left the plant. Those were, "Call me if something comes up that you can't handle." The union insisted that the walkout was a "spontaneous protest of the workers" against management's "unfair actions."

The union also insisted in the meeting that a safety hazard had existed. Management tried to show that operators had worked off these platforms all day with no thought of safety involved. The company would admit that the situation was inconvenient, but not unsafe.

At the conclusion of the hearing, Mr. Palmer said that the company felt that Mr. Maurice should be fired and that the two stewards should be suspended for 30 days. However, if the International and Local union "would recognize their responsibility in preventing such occurrences in the future and not file a grievance," the punishment would be reduced to a 30-day suspension for Maurice and a one-week suspension for each of the shop stewards. After some discussion, Mr. Maurice ceremoniously accepted this decision by tearing an already-typed grievance into shreds. All parties concerned signed a statement accepting the conditions and promised to carry the matter no further.

The company later mailed a written warning to each union employee who had walked out or who had not reported to work as scheduled. A copy of the warning letter was placed in each employee's permanent record file. This letter stated as follows:

TO: ALL MEMBERS OF THE UNITED INDUSTRIAL WORKERS
UNION–LOCAL 1213

I feel it necessary in view of the disruption of plant operations commencing Friday evening, October 6, 19—, to point out your responsibilities as union officers and members in participating and/or directing such demonstrations.

On Friday evening, October 6, there was an interruption of work in the Press Department which later led to all employees in the union local leaving the plant. No scheduled overtime was worked on Saturday, October 7, nor did the same employees report for work as scheduled on Monday, October 9.

Here at Plant 37, we are greatly disturbed that your local union officers would instigate and/or condone such activity in spite of the clear meaning of our contract agreement in this regard. Further, we feel each of you has a responsibility, as a union member, to respect this and all portions of the contract, and we, in turn will do the utmost to administer it in like manner.

I feel we have a fine plant here, and under the right circumstances it could continue to offer full employment to many fine individuals who take pride in their work and their Company. However, we cannot expect our stockholders and top management to continue to invest money in expansion or even maintain our operation, if it will be plagued by slowdowns, work stoppages, and the like, in the future.

Because this recent work stoppage was in direct violation of our contract agreement and because of your obvious participation in it, we intend to make it a matter of record which will be held for review in the event you are involved in any similar act or violation in the future.

Robert Palmer,
Plant Manager

Management hoped that plant efficiency would be improved after the walkout. However, during the first month after the walkout, production was 25% below plant efficiency standards for the previous month of September. Management claimed that it was a "union retaliatory slow-down," but nothing conclusive could be ascertained concerning whether a deliberate slowdown was taking place.

The two suspended union shop stewards did not suffer financially from their one-week suspensions. Union members in their respective departments contributed to a union collection which paid the shop stewards equivalent weekly wages for their week of layoff.

When Mr. Maurice, the local president, returned to work from his thirty-day suspension, management found that the suspension had affected little change in his approach to the in-plant relationship. Several managers stated that Mr. Maurice was deliberately trying to antagonize supervisors by his personal activities.

Production continued to lag in November, and grievances filed by union leaders during the month were higher in number than for any previous month during the year. Management considered most of these grievances to be trivial and "harassment tactics."

Mr. Palmer decided to meet with Mr. Harper and other members of his staff to discuss the plant situation. At a Wednesday morning meeting, Mr. Palmer opened the meeting by stating:

> The situation in this plant continues to deteriorate. Our production efficiency is about 30% below standard. The union is making life miserable for us. The people are openly defiant of our supervisors. We've got to do something—and fast—to straighten this thing out

THE FORSYTHE CHEMICAL COMPANY CASE 56

The Forsythe Chemical Company was a major producer of a general line of chemicals including plastics, organic, and inorganic products. It operated twelve major plants in the United States and plants in Europe, and South America, as well. In 1956 it had net sales in excess of $200,000,000, and its total assets were valued in excess of $300,000,000. Its current operating profit was in the neighborhood of $40,000,000 per year. Although company sales had expanded tremendously in the past ten years and profits continued to be good, Forsythe like other major producers in the chemical field, had begun to experience a profit "squeeze" in the past several years. This had been caused by rising raw-material, labor and power costs, as contrasted with competitive pressures which had forced the company to maintain price levels for most of its products and in some cases even make considerable price reductions.

Of the twelve major plant installations, the majority specialized to some degree within the company's broad product line. The Delaware plant, located in Palmyra, New Jersey on the Delaware River just north of Philadelphia had been acquired in 1938 when the Delaware Chemical Company merged with Forsythe. The old Delaware Chemical Company had produced principally Aluminum Sulfate and limited amounts of other inorganic chemicals for commercial use. In the years following the merger, Forsythe had expanded the operations of its Delaware plant, diversifying the plant's product output to a considerable extent within the general inorganic chemical group and adding some organic products as well. Today, in addition to Aluminum Sulfate this plant produces Aluminum Chloride, Anhydrous Ammonia, Battery Acid, Hydrochloric Acid, Nitric Acid, Sodium Bisulfite, Sulfur, Sulfuric Acid and a number of bleaches, plasticisers and detergents sold under various trade names.

The plant is engaged in continuous-process manufacturing operations and maintains three-shift operation in practically all of its product processes throughout the year. The company presently employs approximately 650 hourly employees and 135 salaried personnel. Within the hourly group the great majority of the workers fall within one of three general classes—(1) maintenance and construction, (2) production operations, and (3) service and transportation. All hourly rated employees are represented by one union, Local 1637 of the International Chemical Workers Union, A.F. of L.-C.I.O.

The last twenty-five years of operation has been a period of tremendous expan-

Case prepared by Professor James H. Mullen of Temple University. Reproduced by the permission of the author.

sion for the Forsythe Chemical Company. In this period, it has acquired through merger, fifteen chemical companies; in addition it has experienced an unusual degree of growth through internal development and diversification of products. Fortunately, the general management of the company recognized the necessity to decentralize administrative control early in this period of development. As a consequence, the company, in recent years, has consistently followed a policy of providing the management of each of its plants with almost complete authority and responsibility for plant operations and administrative procedure within the broad outlines of company-wide policy directives.

The major operating divisions of this company include inorganics, organics and plastics manufacture. The Delaware plant is one of several within the Inorganic Chemical Division. The manager of the Delaware plant, Mr. Joseph Anderson, reports directly to the general manager in charge of inorganic chemicals production who, in turn, reports to the president of the company. Mr. Anderson is responsible to the general manager of his division for over-all plant performance in sales as well as manufacturing efficiency. Within the division there is naturally a lively competition between the several plants.

As it has been mentioned above, Mr. Anderson has considerable freedom in the administration of all phases of the Delaware plant's activities, the development of its sales force of twelve salesmen, as well as customer relations, labor, and public relations.

Virtually all of the manufacturing divisions of the company have experienced some degree of union organization. Company policy has been to maintain bargaining with unions on a local basis wherever possible. This latter policy has committed considerable authority to Mr. Anderson in the field of union-management relations.

Although such a policy placed additional responsibilities and concomitant problems on the shoulders of each of the plant managers, the company believes that in the main it is advantageous since it provides the company with a great deal of flexibility in adjusting to local labor-market conditions and avoiding the cumulative rigidities and sometimes paralysing bargaining strength of company-wide unionism.

DELAWARE PLANT MANAGEMENT

Joe Anderson had come to the Delaware plant two years ago from another manufacturing plant within the Inorganics Division. His educational background was in chemical engineering and he had been with the company seventeen years in various staff and operating capacities. His most recent assignment had been as a plant superintendent in charge of operations within a plant located in Hoboken, New Jersey. In this capacity he had considerable experience dealing with workers, stewards, and local union officers in the informal process of daily consultation over labor-management problems. He also had the opportunity to sit in on local plant negotiations with his then superior, the plant manager.

Joe Anderson was tall, lean, and still youthful at the age of 42. He had a persuasive way of speaking and a direct manner of address which commended itself to dealing with union men. He and the other members of the plant-management group prided themselves on being part of a manufacturing operation. They were accustomed to making frequent tours of the plant to discuss operational problems with supervision and workers alike. In their offices, therefore, they ordinarily wore the heavy shoes and khaki shirt and trousers of the plant personnel. The stitched red letters, "FORSYTHE," above the flap of their shirt pockets proclaimed their membership in the manufacturing team; their white safety helmets and goggles perched on the top of their office coat racks suggested readiness to jump into the mainstream of manufacturing activities at a moment's notice.

Two other members of the plant manager's staff, Jim McDermott, service superintendent, and Bob Weldon, personnel manager, were active in assisting the plant manager in his relations with the union local. Together the three men constituted management's negotiating team and were also management representatives on the plant's joint union-management grievance committee. McDermott, in his late thirties, was a graduate in mechanical engineering from Lehigh University; and Weldon, who was slightly younger, also held an engineering degree and was currently pursuing a law degree in the evenings at Temple University in Philadelphia. Each of these men had experience in line supervisory capacities within the company prior to their present job.

OPERATIONAL PROBLEMS AT THE DELAWARE PLANT

The management of the Delaware plant was certainly aware of the operation of the cost-price "squeeze." This problem had become increasingly difficult for them since 1953. From that year until the present, the manufacturer's price for the great majority of inorganic chemicals had risen less than five per cent. The costs of raw materials, power, labor, and taxes had risen between three and six times as much, during that same period of time.

As Anderson pointed out, the manufacture of inorganic chemicals for industrial use was primarily a high volume, low unit profit business. Narrow profit margins were difficult to protect, particularly in the manufacturing of a standardized product which was chemically indentical to that of competitors. One couldn't pass the increase in costs along and expect competitors to follow suit. The problem was particularly difficult for the Delaware plant because of its high power costs. Bulk-chemical manufacture called for a lot of power, and plants situated close to sources of hydroelectric power could secure power much more economically than the Delaware plant. Taxes, too, were considerably higher for the Delaware plant, located as it was in a large metropolitan district, than they were for some of its competitors.

"Of course," Anderson admitted, "it wasn't all black." The Delaware plant was located close to a good industrial market which included all of the Delaware Valley and the mid- and northern Pennsylvania markets. Its nearest competitors were forty miles south in Wilmington, Delaware, and seventy miles north in Newark, New Jersey. This gave the Delaware plant a cost advantage in transporting its products to customers in these markets. Since inorganic chemicals were low value, high bulk products, transportation costs were a real factor. Anderson also admitted that the location of the plant on the Delaware River where it could receive bauxite and other raw materials directly from ore-carrying ships was an important advantage.

Anderson pointed out, however, that with the cost-price "squeeze," management was forced to look continuously for ways and means of reducing costs.

"Twenty-five years ago, in the chemical industry, if you were looking for a place to cut costs you would concentrate on technical processes. Today, you've got to look to labor costs as well. . . .

"I don't mean to imply that the inorganic technology is completely mature, but with the basic chemical processes we have, we feel we have made most of the mechanical improvements it's possible to make on our present installations. Then, too, we have a fairly old plant here. Process layouts certainly could be improved upon if you were designing the plant from scratch; but without ripping everything apart and starting all over again, we feel we've done most of what we feel can be accomplished technically. . . . The upshot of this is that one of the obvious places where economies can be made is the manning of plant operations."

Jim McDermott pointed out that "the areas where it is possible to economize on labor costs are pretty clearly those in the operational labor grades." He indicated that maintenance work usually increases as machinery become older and technology more complex, and that service and transportation jobs were pretty much a function of the technology and the plant layout.

"With process operators, however, it's different," he said. "In a technology which is almost all continuous process, the major function of the operators is to watch the dials and gauges and make sure that the process is going all right. When all the dials, switches, and gauges are located on one board in one room, how many operators do you need to watch them?"

In many of the plant's operations, the shift crews consisted of three or four men who spent a considerable amount of their time during the shift sitting around a table in the control room drinking coffee and "shooting the breeze."

McDermott pointed out that although there were no manning tables specified in the contract, the union zealously guarded what it considered to be its prerogative to maintain the jobs now in existence. As a consequence, management had concentrated its efforts to reduce the labor requirements mainly to situations where major technological changes were being introduced in present processes or where new processes were being introduced.

Anderson, commenting on the situation, pointed out that "If you're going to live with the union you have got to find ways and means of doing these things without cutting their heads off. After all, we feel we have a very fine relationship with our union and with our individual workers as well. We have had only one strike in the last ten years and our rate of labor turnover is less than one per cent per year. We would not want to do anything to spoil this."

In the last 10 years the plant labor force had been reduced nearly 30%. All of this had been accomplished without "turning a man out on the street."

"You plan your changes and new installations so that you can move the displaced men into other jobs in the plant which become vacant when people die or retire or quit. Of course the boys don't like it any way you do it. When they're transferred to other jobs they lose their departmental seniority and also have to adjust to new people and a new job situation."

THE UNION OFFICERS

Mike Fallon, the president of the local, didn't like it. He had worked at the Delaware plant nearly thirty years and he had seen a lot of changes take place since Forsythe took over. In his book it was the function of the union to protect its membership by protecting their jobs. "When you lose control of the job, you lose control of seniority and then you might as well kiss job security goodbye."

Paul DiMarco, the vice-president of the local, was twenty years Mike's junior. After the war he had started at the Delaware plant as a utility man. Because he was smart and ambitious he had learned quickly. He was now the head operator in the sulfuric-acid installation. Paul agreed with Mike that the union had to control jobs, but he saw it more as a problem of getting the best possible deal without pushing the company to the place where it would "pick up the axe and start chopping away." Besides, he had to admit to himself that there were a lot of guys in the plant who "earned their eight" sitting around the coffee pot.

As a matter of fact, Paul disagreed with Mike about a lot of the ways he had of running the local, and he had discussed this with his friends and occasionally had been outspoken about it at the local meetings as well. He and Mike hadn't exactly run on the same ticket. He had beaten out Mike's man, Jake Bovarnick, two years ago in the election and he knew Mike had tried hard to get Jake back in the number two spot again last election. To make matters worse, a process change in Jake's department had eliminated his job and since he was no longer a union officer with seniority preference in his department, the best he had been able to do bidding around the plant was to land an assistant operator's rate in the newly established sodium bisulfite process.

THE SODIUM BISULFITE PROCESS

In the fall of the previous year, the Forsythe Chemical Company perfected a new process for manufacturing sodium bisulfite in its pilot plant.

Sodium bisulfite in various forms is used as a bleaching agent, an anti-color and a silage preservative. It has a wide market including agriculture, dairying, paper making and the graphic arts industries. As a bleaching agent it is used extensively in the laundry and cleaning industry, leather tanning and by the chemical processing industry which utilizes it in the manufacture of a variety of domestic cleaning and bleaching agents.

After successful production of sodium bisulfite in the pilot plant, company research and technical people experimented for several months on ways in which it might be introduced into full scale production. Full scale production was finally instituted in January of this year at the Delaware plant.

As plant management had fully expected, there were many "bugs" in the operation of the process which had to be eliminated in order to get the sodium bisulfite on an economic production basis. As a consequence, a research engineer, a foreman, and a technician were added to the four hourly operators who manned the installation on each of the three shifts.

Several years previously, management had reached an informal agreement with the union concerning such situations. Management would not determine the final manning of a new process until, in its opinion, the technical problems of efficient production had been ironed out. By the end of May, management felt that all the major problems connected with the production of sodium bisulfite had been solved and it was therefore ready to make permanent worker assignments to the production operation. Again in accordance with an informal understanding between the management and the union, the company approached the local's officers with its proposal in order to get the union's reaction before making its final assignment.

THE NATURE OF THE GRIEVANCE

The production process involved two basic sequences. Soda, sulfur and other raw materials were introduced at the beginning of the process where they were mixed under heat and pressure to produce a wet crystal slurry. The second part of the process involved the production of dry bisulfite crystalline powder. This was accomplished by feeding the slurry into a centrifuge and then to dryers where all remaining moisture was eliminated. After this, the crystalline powder was put through a bulk screening process and then stored in a bulk bin. During the day shift the powder was fed from the gravity storage bin to a bagging operation. Bagged sodium bisulfite was then palleted and stored pending final shipment to customers. All of the dials, gauges and valves necessary for controlling the process are located on the control board in a relatively small control room. The position of the operators and chief operator is normally in this room.

Anderson, McDermott and Weldon had discussed the manning question many times with the research engineers and foremen on the job. During the last several weeks the process had been operated by three men—a chief operator, an operator and an assistant operator. Everyone in the management group agreed that it could be run successfully with two men—an operator and an assistant, who in addition to his operational responsibility could assist moving up pallets and performing other miscellaneous jobs. On the day shift, a filler-shipper could be employed to carry out the bagging operation.

The men in the management group realized, however, that the union would protest violently such an arrangement since four- and five-man teams predominated on other manufacturing processes of a similar nature throughout the plant. Anderson decided, therefore, that the company would establish a three-man operating team plus a bagger-shipper on the day shift. A chief operator would be in charge of the entire operation; a first operator would be responsible for the longer and more complicated second phase of the production cycle; an assistant operator would be placed in charge of the shorter, simpler, crude-slurry phase of the operation.

Joe Anderson called Mike Fallon and asked him and the other members of the local's executive committee to drop into his office that afternoon to discuss the question. Mike accepted with alacrity and Anderson guessed that he was going to have a battle on his hands.

THE MEETING

At two o'clock Fallon, DiMarco, and two other members of the union executive committee walked in the door of Anderson's office accompanied by Warren Jennings, the union steward for the "B" building where the sodium bisulfite process had been installed. Anderson asked them to sit down but no one accepted the invitation. Fallon spoke right to the point:

"Joe, have you reconsidered your decision about manning the sodium bisulfite operation? We think there should be a chief operator, two operators—one for the A and one for the B phase of the cycle, a raw materials handler and a filler-shipper.

"It's a highly complicated process—more so than most of the others in this plant that are using a five- or six-man operating team."

Anderson pointed out that the process had already been running successfully in full-scale operation for over two months with only a three-man team. Fallon countered with the fact that up until the time he mentioned, the process had been backed-up by an engineer, a foreman and a technician and that it was cutting back dangerously on the safety factor to have a man with operational responsibility also doing materials handling work. Fallon pointed out that "the operators on this kind of a job may look like they have nothing to do, but it is easy for management to overlook the fact that if anything goes wrong, an experienced man has to be ready to take quick action and eliminate the cause of the trouble before anything serious or expensive happens."

The exchange continued a few more minutes: Fallon did all the talking—none of the others spoke up. Fallon also raised the issue of the rates. The company had established the following schedule of rates when it went into full-scale production:

	Per Hour
Chief Operator	2.49
Operator	2.26
Assistant Operator	2.16
Filler-Shipper	2.10

Fallon argued that since this was one of the newest and most complicated opperations in the plant, the chief operator should be paid at least ten percent above the prevailing rate for that level job in other similar installations. He suggested $2.72 per hour. He also argued that the responsibilities and the degree of knowledge and experience required for both phase A and B of the operation were the same and that, therefore, both men should be paid the same rate, i.e., $2.51 per hour.

Anderson let them talk themselves out and finally said, "Our decision, Mike, has been made. We're manning the job with three men at the rates which we notified you were in effect."

Mike looked around at his own group quickly and turned back to Joe Anderson.

"All right, Joe, if that's the way you want to handle it, we're filing a formal grievance under Article V, Section Five of the Agreement."[1]

THE MEETING OF THE GRIEVANCE COMMITTEE

The following Monday at two o'clock, Fallon, DiMarco and the other two members of the union grievance committee filed into the conference room down the hall from Anderson's office. Anderson, McDermott, and Weldon were already sitting in their places. They had discussed the strategy beforehand. Weldon had checked the records on all the previous arbitration hearings. They had never arbitrated a wage rate issue before. They had always been able to settle such questions at the third step. Neither had they ever had to test their right to determine the size of a crew under the Management Clause.[2] They decided to listen to the union's presentation and then offer five cents more an hour if they had to in order to settle the matter short of arbitration but to hold the line on the question of manning the job with a three-man team plus a day-shift operator. They were also in agreement that the principle of the differential between the operator and assistant operator should be maintained.

The union made essentially the same points that had been made before at the preliminary meeting. Again Fallon did virtually all the talking.

After a suitable display of hesitation and reluctance, Anderson leaned over the table in a business-like gesture. "All right, Mike, we're prepared to be reasonable as always. We don't like to take these cases to arbitration any more than you do and we don't see any reason why this one should have to go. We're willing to raise the chief operator to $2.54 an hour—that would make him the highest paid operator in the plant—and scale up the others proportionately."

Mike asked quickly, "What about the raw materials handler and equalizing the first and second operator's rates?"

Joe responded without hesitation, "We won't go up to a four-man crew or eliminate that differential. We think there are important principles involved here."

Mike Fallon was about to answer when Paul DiMarco leaned over and whispered something in his ear. Mike called for a ten-minute recess.

When the recess was over, Fallon and the others came back into the room and sat down. Fallon spoke up. "We feel that job should be paid a lot more than you're offering us but we're willing to settle for $2.54 providing you add a materials handler to the crew and equalize the rate on the other two jobs. This is our final proposal. If you can't accommodate us on that we mean to take it to arbitration under Article V."

Joe Anderson shook his head and replied, "Mike, we won't run this process with an extra man we don't need and we've got to maintain differentials where there are real differences in the job."

"O.K., Joe. If that's your answer, you'll receive our written notice of intention to arbitrate tomorrow morning."

[1] See Exhibit A.
[2] See Exhibit A., Article XIV

Anderson thought a moment. "Look here Mike, it is not to either of our advantages to go off half-cocked on this thing. Remember arbitration is expensive and you never know what you're going to get even when you think you have a good case—and we don't think you've thought too much of that part of it either. Why don't you take a week to sift over our offer? We can recess this hearing until next Monday instead of closing the matter here and now. Then you'll still have fifteen days after that under the terms of the Agreement to file for arbitration if you still want to."

The union committee discussed the offer briefly and decided they had nothing to lose by postponing the issue seven more days.

When Fallon, DiMarco and the others had left the room, Anderson turned to McDermott and Weldon.

"We can't just wait around for Fallon and his boys to give us their answer and then think what we should do. We've got to decide on possible alternative courses depending how they decide to play it."

Exhibit A

Excerpts from Forsythe Chemical—United Chemical Workers' Agreement

Article V, (Wage Rates), Section Five

A. Changes in wage rates or classifications may be made during the life of this Agreement only in connection with new operations or changes in existing operations. Such changes shall be discussed with the Union, but if no agreement can be reached, the Company may at its option put such changes into effect and the matter may then be referred for settlement to the third step of the Grievance Procedure as provided in Article XVII of this Agreement.[1]

B. Such changes in rates or new rates shall be based on the requirements of the new job and shall be determined with reference to the requirements and rates of pay of other existing classified jobs as set forth in Schedule A of this agreement.[2]

Article XIV (Management), Section One

The right to employ, assign, promote, discipline, layoff and discharge employees is reserved by and shall be vested in the Company.

Section Two

The products to be manufactured, the location of the plants, the methods and schedules of production, processes and means of manufacture, and the management of the property shall be the function of Management solely and exclusively.

---

[1] Article XVII, Section C provided for the third step in the grievance procedure which consisted of a meeting between management and the union grievance committee. The final decision of the company on each grievance at the third step was to be submitted to the union in writing. The union might submit any matter at this juncture to arbitration. In that event an arbitrator, who is acceptable to both parties, is selected from a list provided by the Federal Mediation and Conciliation Service.

[2] Schedule A consisted of a complete listing of hourly rates classified by department. Chief operator rates in other departments ranged from $2.26 to $2.49 and other rates were paid proportionately.

BEAVER GLASS COMPANY LIMITED   CASE 57

The Beaver Glass Company was a major Canadian firm engaged in the production and marketing of a large range of glass products throughout Canada. At the time of this case, the company had assets of $30 million, sales of $23 million and a net profit of $2.6 million. Head offices were in Toronto, with plants throughout Canada, including a glass container manufacturing plant at Elberton, Saskatchewan.

Depending on the season, the Elberton plant employed from 500 to 600 employees (Exhibit A). Approximately 70% of the employees below the foreman level belonged to the local union which was affiliated with the Glass and Ceramic Workers of America.

Exhibit A
Beaver Glass Company Limited
Elberton Plant

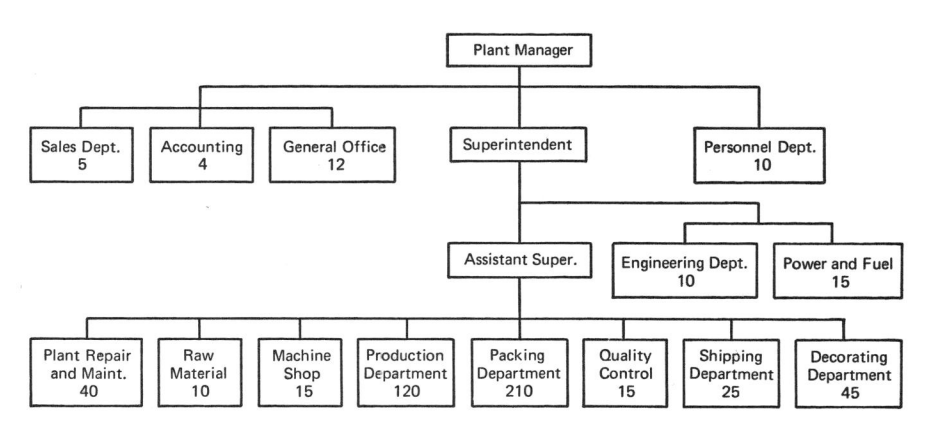

```
                              Plant Manager
                                   │
    ┌──────────┬──────────┬────────┼──────────────┐
Sales Dept.  Accounting  General  Superintendent  Personnel Dept.
    5            4       Office         │              10
                          12            │
                                        ├──────────────┬──────────────┐
                                   Assistant Super. Engineering  Power and Fuel
                                        │            Dept. 10        15
  ┌────────┬────────┬────────┬──────────┼────────┬──────────┬──────────┐
Plant    Raw      Machine  Production  Packing  Quality   Shipping  Decorating
Repair   Material  Shop    Department  Dept.    Control   Dept.     Dept.
& Maint.   10       15        120       210       15        25        45
  40
```

*Breakdown of departments and the approximate number employed in each department.

This industry was such that the plant worked 24 hours per day, seven days per week. Employees worked an eight-hour shift for six days, then had two days off. Each department contained four groups, referred to as "shifts," and each group would alternate from day shift to afternoon to night. The shift hours were as

Reproduced by permission from William S. Preshing, *Cases for Managerial Decision* (Toronto: W. J. Gage, Limited, 1964). All names, places, and dates disguised.

follows: day shift 8:00 a.m. to 4:00 p.m., afternoon shift 4:00 p.m to 12:00 midnight, night shift 12:00 midnight to 8:00 a.m. The switch was made after each group had their two days off.

The "machine end" may be referred to as the heart of the plant (Exhibit B). This was the department where the actual manufacturing was done. In this department there were ten large machines which produced different types of bottles, glasses, jars, etc. These were operated by experienced senior men who were among the highest paid men in the plant.

Exhibit B
Beaver Glass Company Limited
Machine End Organization

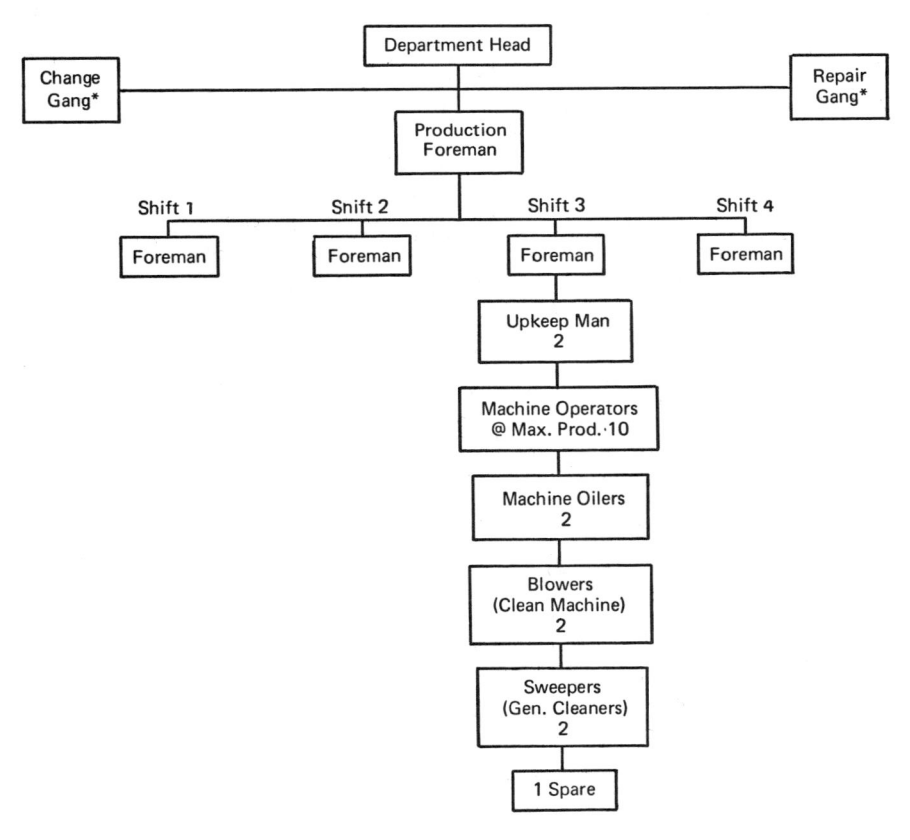

```
                        ┌─────────────────┐
                        │ Department Head │
┌────────────┐          └─────────────────┘          ┌────────────┐
│  Change    │──────────────────┼──────────────────│   Repair   │
│  Gang*     │                  │                  │   Gang*    │
└────────────┘          ┌─────────────────┐          └────────────┘
                        │   Production    │
                        │    Foreman      │
                        └─────────────────┘
        Shift 1        Shift 2        Shift 3        Shift 4
     ┌─────────┐   ┌─────────┐   ┌─────────┐   ┌─────────┐
     │ Foreman │   │ Foreman │   │ Foreman │   │ Foreman │
     └─────────┘   └─────────┘   └─────────┘   └─────────┘
                                      │
                              ┌───────────────┐
                              │ Upkeep Man    │
                              │      2        │
                              └───────────────┘
                              ┌───────────────┐
                              │Machine Operators│
                              │ @ Max. Prod. 10│
                              └───────────────┘
                              ┌───────────────┐
                              │ Machine Oilers│
                              │      2        │
                              └───────────────┘
                              ┌───────────────┐
                              │   Blowers     │
                              │(Clean Machine)│
                              │      2        │
                              └───────────────┘
                              ┌───────────────┐
                              │   Sweepers    │
                              │(Gen. Cleaners)│
                              │      2        │
                              └───────────────┘
                              ┌───────────────┐
                              │   1 Spare     │
                              └───────────────┘
```

*The change gang comprised approximately 8 to 10 men. These men worked straight day shifts and were paid less than operators. Their work was to change and reset machines when the type of job was changed, (e.g., from beer to whiskey bottles).

**The repair gang comprised of approximately 12 men. These men were more highly paid than operators and were usually well trained in repairing and installing the machines. They installed new quipment and handled emergencies in the production end.

The union contract stipulated, in part, that employees should have five statutory holidays per year and that the company would, when possible, close down operations on these days. It also stated that any persons required to work on such days would be paid double time and a half.

During a plant shut-down, the machines were "bedded down" while necessary repairs or replacements were made, by the change and repair gangs. After a shut-down, it normally took three or four hours to get the machinery operating at normal production standards. The change and repair gangs also came early on the morning of start-up to get the machines into proper operating order and to handle problems that usually arose on the start-up.

It was also common practice for the operators, who would normally be working, to come to work to do the actual "bedding down" of the machines. These men were also paid double time and a half for the time worked on these holidays.

Victoria Day, a statutory holiday, was to be observed on Monday, May 20th. The Elberton plant was to close down at 8:00 a.m. on the Monday morning and would resume operations at 8:00 a.m. on the Tuesday morning.

On the afternoon of Saturday, May 18th, the machine end department head, Mr. O'Reilly, received a note stating that the eleven operators whose names were listed did not want to work on Monday, May 20th. The note was countersigned by one of the eleven, Tom Gubrowsky.

O'Reilly consulted Mr. Prentice, Plant Manager, and informed him of the situation. Mr. Prentice contacted Mr. Vann, personnel manager, on Sunday morning and instructed him to investigate the situation.

Mr. Vann contacted O'Reilly to receive further details on the situation. O'Reilly told him that he had personally contacted the eleven operators after receiving the note, and that nine of the eleven definitely stated that they would not work on Monday. O'Reilly said that he had then told the seven senior operators that they were to report to work on Monday to "bed-down" the machines.

When the shift went off work at 4:00 p.m. that Sunday, Mr. Vann interviewed Tom Gubrowsky and two other senior operators. In discussing the situation Vann explained that help was required to do the necessary "bedding down" and maintenance work during the shutdown and there was no question of volunteer help.

The men stated that they had asked their shop steward, Will Benson, if the men could be compelled to work on a holiday, and that Mr. Benson had replied that as far as he was concerned such was not the case. Mr. Vann concluded the meeting by stating that the seven senior operators were to report for work at 8:00 a.m. on Monday, May 20th and that their work could be expected to last until approximately 12:00 noon. He warned that if they didn't, suspension would result.

On the morning of the holiday, Mr. Vann checked the employees' punch cards and found that none of the seven operators had reported for work. He contacted Mr. Prentice and it was decided to prepare a notice of suspension for all seven men. The operators were suspended for a period of ten days, effective immediately, on the grounds that they were absent without authorization. While the suspension would undoubtably cause production problems, it was felt it was a necessary disciplinary action.

Mr. Vann presented the notices to the men when they reported for work the following morning at 8:00 a.m.

The day shift and afternoon shift worked in their normal fashion, but shortly before midnight, the operators on the midnight shift telephoned the plant and informed the foreman that they would not be coming to work. All supervisory personnel were immediately contacted and the plant was hastily shut down.

Mr. Vann contacted union authorities, but they stated they were in no way, nor was the union in any way, involved. He could not find anyone directly responsible.

At 8:00 a.m. Thursday morning all employees on the day shift punched in and proceeded to their departments. The operators in the machine end refused to start work and to operate their machines. Mr. O'Reilly contacted Mr. Vann and informed him of the situation. Mr. Vann went to the machine end and gathered all the operators in the lunch room. He asked them the reason for their refusal to work. A spokesman then stated "No operators are going to work until the men suspended have been fully reinstated and paid for their time lost."

THE FILMORE ELECTRIC COMPANY (B)— THE ASSEMBLY DEPARTMENT

CASE 58

The assembly department of Filmore Electric Company is divided into three major sections. The largest is Section A, known as the "line," where approximately 75 employees assemble standard sizes of fractional horse-power motors. Several units within Section A produce subassemblies, and others complete the final assemblies of various standard motors produced for stock. The other two sections each employs about 25 workers.[1] Section B produces small motors from 1/500th to 1/3000th horse-power in size, and Section C handles all special and custom made motors. Because of the delicate nature of the work and the great number of manual operations in small motor assembly, only the "line" has been able to adopt modified production line techniques.

John Bosch, an industrial engineer assigned to the department, had completed job descriptions and job evaluations for all of the regular positions in the department. The jobs were evaluated and base wage rates were established in accordance with the company's point rating system of job evaluation. It required about one day per week for John to maintain and operate the job evaluation program because of changes in operations and innovations in products and procedures. With the assistance of two time study men who usually worked in other departments, John also had standardized a large number of operations in the assembly work and had instituted a wage incentive program. Using a 100% time premium incentive plan, individual standards and incentive rates were established for approximately 60% of the jobs in the "Line" section and 20 to 30% of the operations in Sections B and C.

Only a few employees in the department were able to work full time on wage incentive jobs. Most of the assemblers could work on incentive jobs for a part of each day, but a number of employees spent full time on tasks which had not been standardized and for which no incentive rates had been established. Most of these day-work jobs, without opportunities for earning incentive pay, were in Sections B and C where the work was highly specialized and did not lend itself to standardization. The wage incentive plan had been in operation for only a few months, but already John Bosch and the departmental foreman, Henry Freitel, had received many complaints from employees who felt that it was unfair for them to be on jobs which did not permit bonus earnings. In general, base rates for assemblers in Sections B and C were 10 to 20% above those of assemblers on the "line." Even with these differentials most Section A assemblers with lower base rates and in-

---

[1] About two-thirds of the employees were women, and this ratio was approximately the same in each section.

centive jobs received larger "take-home pay" than those with higher base rates and no opportunities to earn bonuses.

John Bosch believed it was not feasible to significantly increase the percentage of operations in the department which were standardized and on the wage-incentive program. The frequent changes in styles, sizes, and speeds of the smaller motors assembled in Section B and the custom-order nature of operations in Section C made it practically impossible to put many of the jobs in these sections on standards.

In an attempt to reduce some of the employee complaints, John began to work towards establishing standard operations for certain subassembly work in Sections B and C, with standard times varying with the sizes of materials. John's objective was to make it possible for more of the assemblers to spend at least a part of their time on incentive operations. One of John's first attempts in this direction was to improve and standardize a soldering operation in Section B. A job which the girl assemblers referred to as "pig-tailing" involved the soldering of a small spiral wire to a very small motor brush. After reviewing the method used by the assemblers, (the operation seldom had runs of more than two or three hours in length), John developed a fixture for the soldering iron so that it would be mounted vertically and directly in front of the operator. He developed another fixture consisting of two small storage bins which delivered the spiral wires and the brushes or metal parts to which the wires were soldered. Another improvement in this operation was the development of a drop delivery chute for the completed "pig-tailing" assembly. This permitted the operator to slide the finished part off the table into a chute delivery with a minimum of effort.

After training Mary Horton in the new method for this soldering job, John timed the operation very carefully and established a standard and an incentive rate. About a month later, John learned that only two or three girls had performed the new operation, and then for only about eight to ten hours per week. In discussing his problems with the chief engineer, John pointed out that the standards on the "pig-tailing" job permitted a few girls to earn a bonus of several dollars, but from the company's point of view it was a marginal incentive job. John's comment was, "It is doubtful if the cost savings will ever pay for the time and trouble we've spent in studying the job" ...

As John Bosch was walking through Department B one morning, he stopped at Mary Horton's bench and asked, "How's the pig-tailing job this morning, Mary?"

"Hi, John. I've only been at it for two hours and I don't have much left to do. We all like this new stand you fixed up for the soldering iron, but we're not sure that these wooden fixtures are so good. Maybe we'll get used to them," replied Mary.

"See how it works, Mary, and let me know if you have any trouble;—and let me give you a tip. When you put that soldering paste on with that little paddle, you could save some time if you just used your little finger. Just dab the paste on with your finger and never bother with the paddle."

"What? You want me to put my finger in that old pot of grease? That's terrible—this job is dirty enough without making us handle that stuff," she complained.

"It's up to you, Mary. We wouldn't reduce the time standard and expect you to put the paste on with your finger—but I'm just suggesting you could go a little faster, make a little more bonus if you use your finger."

"Not me, John. I could get dermatitis from that stuff. Besides, what's the big hurry anyway? It isn't worth it for what we get for it."

"I see you have that new girl, Georgia, on pig-tailing now," said John.

"Yes, we call her Peaches and she likes this job. She used to be a beauty operator and she says these "pig-tails" remind her of pinning up curls. She's a lot of fun and she's really fast. Henry says she's made standard faster than anyone he's seen in a long time."

"I thought Henry said some of the girls around here didn't like Georgia."

"Oh, he's probably talking about those bobby-soxers over there on the 'line'. We call those kids at the bench by the wall bobby-soxers; they never wear hose to work and the things they do are terrible! They're not so young, either—in fact, one's a grandmother. They don't really like any of us here in Section B because we dress well and we put on aprons at work. Those kids wear slacks and terrible clothes and never use aprons. It's too bad, but right now they're picking on Peaches."

"What have they got against her?" asked John.

"Oh, Jean over there thinks she can get Peaches into the union—they really go after her."

"Doesn't anyone at this bench belong to the union?" asked John.

"No, only Marge—and she only joined because her husband is shop steward at some plant and practically made her. She's really against the union just like the rest of us back here," Mary explained.

"It's none of my business—but I don't see how they can bother a gal like Georgia."

"Oh, they try all right. The other day Jean and two other organizers had Peaches in the cafeteria trying to get her to sign a union card. They work on all the new girls that way—promising them everything and filling them with everything imaginable. They're really giving us the works these days about the money we should be making over here. But Peaches swears that she won't join a union and she'll quit her job first. Apparently she had some trouble with another union when she had her own beauty parlor."

"Well, I can thank the Lord for one thing," said John, "this union business is none of my worry—I've got enough to do with time standards around here," and with that remark he left Mary and walked down the aisle...

Later in the afternoon John Bosch was talking with Henry Freitel, the departmental foreman. "Mary Horton tells me you have a hot organizing campaign going on for the union now, Hank."

"Yeah—it's getting to be a hell of a situation," said Henry. "Every time some new gal goes to the washroom, Jean and a couple of others take out after her and no telling what goes on behind those closed doors. Sometimes the gals complain about the trouble they have—and I know a lot of them sign the union cards just to get Jean off their backs."

"But Mary tells me that the new girl Georgia, in Section B and some of the others don't really want to join up. How many members do you figure the union has now?"

"I'm not sure," replied Henry, "but I think they've got almost three-fourths of the people on the Line and I just don't know how many in Sections B and C. You know, John, I think they're using this incentive plan of yours as an excuse for raising hell. The people on the line are complaining that we're not paying enough bonus money, and that more jobs should be put on incentive. They're riding the gals in B and C about the fact that assemblers on the line make more money, and then they're saying that a union would see to it that this whole thing would be straightened out.

"I really think that much of the trouble is just a plain difference in people. Those jobs on the line are dirty and monotonous. But those gals back there in B and C are lady-like. They don't want to get their hands too dirty, and they don't want to join a union. Actually, they add a little class to our department. They're always neat and clean—they wear aprons and sometimes put on gloves for dirty jobs. I'd hate to see them forced into the union if they don't want to join. On the other hand, it may not be long before the union could win an election."

"Well how much time can this Jean spend running around the department trying to get people to join the union?" asked John.

"I don't really know," said Henry, "but I talked to her and the kids at her bench the other day—and they just don't like Mary and the gals over in B and C. I told them flatly that they weren't supposed to sign up people for the union on company time. They know I'm watching them all the time—but apparently they don't care. If I tried to fire someone for trying to organize a union I'd probably get into trouble. Besides, most of the organizing seems to be done in the washroom. God knows I can't stop her from doing whatever she wants to in there!"

"Does Jean get paid for all this work she does for the union?" asked John.

"I think they've told her that if the union is recognized, she can be the shop steward—I suppose she would get her own dues paid for collecting from the others. Jean has a lot of enthusiasm and that whole gang at the benches along the wall are all hepped up about the union. Sometimes I think it would be better if we just accepted the union and got rid of all this wrangling and organizing business. The Electrical Union is really not so bad. They boys in the machine shop have their union, and I don't see that they have as much trouble with it as we do without it."

"I'll tell you one thing, Hank," said John, "if the union gets in this department, the old man and the boys in the front office aren't going to like it. It's pretty well known that the boss thinks we can operate better and cheaper without a union."

"Who knows?" replied Henry, "As it is now I have girls fussing at each other, bickering and scrapping among themselves—all because of this. Maybe a union could settle this place down. You know, I met the union agent the other day outside the plant handing out literature. I talked with him and he's really not a bad fellow—but, of course, he tries to make these gals think that they're going to get their pay doubled by joining the union. And then some of the stuff his handouts say about the management is just damn foolishness. He says we're trying to run a sweat shop, bleeding every last ounce of energy out of people without paying them in return. Frankly, it's a hell of a situation,—I don't know why anyone wants to be a foreman in a place like this and I've been here for 25 years."

"Hank, I've got to get back to my own work—all I can do is say that I sympathize with you "

PETRI CHEMICAL COMPANY (D)— THE CASE OF HOWARD EVANS

CASE 59

On a Tuesday afternoon during the spring busy season, Roger Lester, general production foreman of Petri's main plant, received his production quotas for the subsequent two weeks. Since the production of silver nitrate in Building 11 was being increased substantially, Lester had requested five additional men who held the job classification title of "chemical operator." Lester sought assistance from the personnel department to select men for these jobs who had previous experience in producing silver nitrate. Among the men assigned to Lester for the silver nitrate production was Howard Evans, 26 years old, a chemical operator with six years experience at Petri.

On Thursday, Evans received a copy of the posted working schedule for the next week. The schedule indicated that he was to report to Building 11 the following Monday morning to work on the silver nitrate process. About 3:30 that afternoon, Evans walked into Roger Lester's office:

EVANS: Why didn't you pick on someone else to work on silver nitrate? I want to remain on my present job. I was transferred to Building 24 only a few weeks ago. I've just gotten to the point where I understand my new job. Now you are taking me away and putting me back on this job.

LESTER: In other words, Howard, you feel that I am imposing on you by requesting your transfer?

EVANS: I am beginning to believe that you bosses are damn inconsiderate around here. Do you realize that I have been moved six times in the past five months? I haven't been able to learn any of these jobs well. Just as I get to the point where I'm beginning to be able to do the work, one of you guys hauls me off to a different department.

Does everyone get moved around as much as I, or is there something wrong with me? Am I doing such a poor job that all of my bosses are trying to get rid of me?

LESTER: Remember, Howard, I did request that you be assigned to my department. And you do have the job title of chemical operator, which means that we can use you as the demands of our business dictate, so long as you work in jobs that are basically similar in nature. We've always done it this way. You've had prior experience in the silver nitrate production process, and I felt we needed men like you to get over the spot we're in now.

358 *Employee Representation*

EVANS: Can't you fellows plan your work? This is a poor way to run a department. No one shows any consideration for chemical operators. We get moved around like men on a checkerboard. And don't tell me that it's done fairly. No one ever asks us what we want to do.

LESTER: I am sorry to learn that you feel this way about my department. I always thought that we clicked it off in a good manner.

EVANS: Tell me, how long will I be here? Can I count on staying in this department from now on? Or am I going back to Building 24 next week?

LESTER: I can't promise that you will stay here. All I know is that we need production in silver nitrate for at least the next two weeks. I don't know what will happen after that.

EVANS: I think I am getting a raw deal here. I'm going to see my union steward to file a grievance.

Howard Evans had worked in Building 24 for five weeks before being transferred back to Building 11, his former department. He had an excellent work record; in fact, most of his supervisors had given him a top rating on his semi-annual employee evaluations. In recent months, however, several foremen had commented that his previous enthusiasm and spirit on the job had diminished somewhat.

Two days following his conversation with Evans, Roger Lester received a written grievance from the union steward which protested the "indiscriminate transferring of chemical operators from job to job in violation of the contract." In studying Evans' grievance, Lester reviewed the union contract sections governing job transfers in the plant. The most pertinent clauses read as follows:

Section 1—Management Rights

(a) Cooperation between parties and the observance of the contract is the basis of all enduring agreements. The parties to this agreement recognize that stability in wages, working conditions, production, and competency and efficiency of workmen are essential to the best interests of both employees and management and agree to strive to eliminate all factors which tend toward unstabilizing such conditions. It is understood that the administration and operation of the plant including but not limited to the assignment, transfer and disciplining of workmen, and the establishment of production control procedures is the responsibility of management...

Section 21—Transfers

The transferring of employees is the sole responsibility of Management subject to the following...

(b) It is the policy of Management to cooperate in every practical way with employees who desire transfers to new positions or vacancies in their department. Accordingly, such employees who make application to their foreman or the Personnel Department stating their desires, qualifications and experience, will be given preference for openings in their department provided they are capable of doing the job...

Lester pondered what his reply to the grievance should be, and what course of action he should take

PART NINE

The Monsanto Company
Ralston Purina Company
American Cast Iron Pipe Company
The Continental Oil Company
General Mills, Inc.
Union Electric Company
St. Luke's Hospital (St. Louis, Mo.)
Motorola, Inc.
Printing Industries of St. Louis, Inc
    and
Local 252, Lithographers and Photoengravers International Union
U.S. Army Mobility Equipment Command (St. Louis, Mo.)
    and
National Federation of Federal Employees (N.F F.E. Local 405)

Statements of Company Personnel Policies

In Part One of this book, the scope and objectives of personnel management advocated by the authors were presented as follows:

Personnel management consists of those management functions and activities related to the acquisition, development, and maintenance of human resources in a working organization. Successful personnel management implies that these functions and activities integrate the efforts of people with the other resources of an organization in such a manner that the objectives of the company, the goals of individual workers, and the goals of society at large are all attained in the highest degree compatible with the work situation.

Obviously, the perfect attainment of these mutual objectives is extremely difficult, and probably too idealistic to expect in most work situations. The case problems in this book are illustrative of the complexities involved in the human relationships and human considerations of management. Usually there is no one "right" answer to personnel problems, and even the optimal solution to a personnel problem may be at best a compromise of conflicting objectives.

Many companies, recognizing the importance of sound personnel management practices, have provided their managers with guidelines for practice through stated or published personnel policies. In this section, a sampling of company personnel policies has been brought together as representative of efforts of companies in this direction.

These policy statements were taken from various company publications and are reproduced with permission of the companies involved. Some are official policies as printed in company manuals; others are public statements by top executives as to their companies' general philosophies and objectives in personnel matters. Also included as policy statements are two introductory sections to labor agreements, in which both the management and union have contractually stated their mutual objectives and positions guiding their relationships.

Statements of personnel policy serve several important purposes to a business organization. First, policies reflect the values, beliefs, and sentiments of the organization and of the people who direct it. As such, they provide members with guidelines which indicate how they are expected to behave in an organization and how others are expected to behave towards them.

Second, policies enable managers to make decisions more readily than would be the case if each new situation had to be treated as novel.

Third, statements of policy serve to explain the business organization to the larger community. Companies usually disseminate policy statements to outsiders, such as public officials, businessmen, clergymen, teachers, and other community leaders. While many people look upon such dissemination as corporate "window dressing," the authors consider these policy statements essential to the survival of the organization. Through written statements of policy, the business organization is able to explain and justify itself to the larger community of which it is a part and with whose values it must be in compliance. Businessmen feel especially vulnerable to attacks from the community; hence, they utilize the publication of policies as one means for indicating to the community that company values are consistent with those of the community. Thus, policy statements reflect the business organization subculture which must be basically in tune with the broader culture of which it is a part.

The introductory labor agreement sections, too, contain guidelines which in practice may be difficult for both sides to follow. At the same time, however, these contractual statements do reflect policy goals which aid both union and management representatives in their collective bargaining relationships. For example, the *Preamble* excerpt from the Printing Industries of St. Louis—Lithographers and Photoengravers Union Contract was developed over many years of bargaining. During this period it was authored jointly by both parties. These agreements indicate a mutual recognition that the interests of the union (employees) and management are not incompatible, and that both ultimately must cooperate to survive in the competitive society in which they both serve and exist.

In summary, all of these policy statements are particular attempts by business organizations to define the scope and objectives of personnel management in their specific company situations. There is no implication here that these company policies are either "right" or "wrong" or "good" or "bad," but they are presented as the current management thinking of a representative group of successful corporations and institutions. In addition, each statement shows aspects similar to the general statement of scope and objectives of personnel management advocated by the authors of this book. The major problem remaining is the bridging of the gap between purposeful policy statements and the proper utilization of human resources in business. It is toward the solution of this problem that this book has been directed.

THE MONSANTO COMPANY   POLICY 1

A STATEMENT OF BUSINESS PRINCIPLES

Business Principles

Monsanto's objective is profitable growth. Yet, in striving to achieve this objective, Monsanto must live by a set of principles. These principles are as follows:

In our business relations, we will

...act on all occasions in an ethical manner, with honesty and complete fairness.

...direct the company's total manpower resources, technological capabilities and physical facilities to the task of meeting industry and consumer needs successfully, economically and efficiently throughout the world.

...maintain the willingness to pioneer for higher quality, lower costs, better service and broader markets.

...make it desirable and convenient for all customers, potential customers, suppliers and potential suppliers to do business with Monsanto.

...foster autonomy in the divisions and departments under a concept which provides for decentralized operation with top management coordination and control to assure adherence to over-all corporate objectives and policies.

...anticipate and develop new products responsive to the changing needs of civilization.

...buy only on the basis of quality, service and price.

In relations with government, we will

...work vigorously to obtain and to support good government at all levels—federal, state and local.

...strive for governmental policies which encourage economic growth and preserve individual liberties.

...foster a better understanding by our employees, by representatives of government and by thought leaders of the critical economic and political issues that affect industry.

...encourage our employees, on a nonpartisan basis, to take an active part in political and governmental affairs.

...keep ourselves informed on legislative and other trends in government.

In relations with shareowners, we will

...provide them with an optimum continuing return on their investment.

Statement included in the employee brochure entitled, "Facts About Monsanto." Used by permission of Mr. Henry Houser, Training Director, Central Engineering Division, Monsanto Corp.

...strive, on a long-term basis, to improve the investment advantage of Monsanto shares and to attract purchasers of these shares.

In relations with plant communities, we will

...be a good neighbor in all the term implies.

...make our plants safe and attractive places in which to work.

...cooperate with all properly constituted authorities to reduce air and stream pollution.

In relations with our personnel, we will

...stand pre-eminent in the eyes of all people of all nations as a desirable company for which to work and enhance our stature in the business community through the efficient conduct of our operations and our public relations.

...continue our belief that the determining factors in hiring and placing employees are the requirements of the specific job and the qualifications of the individual. Monsanto's policy is to treat applicants equally without regard to race, color, sex, creed, national origin, religion, or political preference.

...utilize and encourage the creativity of the individual by providing special job opportunities.

...define functions and relationships clearly, but not so literally as to hamper initiative, action and growth.

...recognize and develop personnel resources within the company and maintain programs which will ensure the successful future management of the company.

...promote from within, but recruit as necessary to assure growth or to acquire new skills.

...maintain an antinepotism policy in employment practices.

...carry on all employee relations in good faith.

...provide an opportunity for individuals to achieve eminent stature and high level monetary rewards through technical or staff specialist routes as well as the administrative route.

...maintain the most beneficial balance between the importance and well-being of the individual employee and our responsibilities to customers and shareowners.

In our growth, we will

...recognize opportunities in any field where Monsanto capabilities may be applied profitably through the unique skills of management, science and technology, finance, production or marketing.

...grow in specific instances or in specific situations through joint ventures or acquisitions which demonstrably will provide sound economic means of entering a market or business profitably under conditions fully compatible with the law then in effect.

...provide a balanced research program aimed at an optimum return on present capital investment and at providing a steady flow of profitable new products and processes.

...emphasize expansion in areas where the company can achieve and maintain advantages through patents, franchises, marketing, trademarks or other special strengths.

...plan and grow globally with full appreciation of current politico-social movements throughout the world and study opportunities in the light of these developments

RALSTON PURINA COMPANY POLICY 2

CORPORATE OBJECTIVES

Our primary objective is to increase profitability ... to produce maximum long-term profit growth consistent with the balanced best interest of customers, shareholders, employees, suppliers and society at large. To achieve optimum results, we must perform effectively in the following key result areas: a) Customer satisfaction; b) Productivity; c) Innovation; d) Resources; e) Management development and performance; f) Employee attitude and performance; g) Public responsibility.

In achieving this goal we will ...

1. Recognize that the primary purpose of our business is to perform a necessary economic service by creating, stimulating, and satisfying customers. We must be a marketing-oriented company, dedicated to the principle that in order to supply the right product or service at the right time and in the right way, we need first to establish what the customer wants, where, when, how, and at what price.

2. Remain diversified in our operations, multinational in organization, and global in outlook.

3. Dedicate ourselves to the principle of continuous self-renewal so that individuals, organization structure, products, facilities, and systems do not stagnate. We recognize that:

    a) People are the ultimate source of renewal. We will bring to the corporation a steady flow of able and highly motivated individuals and then provide positive, constructive programs of management development.

    b) We must be results-oriented, measured and held responsible.

    c) We must maintain an environment which fosters individual effort and initiative.

    d) Self-criticism is vital to the health of the enterprise. We will welcome constructive criticism.

    e) Organizational structure must be flexible. We will evolve subject only to the yardstick of what is most successful and meets our requirements.

    f) We will have effective and simple systems and procedures to implement organizational structure, and we will evaluate them at regular intervals.

    g) The question "What Next?" is a better road to a greater tomorrow than

Reproduced by permission of Mr. George H. Kyd, Director of Public Relations, Ralston Purina Company.

concentration on a glorious past. We must recognize and manage the accelerating rate of change.

h) The dynamics of an organization is related to motivation, conviction, and morale. We believe and will endeavor to make every employee believe that his optimum efforts make a difference.

i) Analyze assets and functions whose potential is diminishing in terms of contribution to earnings, cash flow, and tie-in value to other units in order to develop a course of action which may include disinvestment.

j) We must create a climate of technology, special knowledges, and services which induces in our customers a desire to buy our products and/or our services.

4. Decentralize by establishing entrepreneurial units with a consistent and systematic effort to delegate decision making authority to the lowest level commensurate with good judgment. Measure qualitative and quantitative results of operating people through a simple control system.

AMERICAN CAST IRON PIPE COMPANY   POLICY 3

INTRODUCTION

American Cast Iron Pipe Company operates under the Eagan Plan which is named for its originator, John J. Eagan, and which involves a unique method of industrial representation and the beneficial ownership of the Company by its employees. For us to participate and cooperate intelligently in the affairs of our Company and discharge fully the responsibilities placed on us by the Eagan Plan, we must all know how, why and what to do.

This book, therefore, has been prepared as an employee's manual in an attempt to give complete data about our opportunities and responsibilities, both for study and for reference. We can achieve our aim to establish and maintain an industry beneficially owned by its employees and operated equally in the interest of the public and its employees only if each of us learns to exercise properly the privileges bestowed and bear the responsibilities imposed on us by the Eagan Plan.

By the terms of the codicil to his will, John J. Eagan placed the responsibility for the success of this industry squarely upon all of us. He believed that industry should operate on a basis of mutual service to the producer as well as the consumer of a commodity. To that end, he gave all of the common stock of our company in trust to representatives of the men in the shop and to representatives of management for the benefit of all employees and with the duty to follow the Plan.

Mr. Eagan's codicil to his will sets out definite rules and regulations as to how the trustees of the common stock of Acipco and the employees of Acipco as the beneficial owners of that stock shall conduct the business and share its rewards, and it is incumbent on each of us who currently enjoy those rewards to become familiar with every facet of the Acipco organization.

JOHN J. EAGAN TRUST

Foreword

> Behind every great enterprise is the character and vision of some outstanding personality. This fundamental truth is clearly illustrated at Acipco by the Spirit and influence of John Joseph Eagan, who during his lifetime laid the foundation of his plan of industrial cooperation under which the American Cast Iron Pipe Company operates.

Excerpts from the *Employees Manual*, pp. 6-10, pp. 18-19. Used by permission of Mr. B. B. Warren, Director of Public Relations, American Cast Iron Pipe Company.

Early in the history of the Company, Mr. Eagan came to realize what a great manufacturing plant operated according to the Golden Rule might mean to industry. He devoted the last fifteen years of his life to creating a permanent organization embodying this ideal. In the codicil to his will, written in 1922, he made permanent a practical plan for carrying out his great purpose, which has come to be known as the Eagan Plan.

When John Joseph Eagan first advanced his plan of business administration according to the Golden Rule, the use of this great principle in connection with the operation of industry was little known.

In order to understand the significance of the Eagan Plan which he put into effect at Acipco, it is necessary to know something of his early life.

A few months after his birth at Griffin, Georgia, April 22, 1870, his father died leaving him and his twenty-five year old mother in moderate circumstances. He was educated in the public schools and entered early in life upon a business career with his uncle, William A. Russell.

In 1899, Mr. Russell died, and the considerable estate he had amassed was left to his nephew, John Eagan. At 29 years of age, Mr. Eagan thus found himself in a position either to dissipate a fortune or put it to work. He chose to put it to work; and in so doing he found opportunity to apply a quality of heart and mind which made his subsequent career unique, and earned for him a place among the great leaders of his day.

The American Cast Iron Pipe Company was organized in October of 1905. Mr. Eagan was president of the Company from 1905 to 1915, when he became chairman of the Board of Directors. In 1921 he reassumed the presidency and held that position until a few days before his death, March 30, 1924.

John Eagan lived the life of a true disciple of Jesus Christ. For 30 years he was superintendent of the Sunday School of the Central Presbyterian Church of Atlanta, Georgia. His concept of the Christian religion and his personal responsibility as a Christian were world-wide. He rendered active service in the work of the Young Men's Christian Association, being for a time a member of its International Committee. During the period of World War I he had charge of the Y.M.C.A. work serving the enlisted men of the Navy.

The life work of Mr. Eagan was not limited to any race, creed, or class of people. This fact is indicated by the support he gave to the Commission on Inter-Racial Cooperation during the years just after World War I. This Commission was formed to help people, both white and black, to understand each other better and to treat each other with fairness and justice. Mr. Eagan's modesty makes any written record of his personal services and financial gifts impossible, since a great number of them were never made known.

Mr. Eagan believed that opportunity for useful, honest work should be given to every one; that workers should be safeguarded against unemployment; that they should be paid a living wage, and given adequate attention in case of accident or sickness; and that provisions should be made for old age pensions. He further believed that the workers should share in the management of the business. All of these objectives have been substantially achieved at Acipco under the Eagan Plan.

Mr. Eagan knew that individual men and women live only a short time at the most, but that a great business enterprise may continue indefinitely. Its life is limited not by the years, but by the quality and the extent of the service it renders to the public. He wanted the practice of the Golden Rule in business to live after him; and it was his desire that his plan be continued indefinitely for the benefit of future generations.

Mr. Eagan had the courage of his convictions which he demonstrated in a practical way by writing, in 1923, a codicil to his will. Within this will, he outlined in detail the principles and objectives which he believed essential to a happy and constructive experience for those who would serve through the medium of organized industry. Through this same codicil to his will, he created a trust of all the common stock of the American Cast Iron Pipe Company in order that the employees of the Company might, through the operation of the Company, demonstrate that it was entirely practical to operate an industrial plant under the Golden Rule and the teachings of Jesus.

The Codicil to Mr. Eagan's Will

On March 30, 1924, John J. Eagan died. In a codicil to his will dated April 3, 1923, he made provision for the perpetuation of the Eagan Plan. He sought through this medium to preserve for the future what he had learned and dreamed in the quarter century since his uncle's fortune came into his youthful hands.

The codicil to his will, which is a most remarkable document, follows:

Georgia
Fulton County

Whereas, I John J. Eagan, did on the 22nd day of April, 1922, sign, seal, declare and publish my last will and testament in the presence of A. E. Ramsaur, Nettie Catoe and H. A. Etheridge, who signed said will and testament as witnesses:

And whereas, I desire to add an additional bequest and devise in said will and testament, I, therefore, make and declare and publish this codicil to said will and testament, to-wit:

I hereby give, bequeath and devise ten hundred and eighty-five (1,085) shares of the common stock of the American Cast Iron Pipe Company, being all of my holdings of said common stock of said Company, to the members of the Board of Management and members of the Board of Operatives of said American Cast Iron Pipe Company, jointly, and their successors in office in said boards, as trustees, in trust for the following purposes, and subject to the directions hereinafter set forth, to-wit:

First: To receive all dividends paid upon said stock and use so much of the dividends thus received, as said trustees in their discretion may deem advisable in supplementing the salaries and wages of the employees of said American Cast Iron Pipe Company in amounts sufficient in the judgment of the said trustees to insure to each of said employees an income equivalent to a "living wage," said trustees to be the sole judges of what constitutes a living wage, and of the amounts, if any, to be paid to each one or any of said employees of said Company.

Second: To use such sums from the dividends received upon said stock, as said trustees in their discretion may deem advisable, in paying an income to any employee, or to the wife and minor children of any employee of said American Cast Iron Pipe Company, at such time as the plant of said Company may shut down for any cause, or at such times as said employee through no fault of his or her own, but through accident, sickness, or other unavoidable causes, shall be unable to work; and said trustees are hereby made the sole judges of the amounts, if any, which shall be paid by said trustees to any employee, or to the members of an employee's family under the provisions of this paragraph.

Third: To vote said certificates of stock in said American Cast Iron Pipe Company at all meetings of stockholders of said Company.

It is my will and desire, and I direct that in determining all questions as to voting said stock and as to carrying out the provisions of the trust created by this codicil, the members of the Board of Management, as trustees, shall vote as a unit, and the members of the Board of Operatives, as trustees, shall vote as a unit, the vote of each group to be determined by the majority vote of the members of the respective boards; and that in the event of the failure of the respective groups of trustees to agree upon any question said question in dispute shall be referred to the Board of Directors, whose decision on said question in dispute shall be final.

Any member of either of said boards, who shall cease to be a member of either boards for any cause whatsoever shall thereupon cease to be a trustee under this codicil of my will, his or her successor upon either of said boards becoming, by virtue of his or her office, a trustee under this codicil, immediately upon his or her acceptance of said trust.

Any employees of said American Cast Iron Pipe Company who shall die, or who shall, voluntarily or involuntarily, for any cause whatsoever other than temporary shutting down of the plant or plants of said Company, leave the employment of said Company, shall immediately thereupon cease to have any interest of any kind whatsoever in any income from, or in any part of the trust estate created by this codicil of my will.

Any person, who may hereafter at any time enter the employment of said Company, shall immediately thereupon become a beneficiary of said trust estate, with all of the rights and privileges enjoyed by the employees of said Company at the time of my death, and subject to the same conditions.

The provisions of the two paragraphs immediately preceding this paragraph shall apply to the wife, or child, or the wife and children of said employee of said Company, if there be a wife, or child, or children, or both, provision having been made for them, in the event of the death of said employee leaving such, under the rules for the management of said Company or its pension fund.

By this codicil to my will and testament, it is my purpose, will and desire to create a trust estate both for the benefit of the persons actually in the employ of said American Cast Iron Pipe Company, and for such persons as may require the products of said Company.

The trustees, appointed by this codicil, in accepting the trust and acting hereunder, will be trustees both for said employees and said persons requiring the products of said Company, through the control of said common stock, shall be guided by the sole purpose of so managing said Company as to enable said American Cast Iron Pipe Company to deliver the Company's product to persons, requiring it, at actual cost, which shall be considered the lowest possible price consistent with the maintenance and extension of the Company's plant or plants and business and the payment of reasonable salaries and wages to all of the employees of said Company, my object being to insure "service" both to the purchasing public and to labor on the basis of the Golden Rule given by our Lord and Saviour Jesus Christ.

This 3rd day of April, 1923.

(Signed) John J. Eagan

ACIPCO ORGANIZATION

The organization of American Cast Iron Pipe Company as originally envisioned and set up by Mr. John J. Eagan during his lifetime and then perpetuated by the provisions of the codicil to his will is believed to be unique in the business world and consists of the several boards described below with their respective duties and functions.

1. Board of Trustees. Mr. Eagan at the time of his death was the sole common stockholder and owner of the Company and when he undertook to bequeath his common stock in such a manner that all employees of the Company, both men working in the plant and the managers of the Company, were made the beneficial owners of the Company, he saw the necessity for establishing some method for achieving this result. He therefore declared in the codicil to his will that all of the common stock is bequeathed to the members of the Board of Management and the members of the Board of Operatives of the American Cast Iron Pipe Company jointly, and their successors in office in said boards, as trustees in trust for the purpose set out in the codicil, the primary one of which is the welfare of all employees and pensioners of the Company. These two boards combine to form the Board of Trustees and in this capacity perform the functions of the common stockholders or owners of the business. This Board of Trustees meets annually to elect the Board of Directors and holds called meetings as desired. The codicil to Mr. Eagan's will provides that the trustees shall vote as two separate units, that is, the Board of Operatives, which is elected by the employees, casts one vote, and

the Board of Management, which is elected by the Board of Directors, casts the other. Should these votes disagree, the question at hand passes from the Board of Trustees to the Board of Directors for final settlement by a majority vote of the Board of Directors.

2. Board of Directors. The general policies and conduct of the business are regulated by the Company's Board of Directors which is composed of representatives of the public, employees, managers, and owners. As above stated, the Board of Directors is elected annually by the Board of Trustees. The Board of Directors may consist of twelve to seventeen members and is presently composed of the members of the Board of Management, two members from the Board of Operatives, one member from the clerical forces of the Company, two members from the Company organization at large, and four members elected from persons not connected with the Company organization, to represent the buying public, invested capital, the religious, social and educational interests, and the financial interests. The board functions in exactly the same way and serves exactly the same purpose as does a board of directors elected by the common stockholders of any usual American business organization. Policies of the Company on sales, finance, manufacturing, advertising, etc., are finally determined by this Board, or delegated to the Board of Management. Officers of the Company are elected by the Board of Directors. The compensation of the President is fixed by the Board of Directors, and the compensation of all other officers is fixed by the President, subject to the approval of the Board of Directors. Officers of the Company are responsible to the Board of Directors and to this Board they make reports on the conduct of their respective departments of the business.

3. Board of Management. The Board of Management consists of the executive officers of the Company who are elected by the Board of Directors to serve for one year. This Board meets as often as is necessary. The active control and the management of the Company's affairs is vested in this Board of Management, which is composed of Company officials highly trained in the various branches of industrial activity. An industry must be properly financed; its products must be well and economically made; its raw materials must be of proper quality; promptly delivered and fairly bought; adequate markets for its products must be developed and maintained; its products must be profitably and justly sold. The men at the head of such activities compose the Board of Management and with their staffs of assistants actually conduct the Company affairs.

4. Board of Operatives. The Board of Operatives consists of twelve employees of the Company who are not officials of the Company and who are elected to the Board of the employees who are employed in the several electoral divisions into which the plant is divided. The members of the Board of Operatives are elected for a term of two years, one-half of the members being elected each year. The Board of Operatives, as previously set out, serve on the Board of Trustees established under the codicil to Mr. Eagan's will, and, further, the Board of Operatives acts as an advisory council to the Board of Management.

THE CONTINENTAL OIL COMPANY   POLICY 4

A PHILOSOPHY OF MANAGEMENT

Introduction

A progressive, diversified, world-wide business enterprise achieves its maximum effectiveness only when all of its employees are working toward common objectives. A good organization structure is essential, but that alone does not assure that all employees will be working toward the same goals.

In addition, it is necessary to have cooperation, coordination, and a guide to orient the actions and decisions of all levels of management in the same direction. Unity of action can be obtained only by having common purposes, objectives, ideas, and ideals—in other words, a PHILOSOPHY OF MANAGEMENT.

The purpose of this PHILOSOPHY OF MANAGEMENT is twofold: (1) to set down the primary, long-range objectives of our organization, (2) to provide criteria which will orient and guide our employees throughout the world—regardless of their level of responsibility—in their conduct, decisions, and actions in seeking to attain the objectives.

CONOCO Objectives

The following statement of objectives is not intended to be all-inclusive. These goals are, however, fundamental to our entire operations and form a core around which other more specific objectives may be established.

> To develop throughout our world-wide management organization a group of individuals who will command respect, not only for their business ability but also for their qualities as people, that is, individuals who have a high standard of integrity and fairness and a true sense of humanity in their dealings with others.

Only by so doing can the Continental organization develop or attract the kind of executive talent required to guide our operations in the future and win the full support of our customers and of the public. Only by so doing can we create the kind of atmosphere in which our people may work with maximum effectiveness and make their best contribution to our common efforts.

Reproduced by permission of Mr. C. Howard Hardesty, Senior Vice President, Continental Oil Company.

> To conduct all our affairs—world-wide—so that Continental organization will always merit the confidence and trust of the many publics, governments, customers, dealers, fellow businessmen, business communities, stockholders, and employees with whom we come in contact.

The integrity of our company is made up of our individual actions, and the ability of our organization to meet the challenges from the world around it depends, in large part, upon the faith others have in us.

> To develop throughout our organization a high level of managerial competence in order that we may realize the maximum possible profits consistent with our other objectives, from our facilities, capital funds, sources of raw materials, market outlets, and opportunities which are at our disposal.

We should continually seek to increase our profits through improvements in our managerial skills. The profit motive and free enterprise have brought to the United States the highest standard of living ever known. Without profits, a company has no opportunity to fulfill any of its other obligations, nor can it long survive. That is why we must be progressive and aggressive, dedicated to making adequate profits by producing our many diversified products at the lowest possible cost. We must be continually aware, however, that pursuit of high profits alone can become socially, politically, and economically dangerous if undertaken without due regard for our other objectives here stated.

> To discharge our joint responsibilities to our stockholders, our employees, and our customers in such a way that the maximum possible benefits will accrue to each group.

We have an obligation to provide *our stockholders* an adequate return on their investment, to make the most effective use of the company's assets, and to assure the future existence and health of the company. To *our employees,* our first obligation is to have a healthy, profitable company in order to insure job continuity. We must also strive to see that they are rewarded properly for their contributions to the company and that they have a working situation in which they may realize the maximum of their potentialities and achieve the maximum of human satisfactions. *Our customers* should be assured of quality products at competitive prices. We should also provide our share of research for the development of new and improved products and for the constant improvement of our national standard of living.

The order in which these objectives have been stated is deliberate, because each in turn can be accomplished only if those that precede it are realized.

GENERAL MILLS, INC. POLICY 5

A STATEMENT OF CORPORATE PHILOSOPHY

General Mills, by the traditions and heritage of its successive managements, has developed a foundation of operation based upon a distinct corporate philosophy, recognizing a three-way responsibility to the stockholders who provide the capital; to the consumers who purchase our products; and to the employees of the company who put the stockholders' facilities to work and produce the goods and services for our customers.

James P. McFarland, President, has said, "It is important to define such beliefs in the modern environment in order to sharpen consistent practices and to inspire individual effort to produce maximum company achievement."

Here is General Mills' philosophy as defined by the President's Office:

Profit growth at a rate representing leadership performance in the sphere of industry within which we compete is our unqualified obligation to our owners— the stockholders.

An essential test of corporate business success is rate and trend of profit production in relation to other businesses within and without a field of enterprise. We attract our basic capital by reason of stockholder evaluation of results (profit).

Full compliance with existing laws and the pursuit of high ethical and moral standards must be inherent in all relationships.

Pursuit of high standards in business conduct (including advertising) will attract more and better customers, employees, suppliers and stockholders. Corporate relationships with each group will be more profitable and enduring because of the healthy standards followed.

Significant environmental forces must be quickly recognized or predicted, then met by an action-oriented willingness to change, innovate and lead.

Leadership in business implies the creation of trends, not the delayed pursuit of trends. We should promptly discern changes in environment affecting our business and the problems or opportunities which these changes create. We should reflect a restless dissatisfaction with the status quo and be willing to change.

Successful business operations result from the establishment of challenging goals and objectives which are achieved by competent, well-trained people at all levels who develop a progressive plan of action supported by adequate financial resources and creative research.

Reproduced by permission of Mr. James P. McFarland, President and Chief Executive Officer, General Mills, Inc.

The achievement of established goals is best met by an organized strategic and tactical plan conceived in detail to reach the end objective. Business goals and implementation plans must be supported by progressive management leading capable people who are backed by adequate financing and creative research.

Authority and responsibility for action should be placed with an individual—not a committee.
The placement of decision-making responsibility with an individual will result in sharp and undiluted decisions, and will avoid delays and compromises characteristic of the committee decision-making approach.

Decisions should be reached promptly on the basis of an objective consideration of the facts and alternatives, then implemented with courage and dispatch.
Intuitive approaches to decision-making in these modern times are frequently disastrous. The careful marshaling of essential facts, appraisal of the relative significance of each and the determination of the alternative courses of action result in sound procedure. This fact-finding approach is the objective approach—an attitude of mind.

Employees should know what is expected of them and should be rewarded or penalized upon the basis of job performance and results.
Through application of the principle of recognition on the basis of job performance, management can inspire maximum motivation, respect and efficiency.

This business succeeds only if our suppliers and customers succeed, and if our ultimate consumers, in turn, are faithfully satisfied by reason of our customer orientation and quality of products and/or services.
The efficient service of the customer requires an intelligent understanding of the customers' needs and the changes he is likely to undergo. If we are to be the best in our industries, we must serve the best in the eyes of our customers. Product quality is essential to good business.

Acquisition, training and development of qualified people, regardless of race, color or creed, is a key to the success of this corporation.
The employees of General Mills are the company's greatest asset. The most effective employee is a well-trained and energetic individual who is challenged to do his best and compensated fairly for the services he renders.

We have corporate and individual citizenship responsibilities which should be met by corporate and employee interest and participation in public affairs at all levels.
The American free enterprise system, the economic system under which we primarily operate, is the greatest in the world and imposes a responsibility upon us to preserve its greatness. The principles of the American democratic system require active participation by its people and its industry. This company and our people should willingly pledge their participation and support.

UNION ELECTRIC COMPANY   POLICY 6

STATEMENT OF POLICY

We are a business enterprise—dependent for success on the high quality and fair price of our service; on the skill, courtesy, and loyalty of our employees; on the confidence of our investors; and on the ability of our management to forecast and provide for the steadily increasing electric power requirements of our area.

In the conduct of our business, we will render service of the highest quality to our customers—promptly, courteously, and efficiently—at the lowest prices consistent with paying fair wages and affording job satisfaction and security to our employees; providing modern facilities for our customers' expanding needs for electric service; and paying a fair return to our investors who have provided the funds to make such service possible.

As a private enterprise entrusted with an essential public service, we recognize our civic responsibility in the communities we serve. We shall strive to advance the growth and welfare of these communities and shall participate in civic activities which fulfill that goal . . . for we believe this is both good citizenship and good business.

From the 1970 *Annual Report,* Union Electric Company. Reproduced by permission of Mr. Charles J. Dougherty, President, Union Electric Company, St. Louis, Missouri.

ST. LUKE'S HOSPITAL (ST. LOUIS, MO.)   POLICY 7

A STATEMENT OF POLICY

In general, it is the policy of St. Luke's Hospital to provide for its employees:

1. Steady year 'round employment.
2. Protection in the form of hospitalization insurance, Workmen's Compensation, Social Security and a retirement plan.
3. Insofar as possible, opportunities for advancement commensurate with the individual's ability, background and performance.
4. Wages, hours of work, vacations, sick leave and other conditions of work at least comparable to those prevailing in other institutions of its type in the St. Louis area.
5. Fair and equitable treatment for all.

GENERAL CONDUCT

Conservation and Economy—Everybody knows about the high cost of living—hospitals have felt these costs just as individuals have. Obviously, it is the responsibility of all of us at St. Luke's to keep these costs as low as possible consistent with a high standard of patient care.

With the help of every employee, the never-ending effort to keep waste at a minimum, conserve supplies and prolong the life of equipment, will be successful—without it, a dismal failure.

Courtesy and Service—St. Luke's was founded on and lives on SERVICE—service not only by those employees who deal with the patients directly, but by all personnel. Just the common garden varieties of plain, old-fashioned courtesy and thoughtfulness are essential not only in our treatment of patients, but in our everyday dealings with each other as well.

GRIEVANCES AND PERSONAL PROBLEMS

In any organization the size of St. Luke's there are bound to be occasions when problems either relating to employment or of a personal nature will arise. Employees are urged first to go to their respective heads of departments on such matters. However, should satisfactory solutions not be reached by this means, the Assistant Administrator is at all times available to either the department head

---

Excerpted "Statements of Personnel Policy" from the employee handbook, *Personnel Policies*. Used by permission of Mr. Harry M. Piper, Managing Director, St. Luke's Hospital, St. Louis, Missouri.

or the employee. If the situation warrants, arrangements for a discussion of the problem with the Administrator can be made.

HOSPITALS ARE PEOPLE

Over and over again, it has been emphasized that hospitals are people. No matter how fine our building—regardless of how modern our equipment, unless there are people like you to run it there is no hospital.

And people are different—their backgrounds, their basic characteristics, their personalities and their temperaments are different. Their lives at home, their family situations also differ. That is why it is almost impossible to devise one set of rules or standards which can be applied rigidly to a large group without occasional unfairness or undue hardship. To avoid as far as possible any such unfairness the Administrator reserves the right to make such exceptions as he sees fit to the policies contained in this booklet although keeping in mind at all times a desire not to "favor" one employee over another or one group over another group.

| MOTOROLA, INC. | POLICY 8 |

HANDLING EMPLOYEE GRIEVANCES AT MOTOROLA

Let's Get It Out In The Open

Here's Motorola's way of settling grievances. If there's something about your job that's bothering you, Let's Get It Out in the Open. Discuss it frankly with the people in Motorola who can and will help you "iron out" your problem.

You can be sure that your complaint will be handled in a "fair and square manner."

Here are the five steps you may take. It's your right and privilege to keep right on going—"to the top," if necessary.

1. As a starter, take up the problem that's bothering you with your supervisor. He works with you each day and is personally interested in your welfare at Motorola. He knows you and your job better than anyone else and knows how to solve your problems promptly and fairly.
   If you are not satisfied with the answer given by your supervisor, you may go on to the next step.
2. Talk your problem over with your foreman if you are in the factory or with your department head if you are in engineering or the offices. Talk to him honestly and sincerely. He's your friend and has been instructed to treat your problem with dignity and respect. He has authority to settle things.
3. If you want further consideration of your problem, then take it to the Personnel Department. Here is your guardian of fair treatment. Personnel is specially trained in handling "human relations" problems and will guide and aid you. You will be helped with any matter you take to the department.
4. You are entitled to a hearing of your problem before the Review Board if you want it. The Vice President of Human Relations, or Director of Personnel at your plant, the Facility Manager, and the Plant Manager of your plant will hear you if you are in the factory. If you are in Engineering or the offices, the Review Board hearing your complaint will be Vice President of Human Relations, or Director of Personnel, Head of your Division, and your department head.
5. As a final step, the door to Chairman Bob Galvin's office is always open to your problem. If you have not been satisfied with the treatment of your

Excerpts from the Employee Handbook, *Welcome to Motorola*. Used by permission of Mr. K. M. Piper, Vice-President, Motorola, Inc.

grievance up to this step, the Chairman will be glad to review it. We all know we can trust his judgment and fairness.

In Conclusion

One last word. You are important to the company. Without you of course, there would be no Motorola. Bob Galvin, Chairman of the Board, has said "Motorola people mold the character of the company."

Whatever your job may be, there are opportunities for you at Motorola. Catch on to the Motorola "family spirit" and build a good future for yourself and your family. Your fine efforts will make Motorola more successful and result in our continued industry leadership.

PRINTING INDUSTRIES OF ST. LOUIS, INC. AND LOCAL 252, LITHOGRAPHERS AND PHOTOENGRAVERS INTERNATIONAL UNION

POLICY 9

ARTICLES OF AGREEMENT

It is hereby agreed by and between the Union Employers Section, Printing Industries of St. Louis, Inc., representing all those Employers whose names are set forth hereto and such Employers who may hereinafter become members of the Association and who subscribe to this Collective Bargaining Agreement, each hereinafter known as the Employer, and St. Louis Local No. 252 of the Lithographers and Photoengravers International Union, hereinafter known as the Union, as follows: (25 Companies)

Preamble

The purpose of this Agreement is to establish and maintain a harmonious relationship between the Union, the Employer, and his employees. The Employer and the Union agree that the fullest cooperation between the Employer and his employees is necessary to permit the maintenance of harmonious relations, and, therefore, set forth herein rates of pay, hours of work, conditions of employment to be observed by the parties hereto, and that they will abide by this Agreement and all mutual understandings contained therein, it being their purpose to settle all differences without disturbances to industrial peace.

The Employer and the Union further agree that the fullest cooperation between the Union, the Employer, and his employees is necessary, in order that the Employer may secure and sustain maximum productivity per employee during the term of this Agreement. The Union is in accord with the objective of achieving the highest level of employee performance and efficiency consistent with safety, good health, and sustained effort.

The Union recognizes the responsibilities imposed upon it as the exclusive bargaining agent for the employees, and realizes that in order to provide maximum opportunities for continuing employment, good working conditions, and better wages, the Employer must be in a strong market position, which means he must produce at the lowest possible cost consistent with fair production standards.

Articles of Agreement, July 1, 1969 to June 30, 1971, Union Employers' Section of the Printing Industries of St. Louis, Inc., and Local No. 252, Lithographers and Photoengravers International Union.

U. S. ARMY MOBILITY EQUIPMENT COMMAND (ST. LOUIS, MO.), AND NATIONAL FEDERATION OF FEDERAL EMPLOYEES (N.F.F.E. LOCAL 405)

POLICY 10

ARTICLE I—GENERAL PROVISIONS...

3. *PURPOSE.* It is the intent and purpose of this AGREEMENT to define certain roles and responsibilities of the parties hereto; to state policies, procedures and methods that govern working relationships between the parties; and to identify subject matter of proper mutual concern to the parties. They have entered into the AGREEMENT:

    a. To provide for employee participation in the formulation and implementation of personnel policies and procedures.

    b. To facilitate the adjustment of grievances, complaints, disputes and impasses.

    c. To improve working conditions including environment, health and welfare, and services.

    d. To provide for systematic employee-management cooperation.

    e. To promote and improve the morale of the employees.

    f. To promote the highest degree of efficiency and responsibility in the accomplishment of their respective objectives.

4. *UNIT AND COVERAGE.* This AGREEMENT is applicable to all civilian UNITED STATES ARMY MOBILITY EQUIPMENT COMMAND employees, classified, professional and wage board, located in St. Louis, Missouri. Employees of all MECOM Facilities located outside of St. Louis are excluded as well as the Materiel Command Project Manager Offices for Beach Discharge and Amphibious Lighters and Mobile Assault Bridge located here in St. Louis; the UNITED STATES ARMY MOBILITY EQUIPMENT RESEARCH AND DEVELOPMENT CENTER employees located in St. Louis, and those employees excluded by regulation. Such employees form the representation unit, and the NATIONAL FEDERATION OF FEDERAL EMPLOYEES LOCAL NO. 405 is the exclusive representative of all employees in this established unit.

5. *REPRESENTATION.* The Employer agrees, in order to permit the Union to discharge its obligations under this AGREEMENT, that duly accredited Union representatives shall be permitted reasonable time to meet at reasonable times and confer on matters pertaining to this AGREEMENT with the Employer's representatives, to process employee grievances, to represent employees and to negotiate supplemental agreements and amendments under this AGREEMENT on official time...

Excerpts from the *Agreement* effective June 24, 1969 - June 23, 1971.

ARTICLE III—RIGHTS AND OBLIGATIONS

10. *MUTUAL RIGHTS AND OBLIGATIONS.* The Employer and the Union, in behalf of the employees it represents, accept the obligations to sincerely and affirmatively negotiate settlement of issues and disputes in accordance with the provisions set forth in this AGREEMENT. The Union and Employer are obligated to negotiate in good faith with the objective of reaching agreement by a diligent and serious exchange of information and views and by avoiding unnecessary protracted negotiations. The Employer and the Union will not change the conditions set forth in the AGREEMENT or supplements except by the methods provided herein.

a. The Employer agrees not to retroactively apply a new policy to any matter under the scope of this AGREEMENT without consultation and participation with the Union.

b. Both the Union and the Employer will oppose any discriminatory practices.

c. Shop stewards and first line supervisors will confer as required to assure uniform interpretation, understanding, and implementation of this AGREEMENT. In the event of conflict in interpretation, both supervisor and shop steward will refer the matter for clarification to their respective higher echelons.

d. This AGREEMENT will be considered as a "living document" and the fact that certain subjects are not listed as appropriate for consultation does not restrict either party from meeting with the other to discuss and to consult on matters appropriate for such consultation.

e. It is further agreed and understood that any prior benefits and practices and understandings which have been mutually acceptable to the Employer and the Union but which are not specifically covered by the AGREEMENT shall remain in force and effect during the term of this AGREEMENT and shall not be changed without prior consultation between the parties.

f. The point of contact between the Union and the Employer for the purpose of discussing questions that may arise concerning the general administration or interpretation of this AGREEMENT shall be: for the Union, the duly elected President or his duly authorized representative; and for the Employer, the Commander's designated representative. In the event of their absence, the duly authorized alternate will serve in their stead.

11. *RIGHTS OF EMPLOYER.* MECOM officials retain the right, in accordance with applicable laws, regulations and Executive Orders, to direct employees; to hire, promote, transfer, assign, and retain employees in positions and to suspend, demote, discharge, or take other disciplinary measures against employees; to relieve employees from duties because of lack of work or for other legitimate reasons; to maintain the efficiency of government operations entrusted to them; to determine the methods, means, and personnel by which such operations are to be conducted, to establish the budget, direct the technology to perform its work; and to take whatever action is necessary to carry out the mission of MECOM in situations of emergency. The determination that an emergency exists rests solely with the MECOM Commander.

12. *EMPLOYER OBLIGATIONS.*
a. The Employer is obligated to confer with the Union as the exclusive representative of all employees in the unit on appropriate matters affecting personnel policies, practices, procedures and other matters affecting the working conditions of the employees in the unit, subject to applicable laws and regulations.

b. Employer agrees to provide the opportunity for the Union to review and comment on proposed policy or regulatory changes affecting employees of the unit. In order to be considered the Union must reply in writing to the Employer in accordance with established suspense dates. This shall not be interpreted as prohibiting any individual employee or the Union from submitting suggestions concerning appropriate matters, such as, Suggestion Programs and Incentive Programs sponsored by MECOM.

c. Employer agrees to take positive and timely action to implement the administration of the conditions and requirements of this AGREEMENT and will orient and instruct all levels of supervision...

15. *UNION RIGHTS.* Under the terms of this AGREEMENT, the Union is the exclusive representative of all eligible employees of the established unit in consultation and negotiation with the Employer regarding personnel policies and practices or other matters affecting general working conditions. The Union has the right to represent any employee in the bargaining unit in connection with a formal grievance, complaint, or an appeal from an adverse action, if the employee involved desires such representation. An employee may handle his own grievance and select his own representative; however, the Union shall be given the opportunity to be represented at discussions between the Employer and employee or employees' representative concerning formal grievances involving these matters and at an appropriate time make the views of the Union known. However, if such discussions involve decisions on personnel policies or other matters which the Employer is obligated to discuss or consult with the Union, such decisions will not be made by the Employer until this obligation is discharged. The Union's right to be present shall not extend to discussion between an employee and supervisory officials when the employee does not desire the presence of Union representatives. Article VI, Grievance Procedures, which further defines the Union's rights as Intervenor to protect the Union's third party interest or its membership at large is applicable. The right of employee representatives to be present during discussion of grievances shall be subject to necessary requirements as to security and confidentiality of information. The Union has the right to expect that its views will receive bona fide consideration by management officials and that dealings will be carried out in a cooperative climate...